Democratizing Global Governance

This book is the result of the Global Governance Reform Project sponsored by:

The School of Social Sciences, La Trobe University, Melbourne

Toda Institute for Global Peace and Policy Research, Tokyo and Honolulu

Focus on the Global South, Bangkok.

Democratizing Global Governance

Edited by

Eşref Aksu
Research Associate
La Trobe University, Melbourne
Australia

and

Joseph A. Camilleri
Professor of International Relations
La Trobe University, Melbourne
Australia

First published 2002 by
PALGRAVE MACMILLAN
Houndmills, Basingstoke, Hampshire RG21 6XS and
175 Fifth Avenue, New York, N.Y. 10010
Companies and representatives throughout the world

PALGRAVE MACMILLAN is the global academic imprint of the Palgrave
Macmillan division of St. Martin's Press, LLC and of Palgrave Macmillan Ltd.
Macmillan® is a registered trademark in the United States, United Kingdom
and other countries. Palgrave is a registered trademark in the European
Union and other countries.

ISBN 0–333–97122–1 hardback
ISBN 0–333–97123–X paperback

This book is printed on paper suitable for recycling and made from fully
managed and sustained forest sources.

A catalogue record for this book is available from the British Library.

Library of Congress Cataloging-in-Publication Data

Democratizing global governance / edited by Esref Aksu and Joseph A. Camilleri.
p. cm.
Includes bibliographical references and index.
ISBN 0–333–97122–1   ISBN 0–333–97123–X (pbk.)
1. Globalization. 2. International organization. 3. Democracy. 4. Security,
International. I. Aksu, Esref, 1969- II. Camilleri, Joseph A., 1944-

JZ1318 .D45 2002
327–dc21   2002022081

10   9   8   7   6   5   4   3   2   1
11   10   09   08   07   06   05   04   03   02

Printed and bound in Great Britain by
Antony Rowe Ltd, Chippenham and Eastbourne

Contents

Part IV Reimagining the Future

List of Figures

List of Tables

Notes on Contributors

Eşref Aksu, co-ordinator of the Global Governance Reform Project and a member of its Working Group, completed his doctoral studies at La Trobe University, Melbourne. His areas of specialization are peacekeeping, international organization, and normative theories. He contributed to *Reimagining the Future: Towards Democratic Governance* (2000).

Joseph A. Camilleri is Professor of International Relations at La Trobe University, Melbourne. He has written a number of important books on international relations theory, international political economy, security studies, and the Asia Pacific region, including *Civilization in Crisis* (1976), *Chinese Foreign Policy* (1980), *The End of Sovereignty* (1992), and *States, Markets and Civil Society in Asia Pacific* (2000).

Stephen Gill is Professor of Political Science at York University, Toronto, specializing in international political economy and international relations. He has been a visiting professor at various universities around the world and held a number of prestigious fellowships. He has published about 50 articles and chapters in edited collections and a number of important books, including *Gramsci, Historical Materialism and International Relations* (1993) and *Globalization, Democratization and Multilateralism* (1997). He is currently completing his new book *The Constitution of Global Capitalism*.

Michael Hamel-Green is Associate Professor in the Department of Social Inquiry and Community Studies at Victoria University, Melbourne. Active on peace and disarmament issues since the 1960s, he has published a detailed analysis of the South Pacific Nuclear Free Zone, and written many articles on regional arms control and alternative security approaches in Asia Pacific.

Adam Harmes recently completed his PhD in the Department of Political Science at York University, Toronto, and is currently a postdoctoral fellow at the Munk Centre for International Studies at the University of Toronto. He is the author of *Unseen Power: How Mutual Funds Threaten the Political and Economic Wealth of Nations*.

Mümtaz Keklik, who holds a PhD in economics, is the principal consultant for the current UNDP Project on Trade and Sustainable Human Development Report. He is the author of *Schumpeter, Innovation and Growth* (forthcoming), and has co-authored several articles including the UNDP publication on 'Budgets As If People Mattered: Democratizing Macroeconomic Policies'.

Kamal Malhotra is Senior Civil Society Adviser at UNDP. He was Co-Founder and Co-Director (1995–99) of Focus on the Global South, Bangkok, known for its progressive policy work in democratizing global finance during and after the Asian crisis. He is the co-author or co-editor of a number of recent books, including *Reimagining the Future: Towards Democratic Governance* (2000) and *Global Finance: New Thinking on Regulating Speculative Capital Markets* (2000).

Marco Mezzera is a Research Associate with Focus on the Global South, Bangkok. He holds a MSc degree in Rural Development Studies, with a specialization in Development Sociology. He has written various papers and articles, and contributed to two books: *Reimagining the Future: Towards Democratic Governance* (2000), and *Global Finance: New Thinking on Regulating Speculative Capital Markets* (2000).

Michalis S. Michael completed his PhD at La Trobe University, Melbourne, where he teaches international relations. In the past he has been employed as both an adviser and researcher for ministers and members of parliament. He has written on the role of the Greek and Cypriot communities in Australia, and is a co-ordinator of the *La Trobe Project*, a Cyprus Conflict Resolution Workshop.

Majid Tehranian, a graduate of Dartmouth and Harvard, is currently professor of international communication at the University of Hawaii, and director of the Toda Institute for Global Peace and Policy Research, Tokyo and Honolulu. His publications include 20 books and over 100 articles. His work has been translated into ten languages. He also edits *Peace & Policy* as well as the Toda Institute Book Series.

Susan Wright, a historian of science, is the co-author and editor of *Preventing a Biological Arms Race* (1990) and *The Biological Warfare Question: a Reappraisal for the 21st Century* (forthcoming) and the author of *Molecular Politics: Developing American and British Regulatory Policy for Genetic Engineering, 1972–82* (1994). In 1998–99, she was a Senior Research Fellow in the UN Institute for Disarmament Research, Geneva. She currently directs an international research project, 'Forming a North-South Alliance to Address Problems of Biological Warfare and Disarmament', at the University of Michigan.

Preface

Countless words have been spoken and written on the subject of United Nations (UN)[1] reform – so far, it seems, with limited effect. There is little reason to think that more words will succeed where so many others have failed. The events of 11 September 2001 and their immediate aftermath have provided graphic evidence, if any were required, of the marginalization of our international legal and political institutions, especially in moments of acute crisis. There is much more to this predicament than the shortcomings of the UN.

Conscious of these limitations, the present study and the Global Governance Reform Project (GGRP) which gave it birth have drawn their inspiration from a much wider agenda. For us the main preoccupation has not been UN reform *per se*, the efficient use of resources, or the speed with which decisions are made, highly desirable though these may be. Nor has it been the reorganization of this or that arm of the UN system, necessary though it undoubtedly is. Rather, our approach has been to rethink the puzzle of global governance by placing it squarely within the context of a globalizing 'economy' understood in its broader (non-economistic) sense.

This larger canvas, we are persuaded, offers the only appropriate analytical framework. It sheds new light on the present institutional fabric of international society and on its future possibilities. It widens our intellectual horizons and at the same time enhances our capacity for sustained initiative. This project, the first results of which appeared in *Reimagining the future* (2000), is therefore concerned first and foremost with meeting the challenges of globalization, with all that this implies for human security. Simply put, its focus is the legitimacy of the emerging system of global governance.

When most people hear the word 'globalization' they often think of a set of mega-trends creating a more interconnected and integrated world. Phrases such as the 'global village', the 'borderless world', the 'end of history' all convey the impression of a massive historical process that is beyond human control. Governments, economies and social institutions, we are told, have no alternative but to adapt to these apparently inexorable forces.

Plausible though it may sound, this view of the world is dangerously simplistic. It conveniently forgets that globalization is not just a set of trends, but also a conscious political project. Global capital and technology flows are not divinely preordained, they are the result of conscious decisions and policies.

Of course, 'globalization' is multidimensional. It involves an intricate mosaic of ideas, images, symbols, fashions and identities. Yet such diversity and complexity cannot obscure the fact that the world's productive assets and the world's trade and financial markets are now dominated by large institutional investors and transnational corporations (TNCs).

As a consequence we have seen the commercialization of almost every facet of social interaction. The legalization of property rights now extends to plants, seeds, genes and various forms of intellectual activity, a process with far-reaching and as yet dimly perceived implications. Ironically, it is unfolding with extraordinary speed but negligible public debate in the very societies that pride themselves on their liberal democratic credentials.

If the notion of global governance is to do justice to the multiple challenges of globalization, then multilateral reform cannot be confined to the UN. To reform the Secretariat and its various departments – or even the Security Council and the General Assembly – is important but clearly not enough. Needless to say, the UN's special funds, programmes and subsidiary organs are all an integral part of the reform agenda. But so are the world's most powerful international institutions, notably the International Monetary Fund (IMF), the World Bank and the World Trade Organization (WTO) which ironically enough have only the most tenuous links with the UN's principal deliberative organs. Regional organizations – some with a predominantly economic focus, others performing a range of security functions – must also be brought into the equation.

Nor can the fate of multilateral institutions be divorced from the actions of their member states or those of other actors on the world stage. Writing more than a decade ago, Sir Sridath Ramphal, then Commonwealth Secretary-General, wrote:

> the paradox and tragedy of recent times is that even as the need for better management of relations between nations and for a multilateral approach to global problems has become more manifest, support for multilateralism has weakened, eroded by some of the strongest nations … . This is most true, of course, of the United States, whose recent behaviour has served actually to weaken the structures of multilateralism, including the United Nations itself.[2]

Much that has happened since the end of the Cold War has confirmed the accuracy of this assessment. There can be little doubt that the United States in particular and the Permanent Five more generally have often allowed narrow self-interest to dictate their actions. Whether by omission or commission, they have tarnished the UN's reputation, and with it the appeal of international citizenship. Yet they are not the only culprits.

Rwanda, East Timor, Sierra Leone, Afghanistan, to name a few, are living reminders of the short-sightedness of states, large and small. The inadequacies of international bureaucracies are numerous and well known. But more significant is the role of large TNCs, banks and financial markets. The enormous, often highly damaging impact of their decisions, is matched only by an almost complete lack of accountability, except perhaps to their shareholders and indirectly at best to their customers. The failure of the mass media to inform and analyse accurately and impartially is itself highly damaging to any prospect for humane governance. Nor can civil-society organizations (CSOs), especially some of the larger non-governmental organizations (NGOs),[3] be regarded as entirely blameless, if one is to judge by their petty rivalries, the priority often given to protecting their own turf, and their frequent failure to consult with the people whose needs are ostensibly their primary concern.

In the face of these institutional bottlenecks, it is time to return to first principles. This is not to dismiss the usefulness of incremental change, or the need for practical reforms. On the other hand, a return to first principles is itself a practical necessity. Without it, it is hard to see how states, peoples and the international community generally will renew their enthusiasm for reform, or indeed how they will oversee over a prolonged period the small but innumerable legal, administrative and financial steps that are needed along the way.

None of this is to say that there already exists or will soon emerge a normative consensus as to the strategic priorities of the reform agenda. Nor does it suggest that the contributors to this volume are themselves in complete agreement either in their analysis or their advocacy. The reader will discern important differences in the way states and civil society are conceptualized, as in the relative weight attached to institutional reform at the various tiers of governance – local, national, regional and global.

All the contributors nevertheless share the view that, to be viable, the reform agenda must adopt an unashamedly radical perspective – not in the sense that it makes revolutionary proposals, but that it keeps the spotlight on a number of fundamental questions:

- Is it possible to democratize national political systems, but also the global (and regional) multilateral system? If so, how? Is democratization compatible with effectiveness and traditional notions of sovereignty?
- Are security and economy separate concerns? If not, how can the necessary connections be made, conceptually and organizationally?
- Is it true that we are seeing the early signs of an emerging global civil society? If so, is such a step to be encouraged? By what practical steps? Can CSOs contribute more effectively to the democratization of global governance? With what consequences for national and multilateral institutions?

The contributors to this volume are of the view that these less conventional but more creative concerns must guide and stimulate the reform agenda. This approach has three far-reaching implications: it forces us to rethink what we mean by success and failure; it helps us formulate more imaginative yet more realistic proposals for change; it sheds new light on the global constituency for multilateral reform.

To grapple with this rather large and potentially unmanageable agenda, the conveners of this project made a number of strategic choices, and commissioned three studies, each of which deals with an area that is important in its own right, but crucially connects with the larger concerns outlined above. The central themes of these three studies (*globalization and global governance*, *global financial flows* and *global peace and security*) are reflected in the first three parts that make up the core of this publication. Given that each of these three themes itself covers a rather large area, the project has had to sharpen its focus by strategically selecting a number of issues for closer examination.

The first part, *Global Governance*, identifies the growing gap between '*de facto*' and '*de jure*' institutions of global governance as the central problem of our time. While the UN system is legally in charge of international peace and security, it is chiefly the actions of well-armed states that exacerbate or settle international conflicts. While state sovereignty is still legally the corner-stone of the international system, it is primarily transnational actors that effectively shape global financial and economic aspects of governance. In other words, global legal institutions have not kept pace with the reach and the power of most influential political and economic actors. If unchecked, current trends, it is argued, weaken still further the social and political fabric of existing states without substituting alternative forms of legitimate governance.

Part II, *Global Financial Flows*, begins with a brief review of the nature and impact of economic globalization, and then proceeds to an equally brief description of the main features of the globalization of financial/capital flows. The part then surveys and evaluates a number of recent proposals for regional and international regulation of financial flows, before setting out the principles that should govern sustainable social and human development at the national, regional and global level. In particular, it concentrates on three key areas which relate to the global level: making the Bretton Woods institutions accountable to a reformed UN system; developing a world financial framework; and integrating civil-society concerns and agencies into the reform of the international financial system.

Part III, *Global Peace and Security*, focuses on issues of conflict prevention, disarmament and peace operations. It spells out the normative and organizational principles that should govern the UN's peace and security agenda. Success or failure, it argues, must ultimately rest on the achievement of such basic principles as minimization of violence, conflict resolution and the lasting relief of unacceptable levels of human suffering. A revitalized approach to peace and security must also give effect to notions of legitimacy and democracy, and be pursued over the short, medium and long terms in ways that are mutually consistent and reinforcing.

The final part of the study, *Reimagining the Future*, brings together the multiple threads of the analysis by arguing for, and giving content to, a sustained programme of structural reform. It returns to the underlying theme presented at the outset, namely the large and growing gap between *de facto* and *de jure* global governance, and examines how that gap might be bridged. It identifies the most likely agents of change and offers new perspectives on available strategic options.

Notwithstanding the many obstacles that lie ahead, there is reason to think that the programme for reform outlined here is likely to resonate with many constituencies. Though still at an embryonic stage, a loose, diverse but potent coalition for global governance reform may soon begin to impact on international discourse and practice. This project will have amply served its purpose if it facilitates, even modestly, the development of such a trend.

It remains to acknowledge the close collaboration of the three sponsoring institutions that made this project possible: the School of Social Sciences, La Trobe University (Melbourne), Toda Institute for Global Peace and Policy Research (Tokyo and Honolulu), and Focus on the Global South (Bangkok). However, the project would not have seen the light of day were it not for the generous support of a great many other organizations and individuals. Special thanks are due to the members of the Working Group: Stephen Gill, Ehito Kimura, John Langmore, Kamal Malhotra, Marco Mezzera, Kinhide Mushakoji, Olle Nordberg, Majid Tehranian, Shibin Yuan; members of the Eminent Persons Advisory Group: Boutros Boutros-Ghali, Gareth Evans, Richard Falk, Noleen Heyzer, Javad Zarif; participants of the consultative GGRP meetings (New York, 21–24 March 2000); Rockefeller Brothers Fund; Ford Foundation; Dag Hammarskjöld Foundation; and Queens College of CUNY. Finally our sincere appreciation of the meticulous work of our copy editor, Janey Fisher.

Notes

1. In this volume, each abbreviation will usually be introduced only once: in the chapter in which it first appears. Subsequent chapters will then automatically adopt that abbreviation. Many abbreviations have been included in the glossary of abbreviations (page xviii).
2. J. Harrod and N. Schrijver (eds), *The UN under Attack*, (Aldershot: Gower, 1988).
3. NGOs, engaged in high profile advocacy in the name of public interest, are a distinctive subset of CSOs which encompass a wider range of voluntary associations, each with its distinctive identity and sense of belonging (for instance, labour unions, scientific and intellectual organizations).

Glossary of Abbreviations

ADB	Asian Development Bank
AGO	alternative government organization
APEC	Asia Pacific Economic Cooperation
ASEAN	Association of South East Asian Nations
ASEM	Asia-Europe Summit
BIBF	Bangkok International Banking Facility
BIS	Bank for International Settlements
BWC	Biological Weapons Convention
CAL	capital account liberalization
CBM	confidence-building measure
CCL	contingent credit line
CIS	Commonwealth of Independent States
CSO	civil society organization
CTBT	Comprehensive Test Ban Treaty
CTT	currency transaction tax
CWC	Chemical Weapons Convention
DPA	Department of Political Affairs
DPKO	Department of Peacekeeping Operations
ECO	Economic Cooperation Organization
ECOSOC	Economic and Social Council of the United Nations
EMU	European Monetary Union
ERM	exchange rate mechanism
EU	European Union
FDI	foreign direct investment
FMCT	Fissile Materials Cut-Off Treaty
FSF	Financial Stability Forum
FTAA	Free Trade Area of the Americas
G7	Group of Seven (Britain, Canada, France, Germany, Italy, Japan, USA)
GATT	General Agreement on Tariffs and Trade
GDI	Gender-related Development Index
GDP	Gross Domestic Product
GEI	Gender Empowerment Index
GNP	Gross National Product
HDI	Human Development Index
ICJ	International Court of Justice
IFI	international financial institution
IGO	inter-governmental organization
IMF	International Monetary Fund
INTELSAT	International Satellite Organization
IOSCO	International Organization of Securities Commissions

LANWFZ	Latin American Nuclear Weapon-Free Zone Treaty
LDC	less-developed countries
MAI	Multilateral Agreement on Investment
MDC	more-developed countries
MERCOSUR	Southern Common Market
MFZ	Missile-free zone
NAFTA	North American Free Trade Area
NAM	Non-Aligned Movement
NATO	North Atlantic Treaty Organization
NESDB	National Economic and Social Development Board
NGO	non-governmental organization
NPT	Non-Proliferation Treaty
NWFZ	nuclear-weapon-free zone
OAS	Organization of American States
OAU	Organization of African Unity
ODA	Official Development Assistance
OECD	Organization of Economic Co-operation and Development
OPEC	Organization of Petroleum Exporting Countries
OSCE	Organization for Security and Co-operation in Europe
PTBT	Partial Test Ban Treaty
SAARC	South Asian Association for Regional Co-operation
SAPRI	Structural Adjustment Participatory Review Initiative
SET	Stock Exchange of Thailand
START	Strategic Arms Reduction Treaty
TFC	transnational financial corporation
TMC	transnational media corporation
TNC	transnational corporation
TRIPS	Trade Related Intellectual Property Rights
UNCTAD	United Nations Conference on Trade and Development
UNDP	United Nations Development Program
UNEP	United Nations Enviroment Program
UNPO	Unrepresented Peoples' Organization
VAT	value added tax
WFP	World Food Program
WHO	World Health Organization
WIPO	World Intellectual Property Organization
WMD	weapons of mass destruction
WMDFZ	weapons-of-mass-destruction-free zone
WTO	World Trade Organization

Part I
Global Governance

1
Globalization and Governance: an Overview

Majid Tehranian

> One of the best ways to explore global governance, what world government we actually have had, is to consider the history of world organizations, those intergovernmental and quasi-governmental global agencies that have (nominally) been open to any independent state (even though all states may not have joined).
>
> Craig Murphy (1994), p.1

Since the Treaty of Westphalia (1648), global governance has been predicated on a territorial state system nested in an international capitalist order. In the twentieth century, the communist, fascist and Third World challenges to that order led to the breakdown of the European, American and Japanese empires. Ultimately, competing national capitalisms and territorial states gave shape to the contemporary institutions of global governance. At the same time, tensions have increased among global capital, territorial states and civil societies. With the collapse of the Soviet Union in 1991 and the end of bipolar rivalries between the American and Soviet camps, a global capitalist regime armed with a neo-liberal ideology has emerged. The neo-liberal project is attempting to integrate the international political economy around the rule of transnational capital. Frictions between global capitalism, the state system and an emerging international civil society are framing the conflicts of the twenty-first century.

Unless a more balanced global governance regime is achieved, violent conflict will continue among and within states. State and counter-state terrorism will also continue to undermine international security. Since trade and investment patterns favour some regions (notably North America, Western Europe and East Asia) in preference to others (notably Africa and parts of Asia and Latin America), widening wealth and income gaps among states are to be expected. But since global capitalism transcends the state system, these widening gaps are also increasingly evident within states. The Quandong Province in China, the Bangalore and Hyderabad regions in India, and Silicon Valley and Orange County in the United States have been growth poles leaping ahead of other regions within their own states while interacting with high-tech industries in a global economy.

Evolution of the capitalist state

Since the Peace of Westphalia, the modern capitalist state has gone through enormous changes. These must be understood in the context of the interplay of four fundamental forces that have framed democratic discourse and practice: the state, the market, civil society and communication networks. The triangle of state, market and civil society floats in a porous circle of national culture penetrated by global economic, military and cultural flows (see Figure 1.1). The public intellectuals in the academic and media worlds, as well as the formal and informal communication networks, serve as the connective nerves of information and analysis in the policy domain. Each of the main stakeholders has gone through an evolutionary process. None of the phases discussed below is applicable to all states, global corporations and civil societies. As the most advanced modern democratic capitalist society, the United States is the best exemplar of some of these developments. Many of the references below will therefore be to American history. Details clearly vary from country to country, but the general drift seems to hold for most parts of the world.

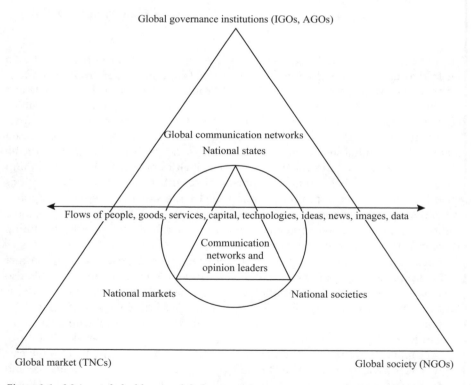

Figure 1.1   Major stakeholders in global governance

Source: M. Tehranian, *Global Communication and World Politics: Domination, Development and Discourse* (Boulder, CO: Lynne Rienner, 1999), p.69.

The modern capitalist state has experienced at least five overlapping and contradictory phases in its evolution. The rise of capitalism prompted the development of a democratic type of state in Western Europe and the United States which called for minimal government interference in business and trade. Adam Smith's 'invisible hand' was part of a classical liberal doctrine that maintained, 'a government is best that governs least'. Historically, however, it was the *visible* hand of the government that, in co-operation with a rising capitalist class, directed the development of national capitalism in a variety of states. Nevertheless, this phase of development of the modern democratic state can be called the *minimalist* state in that government confined itself to the maintenance of national security and a legal framework favourable to capital.

With the rise of monopoly capital in the late nineteenth century, the state went through an important transformation and became a *regulatory* state. The anti-trust legislation passed in the United States during the Progressive Era was a clear effort in this direction, but the return of unbridled capitalism during the 1920s resulted in the Great Crash of 1929 and worldwide depression.

The Great Depression of the 1930s thus ushered in a third shift, from the regulatory to the *social welfare* state. In line with Keynesian economic theories, New Deal policies in the United States took it as axiomatic that the capitalist state must take responsibility for growth and stability, full employment, and a complex array of transfer payments to ensure effective demand for sustained economic development. These transfer payments included unemployment compensation, social security and medical insurance.

The transition from the social welfare to the *warfare* state took place during World War II and its aftermath, the Cold War, when heightened international tensions between the capitalist and communist blocs led to an unprecedented arms race. A perceptive political economist, Joseph Schumpeter, could view capitalism as a relatively peaceful social system prior to this era. But confronted with revolutionary possibilities in its worldwide spheres of investment and trade, the capitalist state consciously turned towards permanent armament.

For the latecomers to industrial revolution, the role of the state in capital accumulation and infrastructure construction has been critical. Although the communist revolutions in Russia, China and other countries espoused a socialist ideology, their centralized state-controlled economies can be more accurately labelled 'state capitalist'. During a period of primitive accumulation, the necessary physical, educational and social infrastructure was built, while civil liberties were suspended and industrialization progressed without significantly raising standards of living. With the introduction of market forces in Russia and China in the 1980s and 1990s, both countries have increasingly entered the global capitalist economy while reducing their antagonism to the West.

Since the fall of the Soviet Union, East–West conflicts have given way to North–South antagonisms. Global capitalism faces no credible threat except from its own domestic and international peripheries in the urban ghettoes, rural hinterlands and such rebellious states as Iran, Iraq and Libya. The rise during the 1980s and 1990s of a neo-conservative and neo-liberal movement to cut government spending on social welfare seems, therefore, to have inaugurated a new era that may be called, in Robert Reich's apt phrase, the *corporate welfare* state. This new era also corresponds to the quickening pace of globalization of the markets and increasing world competition for raw materials, sources of investment and consumer markets. It has consequently led to a new division of international labour in which the previously industrialized countries focus on high-tech industries and services (arms, aerospace, computers, biotechnology, banking and insurance). By contrast, the newly industrialized countries concentrate on labour-intensive industries such as production of raw materials, textiles, microprocessing and automobiles. In the meantime, the transitional-industrialized countries of Central and Eastern Europe are desperately trying to find a niche in this new international division of labour. Each capitalist state has thus been attempting to maximize its competitive position in world markets by formally or informally supporting the efforts of its own indigenous corporations while attracting foreign capital to its own shores.

The new capitalist state, whether among the previously industrialized, newly industrialized or transitional-industrialized countries, is a globalist state. While each capitalist state is committed to the welfare of its own indigenous capital, it cannot ignore the stark realities of an increasingly interdependent world market. When the Mexican and East Asian economies faltered in the 1990s, international capital had no hesitation in bailing out their banking and credit systems by substantial loans from the IMF. These loans were tied to the IMF regime of fiscal and monetary adjustments. The new capitalist state in the age of global capitalism is committed to a triple function: military security, economic growth and corporate and social welfare. These goals all imply an activist state co-ordinating its functions with global capital constantly adjusting to the changing world technological and economic environment. The capitalist state thus continues to re-regulate rather than deregulate while shifting the burden of social welfare spending to the private sector. There is no sign of a shrinking state. On the contrary, government spending as a proportion of GDP has been moving ever upward in all major capitalist countries, with that proportion growing by an average rate of 50 per cent from 1870 to 1996.

Evolution of the capitalist market

Similarly, we may discern an evolutionary process in the changing national and global capitalist markets. The movement from *national* to *corporate* and *global* capitalism has been a less sharply punctuated process than the evolution of the state. Although Marx and Engels correctly argued that capitalism is inherently an internationalist system, World Wars I and II were primarily a product of the intense competition among the old and new capitalist states. Britain, France and the United States had already carved out major parts of the world as colonial or neo-colonial territories before Germany, Italy and Japan were strong enough to challenge them.

The defeat of the Axis powers in World War II ushered in a new phase in the development of capitalism that may be called *corporate capitalism*. Led by US corporate investments in Western Europe, West and East Asia, and Latin America, corporations from Europe, Japan and other newcomers (for example, South Korea, Taiwan, China, Indonesia, Malaysia) soon followed suit. The corporation as a business organization offers several unique advantages when compared to other forms of business. It raises vast sums of capital, and disburses them globally. It frees stockholders of personal liability. Expert professionals rather than family members manage it. It has gained legal status as an autonomous entity with the rights of free speech to advertise, to sue and to be sued. And, because of its enormous size and financial capability, it can muster a vast array of lawyers, lobbyists and accountants to influence state laws and regulations to its own advantage.

In the postwar period, several hundred such national corporations became multinational and transnational in scope, attracting capital from all over the world and operating in more than 100 countries. With the demise of the Soviet Union and the opening of China and East Asia to foreign investment, TNCs have achieved virtually global reach. As a consequence, state regulatory systems can no longer exert significant influence on the behaviour of global corporations. National states have to compete for the favour of global corporations rather than the other way around. Public regulation is increasingly placed at the service of private enterprise. In the absence of effective oversight, global regulatory systems cannot but lag behind the development of global capitalism. Not suprisingly, environmental catastrophes, whether in Bhopal, the Amazon rain forest or Sumatra, and financial disasters, whether it be the Mexican or East Asian currency crash, occur with increasing frequency.

In international economic policy, the trends are clearer. Strategic knowledge industries have been heavily promoted by the advanced industrial states. Their interests are strongly protected under a global intellectual property regime. As Michael Ryan writes,

U.S. patent and copyright business interest groups drove trade-related intellectual property policy in the 1980s and 1990s, although the diplomacy was conducted on their behalf by the U.S. executive branch ... [Related] industries brought the total to 5.72 per cent of GDP. The copyright industries grew at an average annual rate almost double that of the economy as a whole from 1977 to 1994. In 1994 they employed 3.1 million people, and 2.8 million worked in related industries. By 1995 foreign sales grew to more than 10 per cent of all sales by the U.S. copyright industries; they ranked behind only motor vehicles–auto parts and agricultural products.[1]

The strategic alliance between capitalist states and their TNC partners is not new, but the shift to knowledge industries and intellectual-property rights is characteristic of the new phenomenon of global capitalism and informatic imperialism. The locus of decision-making in intellectual property had to be changed from the World Intellectual Property Organization (WIPO) with its one-nation, one-vote procedures to the the General Agreement on Tariffs and Trade (GATT) forum where decisions reflect bargaining based on economic power. When the final GATT agreements were signed in Marrakesh in 1994, the agreement on Trade-Related Intellectual Property Rights (TRIPS) represented a triumph not only for the US copyright industries but also for the emerging international regime of technological innovation and protection.

Less-developed countries (LDCs) wishing to gain access to foreign trade and capital have had little choice but to buy into this new regime. There is much evidence to suggest that TNCs have appropriated local knowledge and products in the LDCs to patent them under new guises and so protect them from competition. The Indian neem tree, the African soapberry and Central Asian cotton provide examples from which a diversity of useful industrial products can be made by learning the local knowledge. By adopting and developing that knowledge in laboratories through genetic engineering, TNCs have established patent monopolies that deny access to competitors.[2] The intellectual property regime thus promoted by TRIPS can perpetuate the dominance of existing patent-holders unless and until the LDCs can break through with their own technological innovations and patenting.

Evolution of global governance

To understand the evolution of global governance, it is necessary to review the development of global institutions. These have sprung up with the intensification of social, political and economic relations across state boundaries. Along with territorial states, global institutions currently shape the rule-making, rule-enforcement, rule-adjudication, rule-communication and rule-surveillance functions of our global civilization. It is useful, however, to draw a distinction between *de facto* and *de jure* global governance regimes. The latter basically consists of the UN system and its complex of international treaties. The former includes the UN system but goes well beyond it, encompassing the governance of the global market, society and communication networks by transnational manufacturing, financial and media corporations, as well as by such transnational NGOs as the Catholic Church and Amnesty International. Table 1.1 provides a schematic view of the *de jure* global governance regimes. (For a schematic view of the *de facto* global governance regime, see the next chapter).

We may distinguish four distinct historical periods in the evolution of global governance: the inter-imperial order, the League of Nations system, the United Nations system, and the post-Cold War (dis)order.

The inter-imperial order, 1814–1914

Craig Murphy has identified the beginning of global governance as the *inter-imperial order*, lasting from 1814 to roughly 1914.[3] This order included the Austro-Hungarian, Belgian, British, Danish, Dutch, French, German, Italian, Portuguese, Russian, Spanish and Swedish empires and their extensions.

The Congress of Vienna and the Holy Alliance began this era. The Congress of Vienna (September 1814–June 1815), initiated by the alliance that overthrew Napoleon, set out to remake Europe in the post-Napoleonic period. To guarantee

Table 1.1   Evolution of global governance: *De jure* aspects

	Inter-imperial 1814–14	League of Nations 1918–40	United Nations 1945–89	Post-Cold War 1989–present
Rule making	International treaties Concert of Europe resolutions	LN resolutions International treaties	UN resolutions International treaties	UN International treaties Regional organizations (NAFTA, EU, CIS, ASEAN ...)
Rule implementation	Imperial states Concert of Europe IGOs	Imperial states IGOs NGOs	Superpowers NATO Warsaw Pact UN IGOs NGOs	Superpower NATO CIS UN IGOs NGOs
Rule adjudication	Permanent Court of Arbitration International Court of Prize	ICJ	ICJ Nuremberg Tribunal	ICJ WTO International Criminal Court ICTY, ICTR
Rule communication	Print media	Print media Radio	Print media Radio TV	Print media Radio TV Internet
Rule surveillance and evaluation	Diplomats Spies Critics	Diplomats Spies Critics	Diplomats Spies Critics	Diplomats Spies Critics

the peace, the Congress created an international balance-of-power system. Diplomatic rights and responsibilities were more precisely defined in European agreements. Such political acts institutionalized the idea of common international zones and inter-state relations.[4]

To preserve their territorial sovereignty, the great powers largely pursued status quo policies based on the balance of power. Whenever international problems arose, they held *ad hoc* conferences collectively known as the Concert of Europe. Spain and Italy both experienced uprisings in support of constitutional government in the years 1820 and 1822 respectively, but the Concert was able to exert its influence and suppress them, although Britain refused to join in the Concert's attempt to intervene in Latin America's revolutions.

The enunciation of the US Monroe Doctrine in 1823[5] prevented European states from gaining control of Latin America.[6] It asserted that the United States did not belong to the European political system, that a distinctive system existed on the western side of the Atlantic, and that the United States saw itself as the protector of independent nations in the Americas.[7] The implication of the Doctrine was that the American states could not participate in the political discussions of the European powers. Although many European nations were reluctant to comply formally with its tenets, the Monroe Doctrine represented one of the first attempts to devise a code of conduct between Europe and the United States, significantly increasing the scope of international governance.

The Concert of Europe lasted for 90 years, during which the Crimean War was the only major international war. Unable to facilitate the peaceful settlement of disputes, the Concert's legitimacy quickly faded thereafter. The Concert did, however, enjoy significant legitimacy for a period of time, during which it provided a communication channel between the European states without infringing on their sovereignty or proposing a common moral consensus. The need for further institutionalization of governance would soon be demonstrated by the outbreak of World War I.

In the meantime, global institutionalization was proceeding in such functional areas as telecommunication and transportation. New telecommunication technologies, in particular, were reinforcing the need for international co-operation. The first of these was the telegraph, which allowed information to be transmitted in encoded form by signals across long distances. The International Telegraph Union (ITU) was formed in 1865 to regulate this technology. The General Postal Union was formed in 1874, and renamed the Universal Postal Union (UPU) in 1875. The Radiotelegraph Union (RTU) was also formed in 1906. These institutions were important in establishing the necessary rules for the more efficient governance of international communication. By signing and ratifying the relevant agreements, sovereign states had consented to the domestic enforcement of these rules.

Another international regime focused on the protection of 'intellectual property' – a phrase which came into usage in the 1840s, a time of rapid technological change. Intellectual property refers to innovations that employ patents, copyrights, licences and trademarks for protection against unauthorized use. The current intellectual property regime may be traced back to the establishment of the United International Bureau for the Protection of Intellectual Property (BIRPI), which itself grew out of a merger between two intellectual property organizations formed during the inter-imperial era.

The emergence of these public international unions thus played a critical role in the globalization of the world. By the nineteenth century, a new world order had been established that divided the world between colonizers and colonized, and produced a new international division of labour that assigned the production of raw materials largely to the colonies and manufactured goods to the colonial powers. While capital, technology and management came from the centres, the peripheries provided consumer markets and cheap or slave labour. Global governance in the form of regulating international functional organizations was no longer a mere ambition. It had become a necessity for the new order.

However, Asia was not fully covered by the public international unions. Developed to manage the 'global' economic system, the unions were still primarily focused on western trade. For example, the International Union for Publication of

Customs and Tariffs, formed in 1890, assisted in the liberalization of trade in the western world by publishing only the current tariffs of its member nations. The nineteenth century may thus be considered a period of European global hegemony. Stavrianos argues that Europe was able to act as a global hegemon partly because Asia was simply not interested.[8] More importantly, however, the key to Europe's success was its modern, capitalist mode of production which rested on the profit motive, scientific and technological innovation, and global expansion. Despite its resistance Asia was forcibly brought into the orbit of the world capitalist system.

The colonization of the Americas also significantly contributed to Europe's hegemonic status, giving it new sources of raw materials and a safety valve for the emigration of its excess labour force. Europe and its various dependencies thus formed the base for the institutions of global governance. The rise of the United States as a world power was a gradual one. Traditionally an anti-colonial country, it would soon rise to imperial status with the support of the doctrine of Manifest Destiny. At the turn of the century, the doctrine would be used to justify US imperial expansion into Cuba, Hawaii and the Philippines.

Over the last hundred years, increasing global connections, mediated largely by NGOs, have added yet another element to global governance. Their function has been to address problems often neglected by governments but of intense interest to an emerging global civil society. International NGOs bring together groups of people from around the world sharing common interests and perspectives, and pool resources available to their members to lobby governments. A number of NGOs act independently of governments, but others are directly or indirectly controlled by governments and to that extent are operating under false pretenses.

Though initially limited to social services that did not challenge the authority of governments, NGOs have gradually entered into such fields as human rights and environmental protection that cross into politically sensitive domains. The World Alliance of Young Men's Christian Associations was founded in 1855, the International Veterinarian Congress in 1863, the International Federation of Metal Workers Organization in 1893, and the International Council of Nurses in 1899. In response to the suffering of the war victims, the Red Cross (ICRC) was established in 1863 to assume a neutral role in relief and rehabilitation. The movement, originally intended to remedy the battlefield conditions at Solferino, subsequently evolved into a worldwide system of relief and rehabilitation in natural as well as human-made disasters.[9]

International law determines and limits the boundaries of state and NGO action. Today, the term 'international law' increasingly refers to a body of more or less formalized rules which regulate inter-state relations, and, to a lesser extent, the interaction between states and other international actors. It is primarily based both on customary usage and on the provisions of multilateral or bilateral agreements. It is also influenced by the writings of jurists, unratified treaties, and decisions of international, and even national, tribunals. It is not enforced by any supranational body; but it is recognized in practice, and enforcement is by virtue of world opinion, third-state intervention, sanctions of international organizations and, as a last resort, war.

The movement to promote the rule of international law also gave rise to several NGOs dedicated to that purpose. The Institute of International Law was founded in 1873 in Ghent, Belgium, by Baron Rolin-Jacquemyns who wished the institution to 'develop and implement international law as a codified science responsible for the legal morality and integrity of the civilized world'.[10] The Institute's goal was to legitimize international law, a concept still in its infancy at that time. The primary channel of enforcement, however, was then and continued to be states themselves.

The League of Nations era, 1918–40

The formation of new global institutions often takes place after particularly horrific tragedies which force states to reconsider past patterns of international behaviour. The League of Nations was formed in response to World War I, with the same goal of promoting peace as the Holy Alliance. The League's 26 articles were the same 26 articles contained in the peace treaties concluded after the war. The great powers leading the League wanted to deny Germany the ability to wage war. The League's Covenant also included the principle of national self-determination as well as the exclusive right of individual states to their own domestic affairs. To resolve the potential contradiction between these two principles the League adopted the idea of collective security. As a principle, collective security commits individual member states to act together when they have identified a threat to international peace and security. The League created two organs, the Council and the Assembly. The Council comprised permanent and non-permanent members whose unanimous agreement was needed for the League to adopt any resolution. The failure of the United States to join the League weakened it considerably. While it achieved minor successes in the peaceful settlement of international disputes and set an important precedent for international co-operation, the League was in practice unable to deter aggression.

A number of significant institutional innovations did nevertheless emerge during the inter-war years. In the area of adjudication, the Geneva General Act for the Settlement of Disputes, adopted by the League in 1928, provided for the settlement of disputes between states by the arbitration of five adjudicators. Between 1902 and 1932, the Permanent Court of Arbitration heard 20 cases. The League also established the Permanent Court of Justice in 1922. As with the Court of Arbitration, its jurisdiction was limited by agreement of the parties in each case.

The League also attempted to regulate the world economy. With funding sorely needed for reconstruction and reparations after the war, the League formed the Financial Commission. Its principal functions were to regulate lending to the defeated powers and the Eastern European successor states, reconcile reparations with financial stability, reduce trade barriers, and reconstruct the international monetary system. The international currency exchange system, which came formally into effect in the late nineteenth century, used gold as the standard of exchange. However, in part because of the inherent limitations to liquidity of the gold standard, the system broke down in 1914 and was replaced by a gold-bullion standard. Individual states were ultimately responsible for the enforcement of these and other rules.

Following World War I, new technological developments boosted economic growth. The output of planes, cars, radios and a range of chemical products rose dramatically. The rapid growth of the working class and the establishment of the eight-hour working day, coupled with the development of mass production, encouraged economic development. However, wartime destruction pushed many European governments to print extravagant amounts of money to finance reparations and pay back their creditors. Spiralling inflation set in without end in sight.[11] Custom barriers went up in Europe in the 1920s, and in the absence of domestic and international regulation of trade and finance, the Great Depression ensued in the 1930s, prompting record levels of unemployment. That in turn caused governments to redouble their protectionist policies, further hindering world co-operation, with international trade and development shrinking to record lows.

In all this, the League was relatively ineffectual. Following Japan's occupation of Manchuria in 1931, China immediately appealed to the League, but the latter could do nothing to stop Japan, which subsequently withdrew its membership. It was similarly unresponsive to Italy's conquest of Ethiopia in 1935–36, being unable to reach agreement on critical oil sanctions because of America's refusal to co-operate. The United States at that time controlled half of the world oil trade, making it an indispensable player in any effort. The League also failed to stop Germany's seizure of Austria in 1938.

The Treaty of Versailles had called for heavy war reparations by Germany. A commission that assessed the losses incurred by the civilian population set an amount of $33 billion[12] in 1921. Economists declared that such a huge sum could not be collected without upsetting international trade and finance. Insisting that Germany must pay, the Allies secured a treaty permitting them to take punitive actions if Germany fell behind in its payments. The harshness of the Treaty fanned the flames of nationalism in Germany, while the allies' subsequent lax enforcement of it paved the way for the upsurge of German militarism in the 1930s. Hitler withdrew Germany from membership of the League in 1933. When he re-militarized the Rhineland in 1936 (a violation of the Treaty of Versailles), the Allies did nothing to stop him, thereby encouraging future German aggression.

A number of inter-governmental organizations (IGOs) did survive the League's failure. One of these was the International Labour Organization (ILO), an autonomous part of the League of Nations, which by 1996 had 174 member states. Its functions were not greatly in need of the League's support. Its goals were to improve labour conditions, raise living standards and promote productive employment. The new IGOs obviously responded to perceived and continuing needs in particular functional areas. The Bank for International Settlements (BIS), founded in 1930 to manage World War I reparations, facilitated co-operation among the central banks. The UPU and ITU would continue to operate as IGOs under the UN system. Together with other IGOs, they would contribute to the development of international regulation in their respective functional arenas.

In co-operation with NGOs working in their own fields, IGOs would also perform research and lobbying functions. This trend began with the development of trade unions, notably the International Federation of Metal Workers. The International Chamber of Commerce was established in 1920. Save the Children was formed in 1919 and became globalized in the 1930s. NGOs served to monitor, lobby and publicize their various causes, which ranged from single issues, as in the case of Save the Children, to broad goals of integration, as with the Federation of International Institutions formed in Geneva in 1929. Their membership was diverse, including a mix of individuals, other organizations and sometimes governmental agencies. Using their research networks, NGOs would provide other channels of information and communication, thus helping to develop and promote international rules and regulations.

The United Nations system, 1945–89

The Great Depression and World War II persuaded the international community that institutions were needed with a greater capacity to manage international peace, security and economic affairs. A change of mind had taken place in the United States regarding international organizations. In the aftermath of the war, the United States stood out as the world's most powerful state, in possession of the nuclear bomb and some 50 per cent of the global gross product. Having experienced a great depression and another world war, the US leadership had renounced unilateral isolationism in favour of multilateralist engagement in world affairs.[13] With the defeat of the Axis powers in sight, the Allied powers (the United States, Britain and the Soviet Union) started making preparations for a postwar order.

Their first significant initiative, the establishment of a new multipurpose global organization to help manage international affairs,[14] was articulated when Roosevelt and Churchill signed the Atlantic Charter in August 1941. The name 'United Nations' was originally used to denote the nations allied against Germany, Italy and Japan, with 26 countries signing the Declaration by the United Nations on 1 January 1942, a document that set forth the war aims of the Allied powers. The United States, Britain and the Soviet Union took the lead in designing the new organization and determining its decision-making structures and functions. Although the Big Three and their respective leaders (Roosevelt, Churchill and Stalin) eventually reached a compromise, political differences that foreshadowed the Cold War hindered agreement. These concerned issues of membership, colonies, and voting formulae in the General Assembly and the Security Council. In the case of membership, the Soviet Union demanded voting rights for its constituent republics, while Britain wanted assurances that its colonies would not be placed under UN control. There was also disagreement over the voting system to be adopted in the Security Council, an issue that became known as the power of veto.

At the Yalta Conference in February 1945, the Big Three laid the basis for Charter provisions delimiting the authority of the Security Council. They also reached a tentative accord on the number of Soviet republics to be granted independent membership status, and on the creation of a trusteeship system to succeed the League's mandate system.

The Big Three agreements formed the basis of negotiations at the United Nations Conference convened in San Francisco on 25 April 1945. It produced the final Charter of the UN, which enshrined the power of veto for the five permanent members of the Security Council (Britain, China, France, the Soviet Union and the United States). The conference also reached compromises on such issues as the line to be drawn between domestic and international jurisdiction for the protection of human rights, promotion of economic and social welfare, status of colonial areas, distribution of trusteeships, status of regional and defence arrangements, and great-power dominance versus equality of states.

Representatives of 50 states attended the San Francisco Conference, including 21 from the Americas, nine from continental Europe, seven from the Middle East, five from the Commonwealth, two Soviet republics (in addition to the Soviet Union), three from Africa and two from East Asia. All geographic areas of the world were thus represented. The UN Charter was unanimously adopted and signed on 26 June and came into force on 24 October 1945. In 2001, UN membership stood at 189 countries.

International functional regimes

The development of specialized agencies and international functional regimes may be considered the most successful aspect of *de jure* global governance. The arenas of technical co-operation are where the divergent interests of states are most likely to converge. These range from global postal services to the allocation of electromagnetic frequencies, the apportioning of space in the geo-stationary orbit, development of international standards in industrial production, and satellite monitoring of weather conditions. For each of these functions and many others, a specialized agency has been created by inter-governmental agreement that sets the rules, assists in their implementation and sometimes adjudication. Understood in this sense, the system is often referred to as an 'international regime'. By adding 'functional' to this appellation, we arrive at a more precise notion of multidimensional tasks performed by these international functional regimes.

The waning of the United Nations?

In the western world in general and the United States in particular, the initial enthusiasm for the UN came gradually to an end as the West lost its numerical majority. The Soviet and Chinese use of the veto and the increasing number of non-western UN members progressively undermined western control. The anti-colonial stance of the LDCs and growing demands for equality in an unequal world also came into direct conflict with western interests and perceptions. On the economic front, continuing US balance of payment deficits resulting from the Vietnam War led the United States to abandon gold convertibility. The Bretton Woods system had pegged the international exchange system to the US dollar at $35 per ounce of gold. That system collapsed once the United States decided in 1971 to float its currency.

All these factors came to a head in the early 1970s when a group of oil exporting countries managed to raise the price of crude oil in 1973. The Organization of Petroleum Exporting Countries (OPEC, established in 1960), seemed able now to impose its will on the oil companies and the importing countries. Crude oil prices were raised 130 per cent at the Tehran Conference of December 1973, producing an 'oil shock' for the importing countries, compounded by a second oil shock occasioned by the Iranian Revolution of 1979. The price of a barrel of crude oil was ultimately raised from $3 in 1973 to $30 in 1980. At the UN, OPEC's success encouraged the LDCs in alliance with the Soviet bloc to call in 1974 for a New World Economic Order. That call was soon followed at the UN Educational, Scientific and Cultural Organization (UNESCO) with a demand for a New World Communication and Information Order. Such calls clearly hit hard at the core of western interests and priorities. The conservative backlash in Britain and the United States in the context of domestic problems and foreign threats helped to bring about the ascendancy of Margaret Thatcher and Ronald Reagan, who advocated conservative policies at home and militarist policies abroad. As a result, the UN and UNESCO came under attack in both countries. The commercial media's assault on UNESCO reached a crescendo in the mid-1980s, with the United States, Britain and Singapore withdrawing from the organization. The United States reneged the timely payment of its UN membership dues. Western states increased their pressure on the UN by calling for its reform. These attacks briefly subsided with the Clinton Administration's support for multilateralism. However, the failures of UN interventions in Somalia, Bosnia and Rwanda-Burundi led NATO to intervene in Kosovo with little reference to the UN.

The inequitable international division of labour between developed and developing countries had for long been a matter of intense debate among political economists. Developed by such neo-Marxist economists as Sweezy,[15] Baran[16] and Frank,[17] the dependency school of economic development emerged out of these debates. It argued that under colonial and neo-colonial rule the international division of labour had imposed the production of raw materials on the LDCs. By contrast, the more developed countries (MDCs) provided capital, industrial goods and financial services. The terms of trade for raw material exports having significantly deteriorated over the years, the LDCs found themselves cheated out of the possibility of using their natural resources for development. In the words of Gunder Frank, the emerging pattern of trade was contributing to the 'development of underdevelopment' in the Third World.[18] The dependency school called for changes to the international division of labour and advised Third World countries to secure an amelioration in the terms of trade, or totally break away from the international market system. The exclusion of agricultural items from the GATT negotiations added fuel to the dependency school's analysis and advocacy. To the developing countries, whose main exports were raw materials, such policies barred them entry into the protected markets of the more-developed countries.[19]

On another front, Germany and Japan as well as the larger LDCs felt under-represented in the UN system where great power politics dominated, and Cold War rivalries heavily restricted the UN's peacekeeping role. The Security Council did little to stop or mitigate the aggression by Iraq against Iran in 1980. Saudi Arabia and Kuwait actively supported Iraq by providing funds, while western powers supplied the arms and ammunitions. As a war of attrition set in, other Persian Gulf states were drawn into the conflict by a tanker war. Ultimately, Iran and Iraq accepted a UN peace plan in 1988, but casualties had risen to over one million dead and one million maimed by the use of chemical and conventional weapons.

The UN system was being bypassed by emerging organizations operating at both the apex and the base of the global governance system.[20] While the Bretton Woods institutions (that is, the World Bank and the IMF) and GATT, which is succeeded by the WTO, served primarily the interests of western powers, other IGOs, for example the International Satellite Organization (INTELSAT), were established on a commercial basis to confer on the first comers the right to use the geostationary orbit for satellites. The new technological environment favoured the advanced economies, yet at the same time a mobilized international civil society was beginning to challenge the legitimacy of hegemonic global governance.

The emergence of NGOs

The growth of international civil society augmented the UN system. To cite one obvious example, rising environmental pollution dramatized the need for supranational monitoring and management. The UN Environmental Programme (UNEP) and the 1958 adoption of the International Maritime Organization (IMO) to undertake surveillance of the world environmental pollution were responses to rising public consciousness. In other areas, the need for transnational monitoring and co-ordination was becoming increasingly apparent. The UN system was too slow to respond to the challenge. As a consequence, international civil society took it upon itself to respond wherever states and IGOs were lax or negligent. Just as domestic interest groups in democratic societies had learned to employ the power of organization to pressure their respective governments, so NGOs were learning to mobilize world public opinion on behalf of their causes.

Expanding global communication

The expansion of global telecommunications would greatly contribute to this process. Computers and satellites opened up immense possibilities for the global society. Once government and private monopolies were re-regulated in the 1980s and 1990s, global telecommunication industries took off. Worldwide telecommunication carriers from diverse regions joined together to form joint ventures that have further extended the potential for world communication. As a consequence, new industries, including telecommunication equipment vendors and value-added services or value-added networks, developed in which private enterprise controlled many aspects of communication, thereby blurring state boundaries. This market has since grown exponentially. Technological innovations on the one hand, and privatization and the competition that comes with it on the other are driving the growing market. Value-added networks provide specialized telecommunication services, including high-speed data networks for large corporations, dial-up packet data networks, and Internet access.[21] The Internet, which has become an integral part of the telecommunication system, originated in a

US Department of Defense programme called Advanced Research Projects Agency (ARPANET) established in 1969 to provide computer communication which was safe and efficient among defence-related research organizations. The programme was to be used for electronic mail or e-mail, file transfers, bulletin board newsgroups and remote computer access or telnet. The system proved so useful that other organizations began to use it. Eventually, the National Science Foundation established a network that was able to handle a much greater amount of electronic information. The expansion of the World Wide Web during the 1990s brought the Internet within the reach of a wide array of people. Allowing its users to navigate the Internet almost intuitively, directing them with pictorial representations and instructions,[22] the growth of the Web has been nothing less than spectacular. Internet hosts increased from 1.3 million mainframe computers in 1993 to 9.5 million in 1996, with subsequent growth continuing at an exponential rate.

The introduction of personal computers in the 1970s and their diffusion in the 1980s and 1990s have broadened and deepened global communication beyond expectations. Although 90 per cent of world computers are concentrated in the hands of 10 per cent of the world's population, the growth of Internet users to over 200 million has created a global network that transcends national boundaries. The far-reaching implications of the communication revolution for governance at all levels is only now beginning to be felt in such developments as the international campaign to ban landmines and the worldwide movement to support the Chiappa resistance in Mexico.[23]

The post-Cold War (dis)order, 1989–present

The end of the Cold War in 1989 ushered in a new era that is still in flux. Diversification of global institutions outside the UN system, the rise of new ethnic and nationalist movements, and the entry of China, Russia and Eastern Europe into the world markets prompted calls for the restructuring of global governance institutions. However, instead of accommodating emerging interests and voices by democratizing those institutions, the great powers have continued a policy of benign neglect, thereby contributing to conflicts that threaten international peace and security.

While the practice of international politics has not substantially changed, the discourse has. The UN-sponsored world conferences of the 1980s and 1990s have sought to develop priorities for the coming decades[24] on such issues as children's and women's rights, the environment, population, social development, crime and racism.[25] Some, like the 1990 Convention on the Rights of the Child and the 1990 World Summit for Children, resulted in treaties that set international standards for child protection. States that are parties to these treaties can now be held accountable. Other conferences, including the 1992 UN Conference on the Environment and Development (UNCED), the 1992 Framework Convention on Climate Change, the 1993 World Conference on Human Rights, the 1994 International Conference on Population and Development and the 1995 World Summit for Social Development have all helped to set guidelines and rules which provide a basis for the further development of global governance. This is not to say that such conferences and gatherings have been devoid of conflict or the pursuit of narrowly defined self-interest. The 2001 World Conference Against Racism, Racial Discrimination, Xenophobia and Related Intolerance was partially side-tracked from its main agenda by the US and Israeli walk-out on grounds of alleged anti-Zionist domination of the conference.

The UN system has thus become the arena for global discourse but also global contestation. Without the co-operation of great powers UN discourse can rarely translate into practice the emerging normative and legal framework. The NGOs also are contributing to the rules that reflect the new priorities. On the forefront of promoting international law, the Institute of International Law began in the 1990s to focus its work on human rights. Transparency International and the Convention Combating Corruption were both formed in 1997. Transparency International, a Berlin-based global anti-corruption organization, publishes an annual Corruption Perception Index (CPI), ranking the extent of individual states' corruption. Publication of the CPI may increase awareness of the corruption of states and politicians, but it will not necessarily deter them. The international community needs to set standards for corporate and state behaviour in financial transactions and enforce them perhaps by using the mechanisms of the WTO. The politics of shame, helpful though it is, may not be enough.

Beyond globalism, the last few decades have witnessed several other striking trends: regionalism, nationalism, localism, environmentalism, feminism and revivalism. Their implications will be more fully explored in subsequent chapters. Suffice it here to say that the growth of TNCs, IGOs, NGOs and alternative government organizations (AGOs) in each of these arenas has greatly magnified the competing pressures impinging on global governance. As the international system grows in complexity, the abuse of loopholes via economic crime and political corruption has become increasingly feasible. Corporate tax evasion, the speculative mania culminating in the 1997 Asian financial debacle, and the growth of crony and mafia capitalism in Indonesia and Russia respectively are clear instances of such abuse.[26]

Yet there are also positive signs of expanding international co-operation. These include the 1989 Montreal Protocol on Substances that Deplete the Ozone Layer, the 1995 formation of the WTO with its rules for the adjudication of trade conflicts, the 1997 Kyoto Treaty on Climate Change, the 1998 establishment of the International Court of Criminal Justice to prosecute crimes against humanity, and the 1997 Treaty to Ban Landmines. All such achievements, however, ultimately require the co-operation of major powers. To the extent that these powers, notably the United States, Russia and China, have refused to become signatories (for example, to the Landmines Treaty) or have withdrawn their support (the United States from the Kyoto Treaty), the prospects for global governance are thereby diminished.

Globalization and its discontents

Despite the enormous complexity of the global system, certain historical trends in the last five centuries can be identified, including global economic integration, cultural fragmentation, and political democratization. These trends have largely taken place under the auspices of capitalism. Understood as a method of commodity production for the market rather than self-consumption, capitalism is certainly much older than its European manifestations.[27] However, with the scientific, technological and industrial revolutions in modern Europe, capitalism became a dominant global system spreading to all parts of the globe. It assumed a variety of institutional forms that have ranged from liberalism to state communism, fascism or Nazism, and communitarian socialism.

What is now emerging globally is a regime that goes beyond the historical features of previous capitalist regimes. Rather than adopt the prevailing political ideologies of territorial states, the new regime operates in a global arena largely beyond the reach of states. It coexists with the national capitalist regimes in a grudging partnership, but its global reach and dominance give it a power and impetus that transcends them.

The new regime may be characterized by the prevalence of three macrotrends: economic globalization, cultural fragmentation and political democratization. Globalization is primarily led by the TNCs which organize, operate and promote the global economy. A TNC typically operates in a large number of countries with centralized strategic planning and decentralized operations. TNCs, also referred to as multinational or global corporations, operate in every sector of the economy, including manufacturing, services and finance. The Commission on Global Governance has estimated their numbers to be around 37,000. Although in the postwar period German, Japanese, Korean and Chinese corporations have reached the ranks of TNCs, these remain primarily Anglo-American in origin. On the other hand, by virtue of joint ventures, interlocking directorships, staff composition, and operations, TNCs increasingly transcend national boundaries and loyalties.

The processes of globalization led by the TNCs are undermining the autonomy and authority of states while fragmenting the population around competing class, status and ethnic groups that gain or lose from the outcome. The territorial state system is thus under strain from both the apex and the base of the global social structure. However, rising income and education are also leading to a third process, namely democratization, led by an emergent global civil society.

Close to 40,000 TNCs, some operating in as many as 150 countries, are the engines of transnational capital. This enables them to influence national regulation and to seek the highest possible profits by locating in low-wage, low-rent, low-tax, and low-regulation countries and localities.[28] The Multilateral Agreement on Investment (MAI) would have allowed TNCs to sue states for any violation of agreements. In the late 1990s, the WTO proposed MAI and then dropped the idea in the face of opposition. In the words of Renato Ruggiero, WTO's director, MAI aimed at establishing 'the constitution of a single global economy'. It would have thus reinforced a global regime of trade, investment and development that favoured transnational capital. From a neo-liberal perspective, this regime can be viewed as a progressive force in transferring science, technology, management and employment to the less-developed world. From the perspective of the marginalized – a perspective articulated at successive demonstrations against globalization beginning with the Seattle protests in 1999 – the transnational agencies must be held accountable to democratic forces. To keep the global capitalist regime socially and ecologically responsible, IGOs, states and NGOs must monitor, regulate and counteract its power.[29]

The globalization of capital is being challenged on several fronts, by regionalism,[30] nationalism, ethno-nationalism, feminism, environmentalism and religious revivalism. Despite the rhetoric of 'end of history',[31] 'triumph of liberal democracy', and 'clash of civilizations',[32] the new world order, which replaced the Cold War, may be best described as a *Cold Peace*. Broadly speaking, Cold Peace can be characterized as rivalry between the trans-state global forces of global capitalism and the fragmented forces of its critics. As the gaps in wealth, income and knowledge within and among states widen, a cold and unstable peace threatens to erupt with rising intensity into flames of violence and terrorism.

On the other hand, those situated at the margins represent a largely disorganized collection of associations and nations which are attempting to resist, change, or otherwise counter, directly or indirectly, the influence of global capitalism on the institutions and processes of global governance. This cluster of forces consists of two main groups: state and non-state actors. The number of states has increased from about 70 in 1945, to about 200 in the late 1990s. Most of the dissatisfied states belong to the Non-Aligned Movement (NAM), launched at the Bandung Conference of 1955. The group has since gathered in numerous conferences and most recently (1998) at the heads-of-state level in Durban, South Africa. Despite its considerable heterogeneity and disunity, this group of states, whose membership considerably overlaps with the Group of 77, shares a common colonial or semi-colonial past, and is struggling for economic development and political democracy. Although membership has grown to 133, and much has changed, not least the end of the bipolar confrontation, the name has been retained primarily because of its historic significance. The group was largely instrumental in the establishment of the UN Conference on Trade and Development (UNCTAD) in 1964 and has since bargained with limited success for special treatment of the LDCs in matters of trade, investment and finance.

Other international interest groups, including OPEC and the Group of 15 (actually 17 developing countries), have been formed to devise and propose alternative policies with respect to prices, production and export, and the broader development agenda. Although OPEC provides a countervailing power *vis-à-vis* the petroleum importing countries and companies, its success has been chequered. While OPEC succeeded during the 1970s in raising the price of crude oil from $1.80 to $24 per barrel, falling prices in the 1990s meant that oil income was now below the levels recorded in the 1960s. In 1998–99, OPEC succeeded in reversing the trend by means of production controls, but rising prices of industrial imports and services have systematically stripped away much of the oil income. The effective transfer of 'foreign aid' from LDCs to MDCs were estimated by the *Economist* to be around $60 billion per annum.

The label 'non-state actors' usually refers to the growing number of NGOs (currently estimated at over 30,000), which point to the emergence of a global civil-society movement. NGOs include such progressive associations as Amnesty International, Greenpeace, Indigenous Peoples' Movement, Campaign to Ban Landmines, and Abolition 2000. Civil society also includes such conservative organizations as the political action committees of the global military-industrial complex, the Christian Coalition, the Trilateral Commission, Commission on Global Governance, and the World Economic Forum. Civil-society forces are thus not uniformly progressive or reactionary. In addition, there is an unknown number of armed AGOs that work openly or clandestinely for a variety of objectives, ranging in legitimacy from drug trafficking and money laundering[33] to national liberation for such repressed groups as the Kurds, Kosovars, Palestinians, Tibetans and Uighurs.

Politically, global capitalism has directly and indirectly subverted the regulatory functions of territorial states to achieve a degree of lop-sided growth that has exacerbated economic and informational gaps within and among nations. While democratic processes are often circumvented through campaign contributions that buy off politicians, the rule of undemocratic states is pre-empted through a combination of inducements and constraints. Indirectly, the commercial media's uncritical promotion of neo-liberal ideology fosters the impression that there is only one cultural basis for self-identity, namely fame and fortune. The central message of global advertising is that money and consumption are the keys to personal success and fulfilment. Neo-liberal ideology has thus combined with acquisitive individualism to justify *commodity fetishism*.

In reaction to this discourse and practice, those at the periphery have resorted to cultural politics and *identity fetishism*. The post-Cold War rise of ethnic, religious and nationalist movements around the world suggests that the neo-liberal project will continue to face increasing fragmentation and resistance from those who are marginalized and excluded from its fruits. James Mittelman among others has provided a thoughtful analysis of the dialectic of domination and resistance as it operates under the globalization regime.[34] In that dialectic lies perhaps the key to the protracted, borderless global war of terrorism and counter-terrorism in which innocent civilians are the prime victims. The phenomenon may be viewed as an incipient World War III. Given the increasing proliferation of nuclear, biological, and chemical weapons of mass destruction (WMDs),[35] this century may come to witness tragedies even greater than those of the twentieth century. Unless a democratic dialogue on global governance is placed high on the international agenda, the spiral of violence may move towards dysfunction or even system breakdown.

The emerging imbalances

September 11, 2001 will be remembered as a defining moment in world history. The world's only superpower, historically protected by two vast oceans, was no longer immune to the new weapons of terror. As the weapon of the weak, terrorism proved a deadly one. The strong were now seen, and saw themselves, as vulnerable.

The root cause of violence may be found in the alienation, dualism and antagonism generated by systemic marginalization of vast segments of the world population. However, every major tragedy brings with it an opportunity for reflection and reconstruction. Historical leaps often result from major human disasters. Societies often learn through pain and suffering. The League of Nations resulted from World War I. The UN emerged out of World War II. This time, the catalyst may be global terrorism.

Despite their profound differences, orthodox liberal, marxist and religious fundamentalist views of power have one thing in common. They are all captive to the Machiavellian ethics which rests on the separation of ends and means. Theorizing at the onset of the modern world, Machiavelli – and since then the school of international politics known as realism – argued that the state stands above morality. Relatively self-contained and possessing a monopoly on the legitimate use of violence, the state, we were told, should be free to pursue its ends by all available means.

The new global reality is sharply at odds with this traditional view. The world is economically interdependent, politically entwined, and territorially vulnerable to hegemonic, resistance, terrorist and criminal movements. Separating ends and means is no longer politically or ethically feasible. In the struggle against terrorism a new global politics and ethics must be learned. The new world view will perhaps receive its moral and political inspiration from the pioneers of non-violent political action, notably Mahatma Gandhi, Martin Luther King, Nelson Mandela and Vaclav Havel. In this view, ends and means are part of an unbroken chain. All political institutions (states, corporations and voluntary associations) must act in accordance with the law which itself must reflect widely accepted moral precepts. In a globalized world, such precepts and laws must be carefully negotiated among different traditions of civility.

Economically, creeping world recession has demonstrated how a continuing lack of transnational regulation can lead to economic breakdown in the most vulnerable countries (witness Indonesia). The Bretton Woods institutions were not designed for the accelerating scale and velocity of international economic activity which followed the privatization and deregulation policies of the 1980s and 1990s. By continuing to preach the gospel of neo-liberal capitalism without regard to its social and political consequences, these institutions have sometimes exacerbated economic downturns.[36] In addition to their regulatory role, the G7, OECD, EU, ASEAN, APEC, OPEC and other economic groupings have attempted with mixed success to set agendas and intervene on behalf of special group interests. But the new capitalist states of East Asia and Eastern Europe have yet to develop institutional defences against the internal and external excesses of primitive accumulation. Such excesses have come to be known as 'robber baron' capitalism in the United States, 'crony capitalism' in East Asia and 'mafia capitalism' in Russia. It is not just that since 1950 world trade has increased 16-fold.[37] According to the IMF, between $500 billion to $1.5 trillion (or 5 per cent of gross world product) may now be laundered every year. The result of such plundering by design has been called 'casino capitalism'.[38] Susan Strange predicted the Asian financial crisis of 1997 a decade earlier by identifying the causes of bank failures, financial fraud, political corruption, money laundering and the general volatility in world financial markets. The rapid globalization of financial markets during the 1980s and 1990s in the absence of effective global regulation was itself prompted by the rise of global capitalism. In search of profits, TNCs adroitly played states off against one another as they sought to take advantage of tax holidays, low wages and lax government regulation.

Population growth and labour-saving technological change have in the meantime created pockets of structural unemployment in various regions. In the United States, about 20 per cent of the population is considered not only structurally unemployed but also unemployable in the current technological environment. Corporate mergers, acquisitions, downsizing, outsourcing and layoffs are constantly adding to the army of unemployed and underemployed.[39] Moreover, an ageing population in the MDCs and the demographic explosion in the LDCs means that large numbers of people will increasingly need to be supported by welfare or face an unpleasant future. Dramatic increases of 6 to 9 per cent in the workforce in parts of Africa, Asia and Latin America will present enormous challenges to employment opportunities.

The addition of women to the labour force is at the same time changing gender relations. By the year 2010, more than 40 per cent of the paid workforce will be women,[40] although, as Human Development Reports data indicate, the situation varies enormously from country to country. Recent evidence suggests that economic power does not automatically lead to social and political power. It does, however, create the necessary conditions for the transformation of gender relations.[41] Women's rights have been violated in three main areas. First, discrimination in economic, social and political opportunities has historically hampered women's progress. Secondly, inequality in family life has limited women's rights in marriage, divorce and reproductive decision-making. Thirdly, gender-based violence in times of war and peace has dishonoured women's dignity and security. Changing norms, laws and international agreements on women's rights to security, reproduction, education and employment are gradually improving their conditions. But as the recent reversal of women's rights in certain societies (notably Afghanistan under the Taliban) demonstrates, without international support domestic struggles are not guaranteed durable success.

Environmentally, the scale and speed of industrial expansion dramatizes the deficiencies in existing institutional mechanisms to protect the global commons. As a consequence, the biosphere, air, land, water and other limited resources are under increasing pressure. Rapid expansion in major growth poles has failed to protect the quality of life as reflected in people's health and well-being. The scale of the Malthusian trap is awesome: demographic trends indicate growing demands on the global commons, making it ever more difficult to provide even the necessities of life. Furthermore, the risk of major environmental catastrophes (for example, ozone depletion, nuclear accidents, acid rain, global warming, drug-resistant microbes, epidemics) is rising. Any of these outcomes could compound global economic or political instabilities, economic or class conflict and terrorism, and might eventually provoke systemic breakdown.[42] Technological capabilities represent a double-edged sword. On the one hand, they hold the awesome potential to create a post-scarcity civilization of abundance. On the other hand, they enable large-scale genocide, unparallelled repression, and even human extinction. Whether the capabilities are put to positive or negative use depends on technological design and application. The absence of democratic governance allows corporate irresponsibility to combine with political corruption to produce deeply felt social discontent that breeds political extremism. Given appropriate conditions, such extremism can in turn unleash nuclear, biological, chemical or cyber terrorism and counter-terrorism.[43]

The only realistic antidote to these possibilities is democratic decision-making. Democratic practices introduce a system of checks and balances which provides early warning on societal problems, together with increased transparency, monitoring and accountability of both public and private institutions. The future of the world system depends on its capacity to endow global regulatory institutions with these democratic practices in order to counterbalance the unfettered power of national states, global capital, or criminal organizations. The task must be undertaken with full participation of the three major stakeholders in global governance: states, TNCs and civil societies, with the world media serving as the nervous system in the global body politic (see Figure 1.1). While states can co-operatively provide for international peace and security, market forces are essential to the production of employment, wealth and income. Civil societies and communication networks, by contrast, must monitor the performance of the system, identify its strengths and weaknesses, and mobilize the public for necessary reforms. Democratic checks and balances at the global level are now largely conspicuous by their absence. Their institution is a *sine qua non* of world survival.

As previously noted, the international community has since 1945 made considerable strides in the development of global governance institutions. However, an even more rapid movement in the globalization of international trade, investment, finance, transportation, communication, tourism, terrorism, crime and arms-trafficking has created what might be called a legal and organizational lag. The development of international law and institutions has not kept pace with the world's rapidly changing technological and economic landscape. A glaring gap has emerged in terms of global reach and power between the *de facto* and *de jure* institutions of global governance. The *de facto* institutions consist of the corporate organizations which dominate the economic and financial arena, and the major states (the United States, Russia, China, Britain, Germany, Japan, India and France) which largely control the political arena. The *de jure* institutions comprise the IGOs and the myriad of declarations and treaties that have been issued and signed by states on human rights, peace and security, environment, humanitarian law and much else. In certain policy areas, NGOs are attempting to bridge the gap between political reality and pious exhortation. However, their reach and leverage pale in comparison with the power and resources of global corporations and major states.

Notes

1. M.P. Ryan, *Knowledge Diplomacy: Global Competition and the Politics of Intellectual Property* (Washington DC: Brookings Institute Press, 1998), pp.8–10.
2. J. Mander and E. Goldsmith, *The Case against the Global Economy: and for a Turn Toward the Local* (San Francisco, CA: Sierra Club Books, 1996), chs 11 and 12.
3. C.N. Murphy, *International Organization and Industrial Change: Global Governance since 1850* (New York: Oxford University Press, 1994), p.3.
4. IB History Page, 'Congress of Vienna Personalities', available online at: <http://kanga.pvhs.chico.k12.ca.us/~bsilva/projects/congress/vienpers.html>   (6 July 1999).
5. 'The Monroe Doctrine', available online at: <http://www.uiowa.edu/~c030162/Common/Handouts/POTUS/Monroe.html> (6 July 1999).
6. IB History Page, 'Concert of Europe: Overview', available online at: <http://www.pvhs.chico.k12.ca.us/~bsilva/projects/concert/concessy.html> (6 July 1999).
7. 'The Monroe Doctrine', Encyclopedia Americana Online (EAO), available online at: <http://gi.grolier.com/presidents/ea/side/mondoc.html> (6 July 1999).
8. L.S. Stavrianos, *A Global History: From Prehistory to the Present* (Englewood Cliffs, NJ: Prentice Hall, 1991), p.457.
9. A. Natsios, 'NGOs and the UN System in Complex Humanitarian Emergencies: Conflict or Cooperation?', in T. Weiss and L. Gordenker (eds), *NGOs, the UN and Global Governance* (London: Lynne Rienner, 1996), p.73.
10. Encyclopedia Britannica Online (EBO), 'Institute of International Law', available online at: <http://members.eb.com/bol/topic?eu=99364&sctn=1> (1 July 1999).
11. PVHS, 'Effects of WWI', available online at: <http://www.pvhs.chico.k12.ca.us/~bsilva/projects/great_war/effects.htm> (6 July 1999).
12. All amounts in this volume are given in US dollars unless otherwise indicated.
13. B. Eichengreen and P. Kenen, *Managing the World Economy – 50 Years After Bretton Woods* (Washington DC: Institute for International Economics, 1994), p.11.
14. EBO, 'United Nations', available online at: <http://www.members.eb.com/bol/topic? eu=115666&sctn=2> (21 August 1999).
15. P.M. Sweezy, *The Transition from Feudalism to Capitalism* (London: NLB; Atlantic Highlands, NJ: Humanities Press, 1976).
16. P.A. Baran, *The Political Economy of Growth* (New York: Monthly Review Press, 1957).
17. A.G. Frank, *The Development of Underdevelopment* (New York: Monthly Review Press, 1969).
18. Ibid.
19. The dramatic success of the Asian tigers in breaking away from the cycle of dependency has led a number of critical theorists to revise their views, see M. Blomstrom and B. Hettne, *Development Theory in Transition – the Dependency Debate and Beyond: Third World Responses* (London: Zed Books, 1984); A. So, *Social Change and Development: Modernization, Dependency, and World Systems Theories* (Newbury Parks: Sage, 1990).
20. Murphy, p.7.
21. H. Hudson, *Global Connections: International Telecommunications Infrastructure and Policy* (New York: John Wiley & Sons, 1997), p.44.
22. EBO, 'Internet', available online at: <http://www.members.eb.com/bol/topic?eu = 1460&sctn = 1> (8 July 1999).
23. M. Tehranian, *Global Communication and World Politics: Domination, Development, and Discourse* (Boulder, CO: Lynne Rienner, 1999), pp.162–5; for global statistics on the Internet, see the *Economist* Survey, available online at: <http://www.glreach.com/globstats/> (24 June 2000).

24. United Nations, *The World Conferences* (New York: UNDPI, 1997).
25. ILO, 'Follow-up on the World Summit for Social Development', available online at: <http://www-ilo-mirror.who.or.jp/public/english/60empfor/polemp/prog4-2.htm> (19 July 1999).
26. See Part II.
27. A.G. Frank, *ReOrient: Global Economy in the Asian Age* (Berkeley, CA: University of California, Press, 1998).
28. 'Disappearing Taxes', the *Economist*, 31 May 1997.
29. M.A. Chen, 'Engendering World Conferences', in Weiss and Gordenker.
30. C. Peck, *Sustainable Peace: the Role of the United Nations and Regional Organizations in Conflict Prevention* (Lanham, MD: Rowman & Littlefield, 1998).
31. F. Fukuyama, 'The End of History', *National Interest* (Summer 1989).
32. S. Huntington, 'The Clash of Civilizations', *Foreign Affairs* (Summer 1993).
33. For an analysis of the global criminal economy, see M. Castells, *The Information Society: Economy, Society, and Culture*, Vol.3 (Oxford: Blackwell, 2000), ch.3; J. Mittelman, *The Globalization Syndrome: Transformation and Resistance* (Princeton, NJ: Princeton University Press, 2000), ch.11.
34. Ibid.
35. See chapters 11 and 12.
36. Notably in East Asia, see Part II.
37. 'Survey of World Trade', the *Economist*, 3 October 1998.
38. S. Strange, *Casino Capitalism* (Oxford: Basil Blackwell, 1986).
39. R. Rifkin, *The End of Work: the Decline of the Global Labor Force and Dawn of the Post-Market Era* (New York: G.P. Putnam, 1995).
40. I. Pearson (ed.), *The Atlas of the Future* (London: Routledge, 1998), pp.70–1.
41. UNDP, *Human Development Report* (New York: Oxford University Press, 2000), p.117.
42. Pearson, pp.18–19.
43. Ibid., pp.30–1.

2
Taming Capital, Holding Peace

Majid Tehranian

Industrialized countries hold 97 per cent of all patents worldwide. The percentage share of the market by the top 10 corporations in each sector in 1998 was: telecommunications, 86 per cent; pesticides, 85 per cent; computers, almost 70 per cent; veterinary medicine, 60 per cent; pharmaceuticals, 35 per cent; commercial seed, 32 per cent. The income gap between the richest fifth of the world's people and the poorest fifth, measured by average national income per head, increased from 30 to one in 1960 to 74 to one in 1997.

UNDP *Human Development Report 1999*

Having examined the development of *de jure* global governance, we now turn to a more detailed analysis of the evolution of the *de facto* regimes of domination. The world faces a daunting challenge: how to tame the economic forces that have produced both majestic successes and horrifying failures.[1] Riding on the waves of accelerating scientific and technological progress of the last century, capitalism has clearly entered a new phase of its development, characterized by a transition from the confines of the territorial state to the global arena. This new phase may be called 'global capitalism'. It is economically driven by the mobility and reach of transnational capital but is politically held back by the fetters of a state system based on territorial sovereignty. The mismatch of the global economic and political systems has retarded the growth of transnational political, economic and cultural institutions to meet the challenges of a global civilization. The development of the institutions of global governance commensurate with the growth of global market forces is the single most important challenge facing contemporary international society.

Unless global governance is democratized, global capitalism will plant the seeds of its own destruction.[2] Global governance must, however, be clearly distinguished from global government. Whereas the world currently lacks global government, it most certainly is ruled by a set of *de facto* as well as *de jure* principles and institutions that together constitute global governance. These principles and institutions include all of the formal declarations, treaties and organizations inherited from the past as well as those more recently established. Global governance also encompasses the transnational forces that have emerged in the postwar period (TNCs, TMCs, NGOs and AGOs) that often operate beyond the reach and power of the territorial state system and its instruments of power. To cite one striking example, organized crime syndicates are estimated to gross $1.5 trillion a year in transactions. The value of the illegal drug trade was estimated at $400 billion in 1995, about 8 per cent of world trade, more than the shares of iron and steel or of motor vehicles, and roughly the same as textiles and gas and oil.[3]

The operations of transnational capital have transformed global governance in several important but different directions. These include an unprecedented period of technological and economic advance, the broadening and deepening of global communication, and a corresponding rise in the level of expectations often frustrated by widening economic gaps and political obstacles to democracy. The regime of global capital has thus succeeded in creating a global market of extraordinary productivity and penetration while failing on two other fronts, namely, to provide sustainable and equitable development and to regulate itself by developing global democratic institutions equipped with the necessary checks and balances.

This chapter proposes first to review the historical evolution of *de facto* global governance, then to analyse the rise of global capitalism, and finally to set out the problem posed by the emergence of a global economic apartheid.

Evolution of *de facto* governance

De facto global governance can be traced back to the rise of modern capitalism.[4] It is precisely the march towards an international system of capital, labour, trade and investment mobility that necessitated the worldwide organization of transportation, communication, and security. The capitalist system, therefore, soon led to a number of competing European and American colonial empires, and an economic division of labour among world centres, peripheries and semi-peripheries. During the inter-imperial period, Africa, Asia and Latin America served as producers of raw materials, cheap labour and consumer markets to industrial Europe and North America.

The transition from national to global capitalism was a by-product of two world wars. During the UN era, national capitalisms under US leadership have learned to co-operate rather than compete ruinously. The destruction of Europe during World War II and the threat of communism posed by the Sino-Soviet camp hastened the integration of national capitalisms into global capitalism. With the fall of the Soviet Union in 1991, global capitalism became the single dominant force in the world.

The hierarchical structure of the world is a continuing characteristic of *de facto* global governance. The global system has gone through three major interlocking phases of hegemonic development, evolving from agrarian to industrial and informatic domination. Similarly, *de facto* global governance may be viewed in terms of the evolution of imperialism from its agrarian to industrial and informatic phases. Table 2.1 provides a schematic view of these three phases with

Table 2.1   Evolution of global governance: *De facto* aspects

	Agrarian imperialism 550 BCE–1648	Industrial imperialism 1648–1991	Informatic imperialism 1991–Present
Economy: Modes of production	Herding, agriculture	Mining + manufacturing + services	Knowledge industries
Polity: Modes of legitimation	Religious	Political	Economistic
Society: Modes of regulation	Multinational agrarian empires + city states + feudalism	Nation-states + nationalist industrial empires	'Super-states', TNCs, TMCs, IGOs, NGOs, AGOs, UNPOs
Culture: Modes of communication	Writing	Print	Electronic
Technology	Religious	Secular	Cosmopolitan
Identity	Local	National	Global
Community legitimacy	Metaphysical	Ideological	Ecological

Adapted from M. Tehranian, *Global Communication and World Politics: Domination, Development, and Discourse* (Boulder, CO: Lynne Rienner, 1999), p.18.

respect to the changing modes of production, legitimacy, regulation and communication. These refer to economic structures and the state system, and their associated ideological and identity configurations. In its first phase, the global system may be characterized as *agrarian imperialism*, marked by the rise and fall of successive multinational empires that thrived on agrarian surplus economies, urban political centres, and capital accumulation through international trade in luxury goods (witness the Silk and Spice Roads). During this phase, the rise and fall of imperial systems can be more generally explained in terms of Ibn Khaldun's theory of history,[5] namely the periodic nomadic conquests of sedentary populations who in turn conquered their conquerors. As the case of the Chinese, Iranian, Indian and Islamic empires demonstrates, the nomads were often sedentarized, then softened by the luxuries of urban life, which in turn led to their dynastic decline and another round of nomadic invasion and conquest. More recent research into comparative global systems shows that four major multinational agrarian empires supported commercial trade and political hegemony: in East Asia (Chinese), South Asia (Indian), Central and West Asia (Persian, Arab and Turkic), and the West (Greek and Roman). Chase-Dunn and Hall have provided a summary of much of this research, accompanied by a rich and diverse cartographic presentation of agrarian empires.[6]

The discovery of sea routes to India, South-east Asia and Japan in the fifteenth and sixteenth centuries led to the decline of the Asian routes and their commercial entrepots.[7] But Asian imperial pretensions continued until military defeats in the eighteenth and nineteenth centuries finally brought about subjugation to the

Europeans. The agrarian imperialist phase came to an end with the rise of the post-Westphalian phase, labelled here *industrial imperialism*. In this phase, the locus of *de facto* global governance shifted sharply to the increasingly dominant industrial economies and nation-states ushered in by the Peace of Westphalia. Large-scale immigration from rural to urban centres and from Europe to the rest of the world gave rise to a number of competing European industrial empires.

The rise of global capitalism

The third phase of world imperialism has yet to run its course. The passage of the most advanced industrial economies into a post-industrial phase[8] has facilitated a new type of capitalism and imperialism based not so much on control of land or capital as on control of information. In contrast to agrarian or industrial imperialism, the new phase of world imperialism may therefore be designated as *informatic*. Control of territory is nowhere near as important during this phase as control of information and the networks of transportation, communication, trade, investment and military-political security. This type of control focuses on the latest copyright, scientific patents and technologies, licences, and their associated knowledge industries.

Eight distinct features characterize the new global capitalist regime.

1. It is global in scope and reach; its loyalties are not to the national flag but to the global marketplace and its profit opportunities.
2. It vitally depends on a global network of information and communication which would have been impossible without the current technological revolution in telecommunications.[9]
3. The new technological and economic environment has made flexible accumulation and just-in-time production possible. Capital is, relatively speaking, liberated from its geographic fetters and can move wherever profit opportunities are most promising.[10]
4. The new flexibility in capital investment has led to a new regionalism focused on politically reliable and economically productive regions of the world (for example, East Asia and certain parts of Latin America) with lower production costs.[11]
5. More effective global communication and the rise of middle classes in Latin America, Eastern Europe, East Asia and China have unleashed democratic movements across the globe demanding civil liberties and political participation.
6. The new global capitalist regime has been supported and celebrated by a neo-liberal ideology encouraging privatization and deregulation.
7. The political ideas of neo-liberalism sometimes contradict its economic interest. Global capitalism has shown a distinct preference for political stability, sometimes achieved by the imposition of military dictatorships as in Iran, the Philippines, Indonesia, Korea and Saudi Arabia during the Cold War years. Nascent democratic systems without the requisite democratic institutions and cultures are often accompanied by political instability, as the cases of Russia, Iran, Indonesia, Malaysia and Korea amply demonstrate.

8. The pressures from below and the opportunities emanating from a new global communication environment have opened the doors to the democratic impulse globally, regionally, nationally and locally as never before.

Three major currents are shaping the world, namely globalization and regionalization from above, fragmentation and tribalization from below, and resistance and democratization at the centre.

A global apartheid?

The optimistic note struck in the foregoing paragraph must be measured against several disturbing trends. Thomas Schelling has aptly compared the growing income gaps among and within nations with that of South Africa under apartheid:[12]

> If we were to think about a 'new world order'... and if we were to think about the political mechanisms that might be developed, what actual nation, existing now or in the past, might such an incipient world state resemble?... what familiar political entity might be our basis for comparison?
>
> I find my own answer stunning and embarrassing: South Africa [during the apartheid regime].

With lopsided world development, the dualistic patterns initiated by colonialism have continued into the post-colonial era. In the past, colonists enriched themselves by exploiting the raw materials and cheap labour of the colonies. Under informatic imperialism, low-tech and high-polluting industries are often located in the LDCs, while high-tech and knowledge industries are kept in MDCs. The profits of foreign-owned corporations are largely transferred to the metropolitan centres where they are re-invested in research and development, further technological innovations, control of patents, licences and copyright, and hence control of the global development process. This pattern can be broken with appropriate global policies and instruments, but only with the greatest difficulty.

The distinguishing feature of globalism is the mobility of capital and relative immobility of labour. Patterns of labour movement often follow capital flows. The process has created a global elite and a global underclass colliding in the major metropolitan centres. The old world centres and peripheries of power were primarily conceived in territorial terms. As we have already noted, the core in Western Europe and North America was assumed to be exploiting the peripheries in Africa, Asia and Latin America in a pattern of 'development of underdevelopment' that reproduced economic and political dependency. However, some former peripheries have now reached the status of world centres (Japan, Singapore and South Korea), while others (Taiwan, Thailand, Malaysia and Indonesia) have made impressive strides, seemingly marred only by the economic recession of 1997–98. The new world centres and peripheries are thus deterritorialized. The new nomads are no longer confined to particular sets of countries defined as developed or developing. A member of the global elite can be in any major world city, whether in the North or the South, and enjoy a lifestyle involving luxury housing, hotels and restaurants while plugged into the global telecommunication network. The world underclass is also making its presence felt in the slums of most major metropolitan centres where violence, crime and drug trafficking prevail.

A system of global apartheid appears to be emerging. Marshall McLuhan's 'global village' is divided between castles inhabited by the lords of the manors, protected by moats of electronic surveillance, and surrounded by teeming, restless peasants living in panoptican societies monitored by the watchmen armed with electronic surveillance systems, from remote sensing satellites to video cameras. As with the South African apartheid regime, global apartheid is not a stable system. Requiring the free flow of goods, services, capital, labour, ideas and information across state boundaries, characterized by porous borders and ethnic divisions, the transnational world economy is vulnerable to sabotage, terrorism, recession and protectionism. In erecting the structures making for a global apartheid, global capitalism may well be sowing the seeds of its own destruction.

Jacques Attali and Susan Strange among others have drawn evocative parallels between the late twentieth century and the early Middle Ages.[13] The latter has set out the problem of global governance in the following terms:

> I am not the first to see the present order as approximating more to that of medieval Europe than to the 'black box' model assumed in many texts on international relations. In medieval Europe, markets functioned under systems of rules, but the authority behind the rules was widely dispersed. It was shared between princes – but princes with very unequal command of resources – the Church, the professional guilds, and the local lords of the manor. What we do not know today, or can perceive only very vaguely, is how authority over world society and economy is shared, where it resides, and over what issues, if no longer so predominantly with the governments of each territorial state.[14]

Perhaps as with the fall of Rome, the dissolution of the European imperial systems in the second half of the twentieth century has assumed the characteristics of a neo-feudal order. Transnational capital in alliance with the world's major states (the United States, Japan, Germany, Britain and France) controls the markets, while the localist, nationalist and ethnonationalist forces of resistance and revolt fight to maintain their porous and vulnerable territorial and cultural spaces. So long as the old Cold War persisted, a rough balance of power enabled the Third World to operate as a buffer zone between the two global systems of capitalism and communism. The end of the Cold War and dissolution of the Soviet Union put an end to these territorial empires. The new forms of domination and resistance have moved on to economic and cultural rather than political and territorial space. Economic and technological globalization from above as well as religious, ethnic and cultural resistance from below are challenging the territorial state. The moral geographies of the territorial state system have shifted from bipolar rivalry to a contestation among competing political and cultural forces.

The last century may be characterized as a century of death by design. Of the 207 million killed during the century, 170 million were civilians killed by governments through deliberate policies of mass extermination, not least in the Holocaust and the Soviet massacre of the Kulaks. Of the 37 million killed in wars, 30 million died in international wars and seven million were victims of civil wars.[15]

Sites of insecurity and resistance

How, then, might we approach the contemporary problem of holding peace in a world that is simultaneously globalizing and fragmenting? We have already analysed the processes of globalization under global capitalism. Now we turn to the major sites of fragmentation and resistance. As previously indicated, seven tension-riddled trends characterize our own era, namely globalism, regionalism, nationalism, localism, feminism, environmentalism and religious revivalism (see Figure 2.1). Each trend contains within it two basic contradictory tendencies, one pointing to conflict and the other to co-operation. The challenge before the international community is how to transform the tensions into a creative process that privileges human security and co-operation rather than hostility and violence. That challenge, in turn, calls for democratizing global governance as a way of accommodating the interests and perspectives of emerging social, economic and political forces.

Global capitalism has not been able to homogenize the world. Despite the cultural power of Coca-Colonization, informatic imperialism faces a world population that is as heterogeneous and resistant to homogenization as ever. The world is becoming increasingly multicultural as information technologies empower previously voiceless groups to assert their cultural identities and political aspirations. Increasing ethnification is a direct consequence of this process.

By its very nature and temperament, modernity creates anomic insecurities. It also privileges the new against the old, the nascent against the dying, and the

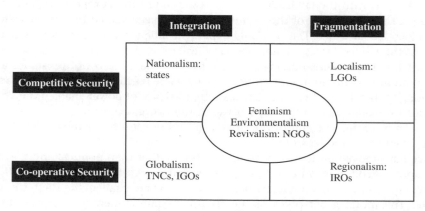

Figure 2.1   Human security and global governance: Mapping trends and tensions

strong against the weak. It thus marginalizes vast segments of the population and induces a conflict of cultures, values and identities which cannot be easily resolved. By de-linking the economy from polity and cultural production, liberal capitalism could until recently manage to quarantine identity negotiations from the political realm. The de-linkage often led to legitimation crises,[16] but periodic elections often defused its systemic impact. However, accelerating globalization of markets and cultures is producing a re-linkage of economy, policy and culture. As witnessed by the increasing costs of campaigning in liberal democracies, both the politicians and the capitalist state are often held hostage to the demands of transnational market forces. Similarly, political resistance against transnational capital is increasingly finding expression in struggles against economic organizations. Resistance sometimes expresses itself against the new regionalism, as in the case of Ross Perot's campaign for the US Presidency in 1992 and 1996, the 1994–96 Chiappa struggle in Mexico against NAFTA, the 1996 Filipino demonstrations against APEC, and the 1996–97 Tupac Amaru takeover of the Japanese embassy in Lima against the transnational encroachments on Peru by Japan. More generally, opposition to globalization has entailed demonstrations against its institutions (G7, WTO, IMF, and the World Bank) in Seattle, Quebec City, Prague and Geneva.

The more recent resistance movements are also couched in cultural and identity terms. Examples include the neo-traditionalist (fundamentalist) movements in India, Iran, Israel, Algeria, Egypt, Turkey, the United States and Europe. Culture has been increasingly politicized, with violence resulting in such diverse settings as Bosnia, Chechnya, Mexico, Kosovo, Macedonia and Tajikistan. The common thread among these conflicts cannot be understood unless we relate them to the larger dynamics of global capitalism.

Informatic imperialism is treading on volatile ground. The impact of global capital on indigenous populations is a mixed blessing. While capital brings with it new technologies, management techniques and possibilities for export-driven strategies of development, it also uproots the traditional nexus of social solidarity and identity. Moreover, it creates dualistic societies torn apart between traditional masses and modernizing elites (witness Iran, Algeria, Turkey and Egypt). It is often the second stratum of the elite among the transitional groups who take the lead in mobilizing the traditional, lower strata of population into a revolt against global capitalism and its compradore elites. It is more appropriate to call these groups neo-traditionalist than fundamentalist. When these groups take power, as the Islamic Ulama did in the 1979 revolution in Iran, their strategy is not to go back to the *status quo ante* but to steer a new course of modernization based on indigenous institutions and ambivalence towards global capitalism (*cum* modernity). The deepening and broadening of political participation in the LDCs inevitably involves layers of society and counter-elites that have a traditional or neo-traditional political orientation. Democratizing national and global polities are thus profoundly linked.

Figure 2.2 puts the foregoing propositions into a schematic portrait of the polarities and spaces of identity negotiation in the new era. In the declining pre-modern societies, the dominant cosmology is ecological and the sources of social

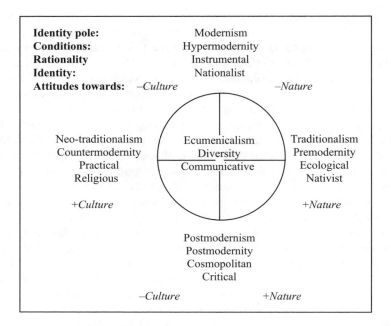

Figure 2.2   Polarities and spaces of identity negotiations

Sources: J. Friedman, *Cultural Identity and Global Processes* (Newbury Park: Sage, 1995); M. Tehranian, *Global Communication and World Politics* (Boulder, CO: Lynne Rienner Publishers, 1999), p.25.

solidarity and identity are primarily nativist (indigenous, tribal, clannish). In modernizing societies, the race to riches is grounded in hypermodernity, the dominant rationality (cosmology) is instrumental, and the sources of social solidarity and identity are secular nationalism. In neo-traditionalist societies and movements, reacting to the onslaught of globalization, rationality is practical and identity formations are based on religious faith and ethnic networks. Finally, in the postmodern world of anti-narrative narratives, rationality is critical and pluralist while identity formation is hybrid and cosmopolitan. We thus live in an economically and culturally heterogeneous world in which democratization cannot be defined solely in terms of liberal democratic norms and practices.

Democracy has many possible modalities. It thrives best at the smallest and most intimate aggregations of human communities – in neighbourhoods, villages, and towns. The level of distortion in communication and representation increases as the distance between the elected and the elector grows. Representative democracy is therefore a necessary but insufficient condition for the devolution of power. New interactive telecommunication technologies have made direct democratic discourse and participation in the form of electronic town meetings entirely possible.[17] Notwithstanding devolutionary trends and emerging technological opportunities, democratization is not guaranteed unless each trend moves away from hegemonic and exclusionist to communitarian and inclusive modalities of power and participation.

Figure 2.1 maps the complex interactions of the seven trends in relation to the emerging patterns in global governance and security. The rows show competitive and co-operative security as the two most dominant orientations in international politics. The columns focus on integration and fragmentation as the twin directions of systemic change. The four spatial trends (globalism, regionalism, nationalism and localism) are placed in the four quarters of the diagram to indicate their primary contribution to competitive as opposed to co-operative security arrangements as well as to integrative as opposed to fragmenting effects. The three substantive trends (feminism, environmentalism and revivalism) are placed at the centre, suggesting once again the potential integration and co-operation on the one hand, and competition and fragmentation on the other.

The figure should be considered a heuristic device providing us with a point of departure for an analysis of the major factors shaping the emerging patterns of global governance and security regimes. Since nationalism and globalism are the oldest of the four spatial trends, the world system has largely incorporated them into its institutional structures through the nation-state system and the political economy of international trade and finance respectively. By contrast, localism and regionalism are relatively new trends that could undermine the dominant world system, with new power centres challenging the centralized states and their inter-governmental institutions. The figure also shows the main actors in each arena. Clearly, a major trend to note in this diagram is the increasing role of non-state actors.

Globalism: Hegemonic versus communitarian

Globalism is the most apparent of all the seven trends. It is particularly visible to the eyes of international travellers at airports, hotel chains, fast food restaurants, and those ubiquitous signs of modern civilization – the Big Mac, Coca-Cola, Sushi Bars, and Hollywood celebrities. The Big Mac has conquered the old world (London, Paris, Moscow and Beijing) for the new. The Coca-Colonization of the world has reached the remotest corners of the globe. Coke is sold on the Great Wall of China as well as in Timbuktu and Katmandu. Following MTV trends, wearing the right brand names may be edging out proletarian solidarity, nationalist fervour and religious devotion. Commodity fetishism and consumerism may be the new global religion that binds all world inhabitants in the cash nexus. Its temples are to be found in the great department stores (Harrods, Macy's), supermarkets, and mass distribution outlets such as Costco and Price Club.

As the main carriers of globalism, TNCs typically follow a global strategy locating wherever low interest, wages, rents and government regulation promise the lowest costs and the highest profits. The sales by the largest TNCs exceed the GNP of many medium-sized economies. Indeed, TNCs constitute more than 50 per cent of the top 100 economic units in the world. The chief technologies of economic expansion have been energy, transportation and telecommunication.

These three have propelled the successive technological breakthroughs that led to three successive long waves of global economic growth. Globalist strategies of conquest involve horizontal, vertical and spatial integration of key world industries from oil to transportation and telecommunication. Its lubricants are the transfers of capital between centres and from centres to peripheries. Globalization mobilizes world capital, allocates it globally, and reduces the risk to private investors. It also produces modernized poverty. In traditional societies poverty is made tolerable by relative equality, by the ethics of self-denial and mutual obligation, and by the bonds of community (see Table 2.2). Modernized poverty in the peripheries is characterized by the ethics of rising expectations, ceaseless identity and status anxieties, mutual irresponsibility, and latent and manifest violence. Modernized poverty feeds on atomistic mobility, social envy, frustration, regression and aggression. The negative internalities of dualistic modernity thus outpace the positive externalities of growth and development. Time-consuming acceleration, illness-producing health care, stupe-fying education, counter-communicative mass communication and information-void news are the symptoms of such negative processes.

Globalism is torn between two hegemonic and counter-hegemonic trends. The ensuing debate on how best to shape the new world order in the post-Cold War era has given rise to four schools of thought: *neo-isolationism, unilateralism, trilateralism* and *multilateralism*.

Neo-isolationism. In the United States, neo-isolationism has never lurked far behind the postwar hegemonic discourse of liberal globalism. With the end of the Cold War and the acceleration of economic globalization, however, neo-isolationism has taken a new lease on life. The movement appears primarily in the form of protectionism against the onslaught of cheaply produced foreign imports from Asia and Latin America. Representing the interests of domestic capitalists and workers respectively, Jesse Helms, former Chairman of the Senate Committee on Foreign Relations, and Richard Gephardt, the Democratic Party leader in the House, have taken up the cause from the right and the left. The neo-isolationist discourse in the United States and Europe has also found new voices in the anti-immigrant sentiments of the domestic unemployed and the threatened sunset industries (witness Le Pen in France). As the case of China amply demonstrates, the human rights violations associated with the cheap-labour countries have also served as a target for such voices.

Table 2.2 Social psychological aspects of poverty: Traditional versus modern societies

Traditional	Modern
Stable expectations	Rising expectations
Status stability	Status anxiety
Identity security	Identity insecurity
Self-denial	Self promotion
Mutual obligation	Mutual irresponsibility
Accepting destiny	Rising frustrations
Bonds of community	Latent and manifest violence

Unilateralism. The unilateralist school views the world in geopolitical and balance-of-power terms. From this viewpoint, the United States as the only power with global military reach must play the role of 'balancer'. From the Napoleonic Wars to World War I, Britain played such a role. The economic corollary to this strategic doctrine is that the United States must also act as the champion of free trade and protector of private capital. This view prevailed in the early post-Cold War years in the Persian Gulf War and President Bush's 'new world order' discourse. The early optimism of the post-Cold War era, however, soon gave rise to increasing pessimism about the limits to power, even for the American 'super-state'. The 'new world order' discourse was replaced with a new discourse on the 'clash of civilizations',[18] in which the United States was perceived as the defender of western values against threats from other civilizations, in particular, a Confucian–Islamic alliance.

Trilateralism. The three major centres of economic power, North America, Western Europe, and Japan together with East Asia, represent the three pillars of the trilateral edifice. Embodied in the G7, the political will of this group effectively determines the international political and economic security agenda. Meeting periodically to co-ordinate policies, the G7 is presumed able to manage the rest of the world. This presumption is beginning to run into increasing resistance as some of the most populous nations (China, India, Indonesia, Russia and Brazil) articulate their distinct economic and political interests with increasing force. Nuclear tests by India and Pakistan and the defiance of the United States by Iran, Iraq, Libya and North Korea, as well as an incipient Russian–Chinese alliance, are early symptoms of such resistance.

Regional multilateralism. Multilateralists have a long tradition of advocating support for the UN and its specialized agencies in opposition to those who consider them a threat to the authority of the world's only superpower. For a brief interlude during the Persian Gulf War, multilateralism of a kind appeared to be the dominant trend. However, subsequent international crises in Somalia, Bosnia, Chechnya, Kosovo and the Persian Gulf have proved too divisive to allow any coherent UN response. Multilateralism, courtesy of such other agencies as NATO, CIS, EU, NAFTA and ASEAN, though still a viable option, hinges on regional rather than global security regimes. As the NATO attack on Yugoslavia in March 1999 indicates, this kind of multilateralism undermines the authority of the UN. The Asian economic crisis of 1997–98 was particularly instructive in highlighting the limitations of regional organizations.[19] Neither ASEAN nor APEC could assist member states in distress. In an age of globalization, national or regional institutions seem poorly equipped to resolve global problems.

Universal multilateralism. Despite its shortcomings, the UN system remains the world's best hope for building a universal, multilateral approach to conflict resolution. However, the UN needs to be reformed on many fronts (see Parts II and III) and its efforts co-ordinated with those of other actors. States, TNCs and NGOs represent the main institutionalized stakeholders which must be integrated with the UN system to achieve a level of global representation and effectiveness commensurate with the rule of global challenges.

Communitarian globalism, or globalism from below, is a force assisted by global communication networks and an emerging international civil society organized around NGOs. There are currently some 30,000 NGOs growing in number and diversity of functions from environmental protection (Greenpeace) to human rights (Amnesty International), to development (Oxfam), to relief (Red Cross and Red Crescent societies). From both above and below, global and local forces are eroding the power of the state. However, the state continues to be a critical instrument of both hegemonic and democratic action. Its demise is somewhat exaggerated. As noted earlier, public expenditure, measured in both absolute and relative terms, remains high. Even in MDCs, where neo-liberal policies have aimed to dismantle the welfare state, increasing costs of 'defence', health and education have led to greater public spending. The Reagan era witnessed the accumulation of the biggest public debt in US history. While that debt fell during the Clinton years, it has since returned to haunt the Bush administration.

Regionalism: Exclusionary versus inclusionary

Given the enormous heterogeneity of the world, global community is best achieved through an interlocking system of smaller and more homogeneous communities. Regionalism is one such trend. Indeed, evidence suggests that we may have entered the 'age of regions'. Regional formations such as the EU, ASEAN, NAFTA and others are establishing new communities of interests, norms, laws and sanctions. The new as opposed to the old regionalism is primarily economic rather than political. Whereas NATO, CENTO, SEATO and the Warsaw Pact were Cold War security systems, the new regional organizations are moving toward common markets. As Mittelman notes, the new regionalism is not an attempt at autarchy.[20] On the contrary, neo-liberal regionalism is based on flexible accumulation that makes 'regional production networks ever more important, because a premium is placed on spatial clustering of suppliers around plants, partly to ensure timely delivery'.[21]

Nevertheless, in recessionary conditions, regional blocs could give rise to intense economic competition and even political confrontation. A revival of protectionism could see Fortress Europe, Fortress America and Fortress East Asia locked in fierce combat. Regionalism, then, can be either exclusionary or inclusionary. It can provide a protective but ultimately divisive shield for its members against global hegemonic projects, or it can be a building-block for democratic global governance.

Nationalism: Totalitarian-aggressive versus democratic-benign

In recent centuries, it has been easier to achieve national than regional integration. The entire history of nationalism is an effort to mould the state in the image of a single nation with a common language, culture, historical memories, economy and political system. Nationalism has proved a relatively successful project precisely because it is closer to the realities of human diversity. However, nationalism has also fostered the fiction of cultural or racial purity and homogeneity. Most states are culturally and ethnically heterogeneous. The modern nation-state has been built on the premise of a nation 'one and indivisible', so the American Pledge of Allegiance would have us believe. The post-Cold War era has shown the falsity of that assumption. Witness the outburst of ethnic conflicts in the former Soviet Union, Yugoslavia, India, Iraq, Iran, Afghanistan, Sri Lanka, Canada and the United States.

Nationalism has gone through at least three distinct historical stages.[22] In the first stage, from the Peace of Westphalia to the end of World War I, nationalism succeeded in integrating the European feudal principalities into a series of relatively homogenous nation-states with their own common languages. Following World War I, the promise of national self-determination in Woodrow Wilson's Fourteen Points injected ideological fuel into the national liberation movements of the colonial world. At the end of World War II, the wars of national liberation intensified, culminating in the fall of the European, Japanese and American colonial empires.

In the post-Cold War period, a third and highly explosive phase of nationalism has burst on to the political stage in the form of ethno-nationalism. With the decline of the universalist ideological pretensions of liberalism and communism, primordial identities have resurfaced as the most potent force in domestic and international politics. Long repressed by dominant majorities, many ethnic minorities clamour for independence and statehood. The Kurds, Croats, Palestinians and Quebecois readily come to mind. Of the 120 violent conflicts currently waged around the world, 72 per cent are ethnic in character. As well as 22 million refugees there are more than 150 million displaced people, most of whom are the victims of protracted ethnic conflicts erupting into violence. The situation in Afghanistan is a telling example. After the ascendancy of the Pushtun-based and Sunni fundamentalist Taliban government in 1995, other ethnic and religious minorities (the Uzbeks, Tajiks, Hezareh and Shiites) were severely persecuted and driven into exile in Iran, Tajikistan, Uzbekistan and Pakistan.

The world is a multi-ethnic and multi-religious place. Policies of forced national integration by 'nation-states' have tried to homogenize state populations into a conforming mass. National language policies are a striking example of how uniformity has been imposed on a diverse world. There are approximately 4,522 living languages in the world, 138 of which have more than one million speakers. Many more languages have unfortunately died. The number of languages in the United States before the coming of Columbus in 1492 was more than 1,000; today it is only 200.[23] Given that every language represents human creativity, much effort will need to go into preserving those languages that live, reviving those that are about to perish, and resurrecting those that have died.

Much to the impoverishment of the world, the forces of colonialism, nationalism and globalism have often homogenized and destroyed cultural diversity. Pan-nationalism, in particular, has often been used as the hegemonic project of a dominant ethnic group to repress a weaker. Nationalism can be democratic and benign, but it can also be totalitarian and malignant, externally aggressive and internally repressive. Swiss nationalism is an example of the former. Nazi German and fascist Italian nationalism provide examples of the latter. More recently, the nationalism of the colonized peoples has demonstrated how the national ideology can be a liberating force in history. The nationalism of the colonizers, on the other hand, justified under such moral claims as 'the white man's burden' or 'manifest destiny', provided a vehicle for European imperialism to exploit and repress subjected peoples. Nationalism has achieved much in art and culture, economic progress and political unity. But it has also produced genocide, including the near-extermination of Native Americans and Native Hawaiians in the United States,[24] the Jewish Holocaust in Europe, and the repression of the Palestinians in Israel.

National identity is often presented as a non-negotiable fact. Much of contemporary violence can be traced to religious, national or racial ideologies which are camouflaging material, economic and political conflicts of interest. Class, ethnicity, race and nationality are so intimately intertwined in a hierarchy of wealth, income and status that politicians are often tempted to transpose conflicting economic interests into ethnic and national passions and violence. While economic conflicts are negotiable, ethnic, racial and national conflicts tend to be treated as non-negotiable. Racism is itself often used as a convenient ideological vehicle for the pursuit of class and status interests.

History is replete with cultural policies that have tried to mould identities to suit reasons of state. Such policies have ranged from extermination to segregation, assimilation, amalgamation and integration. Table 2.3 offers examples of how repressed groups have been treated in different societies and historical eras with respect to their democratic rights. Native Americans in early US history, Jews in Hitler's Germany and Muslims in Bosnia were all victims of policies of extermination. Policies of *de jure* segregation were pursued in the southern United States until the 1960s and in South Africa until the dismantling of apartheid in the 1990s. Such policies continue in many parts of the world through *de facto* social and economic segregation of residential neighbourhoods and workplaces. Assimilation has been the dominant policy of many societies in which a single group enjoys a position of privilege but is willing to co-opt and homogenize talented individuals from other aspiring groups. This has been the dominant policy in most European and North American societies in the postwar period. Assimilated individuals must forgo their own cultural heritage and adopt the cultural norms and practices of the dominant group(s).

Assimilationist policies begin with the premise that, in the words of Theodore Roosevelt, 'we do not need hyphenated Americans'. Amalgamation policies represent the next higher level of tolerance. Since the 1960s, when cultural roots and identities were generally revived in the United States, hyphenated Americans, including Irish–Americans and Japanese–Americans, have become accepted. More than tolerating cultural diversity, integration policies celebrate it. They require a high degree of social and economic levelling, and rely therefore on the institution of equal-opportunity laws and compensatory hiring and social

Table 2.3 Cultural policies with respect to diversity and democracy

	Extermination	Segregation	Assimilation	Amalgamation	Integration
Democratic rights	Denied	Denied	Denied	Limited	Fulfilled
Natural rights: Life, liberty, the pursuit of happiness, including self-determination	Indigenous peoples under colonial rule; Jews in Hitler's Germany; Bahaiis in Iran	Slave societies; The Harijans in India	Colonized peoples; East Timor	Kashmiris in India	?
Civil rights: Suffrage, freedoms of speech, media, assembly, and association	Indigenous peoples under colonial rule; Jews in Hitler's Germany; Bahaiis in Iran	African–Americans in the US South until 1960s; apartheid in S. Africa until the 1990s; women in some societies	Colonized peoples; East Timor	Tibetans in China	?
Social and economic rights: Equal-opportunity employment, unemployment compensation, social security, health insurance	Indigenous peoples under colonial rule; Jews in Hitler's Germany; Bahaiis in Iran	Koreans in Japan; apartheid in S. Africa until 1990s; women in some societies	Colonized peoples	The underclass and slum-dwellers everywhere	?
Cultural rights: Freedoms of identity, language, religion, and customs	Indigenous people under colonial rule; Jews in Hitler's Germany; Bahaiis in Iran	Koreans in Japan; apartheid in South Africa until 1990s	Colonized peoples; immigrants in Europe; Kurds in Turkey; Tibetans in China; East Timor	Immigrants in Britain and United States	?

Note: Columns show the dominant cultural policies. Rows show denial of democratic rights to specific sectors of the population. Due to its brevity, the table should be read with some indulgence.

Source: M. Tehranian, *Global Communication and World Politics* (Boulder, CO: Lynne Rienner, 1999), p.184.

welfare. Although such policies were pursued in the United States and a number of European countries during the 1960s and 1970s, rising unemployment and resentment have placed them in jeopardy.

Nationalism can be both democratic and respectful of difference. At the risk of oversimplifying the complexities of cultural phenomena, Table 2.4 characterizes

Table 2.4   Culture of peace versus culture of violence: A schematic view

Attitudes towards	Tendencies towards violence	Tendencies towards peace
Life	Carelessness or contempt	Reverence
Self	Self-doubt Self-negation Self-hatred	Self-respect Self-affirmation Self-love
Others	Closed Exclusionary Indifferent Greed Revengefulness Exploitative Sarcasm (at others' expense)	Open Inclusionary Compassionate Generosity Forgiving Giving Humour (at one's own expense)
Society	Totalitarian Hierarchical Competitive Conflict generator Monoculturalist Ethnocentric	Communitarian Egalitarian Co-operative Consensus generator Multiculturalist Universalist
Nature	Domination of nature Ecologically irresponsible	Preservation of nature Ecologically responsible
Supernatural	Positivist: letter of the law Sectarian Exclusionary god(s) Transcendence–immanence	Mystical: spirit of the law Ecumenical Inclusionary god(s) Immanence–transcendence
Death	Necrophilic Glorification	Biophilic Remembrance

Source: M. Tehranian, *Global Communication and World Politics* (Boulder, CO: Lynne Rienner, 1999), p.182.

the main cultural tendencies towards violence and peace, tolerance and intolerance. Human attitudes are classified here in seven major categories, that is, attitudes to life, self, others, society, nature, the supernatural and death. The attributes assigned to them are located at opposite extremes of seven continua. No human society, culture or individual consistently possesses all the attributes located at either extreme. Most human societies, cultures and individuals show a complex configuration of attributes, but each has the potential to move in one or other direction. The challenge is to strengthen cultural tendencies that reward peace and conflict resolution, and penalize violence.

Localism: Parochial versus liberal

While nationalism has clearly been a dominant historical force for the past two centuries, localism is a relatively new trend pointing to a deepening of democratic forces. Localism may be defined as the ideology and movement that calls for devolution of power to the local aggregation of human communities, that is, the province, the village, the township and the neighbourhood. The 'local' in this context means any sub-national category. While nationalism in the nation-state centralizes power, localism calls for varying degrees of autonomy from the centre, whether in the context of unitary or federal systems. In the United States, where there has been a tradition of state autonomy, the rise of the 'welfare' and 'warfare' state in the twentieth century has tipped the balance in favour of federal power. Localism is in part an attempt to redress the balance.

The processes of decolonization and democratization that started with the American Revolution in 1776 have now expanded to all corners of the globe. The continuing world democratic revolution has gone through four long waves.[25] The first wave, from 1776 to 1848, was primarily aimed at the overthrow of monarchies and independence for the colonies in Europe and the Americas. The second wave, for which World War I acted as the catalyst, led to the breakdown of the Russian, Austro-Hungarian and Ottoman empires and the weakening of European control over their colonies in the Middle East and North Africa. World War II (the third wave) led to the final breakdown of the British, French, Belgian, Dutch, Portuguese, Japanese and Spanish empires in Africa and Asia. The end of the Cold War in 1989 and the disintegration of the Soviet Union in 1991 may be considered as the fourth wave in a continuing revolution.

A new trend, diffuse but widespread, is focused on devolution of power. Localism is the ideological expression of this trend, emphasizing participation, local knowledge, local initiative, local technologies and local organization. The initiative, it seems, has passed from the great ideological struggles of the nineteenth and twentieth centuries to a new kind of contestation. At the top are the technologues (Bill Gates, Bill Clinton, Tony Blair) of twentieth-century government and business who serve as the shapers and managers of global capitalism. At the bottom are the communologues (Ayatollah Khomeini, Nelson Mandela, Osama Bin Laden) of localist movements that speak in the vernacular of local knowledge, and of epistemic communities that strike a chord with local fears and anxieties. This polarization of the world system is energized by the two dominant fetishisms of commodity and identity or, as Barber has put it, 'McWorld versus Jihad'.

At the same time, the global network has provided channels of communication for a mobilized global civil society. As the slogan 'Think Globally, Act and Dial Locally' implies, the global communication network has brought to local communities the power to link with the global communities of affinity throughout the world. Local initiatives for nuclear-weapons-free zones (NWFZs) increased from 250 in 1982 to 5000 in 1991,[26] reflecting and strengthening the trend which saw 24 countries unilaterally declare themselves NWFZs, and the signing of five formal NWFZ treaties.[27] A global idea, it seems, can find sustenance and inspiration in local movements and organizations.[28] The organization of municipal foreign-policy organizations in a number of US cities is another manifestation of localism, suggesting that local communities may no longer be willing to allow the Department of State to be the sole vehicle representing their international concerns, whether it be in relation to land or immigration.

Localism is caught in a tension between parochialism and liberalism. Parochial localism tends to be narrow-minded, bigoted and persecutionary. The phenomenon of right-wing localism which has emerged in parts of the United States, Europe and Australia is evidence of this trend. Taking advantage of unabashed racism and local prejudice, organizations such as the Ku Klux Klan can strike a powerful chord at times of dwindling resources and diminishing expectations. Le Pen in France and Pauline Hanson in Australia reflect the same phenomenon. The beating of an African-American, Rodney King, by Los Angeles white policemen points to the parochial power of localism. The jurors in Simi Valley in Southern California in handing down a not-guilty verdict simply vented the prevailing local view of the white policeman as protector of law and order. A subsequent trial in a different locale brought forth a different verdict.

Hierarchies of inequality, which place women, minorities and immigrants at the bottom of the social pyramid, can ultimately be corrected through local action and initiative. However powerful global, regional and national forces may be, it is local conditions and power configurations that shape routinized structures of violence, whether in remote villages or in inner-city ghettos. Communities in the American South did not change the scourge of segregation for more than a hundred years, and then only once industrialization had altered the institutional structures at the local level. The same can be said of the dismantling of apartheid in South Africa. The new segregation in urban America relegates one-fifth of the population to an underclass whose chances for upward mobility are marginal. The post-industrial, information society of high technology and fully robotized factories has imposed on this population conditions of structural unemployment and unemployability – some 50 per cent of the black male population of US inner cities is unemployed.

The United States presents one of the most advanced and violent post-urban societies. More than 50 per cent of Americans now live in small towns and suburbs. Only 12 per cent of Americans live in big cities. But, as the *Economist* points out, there are cities within cities:

> Beverly Hills, home of Hollywood's stars, is completely surrounded by the city of Los Angeles. Yet, it has its own mayor, government, police force and tax structure. So does Compton, a poor, largely black slum close to south central Los Angeles. The consequence is that Beverly Hills has lavish municipal services and Compton rotten ones. Redraw the maps, make the areas that can afford to spend and share the burdens with those that cannot, and things may start to grow healthier.[29]

Transportation and telecommunication are making it increasingly possible to live and work in 'edge cities',[30] where high-tech industries, commercial services and shopping malls locate. The city of Los Angeles is a patchwork of such autonomous suburbs connected with the world's most sophisticated freeway system, enabling their residents to bypass the 'undesirable' neighbourhoods while having easy access to urban beaches, theatres, museums and other desirable facilities. While the business districts of the big city and the small edge cities experience revival and expansion, the inner cities decline. Philadelphia, America's fifth largest city, encapsulates this paradox. In the past decade, Philadelphia's skyline in the business districts has been transformed by architecturally exciting new skyscrapers while the ghetto areas have gone into a downward spin. Compared with two million in 1970, the city's population is down to around one and a half million, but its suburbs are ever more populous.

If conditions are to improve, a shift of power to localities must coincide with a shift of resources. In Tajikistan, for instance, the southern provinces of Garm and Badakhshan were starved of resources during the Soviet period while the northern province of Khojand was industrialized. Following independence in 1991, Tajikistan sank into a civil war reflecting regional inequalities and grievances more than ideological differences. Such regional disparities are also typical of other countries. In China, for example, economic growth is proceeding at a furious space in the East Coast regions at the expense of the interior and western parts.

Feminism: Patriarchy versus equality

As the UN Conference on Women held in Beijing in 1995 graphically symbolized, the movement for the freedom and equality of women represents one of the most important turning points in history. Patriarchal resistance to feminist demands indicates that the struggle will continue well into the future, transforming in its wake virtually every facet of domestic, national and international life.

The signs of gender revolution are evident in most parts of the world. There are few countries left today that deny women their rights of suffrage. Women's political participation in elections is increasingly decisive: witness Iran's presidential elections in 1997, and again in 2001 when women voters helped to give Mohammad Khatami, a moderate cleric, a landslide victory. In the 1992 and 1996 US presidential elections women tipped the balance in favour of Clinton, and in the 1997 British parliamentary elections the Labour Party won a decisive victory, again with the help of women's support. Outside the political arena, women are moving into professional positions formerly closed to them. The principle of equal pay for equal work is increasingly recognized world wide. Maternity leave is now deemed a crucial means of bringing women into the labour force. Progressive countries are acknowledging child-rearing and homemaking as social functions that merit reward. More generally, advances in the technology of family planning, greater educational opportunities, and higher levels of employment have put women more in charge of their own lives.[31]

Despite a measure of progress, women are still the subject of extensive discrimination in both advanced and developing countries. The status of women differs greatly both among and within nations. The feminist movement has still a great deal of work ahead of it. The UNDP now provides a balance sheet of women's progress in life expectancy, adult literacy, educational enrolment, share of earned income, and gender empowerment.[32] In most cases, the Gender-related Development Index (GDI) and Gender Empowerment Index (GEI) register lower scores than the Human Development Index (HDI). 'Human development, if not engendered, is endangered' declared the 1995 Human Development Report.[33] Gender equality, the report made clear, should be seen not as an automatic result of economic growth, but as a political and cultural objective that should form an integral part of national development plans. GDI statistics reveal that the Scandinavian countries lead in this respect with a score of about 0.92 compared with a maximum total of 1.0. The next highest scores, which are registered by other advanced industrialized countries, come down sharply to 0.80. A comparison of HDI and GDI reveal that a number of developing countries (Barbados, Thailand, Sri Lanka, Malaysia, Jamiaca and Cuba) have achieved higher levels of women's progress than their level of human development suggests. On the other hand, in several advanced countries, notably Canada, Luxembourg, Netherlands and Spain, women's share of income was significantly lower than men's. In Argentina, Chile, Costa Rica and many Arab states, women lagged seriously behind.[34]

Environmentalism: Exploitative versus protective

Since the 1960s, a new movement has emerged focusing attention on global environmental degradation. Appearing first in the advanced industrial countries, the movement succeeded in changing national and international discourse in favour of environmental protection and sustainable development. In 1972 UNEP was established

> to facilitate international cooperation in the environmental field; to further international knowledge in this area; to keep the state of the global environment under review; and to bring emerging environmental problems of international significance to the attention of the Governments.[35]

UNEP, which prepares an annual report on the 'State of the Environment', has convened a number of major international conferences, including the 1992 Earth Summit in Rio. An unprecedented 178 countries, 115 heads of states, 1,400 NGOs, 7,000 delegates, 9,000 journalists, and 20,000 environmentalists from around the world participated in the summit.

Pollution, now recognized as a universal threat to human security, comes in many guises. As *The Gaia Peace Atlas* puts it,

> It can be injected into the atmosphere as a noxious cocktail of sulfur dioxide, nitrogen oxides, hydrocarbons, heavy metals and ozone; it can be dumped directly into landfill sites as any number of toxic compounds; and it can be flushed into the sea, either as industrial effluent or as agricultural run-off (fertilizers and pesticides). Whatever the route, the hard facts remain: pollution rarely stays put, and it does not go away. Slowly and insidiously, persistent

toxins are entering into our food chains, accumulating in fatty tissues of ani-
mals, contaminating the air we breathe and posing unknown health risks
both for us and future generations.[36]

Pollution knows no borders. The MDCs have grudgingly awakened to the facts
of environmental degradation and taken several corrective measures. The LDCs,
on the other hand, are in urgent need of rapid economic development and tend
therefore to neglect environmental protection. To make matters worse, MDCs are
exporting their pollution-creating industries to the LDCs. This is at best a short-
term strategy, for exported pollution eventually returns home, either indirectly
via the food chains or directly via imported produce.

The ideas of Spaceship Earth,[37] Gaia Hypothesis,[38] sustainable development,
and soft and appropriate technology cannot be dismissed as trendy slogans. They
all suggest the awakening of a global environmental consciousness, the embryonic development of a worldwide movement for sustainable production and
consumption. In response to the onslaught of relentless growth, Green groups
and parties have found in the colour 'green' a symbol for their central ecological
concerns. Destruction of nature is not, however, the only problem. Rapid modernization has inflicted another very high cost: the destruction of the delicate
bonds of community. The traditions of civility and mutual obligation have
eroded under the onslaught of acquisitive individualism and commodity and
identity fetishism. A new balance must be struck between liberty, equality and
community – the three axial principles of modern democratic revolutions. To
attain this balance it will be necessary to reinvent democracy around ecological
and communitarian values.

A great gulf separates the communitarian perspective on globalism from the
hegemonic perspective. The former calls for non-violence, ecologically sensitive
and socially responsible sustainable development, protection of human rights,
the upholding of human responsibility towards all layers of human community
from local to global, and a celebration of cultural diversity. Four elements
seem essential to the construction of an effective world community: common
interests, norms, laws and sanctions. The risks posed by ecological disaster and
genocide have raised the level of global consciousness of common interests. An
emerging normative consensus now recognizes the reality of global political,
economic and ecological interdependence. Global society currently rests on a
fragile moral, legal and political framework. Effective steps are needed to give
shape to a new framework of common interests and norms supported by enforce-
able law.

Revivalism: Sectarian versus ecumenical

We need a new ethics of social responsibility. The acquisitive society has
unleashed boundless human energies and dazzling technologies for production,
but it has failed to institutionalize notions of equity and community. As gaps
widen among and within nations, modernity fails to deliver security not only to

the poor but also to the rich and the middle classes. As a reaction to this moral and political crisis a new religious revivalist movement has emerged in different parts of the world – a movement, however, with two contradictory faces, the one sectarian and the other ecumenical.

During the past decade, countries as wide apart in geography, history, social structure and culture as the United States, India, Iran, Israel and Guatemala have experienced the profound political impact of religious movements.[39] The last few US presidential elections were strikingly influenced by the rise of the Christian Coalition, particularly around the 'Bible belt'. Presidents Carter, Reagan, Bush I, Clinton and Bush II, each in his own unique style, campaigned on political platforms constructed with an eye to the Christian right. Prayer in schools, restrictions on abortion, ban on pornography, limitations on stem cell research, and a general bemoaning of the decadence of a liberal and permissive society assumed high prominence in these campaigns. India's 1991 elections were marked by the spectacular successes of a militant Hindu party in a society constitutionally dedicated to a secular state. In Israel the Jewish religious parties have visibly shifted the balance between the Labour and Likud parties in favour of the latter. In Guatemala, where 70 per cent of the population is Catholic, a Protestant evangelist was elected president in 1990.

Religious revivalism is primarily a response to diverse social anxieties: the unsettling effects of rapid social change (over-modernization in developing countries, post-modernization in the developed world); problems of marginalization, relative material or psychological deprivation, and identity fetishism as a reaction to commodity fetishism. Religious revival is not a passing social phenomenon. It can assume state power as in Iran. It can be frustrated by the superior power of the state, as in Egypt, Syria, Iraq or Algeria. Or it may be gradually integrated into the mainstream of cultural life, as in the case of the Moral Majority in the United States or the Welfare (Refah) Party in Turkey. Alternatively, it can align itself with the ruling elites by identifying with the *status quo* as in Guatemala, Saudi Arabia, and the United States via the Republican Party. Its strategic options include revolutionary *militancy* (to seize total power), *withdrawal* (from mainstream society), *accommodation* (with the rest of society), or a relentless *conservatism* with regard to traditional values and norms. Religious revivalism may have as one of its unintended consequences greater epistemological tolerance between religious and secular world views as each moderates its monopolistic truth claims. Alternatively, it may assume power and rule with an iron fist until it too is chastened by the intractable complexities of human diversity and need for tolerance.

The recent experience of Iran and Afghanistan is instructive in that it suggests that internal and external forces can combine to augment religious fundamentalism. Both countries fell prey to Soviet-American rivalries which left moderate political factions little room for manoeuvre. The 1953 CIA intervention in Iran, by removing an elected and popular nationalist leader, Mohammad Mosaddeq, in favour of Mohammad Reza Shah, imposed a military dictatorship that stifled democratic politics. Following the suppression of communist and nationalist political parties, only religious parties were in a position to oppose the regime. The ensuing Islamic revolution of 1979 threatened to spread to neighbouring countries. To nip the revolution in the bud, Iraq, in alliance with Saudi Arabia and Kuwait and with the tacit approval of the Soviet and western powers, invaded Iran in 1980. The bloody war that lasted until 1988 resulted in some one million dead and another million maimed.

In 1979, partly in response to the Islamic revolution in Iran, a relatively moderate and secular Afghan communist regime invited the Soviet Union to intervene on its behalf. As a result, Afghanistan became the sacrificial lamb in the Soviet–American Cold War. The Soviet occupation of Afghanistan unleashed a war of resistance led by the Mujahedin and supported by American weapons, Saudi Arabian petrodollars, and Pakistani leadership. The defeat and subsequent withdrawal of Soviet military forces in turn gave way to a civil war among the various Mujahedin factions, reducing a beautiful and proud country to rubble. Pakistan, Saudi Arabia and the United Arab Emirates continued to support the Taliban, the most fanatical faction exclusively composed of the Pushtun ethnic group. Having come to power in 1995, the Taliban gave free reign to some 5,000 Arab–Afghans who had supported them. Led by Osama Bin Laden, their organization, operating under the name Al-Qaeda (the Base), were now intent on a global campaign against 'the infidels'. The September 11 attack on New York and Washington was an offshoot of this campaign. Religious fanaticism had given birth to global terrorism.

It cannot be said that with the eradication of world poverty and injustice, fanaticism and terrorism will come to an end. Timothy McVeigh, the Unabomber, and Osama Bin Laden were not poverty-stricken terrorists. They did not suffer material deprivation. When terrorism is the result of a deliberate and organized political act as in the case of the September 11 attacks, it cannot be considered a lone act of insanity. Global terrorism, like most crimes, has its breaking grounds, and must therefore be fought on several fronts. The perpetrators of the crime must be brought to justice. More importantly, however, the sense of social, economic and political injustice that breeds and sustains them must be addressed.

The rise of religious movements also signals a deeper yearning for a spiritual home in a world that ceaselessly generates new wants and anxieties. Though the secular ideologies of progress (nationalism, liberalism and communism) may claim to provide the individual with a sense of community and social responsibility, they have not addressed, let alone resolved, the human conditions of finitude, fragility and moral failure. Marx and Freud considered religion a passing phenomenon, yet religious identities have come back to haunt the political arena. Religion, and more generally culture, as the last repository of collective defence against the alienating onslaught of globalization, has acquired a new force and vitality.

The new world disorder is taking us into uncharted waters. A new trichotomous world system is emerging, consisting of new configurations of First, Second and Third Worlds, which represent historical stages of development from the pre-modern to the modern and postmodern worlds respectively (see Table 2.5). This division does not, however, correspond to what used to be known as the capitalist, communist and non-aligned worlds. Nor does it neatly correspond to the spatial borders between territorial states. Within each state, globalizing forces are dividing localities, regions and communities, either linking them to or de-linking them from global economic, political, social and communication networks. Globalization is privileging the modern and postmodern technocracies of each state while marginalizing the traditional tribal, rural, semi-urban and semi-literate populations. In this new 'order', the status of the individual depends largely on whether or not he or she is logged into the global networks of state, corporate, academic or criminal organizations.

Paradoxically, the world is at the same time discovering a new shared sense of oneness and vulnerability. If that recognition leads states to replace the unilateralist

Table 2.5 Globalization and fragmentation: Interlocking and deterritorialized first, second and third worlds

	Premodern first world	Modern second world	Postmodern third world
Geography	Large parts of Africa, Asia, and Latin America + slum areas in North American and European cities	Parts of Eastern Europe and Asia + South Africa, Argentina, Chile, and Brazil minus the slum rural and urban areas.	Major urban and suburban parts of North America and Western Europe + Australia and New Zealand.
Economy	Herding, agriculture, handcrafts, and underground or criminal economy	Manufacturing, services, and underground (drugs, prostitution and criminal activities)	Knowledge industries and services + underground and criminal economies
Polity	Traditional and authoritarian tribal chiefdoms and monarchies	Centralized and technocratic	Liberal democratic
Military	Small arms with possible access to biological, chemical, and nuclear weapons	Standing military forces with possible access to weapons of mass destruction	Information-intensive, high-technology weapons of mass destruction
Society	Nomadic and rural	Urbanizing	Urban and suburban
Culture and Communication	Oral, kinship and local ties and values	Literate and national ties and values	Electronic, cosmopolitan networks and values
Organization and Identity	Organic, kinship organizations, identity and solidarity	Mechanical, technocratic organizations, identity and solidarity	Super-organic, network organizations, identity and solidarity

pursuit of power with new rule-based multilateral policies and institutions, progress may be possible. The issue at stake is nothing less than democratization of global governance.

Notes

1. For a defence of globalization against its critics, see C. Crook, 'Globalization and its Critics', the *Economist*, 29 September 2001.
2. M. Tehranian, *Worlds Apart: Human Security and Global Governance* (London: I.B. Tauris, 1999).
3. UNDP, *Human Development Report 1999* (New York: Oxford University Press, 1999), pp.221–4.
4. I. Wallerstein, *The Modern World-System*, Vol.1 (New York: Academress, 1974); I. Wallerstein, *The Capitalist World-Economy* (Cambridge: CUP, 1979); T.D. Hall, 'The World-Systems Perspective: a Small Sample from A Large Universe', *Sociological Inquiry*, 66, 4 (November 1996); T.D. Hall, 'The Effects of Incorporation into World-Systems on Ethnic Processes: Lessons from the Ancient World for the Modern World' (Paper prepared for ISA Conference, Toronto, 18–22 March 1997).
5. Ibn Khaldun, *The Muqaddimah, An Introduction to History*, 3 vols, tr. Franz Rosenthal (Princeton, NJ: Princeton University Press, 1967); C. Issawi, *An Arab Philosophy of History: Selections from the Prolegomena of Ibn Khaldun of Tunis (1332–1406)* (London: Murray Press, 1950).
6. C. Chase-Dunn and T.D. Hall, *Rise and Demise: Comparing World-Systems* (Boulder, CO: Westview, 1997).
7. A.G. Frank, *The Centrality of Central Asia* (Amsterdam: VU University Press, Comparative Asian Studies No.8, 1992); A.G. Frank and B.K. Gills (eds), *The World System: Five Hundred Years or Five Thousand?* (London: Routledge, 1993).
8. D. Bell, *The Coming of the Post-Industrial Society: a Venture in Social Forecasting* (New York: Basic Books, 1999).
9. M. Castells, *The Information Society: Economy, Society, and Culture*, Vols 1–3, (Oxford: Blackwell, 1996–2000); D. Schiller, *Digital Capitalism: Networking the Global Market System* (Cambridge, MA: MIT Press, 2000).
10. D. Harvey, *The Conditions of Postmodernity* (Oxford: Blackwell, 1990).
11. J. Mittelman, *The Globalization Syndrome: Transformation and Resistance*, (Princeton, NJ: Princeton University Press, 2000), ch.6.
12. T. Schelling, 'The Global Dimension', in G. Allison and G.F. Treverton (eds), *Rethinking America's Security* (New York: Norton, 1992), p.200.
13. J. Attali, *Millennium: Winners and Losers in the Coming World Order* (New York: Times Books, 1991); S. Strange, 'Territory, State, Authority and Economy: a New Realist Ontology of Global Political Economy', in R.W. Cox (ed.), *The New Realism: Perspectives on Multilateralism and World Order* (Tokyo: UNU Press, 1997).
14. Strange, pp.15–16.
15. R.J. Rummel, *Death by Government* (New Brunswick: Transactions Publishers, 1994); the *Economist Survey* (11 September 1999).
16. J. Habermas, *Legitimation Crisis* (Boston: Beacon Press, 1973).
17. M. Tehranian, 'Communication, Peace, and Development: a Communitarian Perspective', in F. Korzenny and S. Ting-Toomey (eds), *Communicating for Peace* (Newbury Park: Sage, 1990).
18. S. Huntington, 'The Clash of Civilizations', *Foreign Affairs* (Summer 1993); S. Huntington, 'The Clash of Civilizations: a Reponse', *Foreign Affairs* (November–December 1993).
19. See Part II.
20. Mittelman, p.112.
21. Ibid., p.122.

22. F.W. Riggs, 'The Modernity of Ethnic Identity and Conflict' (Paper prepared for ISA Conference, Toronto, 18–22 March 1997).
23. S. Shah, 'The Roots of Ethnic Conflict', *Nuclear Times* (Spring 1992).
24. D.E. Stannard, *Before the Horror: the Population of Hawaii on the Eve of Western Contact* (Honolulu: Social Science Research Institute, University of Hawaii, 1989).
25. K. Tehranian and M. Tehranian (eds), *Restructuring for World Peace: on the Threshold of the 21st Century* (Creskill, NJ: Hampton Press, 1992), M. Tehranian, 'Global Communication and International Relations: Changing Paradigms and Policies', *International Journal of Peace Studies*, 2, 1 (January 1997).
26. E. Boulding, 'The Zone of Peace Concept in Current Practice: Review and Evaluation' (Paper presented at the Inaugural Conference of the Centre for Peace Studies, Curtin University and University of Western Australia, 14–16 January 1991).
27. For a proposal on de-nuclearization, see chapter 11.
28. M. Tehranian, 'Zones of Peace', in D.E. Wells (ed.), *Encyclopedia of War and Ethics* (Westport, CT: Greenwood Press, 1996).
29. The *Economist*, 9 May 1992, p.22.
30. J. Garreau, *Edge City: Life on the New Frontier* (New York: Doubleday Press, 1991).
31. UNDP, *Human Development Report* (New York: Oxford University Press, 1995), chs 3–4.
32. UNDP, *Human Development Report* (New York: Oxford University Press, 1996).
33. UNDP, 1995, p.1.
34. Ibid., pp.1–10.
35. United Nations, *Everyman's United Nations* (New York: UN, 1985), p.240.
36. F. Barnaby (ed.), *The Gaia Peace Atlas* (New York: Doubleday, 1988), p.118.
37. R.B. Fuller, *Grunch of Giants* (New York: St Martin's Press [now Palgrave Macmillan], 1983).
38. J. Lovelock, *The Ages of Gaia: a Bibliography of Our Living Earth* (New York: Norton, 1988).
39. M. Tehranian, 'Fundamentalist Impact on Education and the Media: an Overview' and 'Islamic Fundamentalism in Iran and the Discourse of Development', in M.E. Marty and R. Scott (eds), *Fundamentalism and Society*, Vol.2 (Chicago, IL: University of Chicago Press, 1993).

3
Democratizing Governance

Majid Tehranian

> We use the term governance to denote the command mechanism of a social system and its actions that endeavor to provide security, prosperity, coherence, order and continuity to the system…Taken broadly, the concept of governance should not be restricted to the national and international systems but should be used in relation to regional, provincial and local governments as well as to other social systems such as education and the military, to private enterprise and even to the microcosm of the family.
>
> King and Schneider (1991), pp.181–2

To propose reforms in the present system of global governance is a hazardous task. However, given the enormous inequities and inefficiencies of the present system, the task is unavoidable. It would be best if a variety of interest groups in government, business, and civil society could put their considered proposals before the international community. Ultimately, no reform can take place unless a consensus emerges among the major states. For this reason, a period of intense dialogue involving government, corporate, and civil-society experts and the public at large is necessary. Some proposals may be rejected, others may be adopted, and others still may be tried experimentally.

The proposals that follow are premised on the desirability and practicability of a greater level of global democracy than currently prevails. This chapter focuses first on the problems and prospects for global democracy, before addressing the need for greater balance in the distribution of power among state, market and civil-society forces.

Global democracy

Democratic development is a long historical process. It may be considered to have begun when the great spiritual leaders of humanity first spoke for human dignity, freedom and equality as the cardinal principles of their faiths. Major lawgivers in history – Hammurabi, Moses, Muhammad, Confucius and others – pushed the process forward by establishing the rule of law rather than arbitrary government as the normative basis for political organization. Landmark documents such as

Magna Carta, the American Declaration of Independence, the French Declaration of the Rights of Man and the Citizen, and the Universal Declaration of Human Rights established lofty democratic norms. In different periods of history, notably the Age of Pericles in Athens, and colonial New England, democratic principles were partially practised in direct democracy by a limited number of citizens. In the modern popular imagination, the Agora and the New England Town Meeting have become the archetypes of such pure forms of democratic practice. However, it is important to note that in ancient Greece, women and slaves were excluded from citizenship while in New England, citizenship was limited to property owners.

In modern times, the democratic movement has gone through at least four historical waves. The first wave consists of the rise of modern representative government in Britain, France and the United States through a series of democratic revolutions, namely the English Revolution of 1688, the American Revolution of 1776, and the French Revolution of 1789. This first wave filtered throughout Europe by means of the democratic revolutions of 1848. While a rising industrial bourgeoisie led the first wave, the second wave of democratic development was set in motion by the rise of an industrial working-class movement in the nineteenth century, whose struggles gradually led to labour and social-welfare reforms in advanced industrial countries. The second wave also led to a series of communist revolutions in Russia, China, Korea, Cuba and Vietnam, that focused on equality rather than freedom as the axial principle of democracy. The third democratic wave appeared in the European colonies with the rise of the national liberation movements of the nineteenth and twentieth centuries. Two world wars weakened the grip of European, American and Japanese colonialism, paving the way for the independence of Asian, African and Latin American states. A fourth wave of democratic movements has assumed momentum with the end of the Cold War in 1989. Repressed ethnic minorities which have been kept largely in check by powerful states, whether the Soviet Union, China or Turkey, indigenous peoples throughout the world, and repressed religious groups such as the Shiites in Lebanon and Iraq are pressing for their democratic rights.

A fifth democratic wave may be on the way in the wake of the Asian financial crisis of 1997–98.[1] A succession of financial crises, which subsequent chapters will examine further, have made it apparent that the institutions of global governance are lagging far behind the expanding but increasingly unregulated capital flows. Quite apart from issues of financial and economic management, such global problems as genocide, the proliferation of weapons of mass destruction, environmental pollution, and protection of the natural and cultural heritage of humankind appear to fall outside the competence of the present state system.

As Daniel Bell put it aptly, 'the territorial state is too small for the big problems and too big for small problems'.[2] Global democracy has to move therefore in two different directions simultaneously: it must deepen democratic participation at the lower levels (local, national, regional), while broadening it at the higher level of global decision-making. In this process, democracy is hostage to the competing ideological contestations of libertarianism, egalitarianism, communitarianism and authoritarianism. Each ideological school tends to opt for a different axial principle of political organization emphasizing, respectively, the role of freedom, equality, community and order. The challenge is to *optimize* the mix of these competing but complementary norms, not to maximize any one of them at the expense of the others.

In order to represent these ideological contestations, Figure 3.1 re-maps the conventional half circle of the political spectrum into a full circle around the

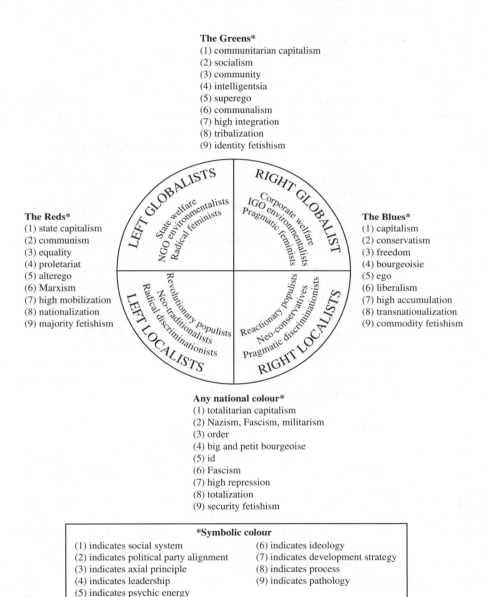

The Greens*
(1) communitarian capitalism
(2) socialism
(3) community
(4) intelligentsia
(5) superego
(6) communalism
(7) high integration
(8) tribalization
(9) identity fetishism

The Reds*
(1) state capitalism
(2) communism
(3) equality
(4) proletariat
(5) alterego
(6) Marxism
(7) high mobilization
(8) nationalization
(9) majority fetishism

The Blues*
(1) capitalism
(2) conservatism
(3) freedom
(4) bourgeoisie
(5) ego
(6) liberalism
(7) high accumulation
(8) transnationalization
(9) commodity fetishism

Any national colour*
(1) totalitarian capitalism
(2) Nazism, Fascism, militarism
(3) order
(4) big and petit bourgeoise
(5) id
(6) Fascism
(7) high repression
(8) totalization
(9) security fetishism

*Symbolic colour	
(1) indicates social system	(6) indicates ideology
(2) indicates political party alignment	(7) indicates development strategy
(3) indicates axial principle	(8) indicates process
(4) indicates leadership	(9) indicates pathology
(5) indicates psychic energy	

Figure 3.1 Re-mapping the global political spectrum

four polarities and norms. World politics has been characterized by a struggle among the proponents of the four paths to democracy and order. The Blues, or the pioneers of the industrial revolution (England, France and the United States), took the liberal democratic, capitalist road. The industrial bourgeoisie, preoccupied with the rights of private property and individual freedom, led the transition by following a high accumulation strategy of development and free trade policies designed to open up the markets of the rest of the world. The Reds, or communists, were led by the revolutionary working class and intelligentsia aiming at the same goal, namely industrial revolution, but through national planning with the stress on social equality, national self-sufficiency and high-mobilization strategies of development and self-sufficiency. The Greens, led by the intelligentsia, have argued for socially, culturally and environmentally responsible strategies of development, prizing 'community' and high-integration strategies of development. The communitarians range in perspective from Gandhian revolutionaries in the LDCs (India, South Africa and Sri Lanka) to social democratic and socialist parties in the West.

This conceptual map situates within the international political spectrum a complex range of right and left globalists as well as right and left localists. All democratic paths have shown themselves prone to totalitarian temptations, though some more than others. During the inter-war years, Germany, Italy and Japan fell under totalitarian regimes. Under Stalin's regime (1927–52), Soviet communism assumed totalitarian forms. In the early 1950s, liberal capitalism in the United States came close to that in the Red Scare of the McCarthy era. Under Mao's Cultural Revolution (1966–76), China also succumbed to a totalitarian system of terror, mass arrests and murders. Since the occupation of the West Bank in 1967, Zionist communitarianism in Israel has unleashed terror on Palestinian Arabs. Similarly, Hindu militancy in India and Islamic militancy in Iran has meant terror and persecution for religious minorities in those countries. Totalitarian regimes propelled the latecomers to industrial revolution (Germany, Japan, Italy, Spain, Argentina) and employed national or party colours (brown for Nazism, black for Fascism, yellow for Japanese militarism) to mobilize their respective societies around a new, highly repressive 'order' that glorified national myths of superiority.

The eternal triangle

Though the structure and processes of global governance are complex, a schematic account is nevertheless possible. As has been noted more than once, the key stakeholders – the state, market and civil society – may be said to form an eternal triangle. The global communication networks, including the flows of people, goods, services, technologies, ideas, news, images and data have increasingly penetrated the territorial state. These networks range from the most informal social relations to the highly evolved political, economic, social, cultural and media institutions. Territorial states, no matter how large and powerful, are not immune to the pressures of global communication, not least the flows of international finance capital that can make or break smaller states, as witnessed in the recent East Asian economic crisis. We are dealing then with a complex web of states (great, small and middle powers), non-state actors (TNCs, TMCs, TFCs, NGOs, AGOs), and IGOs (UN, specialized agencies, regional and functional organizations).

We may view the relations between state, markets and civil society from two diametrically opposed perspectives: authoritarian and democratic. In Figure 1.1 (see Chapter 1, page 4) the state was portrayed as dominating both market and civil society in a pyramid nested within the larger pyramid of global governance institutions. However, the national state can, as shown in Figure 3.2, be an equal partner with market and civil-society forces in a democratic system represented by the interlocking circles.

Clearly, the two models are merely indicative of the theoretical possibilities, authoritarian regimes at one end of the spectrum and democratic regimes at the other. Reality, however, is more complex and constantly evolving. Relations between the local, national, regional and global tiers of governance are similarly complex and dynamic, and conflicts between these various tiers are becoming more frequent and more acute. Democratization is itself contributing to this dynamic process.

Two international campaigns, one against apartheid in South Africa and the other against the military dictatorship in Myanmar (Burma) are indicative of the impact of democratization on the various tiers of governance. In the 1980s, local governments and state pension funds in the United States helped lead the fight against South African apartheid by withdrawing investment funds from companies that continued to operate in that country. In the 1990s, more than 20 local governments, from the city of Los Angeles to the State of Massachusetts, waged similar campaigns against Myanmar's repressive regime.[3] However, these latter efforts have run into opposition from two powerful sets of actors, the EU and the TNCs. The EU filed a suit in the WTO, claiming that Massachusetts law violated US treaty obligations to base government procurement solely on performance. The National Foreign Trade Council, an alliance of major US exporters, persuaded a federal judge to invalidate the Massachusetts law on the grounds that it impinged on foreign policy-making, a federal prerogative. Aung San Suu Kyi

Figure 3.2 Global policy stakeholders: a democratic vision

disagreed. She strongly welcomed the Massachusetts decision: 'We would like to see more of this…It's consumer power…I think in some ways it's better to have the people of the world on your side than governments'.

The Clinton Administration was torn between its global human rights policies in support of democratic movements and its global economic policies of encouraging freedom of trade and investment. US officials complained that state and local sanctions complicate their dealings with allies. But New York's threat of sanctions against Swiss banks undoubtedly helped the United States to negotiate a better deal for Holocaust victims. Secretary of State Madeleine Albright recognized the state and local officials' authority 'to determine their own investment and procurement policies, and the right – indeed, their responsibility – to take moral considerations into account as they do so'. The tendency, however, was for US economic policy-makers to side with TNCs in their efforts to keep international trade and investment out of local or state government hands.

The foregoing examples reveal the actual and potential tensions among the main stakeholders of global governance. Some 200 territorial states occupy a central place, primarily as regulators of the game, pursuing their national interests on the international stage bilaterally and through IGOs, and communicating to the rest of the world through government-controlled or regulated media. Next to states, and probably surpassing them in global reach and power, markets perform the central function of resource allocation (land, labour, capital, information and management). Engaged in global competition, some 40,000 TNCs occupy the commanding heights of the world economy, communicating with the public through public relations firms and advertising agencies.

In contrast to states and TNCs, which tend to be vertically organized, civil societies usually have a horizontal structure. They function as mobilizing and democratic agencies, checking and balancing the power of states and markets. They are represented by some 30,000 NGOs.

Transnational media corporations (TMCs) constitute perhaps a more visible set of global actors. Their central function may be said to be the legitimation of competing interests and perspectives in global society. Since most of TMCs are allied to TNCs through corporate linkages and advertising revenues, it is hardly surprising that they should act primarily as legitimizing agents of global capitalism.

Mention must also be made of transnational financial corporations (TFCs), whose role in the mobilization and transfer of savings and capital resources has made them central to the workings of the entire financial system. Served by the trade and investment media, TFCs reflect in their increasing numbers and diversity the mounting complexity and importance of financial instruments in world capital markets.

Finally, we have the lobbying groups, some visible, others not. These AGOs have their own channels of command, control and communication, which range from governments in exile to an alternative UN comprising the Unrepresented Peoples' Organization (UNPO), to drug cartels and criminal organizations. Although varying greatly in their claims to legitimacy, these organizations have one characteristic in common: according to the rules of state sovereignty, they operate outside the law.

Global policy-formation process

Global policies emerge from the complex interaction of diverse actors operating in diverse domains. At the global level, states are represented by IGOs, civil societies by NGOs and AGOs, and markets by TNCs, TMCs and TFCs. Each set of actors is equipped with its own media outlets, as they attempt to influence the global, national and local spheres of public discourse. Table 3.1 provides a schematic view of the global policy formation process, including policy definition, formulation, legislation, legitimation, implementation, regulation, adjudication and evaluation.

As a system of power and representation, the state legislates, executes, adjudicates and regulates. The increasingly globalized market, under the leadership of TNCs, allocates scarce resources (land, labour, capital, information and management) to competing demands. Political lobby groups attempt to influence the state in whatever way they can. To the extent that they exist and act autonomously, civil societies mobilize popular sentiment around such issues as environmental protection, health, education and social welfare. The mass media, largely owned and controlled by TNCs, play a pivotal role in legitimizing the dominant global political and economic system.

The global elite media serve as intermediaries in the twin processes of reality construction and public discourse. Such global newspapers as the *International Herald Tribune*, the *Wall Street Journal*, and the *Financial Times*, publishing simultaneously in more than ten cities around the world, are also available online. Weekly magazines such as the *Economist, Time, Newsweek, Der Spiegel*, and their equivalents in different countries provide context for the news. Journals of opinion such as *Foreign Affairs, Foreign Policy*, and *World Policy Journal* identify the emerging issues and controversies for their constituencies.

As for policy formulation, it is mainly the G7, IGOs, TNCs and TFCs that set global policy, often in concert, sometimes in conflict. For decades before and after World War II, for instance, the Seven Sisters of the international petroleum cartel single-handedly set oil prices and the level of exploration, production and distribution.[4] In the mass-media industries, Britain and the United States took the lead in the nineteenth century, and their TNCs have maintained their dominant position to this day.

Policy legislation is a complex process which concerns primarily national legislatures and foreign ministries. It gives rise to diverse international agreements and treaties, which upon ratification are passed on to IGOs for implementation by international administrative agencies, for example the ITU and the WTO. From the opposite end of global organization, revolutionary movements, governments-in-exile and such agencies as the UNPO become sources of resistance. The global telecommunication laws and covenants (such as copyright, spectrum and orbit allocation, and technical standards) set the scope and limitations for freedom and balance in global information and communication flows. The informed sectors of the world population with material interests at stake are the most influential in global legislation. TNCs, as major stakeholders in national and international legislation,

Table 3.1 The global policy formation process: a schematic view

Resources	Problem definition	Policy formulation	Policy legislation	Policy legitimation	Policy implementation, regulation, adjudication and evaluation
Top-Down Process: Generated by the interests and policies of the great powers and TNCs					
Natural, technological and human resources	Think tanks, foundations and commissions, e.g. Rand, Rockefeller, and Trilateral Commission	Great powers and transnational corps, e.g. G7 + Russia and China, Esso, AT&T, Brit. Telecom, Mitsubishi	National Legislatures and IGOs	Politicians, publicists, press and broadcasting	TNCs, IGOs, national govt agencies, regulatory commissions and the courts
Mediation process: Generated by the media constructions of reality and discourses in response to governments and oppositions					
Global telecom networks	Global elite press, e.g. *International Herald Tribune, Wall St. J., The Economist*	Media owners and editors	National media laws, and international covenants on copyright, spectrum and orbit allocation, technical standards	Global media networks, e.g. elite press, CNN, news agencies	Media associations, e.g. Int. Press Inst., Int. Publishers Ass.
Bottom-Up Process: Generated by the small and medium powers, revolutionary and opposition parties and associations					
Human, natural and technological resources	Revolutionary movts, NGOs and related foundations, think tanks and civil and religious networks, e.g. Amnesty International, World Council of Churches	Small-medium powers and global lobby groups, e.g. Group of 77, Physicians for Social Responsibility, American Friends Service Committee, Greenpeace, etc.	States in exile, revolutionary movts, e.g. PLO, Tibet govt-in-exile, UNPO, etc.	The alternative and underground media; the informal networks of gossip, rumour, civic and religious associations	Voluntary associations, labour unions, religious institutions, out-of-power political parties

Source: M. Tehranian, *Global Communication and World Politics: Domination, Development and Discourse* (Boulder, CO: Lynne Rienner, 1999), pp.79–80.

employ vast teams of lawyers and public relations officers to influence lawmakers and executive agencies. The informal ties of common neighbourhood, affiliation and education are often critical to this process.

Policy legitimation is primarily the task of politicians and publicists operating through the print and electronic media. Policy delegitimation is mainly the function of alternative and underground media and informal gossip and rumour networks. Other informal networks, including Internet electronic clubs and *listservs*, play a growing role in challenging the accuracy and legitimacy of mainstream sources of information.

Policy implementation, regulation, adjudication and evaluation are tasks performed in the main by TNCs, IGOs, national government agencies, regulatory commissions, and national and international courts. Citizens, whether through individual or collective litigation, can challenge the way these functions are performed, often with the help of voluntary associations, labour unions, religious institutions, and oppositional parties and groups. The role of the world media in such conflicts is often problematic. While national and international media professional associations set codes of conduct for media reporting, it would be naïve to assume that media are neutral bystanders. Despite the efforts of courageous and public-spirited journalists, media stories are often framed within the broad interests of media owners and managers. The structure is the message. In other words, media messages tend to reflect the structures of media ownership and the interests of editorial gatekeepers. Commercial media are in the business of competing for advertisers, audiences and ratings in order to maximize profits. As a consequence, they follow the most sensational or entertaining stories, and cater to the lowest common denominator. Government media toe the government line. Public media tend to follow elite tastes and shy away from sensationalism. Community media reflect the interests and views of the community groups (churches, trade unions, civic groups) that own and operate them.

Pluralism in structure may thus be considered the main guarantee of pluralism in content. Media systems such as those in Western Europe and Japan, which have equally strong commercial and public media, generally provide greater diversity in news and entertainment than the US media system, which is overwhelmingly dominated by commercial media. The proliferation of television channels – over 100 in some US cities – is an attempt to cater for diverse audiences, but commercial considerations invariably intrude.

A democratic drift?

In response to the globalization processes of the last two decades, scholars are increasingly coining such terms as 'humane governance',[5] 'cosmopolitan democracy',[6] and 'Pax Democratica'[7] in a conscious effort to go beyond inter-state relations and encompass the role of non-state actors. An important new development is research that seeks to make sense of the competing trends of globalization and fragmentation. Democratic governance at the national and global levels is often caught between the economic forces of globalization from above, the political forces of tribalization from below, and the weaker mediating forces of democratization from the centre.

At the national level, the development of democratic institutions of accountability has served as the major barrier to unbridled capitalism. The rise of a civil society of voluntary and religious associations, trade unions and political parties is the backbone of all modern democratic polities. Representative democracy without a flourishing civil society has proved to be a sham. Elections in which dictators win 99 per cent of the votes or in which only about 30–40 per cent of the electorate participates (as in the United States) indicate the absence or weakness of civil society.[8] In such circumstances, special-interest groups often present themselves as the sole defenders of 'the public interest'.

Civil-society institutions have gone through an evolutionary process that is no less remarkable than that experienced by state and market institutions – a trend described in Chapter 1. This evolution may be characterized as an overlapping movement that extends from religious to professional, civic, political and global associations. De Tocqueville was perhaps one of the earliest democratic theorists to recognize the central importance of voluntary associations to the daily operation of democratic societies.[9] In recent years, other democratic theorists, while posing the question differently, have come to much the same conclusion.

Robert Putnam, for example, has pointed to the decline of voluntary associations as one of the factors contributing to the weakening of democracy in the United States.[10] Organic associations based on kinship, characteristic of premodern societies, gave way to mechanical associations in modern societies based on functional roles such as labour unions, professional organizations and political parties. The decline of labour unions and political parties has been matched by the rise of a global network society with far-reaching consequences for democratic possibilities.[11] The central question for the democratic prospect is how to invest public trust in voluntary associations and networks, which is a necessary foundation for more responsible governments and robust economies.[12]

It is clear that globalization has created a political gap between national democratic checks and balances and transnational corporate power.[13] It has also created a serious psychological and political fracture between a primarily pre-modern and poverty-stricken world and an affluent postmodern world of high technology, cosmopolitan identities and permissive culture.

Can global civil society and a network of IGOs fill some of those economic, political and cultural gaps?[14] On the positive side, global civil society in collaboration with the UN has successfully problematized a number of international issues, including environment, human rights, security[15] and racism. On the negative side, the refusal of the great powers to support many of these efforts is a discouraging sign. The actual or threatened withdrawal of the United States from the Kyoto Protocol on global warming, the ABM Treaty, and the UN Conference on Racism are indicative of a unilateralist tendency. The refusal of several states (China, Russia and United States) to sign the Landmine Ban Treaty, and the reluctance of some countries to accept the International Criminal Court point to the obstacles ahead.

Humane governance is hostage to state and market fundamentalism from above and religious and ethnic fundamentalism from below. The future of humane global governance thus depends on the strengthening and reform of the UN system, and the growth of the international civil society. NGOs now perform multiple and increasingly important functions. They are playing an active role in UN and regional conferences. They are acting as gadflies (shaming governments on human rights), postal pigeons (multiple-track diplomacy), watchdogs (production and dissemination of critical information on the environment, and so on), advocacy groups (for example, against WMDs), pressure groups (political actions committees), and direct action groups (for example, Grameen Bank, peace and environmental protests, public health or development projects). These roles are not mutually exclusive.

Expanding global communication networks may be considered another positive development for democratic prospects. The missing link in our knowledge of democratic theory and practice relates precisely to the role of information, communication and media more generally. Despite the visible impact of instantaneous communication on the political process, whether through broadcasting, satellites or computer networks, that role is not yet fully understood. Much of the literature in the field reflects conflicting views on technology in general and information technologies in particular.[16] Hence the sharply contrasting interpretations offered by technophiles or technophobes, techno-neutralists or techno-constructivists.

Much of the literature is dominated by a technological determinist view imputing to technology an independent will or logic of its own, tending either towards dispersions or concentrations of power (technophiles and technophobes). However, as the other two schools of thought (techno-neutralists and techno-constructivists) well understand, technological impact is always mediated by social constructions of technology. Radio waves could be used for interactive communication among ships (as they were originally) or as one-way broadcast messages. While techno-neutralists tend to be consultants at the service of their clients, designing technologies for proprietary applications, techno-constructionists are analysts focusing on the social construction of technologies.

Global communication has clearly benefited from enormous technological breakthroughs (printing, telephony, photography, film, radio, television, computers, satellites), and the convergence of all these into multimedia and the Internet. Digitalization, miniaturization, diminishing costs and increasing access have also created multiple social constructions and effects. That is why a balanced assessment of the role of communication in democratic governance must emphasize its multiple effects as a key to understanding the complexities of the present conjuncture. The following propositions may serve as a starting point:

- Public communication empowers those who have communicative competence and access to the means of communication.
- Systematic distortions in public communication, prompted by ideologically biased discourses, disempower those who have no access to the media.
- Equal and interactive communication contributes to community building and democratic will formation.
- Unequal access to the media and systematic distortions in communication have a disintegrating effect on community and democratic will formation.

- Distantiation in communication (through one-way mass media) tends toward distortion and disintegration of the political community.
- Communication through interactive media (for example, the Internet) allows for integration of views of electronic communities.
- Media programming and effects often follow their structures of ownership and editorial management with commercial media going for high ratings and entertainment, government media focusing on government perspectives and propaganda, public media mostly catering to elite tastes,[17] and community media responding to their own particular constituencies and audiences.

Demassification of the mass media in the form of cable narrowcasting has resulted in a plurality of channels catering to different interests and tastes. However, because of the primacy of commercial interests, plurality of political and social views is not reflected in the diversity of channels. Instead, we have more and more light entertainment catering to different audiences, ranging from lovers of sports, finance or comedy, to children, women and shoppers.

The use of micromedia and mesomedia by social and political movements has in a number of instances contributed to democratic empowerment. These include the use of audio-cassettes and photocopy machines in the Iranian revolution, fax machines in the democratic movement in China, computer networks in the dissolution of the Soviet Union, and video cameras in capturing and disseminating censored news.

In co-operation with voluntary associations and electronic communities, interactive technologies such as the Internet and World Wide Web can facilitate democratic discourse, integration and will formation. However, pluralization of media structures of ownership and management remains the key to the realization of the democratic potential of modern media technologies. So long as a society is subjected to monolithic media ownership and control, whether it be in the commercial, state, public or community domain, democratic processes and institutions are unlikely to flourish. As we have already observed, structural pluralism is thus a precondition of content pluralism.

Global communication has placed the democratic norms of order, freedom, equality and community on the political agenda of most countries. The central task of the media in a democratic society may be considered a twofold one: first, to allow the diversity of voices in society to be heard, and second, to channel that diversity into a process of democratic integration of public opinion and will formation. Without free and vigorous debate among competing views, no society can achieve the level of integrated unity and determination necessary for it to act in the public interest. Generally speaking, media pluralism will serve these purposes better than a media system exclusively or largely dominated by state, commercial, public or community media. Pluralism in structures of ownership and control are therefore needed in order to obtain pluralism in perspectives and messages. Separation of editorial from ownership structures may guarantee a measure of editorial autonomy, but evidence shows that such separation often leads merely to editorial self-censorship. In any case, structural pluralism is hostage to the presence of independent market institutions and voluntary associations (political parties, trade unions, religious and civic organizations). The existence of a robust civil society to counter the power of the state and the market is itself a precondition for media pluralism.

As we have argued in this study, growth in communication and information technologies does not necessarily lead to democratic outcomes. Technologies in general and communication technologies in particular are double-edged swords. They can be employed for democratic as well as counter-democratic purposes. The surveillance potentials of communication and information technologies are immense, hence the need to ensure the legal protection of civil liberties. Similarly, the proliferation of mass media channels of communication is no guarantee of intellectual or cultural pluralism. Democratic discourse is dependent on a plurality of sources of information and power which are willing and able to counterbalance each other.

Concluding observations

The foregoing chapters have critically reviewed the historical evolution of global governance. Attention has been primarily directed to contemporary trends, and more specifically to the emergence of a transnational system of governance in the era of global capitalism. As senior Coca Cola executive R.C. Goizueta has argued, the institutions of global governance are increasingly dominated by global capital:

> Four prevailing forces – the preeminence of democratic capitalism, the desire for self-determination, the shift in influence from regulation to investment, and the success of institutions which meet the needs of people – reinforced by today's worldwide communications and dramatic television images ... all point to a fundamental shift in global power. To be candid, I believe this shift will lead to a future in which the institutions with the most influence by-and-large will be businesses.[18]

Striking a somewhat different tone, another business leader, George Soros, has acknowledged the dangers of market fundamentalism:

> Although I have made a fortune in the financial markets, I now fear that untrammeled intensification of laissez-faire capitalism and the spread of market values to all areas of life is endangering our open and democratic society ... The doctrine of laissez-faire capitalism holds that the common good is best served by the uninhibited pursuit of self-interest. Unless it is tempered by the recognition of a common interest that ought to take precedence over particular interests, our system ... is liable to break down.[19]

Many scholars have also described the emergent landscape as fraught with ambiguity. James Rosenau has observed:

> ... in this time of continuing and profound transformations, too much remains murky to project beyond the immediate present and anticipate long-term trajectories. All one can conclude with confidence is that in the twenty-first century the paths to governance will lead in many directions, some that will emerge into sunlit clearings and others that will descend into dense jungles.[20]

What are we to make of these contrasting views?

The argument here is that while the dominant trend is towards corporate domination of global governance, there are important and emerging sites of resistance pointing to greater fluidity and uncertainty. Table 3.2 draws from Goizueta, Soros, and Rosenau to demonstrate the complexity of global governance formation. It focuses on the transnational, international, national and subnational forces, whether already institutionalized or nascent. The table does not show the hierarchy and direction of power formations. It does, however, illustrate the problem of global power and the probable direction of global change. Central to the analysis developed here is the proposition that global capitalism as distinct from previous hegemonic systems vitally depends for its supremacy upon control of information and knowledge industries. This, in turn, is based on a global market driven by information technologies, patents, licences, trademarks and copyright managed by TNCs. While the territorial state continues to play an

Table 3.2 Global governance formation: Transnational, international, national and subnational forces

	Institutionalized	Nascent
Transnational	TNCs, TMCs, NGOs, AGOs, TROs, Internet, credit-rating agencies	Transnational social movements Epistemic world communities Electronic world communities
International	IGOs, G7, Group of 77, G15, NATO, RGOs, OPEC	Religious revivalism Environmentalism Feminism
National	Territorial states GATT negotiations	Civil wars National liberation movements
Subnational	Pressure groups, state and municipal governments	Ethnic minorities
Combinations	UN election monitoring Human rights regime	New issues Cross-border coalitions Agreements on foreign investment

Derived from: R.C. Goizueta, 'The Challenges of Getting What You wished For', remarks presented to the Arthur Page Society, Amelia Island, Florida, 21 September 1992; J.N. Rosenau, 'Governance in the 21st Century', *Global Governance*, 1(1995), pp.13–43; G. Soros, *The Crisis of Global Capitalism: Open Society Endangered* (New York: Public Affairs, 1999).

important role in the management of inter-governmental affairs, non-state actors (TNCs, TMCs, TFCs, IGOs, NGOs and AGOs) have assumed an increasingly important role in the new system. The world appears to have entered a post-Westphalian global system in which state sovereignty and territorial borders are eroded by subnational forces from below and transnational forces from above.

Visions of the future are as diverse as accounts of the contemporary situation. Three basically different scenarios have been proposed: *continuity, collapse* and *transformation*. Table 3.3 provides a schematic review of the three scenarios and their variants as reflected in the literature. Continuity scenarios envisage more of the same. In typical capitalist busts and booms, the world system will continue to grow unevenly across the globe, with certain regions and countries growing faster than others. The basic structures of global capitalism, however, will not change. Liberal democracy will remain the most successful form of governance, while dictatorships will have to democratize as the working class demands higher wages and the new middle classes insist on their freedoms.[21]

The collapse scenario, by contrast, foreshadows widening gaps within and between countries and regions of the world. These gaps will inevitably produce their own tensions and conflicts. These may erupt on a massive scale or continue to simmer below the surface, breaking out from time to time as low-intensity warfare, or as various forms of terrorism and counter-terrorism.[22]

The transformation scenario regards neither of the above two scenarios as inevitable. Education and political action of various kinds can avert disaster. As H.G. Wells put it aptly, 'civilization is a race between education and catastrophe'. Such interventions may take radically different forms. One approach might be to establish global law and order through a federated world government (the World Federalists). At the other extreme are those who view all governments as embodiments of domination and exploitation (classical Marxists and anarchists).

Alternatively, the transformative project for a more just world order can proceed by incremental and reformist steps. It can focus on the rule of law as the necessary building-block of world governance.[23] Or it can concentrate on the construction of interlocking communities of interest, knowledge and meaning in a variety of spaces, from the local to the global.[24] Clearly, these different approaches are not mutually exclusive. Nor are the three predictions likely to prove entirely right or entirely wrong. We cannot change the past, but by changing the present, we can change the future.

Global democracy is a necessary but not sufficient condition for regional, national and local democracy. Visions of global democracy are as diverse as the three main historical vehicles of democratic revolution (libertarian, egalitarian and communitarian democracy). David Held has forcefully argued for 'cosmopolitan democracy':

All groups and associations are assumed to have a capacity for self-determination which can be specified by a commitment to the principle of autonomy and specific clusters of rights and obligations. These clusters cut across each network of power and are subsumed under the following categories: health,

Table 3.3   A schematic view of post-Cold War future scenarios

Scenarios	Sources
CONTINUITY SCENARIOS	
• **State system scenario** Continuity and restoration of the states system requiring a balance of power through military strength.	Kissinger, Waltz
• **End of history senario** Global triumph of liberal capitalism requiring progressive worldwide democratic and market institutions.	Fukuyama
• **Corporate hegemony scenario** Transnational corporate domination of the world requiring democratic resistance.	Barnet, Cavanagh
• **Regionalist scenario** Intraregional co-operation and interregional competition for trade and development requiring such organizations as NAFTA, EU, MERCOSUR, ASEAN, APEC, SAARC, CIS and ECO.	Fawcett and Hurrell
COLLAPSE SCENARIOS	
• **Growing gaps scenario** A widening bifurcation of the world system between rich and poor leading to increasing intrastate and interstate clashes.	Attali, UNDP
• **Clash of civilizations scenario** Future conflicts will be among civilizations, notably between the West and the rest.	Huntington
• **Chaos scenario** Disintegration of the world system into anarchy requiring strict anti-terrorist strategies.	Kaplan
TRANSFORMATION SCENARIOS	
• **End of state scenario** Abolition of social classes and withering away of the state requiring revolutionary struggle.	Marxists
• **Anarchist scenario** Dissolution of the state into a libertarian laissez-faire system requiring progressive devolution of power.	Anarchists Libertarians
• **World government scenario** Evolution toward a federal system of world government through a democratic federal constitution.	Tinbergen World federalists
• **Just world order scenario** Rule of law and conflict resolution through peaceful means requiring institutionalization of conflict resolution and legal methods of dispensing justice.	Falk WOMP
• **Communitarian scenario** Co-operation for peace, development and justice on the basis of shared values and interests requiring world integration and building of dialogical security communities at national, regional and global levels.	Deutch Etzioni Tehranian

social, cultural, civic, economic, pacific and political. Together, they form the basis of an empowering legal order – a cosmopolitan democratic view.[25]

Held's universal vision of democracy is at odds with Huntley's vision of 'Pax Democratica'.[26] Huntley argues for an intercontinental democratic community with NATO and OECD members as its core. His criteria for membership include an advanced state of democracy, advanced global market economy, knowledge-based economy and society, modern humane society, understanding of common vital interests, proven capability for joint undertakings, substantial core of available leadership for international tasks, and economic weight and power.

Huntley has succinctly outlined the neo-liberal project, or as we have called it 'informatic imperialism'. While Huntley's vision may suit the interests and perspectives of global capital, the democratic visions offered by David Held, Richard Falk and James Mittelman among others offer more promising avenues to the future. The transition from a vision of the desirable to the practicalities of the possible is a difficult one. It must take into account the larger forces at work. Three macro trends characterize our own era and perhaps the rest of the twenty-first century: *globalization, regionalization* and *democratization* (see Tables 3.4–3.6 on page 72). All three trends may be viewed in terms of domination or resistance. Their historical formation in the three tables have been thus labelled *hegemonic, counter-hegemonic* and *democratic*.

As we have seen in the historical overview, globalization is perhaps the best known of the three trends, and has already been subjected to detailed analysis. Regionalization has an equally long history, assuming different forms in different periods. Western Europe pioneered the new regionalism by establishing the EEC, now the EU. Other regions of the world have followed suit, giving birth to NAFTA, MERCOSUR, ASEAN, SAARC, CIS, ECO, and many others. The trend continues in a variety of modalities in different regions and sub-regions.

In the post-Cold War era, regionalism has taken more complex forms. However, regionalism has clearly shifted from primarily political to economic objectives. In an age of globalization, states in any given region face a stark choice. Either they hang together or are hanged separately. The question is not whether to engage in regional formations but when, how, and with whom. In countries characterized by enormous ethnic diversity within their borders, regionalism has also a compelling security logic. It can reduce ethno-nationalist conflicts and remove the constraints on population movements and trade across borders.

The democratic project has entered a new and important phase. Globalization and regionalization have increasingly demonstrated that without democratic checks and balances at the global and regional levels, national democracy is likely to prove a declining phenomenon. In recent decades, global capital has been able to bypass unfavourable national regulations in taxation, labour standards and environmental protection by relocating elsewhere. In liberal democracies such as the United States, as the cost of political campaigning rises, politicians are increasingly made hostage to their campaign fund donors. The nexus between global capital, political advertising and legislation is growing

Table 3.4   Globalization: Structures and processes

Globalization	Economic	Military-political	Cultural
Hegemonic	Corporate oligopolies: technology, finance, investment, trade	WMDs; Industrial oligopolies	Communication and media oligopoly
Counter-hegemonic	Self-reliant development and micro-credit banking	Local and regional organizations for WMDFZs	Revival of indigenous cultures, languages and media
Democratic	Global movement for sustainable development	Global movement for peace and disarmament	Ecumenical movements for culture of peace, multiculturalism and human solidarity

Table 3.5   Regionalization: Structures and processes

Regionalization	Military regionalism	Political regionalism	Economic regionalism	Comprehensive regionalism
Hegemonic	NATO, SEATO, CENTO, Warsaw Pact		APEC, NAFTA	
Counter-hegemonic	NAM	Arab League, OSCE, GCC	MERCOSUR, ASEAN, SAARC, RCD, ECO	
Democratic	EU	EU	EEC	EU

Table 3.6   Democratization: Structures and processes

Democratization	Economic	Political	Cultural
Liberal democratic	Private enterprise	Civil liberties	Nationalism and neo-liberal internationalism
Social democratic	State regulation	Social welfare	Assimilationism
Communitarian democratic	Worker participation	Devolution	Multiculturalism

steadily stronger. The levers presently available at the national or regional level are proving patently insufficient to tame global capital. In LDCs, the task is even more daunting, as global capital is often able to infiltrate national institutions, taking advantage of the political, economic and military leverage of powerful foreign states, or the informal avenues offered by domestic political corruption.

Global democratization must therefore be pursued as an end in itself, but also as a means to local, national and regional democratization. Using financial flows and security policy as major case studies, the chapters that follow develop in greater detail how and why global governance reform can enhance and hasten that process.

Notes

1. See Part II.
2. As quoted by Senator Allan Cranston at the State of the World Forum, San Francisco, 1995.
3. F. Hiat, 'Europe Blasts Massachussetts for Taking on Burma', *Honolulu Advertiser* (7 February 1999), B3.
4. A. Sampson, *The Seven Sisters: the Great Oil Companies and the World They Made* (New York: Viking Press, 1975).
5. R. Falk, *On Humane Governance: Toward a New Global Politics* (University Park, PA: Pennsylvania University Press, 1995).
6. D. Held, *Democracy and the Global Order: From the Modern State to Cosmopolitan Governance* (Stanford, CA: Stanford University Press, 1995).
7. J.R. Huntley, *Pax Democratica: a Strategy for the 21st Century* (New York: Free Press, 1998).
8. R.D. Putnam, 'What Makes Democracy Work?', *IPA Journal*, 47, 1(1994).
9. A. de Tocqueville, *Democracy in America* (New York: Mentor Books, 1956; abridged and edited by R.D. Heffner).
10. See Putnam.
11. M. Castells, *The Information Society: Economy, Society, and Culture*, Vols 1–3 (Oxford: Blackwell, 1996–2000); M. Tehranian, *Technologies of Power: Information Machines and Democratic Prospects* (Norwood, NJ: Ablex Publishing Corporation, 1990).
12. F. Fukuyama, *Trust: Social Virtues and the Creation of Prosperity* (New York: Free Press, 1995).
13. See Held.
14. Commission on Global Governance, *Our Global Neighbourhood* (Oxford: OUP, 1995).
15. M. Tehranian, 'Global Communication and International Relations: Changing Paradigms and Policies', *International Journal of Peace Studies*, 2, 1 (January 1997); M. Tehranian, 'Human Security and Global Governance: Power Shifts and Emerging Security Regimes' (Paper presented at the Toda Institute Conference, Honolulu, 6–8 June 1997).
16. M. Tehranian, 'Communication, Peace, and Development: a Communitarian Perspective', in F. Korzenny and S. Ting-Toomey (eds), *Communicating for Peace* (Newbury Park: Sage, 1990).
17. As advertising replaces licence fees and government sources of revenue, public broadcasting is succumbing to mass tastes just as much as commercial media.
18. R.C. Goizueta, 'The Challenges of Getting What You Wished For' (Remarks presented to the Arthur Page Society, Amelia Island, FL, 21 September 1992).
19. G. Soros, 'The Capitalist Threat', *Atlantic Monthly*, 279, 2 (1997), pp.45, 48.
20. J. Rosenau, 'Governance in the 21st Century', *Global Governance*, 1(1995), p.39.
21. F. Fukuyama, *The End of History and the Last Man* (New York: Free Press, 1992).
22. R.D. Kaplan, 'The Coming Anarchy', *Atlantic Monthly* (February 1994).
23. R. Falk, *On Humane Governance: Toward a New Global Politics* (University Park, PA: Pennsylvania State University Press, 1995).
24. K.W. Deutsch et al., *International Political Communities: an Anthology* (New York: Anchor Books, 1966); K.W. Deutsch, *The Analysis of International Relations*, 3rd edn (Englewood Cliffs, NJ: Prentice-Hall, 1988); K. Tehranian and M. Tehranian (eds), *Restructuring for World Peace: On the Threshold of the 21st Century* (Cresskill, NJ: Hampton Press, 1992).
25. Held, p.271.
26. See Huntley.

Part II
Global Financial Flows

4
The Political Economy of Globalization: the Old and the New

Stephen Gill

Globalization as a trend and globalization as a political project

When most people hear the word 'globalization' they think of a set of mega-trends and processes creating a more interlinked and integrated world. Perhaps unintentionally, phrases like 'the global village', 'the information society' and 'one world, ready or not!' convey the impression that globalization is a massive historical and evolutionary process that is beyond human control. Some theorists see the mega-trends of globalization as unstoppable. It is claimed, therefore, that governments, societies and social institutions have no alternative but to adapt to these apparently inexorable forces. At its extreme, this view gives rise to what one Canadian journalist, Linda McQuaig, has called 'the cult of impotence'.[1] What she means is that government leaders have convinced themselves they are powerless in the face of global financial markets and freewheeling investment or capital flows across borders. This is the 'myth of powerlessness in the global economy' and this myth reflects a form of 'historical determinism'. This is the essence of the 'end of history' thesis as it applies to globalization. Thus globalization is inevitable, necessary and irreversible. Governments have lost power to market and technological forces. However, globalization is not just a set of trends, but also a conscious political project.

Globalization as a political project refers to a deliberate attempt – which of course can never be fully successful because of different forms of resistance to it from Right and Left – to construct a free-enterprise capitalist market system at the global level. It involves conscious political choices. Perhaps the most obvious way to make this argument is to say: globalization is not new. It has come and gone before. In a similar fashion to today, globalization also existed in the nineteenth century. For example, for 17 industrial countries for which there is data, exports as a percentage of GDP in 1913 were 13 per cent; not much below the 1993 level of 14.5 per cent. In 1996 capital transfers as a share of industrial-country GDP were still smaller than was the case in the 1890s.[2] However, the scale of globalization today is very much greater. The stock of foreign direct investment in 1914 was $143 billion (in 1990 dollars), compared with well over $2 trillion in 1993.

Globalization in the nineteenth century was not simply the result of techno-logical developments such as the invention of the telegraph. Rather, amongst other things it involved two conscious political choices by rulers and govern-ments: first, the decision to free capital flows across borders; secondly, the choice of conservative macroeconomic policies that were locked in through adherence to the fixed exchange rate system of the international gold standard.

This meant that from the 1870s until the outbreak of World War I in 1914, macroeconomic policies were relatively uniform across the major countries. In fact, these policies were similar to those which prevail today. The gold standard required that governments defend the value of their currencies, by raising inter-est rates. In the nineteenth century, democracy was in its infancy. Governments were under little pressure from popular forces that might limit their ability to raise interest rates when necessary – even if this meant higher unemployment. In other words, the question of political legitimacy as it is understood in today's more democratic world was not an issue in the making of macroeconomic policy. This enabled international financiers and governments to maintain the inter-national gold standard.

Economic development and political legitimacy in a globalized world

The development of the world economy in the nineteenth century involved the free movement of capital as well as relatively free movement of labour. However the dislocations of the free market and World War I produced a growing crisis of legitimacy for the old order and growing demands for democracy. Millions had been sacrificed during the Great War, and the Russian Revolution of 1917 demon-strated to European and US governments that the threat of communism was real – especially in Europe. So after 1918 there was greater democracy, although women were generally excluded from the franchise.

Nevertheless, the growth of democratic and popular forces in the 1920s meant that when efforts were made once again by what Karl Polanyi, writing in 1944,[3] called *haute finance* and the governments to restore the international gold standard and free-trade, this took place in new political conditions. At the same time, what had once been the political and economic orthodoxy of the nineteenth century now began to take the form of what the wealthy New York financier George Soros, has called 'market fundamentalism'.[4] Indeed, not only the big international bankers and conservative political leaders, but also the leaders of labour and social-ist parties all began to treat the international gold standard – and the conservative macroeconomic policy that it implied – as if it were an 'article of faith'.

Indeed, it was only when the dislocations reached chronic proportions that countries like Great Britain and the United States, who, up to that point, had been committed to the global market system of the time, finally went off gold and tried new types of measures to deal with the slump. As governments began to abandon market fundamentalism the immediate crisis of economic stability began to be resolved, but in the United States, for example, it took wartime mobilization to restore health to the economy. Other governments used various measures of state intervention to stimulate their economies and deal with the slump. However, the crisis of legitimacy for capitalism as a system took much longer to resolve – this occurred after the experience of Fascism and Nazism and the most destructive war in history.

Political legitimacy and the restoration of capitalism after 1945

So how was this legitimacy crisis addressed? During World War II, Allied leaders sought to create a postwar economic order that would avoid the disastrous economic and political consequences of the 1930s and allow them to construct a more democratic system. Allied leaders resolved to design an international economic framework to allow for rapid postwar reconstruction and stable, growth-oriented macroeconomic management. They realized that the collective sacrifices made in the war effort meant that, more than ever before, political representation would have to include the interests of workers – even if this meant government controls over the freedoms of wealthy financiers and investors.

Thus a new framework for world capitalism was developed in 1944 at the Bretton Woods conference and it involved the use and ratification of new forms of state power to control capital. The discussions were influenced by Lord Keynes, the British negotiator, and by Harry Dexter White, who led a US team dominated by the Treasury, which had been a bastion of New Deal thinking. The agreements made were premised on the need for state intervention in the economy to compensate for market failures and the consequences of market fundamentalism. This included control over the freedom of movements of capital, especially speculative, or 'hot money' flows which they felt would be destabilizing for national economic policy-making. Thus hot money or 'vicious flows' of capital were to be regulated, for example by capital and exchange controls and other administrative measures, whereas 'virtuous flows' of capital which are used to finance trade and production were to be allowed. It was in this context that US Treasury Secretary Morganthau stressed that finance should be made the 'servant' rather than the 'master' of production.[5]

The new system helped to produce the longest boom in economic history, and the absence of severe economic crisis, at least in the major capitalist nations of the world. It was during this period that much of what we identify with the American dream became a reality: automobiles, televisions, new labour-saving appliances, and a growing consumer culture throughout the capitalist industrialized world, although of course this did not mean equal life-chances for all.

One result of these initiatives is that in their post-1945 phase, the processes of globalization are unparallelled, at least in terms of their scale and extension: there have been massive increases in productive power and compression of time and space. This has occurred in the context of tremendous and unprecedented population growth which began to rise significantly, again from the late eighteenth century onwards and has continued to do so. Indeed, according to Eric Hobsbawm, globalization is one counterpart to an unprecedented social and cultural revolution, at least in the OECD nations where the peasantry as a class have been effectively eliminated – thus bringing to an end the seven or eight millennia of human history in a major portion of the world. Whilst the situation in the Third World differs – the peasantry still constitutes the most numerous social class – there is a world-wide trend towards a more urbanized, rationalized and marketized form of economy. For the first time in history there is 'a single, increasingly integrated and universal world economy largely operating across state frontiers ("transnationally") and therefore increasingly across the frontiers of state ideology'.[6]

The forms of globalization today

The form of today's globalization began to take shape in the 1970s, after the strong economic growth of the 1950s and 1960s began to come to an end. Conservative political leaders began to press for free market policies including freedom of capital movements and deregulation of markets for goods, capital and labour, and, along with them, for new forms of neo-liberal state with new powers to liberate capital. They advocated 'sound' macroeconomic policies premised upon reducing inflation – even at the cost of much higher unemployment – and these policies were increasingly adopted during the 1980s and 1990s.

One key aspect of the structural developments that generated support for these changes is the enormous recent growth in capital mobility, which includes the emergence of offshore markets as well as the gradual abandonment of the postwar capital and exchange controls during the 1980s. Some estimates suggest that up to 50 per cent of total global or cross-border transactions now go through offshore centres – as a legal means of avoiding taxes, regulations or indeed public scrutiny or accountability.

Since governments now compete – as competition states – with each other to provide a low-inflation investment climate that is attractive to investors, the brave new world of capital mobility places restrictions on the ability of governments to pursue the type of economic policy typical of the 1950s and 1960s. Even where this is seen as desirable by political leaders, it is now increasingly difficult for governments to use fiscal and monetary policy to combat higher unemployment, or to use redistributive fiscal transfers to deal with social and some environmental problems. Indeed, because of footloose capital, governments have reduced taxes on capital gains and on profits, moved away from progressive income taxes, and removed certain types of regulation in their quest to create a free market. In this sense, the situation is similar to that which prevailed under the international gold standard, and it represents a victory for the holders of property over the majority of the citizens.

So what does this mean today? When governments are forced to compete to attract money from the vast pools of footloose capital it has an impact on both government policy and upon the distribution of income within and across societies. It is no coincidence that as capital has become more mobile, social inequality has increased throughout the world. Recent figures released by the UN show this trend is accelerating and has reached unprecedented proportions, as the following three examples indicate:

1. UNDP estimates showed that the world's 225 billionaires had a combined wealth of over $1 trillion, equal to the annual income of the poorest 47 per cent of the world's people (2.5 billion).[7] Indeed, the three richest people in the world had assets greater than the combined annual output of the 48 least-developed countries.
2. One billion people had no access to safe drinking water; 842 million adults were illiterate; 158 million children under five were malnourished. In 1996 there were 1.3 billion poor in the world: 20 per cent of the world's population lived below the income poverty line. In some respects this situation improved during the late 1990s so that 1.2 billion (half in South Asia) lived on $1 a day or less, although inequality of incomes continued to accelerate. The poor continue to bear a disproportionate burden of taxation, which has become increasingly regressive since the widespread introduction of sales and value added taxes in the 1990s.[8] Moreover, the distribution of poverty is highly gendered and racialized and it is accompanied by legal, political and other dimensions of human insecurity.
3. At the same time, unemployment has been rising throughout the world. The ILO estimated that in 1996 about one billion people were unemployed. They note that this global unemployment crisis began in the early 1980s.[9]

These developments are raising major legitimacy problems for globalization throughout the world. Even in the affluent United States, the wage gap is widening between high and low income earners. According to the UNDP Human Poverty Index, the United States, with the highest average incomes of any major country, also has by far the highest population share that experience poverty, now 17 per cent of total population.[10] At the same time, as John Kenneth Galbraith has shown, the privileges of the politically powerful and economically strong have been reinforced in the OECD nations since the late 1960s,[11] often to the detriment of the vast majority of the population, although even here downsizing and job insecurity haunt the global middle classes as an economic spectre, and their confidence as consumers (for example, as tourists) has been hit hard by the terrorist attacks on the World Trade Centre and the Pentagon.

The neo-liberal shift in government policies has tended to subject the majority of the population to the power of market forces (most workers, and small businesses) whilst preserving social protection for the strong (for instance, highly skilled workers, oligopolistic corporate capital and those with inherited wealth). In the Third World, the counterpart to Galbraith's 'culture of contentment' are urban elites and ruling and emerging middle classes who benefit from the consumption patterns and incorporation into financial and production circuits of transnational capital. A recent growth in enclave residential development, private provision of security (for example, the massive growth in numbers of private police relative to public law officers), and private insurance and healthcare (as well as private prisons) suggests that access to what were often considered to be public goods under socialized provision is now increasingly privatized, individualized and hierarchical in nature. More broadly, there has been a transformation of the socialization of risk towards privatization and individualization of risk assessment and insurance provision. Nevertheless, this process is hierarchical, not only because some people can have platinum credit cards and others only green ones (the former provide cheaper credit to higher income earners and *vice versa*) but also in so far the burdens of risk are redistributed, marketized and individualized (for example, associated with illness, old age and pensions) as opposed to being fully socialized through collective and public provision.[12]

Thus globalization is part of a broad process of restructuring of the state and of political and civil society, and of the political economy and culture. It is also an ideology largely consistent with the world view and political priorities of large-scale, internationally mobile forms of capital. Politically, its dominant values are consistent with the outlook of affluent minorities in the OECD and in the urban elites and new middle classes in the Third World.

Of course, 'globalization' as a process is not amenable to reductionist forms of explanation, because it is many-faceted and multidimensional and involves ideas, images, symbols, music, fashions, and a variety of tastes and representations of identity and community. Nevertheless, in its present mythic and ideological representations, the concept serves to reify a global economic system dominated by large institutional investors and transnational firms that control the bulk of the world's productive assets, and are the principal influences in world trade and financial markets. This seems to be what Tehranian calls 'global capitalism'.[13] However, it is not so much that the dominance of the globalizing political economy depends upon control over information and knowledge industries as such (this was just as much the case for capital in the nineteenth century as it is today). Rather, the power of capital is very specific and it depends on retaining ownership and control over contracts, leading industrial processes, brands or core technologies, and a range of other endeavours whilst sustaining the consumerism that drives the circuits of accumulation. The former is principally achieved by using political and juridical power to lock in the rights and freedoms of investors and owners. This involves private property rights generally (not just intellectual property rights), which include the freedom to move capital across borders (capital mobility is a key private property right in the world today as it was in the era of the international gold standard). The latter involves the promotion of consumption and measures to support 'consumer confidence'.[14] Moreover capital still makes large profits in the largest (and old-economy) consumer sectors such as automobiles, oil, textiles and apparel, as well as from food and drink (for example, Coca Cola).

Thus in 1992, the 300 largest TNCs controlled about 25 per cent of the world's $20 trillion stock of productive assets; the top 600 corporations with annual sales over $1 billion accounted for over 20 per cent of the world's total value added in manufacturing and agriculture.[15] There were about 37,000 TNCs by 1992, with 170,000 affiliates (up from 7,000 in the early 1970s). These firms had cumulative FDI of about $2 trillion, one third controlled by the 100 largest corporations. The top 100 had global sales of $5.5 trillion, a sum roughly equal to the GNP of the United States. The 1992 value of world exports of goods and non-factor services was around $4 trillion, of which a third was intra-firm trade, between parents and affiliates of transnationals.[16] TNCs are large capital-and knowledge-intensive firms which employ about 72 million people, of whom 15 million are in developing countries. Most workers of TNCs are well paid, and tend to enjoy better working conditions than those in local firms. Directly and indirectly TNCs perhaps account for 5 per cent of the global workforce, although they control over 33 per cent of global assets.[17]

The neo-liberal concept of 'globalization' suggests that privatization and transnationalization of capital are either inevitable or desirable from a broad social viewpoint. In this sense, the concept of globalization exhibits positive and negative forms of ideology. A positive aspect is the equation of free competition and free exchange (global capital mobility) with economic efficiency, welfare and democracy, and a myth of virtually unlimited social progress, as represented in TV advertising and other media, and in World Bank and IMF reports. As we noted earlier, George Soros, the wealthy financier, has called the extreme version of this thinking 'market fundamentalism'. A negative aspect is the way in which neo-liberal market forces are often said to have marginalized non-market alternatives, especially from the political left, so that there is no alternative to globalization – what we earlier referred to as the 'cult of impotence' is an example of this type of historical determinism.

Historical determinism of this type seems particularly reprehensible in an ethical and political sense if one considers how, despite enormous increases in global output and population since World War II, central to the restructuring process of the last twenty years has been a significant polarization of income and of life-chances: on the one hand there is a growing plutocracy of multi-billionaires, some of whom are authoritarian political leaders, whilst on the other there is social disintegration and a global unemployment crisis of chronic proportions. In this contradictory situation we can see the formation of a global class structure; for example, for the 800 million or so affluent consumers in the OECD, there is a counterpart number starving in the Third World, with one billion more that have no clean drinking water or sufficient food to provide basic nutrition.[18] More than half Africa's population lives in absolute poverty. In the 1980s, the income of two-thirds of African workers fell below the poverty line. A disproportionate burden of adjustment to harsher circumstances has fallen on women and children, and weaker members of society – the old and the disabled.[19] Many of these people also live in war-torn societies, where huge quantities of cheap mass-produced conventional weapons have accumulated, including 'weapons that never miss': over 100 million landmines. One million landmines have exploded under Third World victims in the last 15 years.[20]

The resurgence of epidemics – similar in some sense to the situation that prevailed in the nineteenth century and before – is a crucial indicator of the condition of our globalized world, not only in terms of human suffering, but as an indicator that capital accumulation and scientific progress do not necessarily lead to human development and human security. Epidemics imply the breakdown of the social controls and government programmes/infrastructures that might prevent such diseases – clean water, hygiene, nutrition, healthy populations who are resistant to infection, immunization programmes and housing.[21]

Prices of many medical products marketed by transnational pharmaceuticals firms have risen and the relaxation of trade barriers and other market forms of restriction and regulation has made it simpler to dump expired or unsafe medicines in parts of the Third World.[22] Globally, public health and educational provisions have been reduced, partly because of the neo-liberal structural-adjustment pressures on most governments to exercise monetary restraint, cut budgets, repay debts, balance their international trade, devalue their currencies, remove subsidies and trade and investment barriers and, in so doing, restore international credit-worthiness and thereby extend the market civilization globally. Such pressures emanate from agents in the global financial markets, from international organizations such as the World Bank and IMF, and from within these societies themselves.

More and more aspects of everyday life in OECD nations have come to be premised upon or pervaded by market values, representations and symbols, as time and distance are apparently shrunk by scientific-technological innovation, the hyper-mobility of financial capital and some types of information flows. Commercialization has configured more aspects of family life, religious practice, leisure pursuits and aspects of nature. Indeed, processes of commodification have progressively encompassed aspects of life that have been in the past viewed as inalienable.[23] Increasingly, patent rights over human genes and tissue, plants, seeds and animal hybrids are obtained routinely by pharmaceutical and agricultural corporations, including the DNA of 'endangered peoples', that is aboriginal or native peoples. Despite limited mainstream debate on the repercussions of biotechnology and genetic innovation, to say nothing of the privatization of life-forms, peasant farmers, women's organizations, environmentalists and other activists are engaging in public protest,[24] and organizing and forming alliances in a broad ranging process of democratization.[25]

By implication, this situation involves methods by which patterns of privilege can be defended from encroachment and possible expropriation by those subordinated and marginalized. In the terminology of Fred Hirsch, privileged consumption and production patterns of a small section of the world's population are, in effect, the 'positional goods' of the global political economy which the contemporary systems of policing and military power, used in the 1991 Gulf War and later the NATO military apparatus in Serbia/Kosovo, are designed increasingly to protect.[26]

Thus it is crucial to identify the dominant form of globalization – what we call here disciplinary neo-liberalism – and the way that this is central to a deepening and extension of the power of capital and the most powerful G7 states on a world scale. Such power is not purely economic – it is also political, military and juridical, and indeed cultural. Substantial political and constitutional restructuring links accumulation and legitimation. It seeks to harmonize the orientations of the legal structures of disparate nations into a global quasi-constitutional structure of laws, rules, regulations and standards to create a 'constitution for global capitalism'. The aim is to create long-term frameworks to insulate capital from democratic rule and accountability, although this is difficult given the persistent instability and crises we have witnessed in the global political economy over the past two decades.[27]

The world economic crisis of the 1990s: Economic stability and political legitimacy

In addition to the long-term challenges to political legitimacy building up in the world that are linked to the contradictions of globalization, the Asian economic crisis of the late 1990s, which spread world wide to encompass Russia and eventually the American and global financial systems, was merely the most immediate of an increasing number of international financial crises seen in the past two decades. Each of these has posed immediate questions of short-term economic stability. In discussing proposals for the reform of the UN, however, we should be clear that the real question at the heart of the problem of neo-liberal globalization today is the legitimacy of global capitalism.

We should note initially that, as in the 1930s, the world economic situation in the late 1990s included falling commodity prices and oversupply in many industries, at the same time as capital was free to move into and out of different countries. When the countries in difficulty turned to the IMF for assistance, not only did the IMF insist on its usual formula of shock therapy and austerity through higher interest rates to restore currency parities, it also began to demand political changes in these countries.

According to one interpretation, the Asian contagion was a classic example of the effects of what Keynes and Dexter White in 1944 had called 'vicious' flows of short-term capital. It started with a devaluation of Thailand's currency and it spread rapidly to other East Asian countries. Whilst the jury is still out, the Thai devaluation seems to have been precipitated by banks, hedge funds and speculators who sought to make quick profits by selling the currency.[28] Other investors panicked and got their money out, creating a bandwagon effect. The huge fall in currency values then precipitated an economic collapse. The contagion spread to Russia and to Latin America. As of the late 1990s Brazil was its latest victim. As Harvard economist Jeffrey Sachs has argued, the IMF measures were the equivalent of yelling 'fire' in a crowded theatre, causing investors to panic.

In a similar fashion to the Great Depression, what was initially in East Asia a crisis of economic stabilization turned into a massive collapse as a result of the IMF's application of market fundamentalism. The Fund prescribed higher interest rates and cutbacks in industrial subsidies, but also reductions in food subsidies to the poor in an effort to restore soundness to the currency and improve government finances. As might be expected, there was fierce resistance to the application of IMF policies, and as a result some of them were modified.

However, in contrast to the 1930s the US Federal Reserve, recently a bastion of market fundamentalism, quickly moved to lower interest rates to restore liquidity to the markets in 1998 when its own financial system was threatened with collapse (it did the same in 2001 when terrorists struck the command and control centres of American government and its financial system). In 1998 the US problem was triggered by the bankruptcy of Long Term Capital Management (LTCM), a private and secret hedge fund, based in the Cayman Islands offshore centre. LTCM had the services of two Nobel prize winners in Economics who specialized in financial market risk, as well as a large number of PhDs in Mathematics who crunched the numbers. LTCM had leveraged about $5 billion in capital (mainly the holdings of super-wealthy individuals and large banks and financial services firms) into a huge and complex pyramid of assets of about $1.5 trillion, a sum that is roughly twice the size of Canada's annual GNP.

The firm's strategy rested on making profits from leveraged investments based on complex financial products called derivatives. When Russia defaulted on its debts it was exposed and could not meet its obligations. When the US Federal Reserve Bank organized a bail-out by its private creditors LTCM almost brought about the collapse of the US financial system. Unbelievably LTCM had failed to hedge against the possibility of a Russian default despite the catastrophic condition of the Russian economy and the chaotic state of Russian politics.

So, in contrast to the 1930s some lessons had been learned about economic stabilization and, like the 1930s, this meant methods that did not strictly conform to market fundamentalism. However, the other lessons which Keynes and Dexter White learned on the need to control vicious flows of short-term capital have yet to be applied.

These examples show that whilst the OECD was relatively insulated from the effects of the most recent financial crisis in 1998, the complexities of the new global financial system, with its complex derivatives and high leverage, pose continuing threats to stability. Moreover, in the longer term OECD countries cannot avoid some of its effects. In particular, the Asian crisis amplified an emerging global crisis of legitimacy. This is evident in the backlash that is now gaining momentum against economic globalization generally, and unregulated capital flows in particular. Indeed, following the attacks on New York and Washington even the Bush Administration, which is stridently opposed to greater international financial regulation (and specifically regulation of the offshore world and money laundering), in co-operation with its key allies in western Europe and elsewhere, began to freeze assets of suspected terrorists and their supporters, showing at a stroke the capacity to regulate finance heavily and suspend private property rights and international capital mobility when the authorities choose to do so. The issue of footloose capital flows is a political not a technical one.

The crisis is not simply one of economic stability, but more fundamentally an ethical and political crisis – a crisis of legitimacy – that calls for more long-term political solutions, which is not to say that the practical question of immediate reform should not also be addressed, or for that matter cannot contribute to the long-term solution.

Reform proposals

In considering the nature of reform we should bear the following in mind:

1. Globalization, especially capital mobility, is not new – it came and went in the nineteenth century.
2. When we examine globalization in the nineteenth century we see that it was not simply the result of technological trends and the evolution of history. Rather, it was the result of a deliberate political project that consciously chose to construct a global market through the freeing up of cross-border investment, labour and to a lesser extent trade flows.
3. The form of globalization that existed from the nineteenth century until the 1930s was inherently unstable and contradictory, and it produced first, a crisis of political legitimacy, and second, a crisis of economic stability in the form of the Crash of 1929 and the Great Depression.
4. Finally, the immediate crisis of economic stability and the deeper crisis of political legitimacy were resolved only when market fundamentalism was abandoned.

Today, a crucial reason for proposing more inclusive methods of collective global security in a UN reform process is connected to the vexed questions of humanitarian intervention and controlling capital flows. The ultimate aim is to prevent further economic instability coupled to policies that promote social inequality, in order to contain political polarization and social disintegration. Reforms in the economic and military spheres are needed politically to inhibit the widening use of organized violence within and between societies. We must challenge the cult of impotence, which also means challenging those who simply argue for superficial, marginal changes in the systems of global governance. Since neo-liberal globalization is the product of patterns of human thought and action, it can be channelled, controlled and changed by collective action.

One practical example shows the links between economic and security dimensions of globalization – a theme which subsequent chapters will further elaborate. As Chapter 7 indicates, one way to promote both economic stability and political legitimacy would be to tackle the problem of 'vicious' flows of capital. Indeed, a number of nations and organizations, that reflect the interaction between states and civil societies worldwide are actively considering whether to impose a tax on transactions in the $1 trillion-a-day currency markets. A tax proposed by the Nobel Laureate in Economics, James Tobin of Yale University, would levy a charge of much less than 1 per cent on each transaction. It would therefore discourage short-term movements of money into and out of currencies. The tax was discussed in the preparation for the 1995 G7 summit in Halifax, Nova Scotia, and it is the subject of increasing attention by a variety of influential international organizations and forums (for example, the UNDP, the ILO and the Commission on Global Governance) and by G7 members such as France and Canada. The tax is supported by many development NGOs throughout the world. A modified version of this tax and a number of other proposals are outlined in Chapters 9 and 15.

In the long term the wealthy powers cannot continue as islands of prosperity, protected by their superior military technologies and capabilities, but increasingly surrounded by oceans of poverty and conflict. More generally, as the violent history of the twentieth century shows, crises of legitimacy – for example those in the 1930s linked to the collapse of the capitalist world economy – can produce extremism and war. The Tobin Tax and the numerous other proposals elaborated in this volume, by building on existing computerization and surveillance of data and financial flows that are already central to the operation of world capital and currency markets, simply make the point that there are political alternatives to market fundamentalism. The introduction of a relatively modest tax could go a long way towards funding a renovated UN system with effective and well-financed institutions of collective human security, linked to a broader vision of human development and human rights.

Notes

1. L. McQuaig, *The Cult of Impotence: Selling the Myth of Powerlessness in the Global Economy* (Toronto: Viking Press, 1998).
2. UNDP, *Human Development Report 1997* (New York: Oxford University Press, 1997), p.83.
3. K. Polanyi, *The Great Transformation: Political and Economic Origins of Our Times* (NY: Octagon Books, 1975).
4. G. Soros, *The Crisis of Global Capitalism: Open Society Endangered* (New York: Public Affairs, 1998).
5. S. Gill, 'Global Finance, Monetary Policy, and Co-operation among the Group of Seven, 1944–92', in P. Cerny (ed.), *Finance and World Politics: Markets, Regimes and States in the Post-Hegemonic Era* (Gloucester: Edward Elgar, 1993).
6. E. Hobsbawm, *Age of Extremes: the Short Twentieth Century – 1914–1991* (London: Michael Joseph, 1994), p.11.
7. UNDP (1997).
8. UNDP, *Human Development Report 2000: Human Rights and Human Development* (New York: Oxford University Press, 2000).
9. K. Moody, *Workers in a Lean World: Unions in the International Economy* (New York: Verso, 1997), p.41.
10. UNDP (2000), p.34, Table 2.1.
11. J.K. Galbraith, *The Culture of Contentment* (Boston MA: Houghton Mifflin, 1992).
12. The IMF and World Bank have pressed consistently during the 1990s for privatization of public pension provision, especially in the Third World, particularly to create larger local capital markets. See for example E. James, 'Averting the Old-Age Crisis', *Finance and Development*, 32, 2 (1995), pp.4–7 and the rest of the special edition of this World Bank/IMF journal.
13. See Part I.
14. Thus the world's biggest industry (at least until the terrorist attacks on the World Trade Centre and Pentagon on 11 September 2001) is tourism. Because the climate for personal security has deteriorated, tourism may now decline rapidly with very negative effects on global economic activity.
15. 'A Survey of Multinationals', *Economist*, 27 March 1993.
16. UNCTAD, *World Investment Report* (Geneva: UNCTAD, 1993).
17. UN Research Institute for Social Development (UNRISD), *States of Disarray: the Social Effects of Globalization* (Geneva: UNRISD, 1995), p.154.
18. There has of course been substantial improvement in basic living conditions. The UNDP showed that nearly 70 per cent of world population lived in 'abysmal' conditions in

1960; by 1992, only 32 per cent suffered such conditions. Global GNP rose seven-fold since 1945 from $3 trillion to $22 trillion. World population more than doubled from 2.5 billion to 5.5 billion; per capita income more than tripled; see UNDP, *Human Development Report 1994* (New York: Oxford University Press, 1994). However, the same UNDP report adds, 'we still live in a world where a fifth of the developing world's population goes hungry every night … and a third lives in abject poverty – at such a margin of human existence that words simply fail to describe it … the richest billion people command 60 times the income of the poorest billion … Poor nations and rich are afflicted by growing human distress … food production must triple if people are to be adequately fed, but the resource base for sustainable agriculture is eroding'; see pp.1–2.

19. UNRISD, pp.110–26.
20. Ibid., pp.48, 114.
21. Ibid., p.26.
22. Ibid., pp.26–7.
23. H. Gottweis, 'Genetic Engineering, Democracy, and the Politics of Identity', *Social Text*, 13 (1995), pp.127–52.
24. J. Vidal and J. Carvel, 'Like Lambs to the Gene Market', *Guardian Weekly* (1 January 1995), p.17. On the commodification of the human body involving the sale of eggs, sperm, kidneys and the patenting of genes, see A. Kimbrell, 'The Body Enclosed: the Commodification of Human "Parts" ', *Ecologist*, 25, 4 (July–August 1995), pp.134–40. I am grateful to D. Law for this reference.
25. S. Gill, 'Globalisation, Market Civilisation, and Disciplinary Neoliberalism', *Millennium*, 23, 3 (1995), pp.399–423.
26. F. Hirsch, *The Social Limits to Growth* (Cambridge, MA: Harvard University Press, 1976), pp.27–54.
27. S. Gill, 'New Constitutionalism, Democratisation and Global Political Economy', *Pacifica Review*, 10, 1 (1998), pp.23–38.
28. See Chapter 7.

5
Financial Globalization: the State, Capital and Policy-making

Kamal Malhotra, Marco Mezzera and Mümtaz Keklik

Globalization in its contemporary setting

As convincingly elaborated by Gill in the previous chapter, globalization is not a new phenomenon. It is its form that has changed in an attempt to adapt to the complex international environment in which it now operates. According to the OECD, the term globalization was first used in 1985 by Theodore Levitt to characterize the vast changes to the international economy over the last two to three decades.[1] Levitt had in mind the rapid and pervasive changes in the global system of production, consumption and investment resulting from economic and financial liberalization, structural adjustment programmes and the dramatically diminishing role of the nation-state as the pace-setter in economic and social policy formulation. There is, however, another important dimension to globalization, which is integral to technological change, and which Giddens has aptly characterized as 'the intensification of world wide social relations which link distinct localities in such a way that local happenings are shaped by events occurring many miles away and vice versa'.[2]

Global versus local processes

Globalization cannot be conceived of as independent of a parallel process of internalization in a given national context or structure. In this respect Bonanno affirms that local and global activities are dialectically related, and that this process can often be confrontational, leading to a series of actions whose different interests and ends need to be politically negotiated between the global, national and local levels.[3] The global landscape should be considered as composed of different integrated spheres, spatial and temporal, where local activities are recomposed at the global level. At first sight one could conclude that world markets are so interconnected that 'huge chronic surpluses from exporting countries compete on the international market and depress world commodity prices'.[4] While there is truth in this, it is equally true that the new global organization of society remains a multi-centred process in which state and local regulation of global processes remain crucial. Here it is worth recalling Polanyi's warning, issued as far back as 1944: 'there is no such thing as a self-regulating market and markets cannot exist outside the web of social relations for long without tragic consequences'.[5] The effects witnessed in South-east Asia in the late 1990s are perhaps a case in point.[6] The crucial question, therefore, is: 'how do international economic processes and policies become embedded in local production systems, and what room for manoeuvre do local actors have?'[7]

The role of the state

Caught amid different but mounting pressures to make way for international and global actors, the state is faced with the challenge of maintaining its position and relevance on a wide front constituted by a myriad of complex social issues and actors. Although recent dominant globalization trends suggest the marginalization of many of the traditional economic and social policy-formulation responsibilities previously fulfilled by the state, it would be a serious mistake to assume that this is indeed an irreversible process. It is naive to believe that the role of the state is on its way to extinction.

Indeed, the global dominance of the corporate world and its attempts to exert total control over the rules of the game in the global market provide renewed justification for the existence of the state and for its intervention in matters concerning the public good. Until now many governments have been silent partners, supporters and even salesmen for global corporate actors and their interests, rather than monitors and regulators on behalf of the public good. Because of this complicity, TNCs have been relatively free to engage in the new practices of global sourcing and to devise new forms of exploitation and value extraction from productive processes on a world scale, regardless of geographical barriers. The state has continued to intervene in these processes, but its actions have too often been focused on fostering and sustaining elite interests in capital accumulation. Much less effort has gone into introducing corrective mechanisms, for example by legitimizing the needs and rights of weaker groups in society, or by assuring equitable social reproduction and human development.

Governments have been induced 'not only to adopt free market policies, but also legal and political structures to both redefine and internationally guarantee private property rights'.[8] In so doing they have made it easier for corporate actors intent on 'developing policies to extend... the fictitious commodities of land, labour and capital, on the one hand, and defining the terrain of competition through the adoption of liberal macroeconomic and regulatory policies, on the other'.[9] The intrinsic link between the rise of capital and the coercive capacity of the state is, on the other hand, and from an historical perspective, nothing new. The transformation from a mercantilistic to a liberal society, which took place between the sixteenth and nineteenth centuries (eloquently outlined by Tehranian in Part I), required the 'capture of the state apparatus by the bourgeoisie and the design of constitutional forms to underpin the power of capital'.[10]

Assuming that at the national level the state is meant to fulfil at least four major functions (accumulation, legitimization, mediation of inter- and intra-class conflict and social reproduction),[11] it is up to its 'managers' to determine the course to follow, that is, whether to protect the interests of the dominant classes or those of the less advantaged.

Unfortunately, the state almost everywhere seems to have privileged the destinies of the bourgeoisie above those of the working classes. It is the state that maintains the conditions necessary for the reproduction of capital, thereby ensuring the accumulation of capital and the rule of the bourgeois class in society. The state also legitimizes the accumulation of capital and obtains its financial resources from the taxation of revenues generated through the accumulation process. 'The continuous existence of the accumulation process is [therefore] paramount for the existence of the State'.[12]

A regrettable aspect of the role and functions of the state in the current globalization context is that social policies have been the first to suffer in times of economic difficulty, often as a result of the lending policies of international financial institutions (IFIs). Priority has been given to programmes of strict fiscal balancing in what Amartya Sen has called 'anti-deficit radicalism'.[13] The net effect has been to subordinate and integrate social policy into economic policy.[14] The recent cure enforced by the IMF on crisis-stricken, export-oriented countries, such as Thailand, Indonesia and South Korea, is a clear case in point. In most LDCs, reduced social expenditures are frequently the result of externally imposed conditionalities which accompany the stabilization and structural adjustment programmes of the Bretton Woods institutions.[15]

Another distinctive and, from a developing country perspective, problematic feature of the ongoing globalization process has been the standardization strategy applied by industrialized countries in a wide range of areas connected to production, processing, trading and consumption activities. Here, it is worth highlighting the current attempts by different international bodies and fora to propose a core set of internationally recognized standards. These cover issues ranging from the Basel Standards on capital adequacy to sanitary and phytosanitary standards on the flow of goods and services in the WTO. Standards are essential to the accumulation activity of global capitalist enterprises, because they ensure predictability, facilitate the exchange of goods and encourage foreign investments flows. Without such a common framework, each transaction would have to be individually negotiated and distinctive standards would need to be set. Traditionally, it is the national government that has set such standards, taking into account a country's stage of development. However, international standards often fail to do this, to the detriment of developing countries.

The nation-state versus transnational capital

The ground left unguarded by a weakened nation-state has in many cases been occupied by TNCs. Power and control have clearly shifted from the sphere of influence of the state to that of transnational capital. In 1998, for example, approximately 70 per cent of global trade was controlled by just 500 TNCs, a scant 100 TNCs controlled one-fifth of all foreign-owned assets in the world, and a mere 1 per cent of TNCs were responsible for half the total FDI in the world.[16] The cumulative result of these trends is illustrated by another statistic that shows that of the world's largest 100 economies in 1998, only about half were states; the rest were TNCs.

The growth of TNCs has been nothing less than dramatic in the last three decades. In 1970, there were only 7,000 TNCs globally, but by the beginning of the 1990s the number had grown to 37,000 (24,000 of which had home bases in the 14 largest OECD countries). According to UNCTAD's *World Investment Report 2000*, the number of TNCs in 1999 had risen to 63,000 parent firms with approximately 690,000 foreign affiliates. While they accounted for a high proportion of global FDI, these corporations contributed less than 5 per cent to global employment in 1996, even after including their sub-contractors. Worse still, only one-fifth of those employed by TNCs were in developing countries in the early part of the last decade (15 million in 1990).

The steep rise of corporate power in the global economic arena points to patterns of 'contradictory convergence', in which transnational expansion of state action is demanded by TNCs and subordinate classes alike.[17] This demand, however, is contradictory because the transnational bourgeoisie wishes to avoid state action that intrudes too deeply in its relations with labour. The state is therefore welcomed only insofar as it facilitates private capital accumulation and economic growth but not when it becomes involved in matters of social equity. Although many TNCs have sales equal to or greater than the national product of some countries, they cannot exercise direct state power and cannot therefore formulate or implement legislation. As a consequence, they invest heavily in influencing the state and feel obliged to co-operate with national governmental institutions.

The state's role in financial regulation?

The contemporary state has almost everywhere supported financial liberalization and deregulation. Though the interventionist wave, symbolized by Mahathir's decision to introduce controls on capital outflows, appeared in 1998 to be a long-term one, many in the international financial community remain strongly wedded to the loosening of barriers to capital flows and transactions. It is as if governments now have to choose between isolationism on the one hand and opening to market forces on the other. The September 1998 decision by the Chilean central bank to eliminate its capital reserve requirement, which had stood at 10 per cent[18] in the aftermath of the Asian crisis, was clearly a reaction to the same competitive global pressures. Gill aptly describes this phenomenon as 'competitive deregulation' of national capital markets.[19] He goes on to observe 'that the *investment climate* of one country will be judged by business with reference to the climate which prevails elsewhere...As a result, governments are increasingly constrained in their freedom of manoeuvre by the economic policies of other states'.[20] In a period of intense competition, vast global capital flows and financial instability, governments are increasingly forced to compete for foreign investment.[21] Set in this context, any barrier to the free inflow of the desired capital injections is considered detrimental to the national interest and therefore under pressure to disappear. Previously nourished long-term objectives give way to more immediate and ephemeral targets. Transnational elites tend to support such policies and those by the state which they believe are needed to ensure a stable economic and political framework within which they can operate. In the words of George Soros: 'One thing is certain: political instability is not conducive to investment'.[22]

Communications and information technology

Globalization processes do not relate only to issues of changing political, economic or social power balances, but also to technological and scientific innovations. It is in this realm that one of the defining and driving characteristics of globalization, the so-called global communications revolution can be observed. This phenomenon is extensively and comprehensively elaborated in Tehranian's chapters in Part I. New power balances have appeared as a result, with the control and management of information and knowledge as the focal point. In the financial system, developments in information technology have produced immediate information links among different markets and countries. As a result, financial services markets and trade in commodities have become fully integrated on a global scale. At the same time, the cost and time needed to conduct particular transactions has been dramatically reduced, allowing for a massive expansion in the volume of transactions. The Asian financial crisis and its ripple effects on the Hang Seng index in Hong Kong, and on the stock markets in Wall Street, Japan and other parts of North-east Asia, Europe and even Brazil, are illustrations both of this global integration in financial decision-making and of its contagious effects.

Globalization of finance and capital flows

As should be evident from this and previous chapters, economic and financial processes have had and continue to have a pre-eminent role in both stimulating and shaping dominant trends in production, trade and investment. These globalizing processes are clearly of benefit to those with considerable amounts of accumulated capital, or certain professional skills to sell or trade in the marketplace. Those without any such assets, notably the poor and those already at the fringes of both industrialized and developing societies, are further disempowered and marginalized by these trends. This is true *between* countries (traditional North and South), *within* countries (the North and South within each of the LDCs), and globally among certain social categories such as gender, age and skill groups (non-indigenous versus indigenous peoples, men versus women, professional versus unskilled labour and so on).

The demand, led by the IMF and by most of the industrialized countries, for developing countries to liberalize their capital accounts fully in a telescoped period, is an example of how the process of financial globalization is being operationalized. The irony of this specific demand is that it comes from countries that enjoyed accumulation of capital over centuries and did not undergo financial liberalization until fairly recently. The United States instituted full capital-account convertibility only in the early 1970s, Sweden in the late 1980s, and Spain only in the early 1990s. This pressure cannot but exacerbate the traditional North–South divide.

The global rush of the last decades towards trade liberalization, coupled with the adoption of internationally accepted standards, has facilitated and increased the flow of capital across national borders. Production of goods and services has been slowly but steadily disappearing from the centre stage of the global economy, and its primary role has been taken over by international finance. The scale of the trend is instructive: the volume of capital processed daily in the largest international exchange markets stood at about $188 billion in 1986, but by 1995 that volume was close to $1.2 trillion (see Table 5.1). In 1998, between $1.5 and $2 trillion was said to be transferred around the world every day as a result of financial deregulation and the computing and information technology revolution. In search of the highest returns in the shortest possible time period, these predatory, highly mobile, massive short-term movements of capital have dwarfed the more traditional and long-term investment flows (FDI).

As a consequence, total private capital flows, including FDI and portfolio speculative capital, to developing countries increased nearly five-fold from $62.1 billion to $299.8 billion between 1991 and 1997 (see Table 5.2). The same table also shows the enormous impact that the Asian financial crisis had on the net flow of private capital to developing countries. In just one year, 1997–98, such flows decreased by 7 per cent. This negative trend continued throughout 1999, with recovery beginning only in 2000. An early warning of this 'reversal of fortunes' was evident by end-September 1998, when the British Chancellor of the Exchequer, Gordon Brown, openly admitted a significant decline in net private capital flows to emerging economies in 1997, returning to levels close to those registered in 1994.[23] In the specific case of the Asian markets, according to the same source, what had been a net inflow of $40 billion in 1996 dramatically changed to a net outflow of $30 billion in 1997.[24]

Global official development assistance (ODA) flows during the same period, on the other hand, declined to around $45.3 billion in 1999, from $60.9 billion in 1991, with global ODA in 1998 ($34.7 billion) considerably smaller than private capital flows to just one Asian country, the People's Republic of China (PRC),

Table 5.1 Foreign-exchange trading

	1986	1989	1992	1995
Global estimated turnover[a] ($ billion)	188	590	820	1190
As a ratio of:				
World exports of goods and services (%)	7.4	15.8	17.4	19.1
Total reserves minus gold (all countries, %)	36.7	75.9	86.0	84.3

[a] Daily average turnover, on spot, outright forward, and foreign-exchange swap transactions, adjusted for local and cross-border double counting and for estimated gaps in reporting. Figures are based on surveys of activities in the three largest exchange market centres (London, New York and Tokyo) in 1986, and markets in 21 countries in 1989 and 26 countries in 1992 and 1995. The London, New York and Tokyo markets accounted for 57 per cent of global turnover in 1989, 54 per cent in 1992 and 56 per cent in 1995.

Source: K. Singh, *A Citizen's Guide to the Globalization of Finance* (Public Interest Research Group, Delhi: Madhyam Books, 1998).

Table 5.2   Net long-term resource flows to developing countries, 1991–2000 (billions of dollars)

Type of flow	1991	1992	1993	1994	1995	1996	1997	1998	1999	2000[a]
Official flows[b]	60.9	56.5	53.6	48.0	55.1	31.9	42.8	54.6	45.3	38.6
Private flows	62.1	99.3	166.8	175.7	206.1	279.3	299.8	280.3	219.2	257.2
Capital markets	26.3	52.2	100.2	85.6	99.1	147.8	127.2	103.5	33.8	79.2
Debt flows	18.8	38.1	49.2	50.5	63.0	98.7	97.0	87.9	−0.6	31.3
Bank lending	5.0	16.2	3.4	8.7	30.5	33.7	42.5	50.0	−24.6	0.7
Bond finance	10.9	11.1	36.6	38.2	30.8	62.5	49.0	40.9	25.4	30.3
Other	2.8	10.8	9.2	3.6	1.7	2.4	2.7	−3.0	−1.6	0.3
Equity flows	7.6	14.1	51.0	35.2	36.1	49.2	30.8	15.6	34.5	47.9
FDIs	35.7	47.1	66.6	90.0	107.0	131.5	172.6	176.8	185.4	178
TOTAL	123.0	155.8	220.4	223.7	261.2	311.2	342.6	334.9	264.5	295.8

Note: Developing countries are defined as low- and middle-income countries with 1995 per capita incomes of less than $765 (low) and $9,385 (middle).
[a] Estimated.
[b] Based on OECD/DAC Geographic Distribution of Flows
Source: World Bank, *Global Development Finance*, 2001.

which in 1996 received a record $42.3 billion. The astonishing increase of private capital flows was reflected in the ratio between such flows and ODA of 15:1 in 2000, a dramatic reversal from the 0.74:1 ratio just a decade earlier.

An increasingly larger part of the total amount of capital flows to developing countries is short-term. In 2000 even portfolio speculative capital or equity flows ('hot money') to developing countries exceeded global ODA, having grown rapidly after financial liberalization took hold in many 'emerging market' countries in the early 1990s. Despite the reversal of the situation in 1997, the 2000 estimates show that ODA was falling behind equity flows once again by about $9.3 billion (see Table 5.2). Asia alone accounted for 53 per cent of equity flows to developing countries in 1995. The role and impact of short-term, speculative portfolio capital in the 1990s became increasingly important in 'emerging market' countries (where it largely concentrated), thereby contributing to both short-term 'booms' and big 'busts'.

One feature of the increasing importance of short-term capital flows in emerging markets during the 1990s was the growing presence of hedge funds (see Table 5.3). These funds are generally structured as limited, often offshore, investment partnerships, which target all kinds of underlying assets, including stocks, bonds and currencies. Generally in search of the most liquid funds, this approach makes the foreign exchange market (the most liquid market in the world) their favourite target.[25] The underlying strategy is to identify an economic contradiction, such as the fixed exchange rate between the Brazilian *real*, or the Argentinean *peso*, and the US dollar. Such inconsistencies trigger a subsequent bet by the hedge funds (and by other speculators) that the situation is unsustainable in the longer term. Instead of using the negatively charged label of speculators, many hedge funds prefer to describe themselves as 'arbitrageurs'. They insist that they merely play a corrective function for those 'assets whose prices are

Table 5.3 The rise of emerging market hedge funds, 1992–97

Year	Number of funds	Assets (billions of dollars)	Asset-weighted return (%)
1992	5	0.7	7.0
1993	9	1.0	69.6
1994	16	3.2	3.1
1995	29	3.4	8.8
1996	38	4.6	30.9
1997[a]	57	7.1	64.0

[a] As of July.

Source: World Bank, *Global Development Finance* (Washington DC, 1998).

temporarily out of line with their fundamental values'.[26] However, by directing large amounts of money, often larger than the targeted country's foreign reserves, towards specific markets and assets, hedge funds are frequently in a position to secure desired outcomes.[27] This particular feature of the hedge funds' *modus operandi* was the main reason which prompted Mahathir to blame them for the depreciation of the *ringgit*, and eventually led to the Malaysian decision to peg its national currency to the US dollar. After the outbreak of the crisis, even Taiwan felt it necessary to impose a ban on all funds managed by George Soros. The common resentment towards hedge funds would reach new heights during the crises that affected Russia and Brazil.

Although measured in absolute terms hedge funds dedicated to emerging markets 'have only a small share of worldwide hedge fund assets, which are estimated at US$300 billion', their focus on those markets has grown enormously during the 1990s. It is no coincidence that in the second half of 1998 the greatest financial distress occurred in the 'specialized market sectors' targeted by the hedge funds, namely 'distressed debt, Latin American bonds, or Russian stocks'.[28]

The increasing global reach and impact of short-term capital is vividly illustrated by the following statistic: of the $279 billion private capital which flowed to developing countries in 1996, only $131.5 billion was longer-term foreign direct investment – FDI (see Table 5.2). The gap started closing in 1997, after the first effects of the financial crisis in Asia were felt and short-term capital quickly left Asia. However, once the worst effects of the financial crisis had receded, the gap began to widen again in 2000. The volume of FDI to developing countries continued to grow steadily until 1999, but in that year, debt flows saw a sudden collapse and even a dramatic reversal of direction. Portfolio equity flows (the most volatile of the private flows) collapsed by 37 per cent in 1997, and started recovering only in 1999.

Even FDI, which is widely regarded as more beneficial than short-term speculative capital because of its long-term and more productive potential, reflects the highly concentrated nature of total private capital flows, with almost three-quarters of net FDI flowing to just ten 'emerging market' developing countries

Table 5.4   FDI flows to the top ten recipient developing countries, 1991, 1994 and 1997 (billions of dollars)

Country	1991	Country	1994	Country	1997[a]
Mexico	4.7	China	33.8	China	37.0
China	4.3	Mexico	11.0	Brazil	15.8
Malaysia	4.0	Malaysia	4.3	Mexico	8.1
Argentina	2.4	Peru	3.1	Indonesia	5.8
Thailand	2.0	Brazil	3.1	Poland	4.5
Venezuela	1.9	Argentina	3.1	Malaysia	4.1
Indonesia	1.5	Indonesia	2.1	Argentina	3.8
Hungary	1.5	Nigeria	1.9	Chile	3.5
Brazil	1.1	Poland	1.9	India	3.1
Turkey	0.8	Chile	1.8	Venezuela	2.9
Top ten share in FDI to all developing countries (%)	74.2		76.1		72.3

[a] Preliminary.

Source: World Bank, Global Development Finance (Washington DC, 1998).

(see Table 5.4). Another bias worth noting in the concentration of FDI is that most of the top recipients of FDI are middle-income countries. In 1997 the only low-income countries in the top ten were China and India.

According to UNCTAD's *World Investment Report 2001*, Africa's share of global FDI flows, estimated at a mere $5 billion in 1996, plummeted from 2.3 per cent in 1997 to 1.2 per cent in 1999. By comparison the total FDI to developing countries in South, East and South-east Asia rose by 25 per cent to $81 billion in 1996, or two-thirds of all FDI to the developing world.[29] While total FDI (to both industrialized and developing countries) stood at $349 billion in 1996,[30] it is worth noting that FDI captures only a part (perhaps no more than one quarter) of the total volume of financial resources directed to international production. The total value of investments made by TNCs abroad was estimated by UNCTAD at $1.4 trillion.

Apart from financial deregulation and the technological revolution, the other key factor in the dramatic increase in private capital flows was economic liberalization. *World Investment Report 1997* indicates that of the 599 changes in regulatory regimes relating to FDI made by governments between 1991 and 1996, 95 per cent were in the direction of liberalization. In 1996, on average, one bilateral investment treaty of this kind was concluded every day.

The thrust towards financial liberalization, already pursued assiduously before the outbreak of the economic crisis in East Asia, received added impetus even while the crisis unfolded. The cause was often the herd-like reaction of monetary authorities in most emerging markets as they attempted to capture much-needed and increasingly scarce capital from other crisis-prone emerging market countries. Another, perhaps equally important reason why national authorities unhinged financial restrictions on foreign capital flows had to do with the conditionalities attached to various IMF bail-out plans. The trends towards financial liberalization are clearly observable in Tables 5.5 and 5.6.

The above analysis suggests that in this new global context small- or medium-sized developing countries (and such industrialized countries as Sweden in the early 1990s after its capital account liberalization), even if their economies are relatively strong in growth terms, have less and less control over their destinies. Those with weaker economies, or those dependent on low-end value-added labour-intensive exports, are even more vulnerable to external shocks.

Similarly, countries with a higher dependence on export markets, external trade and financial flows (for example, Thailand and Malaysia, whose trade in 1998 as a percentage of GDP was respectively around 80 per cent and 200 per cent) are more vulnerable than those that have large internal markets and for whom trade is a relatively small proportion of their GDP, such as China and India. Moreover, given that financial markets tend to exaggerate shocks and over-react negatively in times of crisis, the likelihood is that such external trade dependent countries will be especially at risk in times of crisis, as evidenced by the exaggerated depreciation of some Southeast Asian currencies during the Asian crisis.

The current dominance of financial criteria in evaluating economic success, in addition to marginalizing social development objectives, leads to a natural bias in favour of short-term horizons and unemployment. To generate high employment, on the other hand, requires expansionary policies, with interest rate implications in directions that financial markets do not like. Similarly, such markets do not generally welcome investments in health, education and care for children because the gestation period for the investment to bear fruit (perhaps twenty years) is considered too long for their planning strategies, which are intent on quick returns.

Envisioning new globalization: Trends for the future

There is nothing to suggest that the current patterns of globalization will automatically reverse themselves or fundamentally change in the next two to three decades. Yet, as already indicated, current forms of globalization are neither inevitable nor an act of nature. Neither is Fukuyama's vision of 'the end of history', that is, the nirvana of total financial liberalization, inevitable or even likely.

An optimistic but not improbable scenario is that the economic liberalization pendulum will swing back towards greater regulation over the next few decades. Even leading capitalist and 'currency speculator', George Soros, conceded the need to slow down the current pace of economic and especially financial liberalization, while Joseph Stiglitz, former Chief Economist of the World Bank, argued for a post-Washington consensus.

The rise of global protest indicates a growing demand emanating from below for a new kind of globalization based on equity. As Michael Hardt and Antonio Negri aptly put it, 'the protesters are indeed united against the present form of capitalist globalization, but the vast majority of them are not against globalizing

Table 5.5 Investment regulations and restrictions in emerging equity markets (as of end-1997)

Market	Foreign investment ceiling (%)	Withholding taxes			Investment regulations for entering and exiting		
		Interest (%)	Dividends (%)	Long-term capital gains on listed shares (%)	Entry[f]	Exit[g] (Repatriation of income)	Exit[g] (Repatriation of capital)
Argentina	100 in general	0	0	0	Free[h]	Free	Free
Brazil	49 common stocks; 100 preferred stocks; 0 for bank ordinary shares	15	0	0	Free	Free	Free
Chile	100 in general	15	15	35	Relatively free	Free	After 1 year
China	100 only for B- and H-class shares	0	20	0	Special classes of shares	Free	Free
India	24 in general	20	20	10	Authorized investors only	Free	Free
Indonesia[a]	100 in general; 49 banks; 85 for securities companies	20	20	0	Relatively free	Some restrictions	Some restrictions
Korea[a,b]	55 in general; 25 for KEPCO and POSCO; 33 for SK Telecom	13.2	16.5	0	Relatively free	Free	Free
Malaysia	100 in general	15	0	0	Free	Free[i]	Free[i]
Mexico	100 in general	0	0	0	Free	Free	Free
Pakistan	100 in general	10	10	0	Free	Free	Free
Philippines[c]	40 in general; 30 for banks	20	15	0.5	Special classes of shares	Free	Free
Poland[d]	100 in general	40	20	0	Free	Free	Free
Russia	100 in general	15	15	20	*	*	*
Sri Lanka	100 in general; 49 for banks	0	15	0	Relatively free	Some restrictions	Some restrictions

Taiwan[a]	30 in general	20	35	0	Authorized investors only	Some restrictions	Some restrictions
Thailand	10–49 depending on company by-laws	15	10	0	Relatively free	Free	Free
Venezuela[e]	100 in general	0	0	1	Relatively free	Some restrictions	Some restrictions

Notes:

[a] Markets that showed changes in their foreign investment ceilings in comparison with the data reported in the same publication in the year 1996. In all the cases the changes clearly moved towards an increased liberalization of the market. In Indonesia the situation changed from a previous general ceiling of 49 per cent to a new general ceiling of 100 per cent, with some adjustments added for banks and securities companies. In Korea the general ceiling grew from 15 to 55 per cent, with some correction for specific companies there too. In Taiwan the general ceiling was brought up from a previous level of 15 per cent, to a 30 per cent level. It does not seem to be a coincidence that all these changes took place in the crisis-afflicted South-east Asia. After all, the introduced market openings followed the lines drawn by the IMF.

[b] Withholding tax rates are for funds in which US investments total more than 25 per cent. Tax rates shown include 10 per cent resident tax applied to base rate.

[c] Transaction tax in lieu of a capital gains tax.

[d] No withholding tax on interest for individuals.

[e] Transaction tax.

[f] Free entry: no significant restrictions to purchasing stocks. Relatively free entry: some registration procedures required to ensure repatriation rights, or significant limits on foreign ownership. Special classes: foreigners restricted to certain classes of stocks, designated for foreign investors. Authorized investors only: only approved foreign investors may buy stocks.

[g] Repatriation of income: dividends, interests, and realized capital gains. Repatriation of capital: initial capital invested. Free: repatriation done routinely. Some restrictions: typically, requires some registration with or permission of Central Bank, Ministry of Finance, or Office of Exchange Controls that may restrict the timing of exchange release.

[h] Some industries in some countries are considered strategic and are not available to foreign or non-resident investors. The level of foreign investment in other cases may be limited by national law or corporate policy to minority positions, not to aggregate more than 49 per cent of voting stock. The summaries above refer to 'new money' investment by foreign institutions. Other regulations may apply to capital invested through debt conversion schemes or other sources.

[i] The fast pace of the events that followed the outbreak of the financial crisis has of course already made out of date some of the figures reported in the table. In the case of Malaysia, however, the situation was made particularly interesting and worth mentioning, because of the choice against the stream made by the Mahathir government. In fact, on 1 September 1998, Malaysia imposed a one-year ban on the repatriation of income and capital. In February 1999, a correction to that measure, motivated by sudden fears that by September 1999 an exodus of foreign funds would have taken place, transformed the one-year requirement into an exit tax. The tax presents a uniform 10 per cent level to be applied only on repatriation of income.

* Data not available.

Source: IFC, *Emerging Stock Markets Factbook 1998*, 1998.

Table 5.6 Investment regulations and restrictions in emerging equity markets (as of end-2000)

Market	Foreign investment ceiling for listed stocks (%)	Withholding taxes			Investment regulations for entering and exiting		
		Interest (%)	Dividends (%)	Long-term capital gains on listed shares (%)	Entry	Exit (Repatriation of income)	Exit (Repatriation of capital)
Argentina	100 in general	0	0	0	Free	Free	Free
Brazil	100 preferred stocks; 100 for common stock in general[a]	15	0	0	Free	Free	Free
Chile	100 in general	35	35	15	Relatively free	Free	Free
China	100 only for B- and H-class shares and red chip stocks	20	20	0	Special classes of shares	Free	Free
India	24 in general; 20 for banks	20	0	10	Authorized investors only	Free	Free
Indonesia	100 in general	15	15	0.1	Relatively free	Some restrictions	Some restrictions
Korea[b]	100 in general; 40 for KEPCO and POSCO; 19.44 for SK Telecom	27.5	27.5	27.5	Relatively free	Free	Free
Malaysia[c]	100 in general	0	0	0	Relatively free	Free	After 1 year
Mexico[d]	100 in general	4.9	0	0	Free	Free	Free
Pakistan	100 in general	10	15	0	Free	Free	Free
Philippines[e]	40 in general	25	25	0.5	Special classes of shares	Free	Free
Poland[f]	100 in general	30	15	0	Free	Free	Free

Country							
Russia	100 in general; 9 for Gazprom, 25 for UES; 12 or central bank approval for banks	0	10	–	Free	Free	Free
Sri Lanka	100 in general; 60 for banks	0	15	0	Relatively free	Some restrictions	Free
Taiwan	Limits to the maximum holdings of total shares outstanding by foreigners[g]	20	20	0	Authorized investors only	Some restrictions	Some restrictions
Thailand[h]	10–100 depending on company by-laws	15	10	15	Relatively free	Free	Free
Venezuela[i]	100 in general	1	0	1	Free	Free	Free

Notes:

[a] Except 0 per cent for banks, 20 per cent for air transport, 49 per cent for cable television and 20 per cent for highway cargo transport, 0 per cent for newspaper, radio and TV broadcasting companies and 50 per cent minus one share for Petrobas.

[b] Rates applied when there is no tax treaty. For capital gains, the rate is 27.5 per cent on capital gains or 11 per cent on the gross proceeds, whichever is less. Tax rates shown include a 10 per cent resident tax.

[c] Capital gains subject to a flat 10 per cent levy upon repatriation.

[d] Government debt is exempt. For private debt interest the 4.9 per cent tax is not applicable if the beneficiary resides in a member country of the OECD in which the income tax applicable is equivalent to that applied in Mexico, or in a country with which Mexico has a treaty.

[e] Transactions tax in lieu of a capital gains tax.

[f] No withholding tax on interest or capital gains for individuals. Taxes are subject to treaties to avoid double taxation for foreigners.

[g] Sector foreign investment ceilings of 50 per cent for cement, 0 per cent for domestic transportation, 33 per cent for aviation, 50 per cent for aviation logistics, 20 per cent for telecommunications, 50 per cent for natural gas, 40–50 per cent for some banks and insurance companies.

[h] Capital gains are tax free for individuals.

[i] Transactions tax.

Source: Standard & Poor's Emerging Stock Markets Factbook 2001, 2001.

currents and forces as such; they are not isolationist, separatist or even national-ist'.[31] The heart of the problem is that the current form of globalization has no democratic institutional mechanisms for representation, and no public forum for debate.

Mainstream concerns and proposals, on the other hand, while useful from an incremental perspective, tend to operate on the assumption that globalization and the laissez-faire capitalist drive can be harnessed for positive, human-centred development. The evidence suggests that this view may be somewhat naive or overly optimistic, and that bolder alternatives are required.

There is now general agreement among those who advocate democratic forms of globalization on the following key issues: first, 'globalization from below' is needed to ensure that living standards are improved and equality among social categories is established; secondly, globalization must be transformed into a process which favours inclusion and participation in decision-making and imple-mentation,[32] and replaces the exclusionist practices that lead to poverty and con-flict; thirdly, globalization must be reshaped by new international norms and multilateral institutions conducive to global democratic governance. These key principles resonate well with those articulated in Tehranian's earlier chapters (Part I).

To this end, global alliance-building amongst progressive civil-society groups in both North and South must accelerate, based on an agenda which offers a rad-ical alternative to humanizing laissez-faire capitalism and current forms of glob-alization, and on proactive rather than the largely reactive strategies of the past.

Notes

1. T. Levitt, 'The Globalization of Markets', in A.M. Kantrow (ed.), *Sunrise... Sunset: Challenging the Myth of Industrial Obsolescence* (New York: John Wiley & Sons, 1985).
2. A. Giddens, *The Consequences of Modernity* (Cambridge: Polity Press, 1990), p.64.
3. A. Bonanno, 'Diversity and Globalization: the Homogenization of Heterogeneity' (Paper prepared for presentation at the seminar: The Production of Diversity in a Global Context, Wageningen, The Netherlands, 26–8 October 1994), p.21.
4. L.L. Sfeir, 'Towards Globalization of Agricultural Policies?', in A. Bonanno, *The Agricultural and Food Sector in the New Global Era* (Concept Publishing Company, 1993), p.81.
5. K. Polanyi, *The Great Transformation: Political and Economic Origins of our Times* (New York: Octagon Books, 1975).
6. For a detailed account of the role played by institutional investors in the Asian crisis see Chapter 7 of this book. For a detailed account of the Asian crisis see Chapter 6.
7. T.K. Marsden and A. Arce, 'Constructing Quality: Emerging Food Networks in the Rural Transition', *Environment and Planning A*, 27 (1995), p.1263.
8. S. Gill, 'New Constitutionalism, Democratisation and Global Political Economy', *Pacifica Review*, 10, 1(1998), p.26.
9. Ibid., p.26.
10. Ibid., p.27.
11. W.H. Friedland, 'The Transnationalization of Agricultural Production: Palimpsest of the Transnational State', *International Journal of Sociology of Agriculture and Food*, I (1991), p.57.

12. A. Bonanno, 'The Globalization and Theories of the State of the Agricultural and Food Sector', *International Journal of Sociology of Agriculture and Food*, I (1991), p.18.
13. A.K. Sen, *Development as Freedom* (New York: Vintage Anchor, 2000).
14. N. Cagatay and D. Elson, 'The Social Content of Macroeconomic Policies', *World Development*, 28, 7(2000).
15. A. Bhaduri, 'Implications of Globalization for Macroeconomic Theory and Policy in Developing Countries', in D. Baker, G. Epstein and R. Pollin (eds), *Globalization and Progressive Economic Policy* (Cambridge: Cambridge University Press, 1998), pp.149–58.
16. For more extensive discussion of TNCs, see Chapters 3 and 7.
17. Bonanno (1991).
18. At the same time the central bank decided to raise the interest rates to 14 per cent.
19. S. Gill, *Global Hegemony and the Structural Power of Capital* (Essay presented at the XIV Congress of IPSA, Washington DC, 1988), p.5.
20. Ibid., pp.10–11.
21. On the issue of 'competition states', see also Gill's elaboration in the previous chapter.
22. G. Soros, with B. Wien and K. Koenen, *Soros on Soros: Staying Ahead of the Curve* (New York: John Wiley & Sons, 1995), p.158.
23. To be more precise, Gordon Brown mentioned a level of net private capital flows to emerging markets equal to $174 billion.
24. G. Brown, 'New Global Structures for the New Global Age' (Speech by the Chancellor of the Exchequer to the Commonwealth Finance Ministers meeting in Ottawa on 30 September 1998), HM Treasury News Release, 158/98, available online at: **<http://www.hm-treasury.gov.uk/press/1998/p158_98.html>**
25. As shown by the speculative attacks on some of the Southeast Asian currencies that triggered or worsened the crisis, and also by similar subsequent attacks on the Russian rouble and the Brazilian *real*.
26. The *Economist* (London), 'The Risk Business' (17 October 1998), pp.21–3.
27. For a comprehensive analysis of the way institutional investors operate and their role during the Asian financial crisis, see Chapter 7.
28. World Bank, *Global Development Finance* (Washington DC: World Bank, 1998), p.17.
29. UNCTAD, *World Investment Report* (Geneva: UNCTAD, 1997).
30. Ibid.
31. M. Hardt and A. Negri, 'What the Protesters in Genoa Want', *New York Times*, 20 July 2001, available online at: **<http://www.nytimes.com/2001/07/20/opinion/20HARDT.html?searchpv=nytToday>**.
32. Such a process of inclusion should not happen through a process of 'globalization from above'. New rules of governance of the global economy will need to be sketched before equitable inclusion can be guaranteed.

6
The Asian Financial Crisis and IMF Intervention

Marco Mezzera and Kamal Malhotra

Cyclical financial booms and busts

Financial crises are closely interrelated with the phenomenon of business cycles. Indeed, a financial crisis may be considered the natural death which frequently follows a phase of strong economic expansion. The business cycle tends to exhaust itself in a last, desperate and self-destructive attempt to reach for higher levels of economic achievement. This speculative excess is what Kindleberger called 'a mania'.[1] Each mania is followed by an historically common, if not inevitable, recurrence of crises, crashes and panics.

Given such tendencies, even assertive intervention on the part of national and international agencies cannot guarantee peaceful crisis resolution. On the other hand, the knowledge that such agencies may be willing to provide 'bail-outs' tends to increase the moral hazard which continues to insulate irresponsible market actors from the full costs of their lending decisions.

The common thread connecting all major recent financial crises is their cyclical nature. They are intrinsic to the capitalist development model and not just aberrant variations in an otherwise perfect symphony. To fail to recognize them as fundamental components of the modern economic system would be to ignore one of its basic tenets.

From this analysis, it emerges that the appearance of speculative manias before the actual onset of crisis is a factor common to all past crises. While the financial and economic disruption that occurred in Asia and Mexico during the 1990s may have been triggered in each case by different factors and assumed different characteristics, strong and unrestrained speculative tendencies clearly played a key role.

When drawing comparisons between the crises that hit East Asia in the late 1990s and those that afflicted Mexico and other parts of Latin America during 1994–95, analysts often emphasize the role of private debt in the former case and public debt in the latter case. This is essentially a difference in 'presentation'. In both cases, the crisis was caused by speculative manias, encouraged by domestic monetary measures. Mexico's technocrats had discovered the efficacy of maintaining high interest rates in order to 'suck in foreign capital', especially from the United States.[2] By offering stocks and short-term government notes at rates double those available in the United States, Mexican monetary authorities succeeded in attracting huge flows of portfolio investments despite low economic growth in the country. This was a short-term strategy based on highly unstable and volatile speculative capital. Once the mania reached its peak, the economy became vulnerable to reversals of investment decisions and other destabilizing events. The coincidence of speculative attacks on the Mexican *peso*, high inflation, a peasant revolt, the assassination of a presidential candidate and an earthquake threw the system out of equilibrium and 'led to a massive capital flight and depreciation of the peso'.[3] Panic got hold of the Mexican financial market and prepared the way for yet another crash in the international financial system.

Mexico, which had already confronted a serious debt crisis in 1982, appeared to have quickly forgotten the dangers of relying on 'hot money' for its economic development. When syndicated bank lending to the Third World collapsed and the 'binge' of Third World borrowing came to an abrupt end, Mexico as well as Argentina, Brazil and Chile went into recession and had to face bankruptcy.

Speculative financial crises do not affect only developing countries. They dot the recent history of many industrialized countries. The stock market crash of 1929 was the pre-eminent financial crisis of the twentieth century. More recent examples include the Wall Street stock exchange crash of 19 October 1987, the parallel bubbles in the stock markets of Sweden, Finland, Norway and Denmark in the late 1980s and early 1990s and the breakup of Europe's exchange-rate mechanism in 1992–93.

The origins of the Asian financial crisis[4]

The Asian crisis was one in which dominant aspects of the globalization process combined with different versions of the East Asian 'economic miracle'. Three sets of actors played a decisive role: 'foreign direct investors seeking low-wage production sites; portfolio investors seeking high yields on their investment with a quick turnaround time; and technocratic and economic elites in Southeast Asia' in search of 'prosperity for themselves'. Their converging interests created the illusion that neo-liberal economic development strategies could be successfully and instantaneously applied to most Southeast Asian economies. The dominant globalization model advocated 'high-speed growth fuelled, not principally by domestic savings and investment ... but mainly by huge infusions of foreign capital'.[5]

To better understand the crisis, it must be placed in the historical context of the 1985 Plaza Accord, which was imposed on Japan by the United States as a way of dealing with the Japanese trade surplus. The Plaza Accord led to a flow of between $15 and 20 billion in Japanese FDI into South-east Asia between 1986 and 1990. By 1996, the total amount of Japanese direct investment in Indonesia, Singapore, Malaysia, Thailand and the Philippines had reached $48 billion.[6] Additional capital flowed into the region, in the form of ODA and financial capital, especially from South Korea and Taiwan. The same accord allowed South-east Asia to avoid the classic structural adjustment programmes (SAPs) which the IMF and the World Bank had prescribed for Latin America and Africa in the 1980s.

In the early 1990s, the FDI flow into the region began to level off, essentially as a result of the economic recession that was starting to hurt Japan. To continue to have access to foreign capital, on which high economic growth in the region now depended, financial technocrats attempted to attract portfolio investment. Financial liberalization, together with high interest rates and fixed exchange rates, became the three elements of an immensely successful formula to attract portfolio capital in the short term.

Such speculative capital flows were encouraged and lauded by the IMF, the World Bank and the US commercial banks. Depressed US interest rates and the communications technology revolution also facilitated such capital flows. The World Bank's assessment of the pre-crisis economic performance of most of the South-east and East Asian countries is highly instructive. In a 1997 policy research report, the World Bank stated that

> the surge in flows [see Table 6.1] reflected these countries' strong economic performance, including rapid growth, sustained improvements in macroeconomic balances (public sector balances, inflation), and structural changes that have fostered a market-led, outward orientation since the late 1980s'.[7]

The positive tone of that commentary was in striking contrast with the Bank's subsequent position, as reflected in the 1998 edition of *Global Development Finance*. The latter report, though underlining 'the good macroeconomic track record of the East Asian countries', admitted that at least 'three sources of vulnerability' had emerged in the system: 'large current account deficits and misallocated investment, bad loans and currency and maturity mismatches, and misaligned real exchange rates and lost competitiveness'.[8]

The enormous growth of debt and portfolio equity flows, especially when compared with the declining amounts of official developing finance,[9] was channelled mainly into the stock market, consumer credit and real estate business. The only rationale behind this investment activity was the search for the highest returns in the shortest period. Investment or reinvestment of capital in the productive sectors of the economy, notably agriculture and industry, was neglected. The serious lack of 'market discipline' in lending decisions and the inability of various central bank authorities to fulfil their regulatory tasks led to an over-supply in real estate, asset inflation in stocks and property values, and high consumer debt.

Table 6.1   Net private capital flows to East Asia, 1994–96 (percentage of GDP)

	1994	1995	1996
Indonesia	0.3	3.5	6.1
Korea, Rep. Of	1.2	2.0	4.9
Malaysia	1.2	6.2	8.4
Philippines	7.9	8.4	12.7
Thailand	14.3	17.3	14.5

Source: World Bank, *Global Development Finance*, 1998.

As pointed out in the G-22 Report on the International Financial Architecture, a 'weak banking system ... [had] contributed to the misallocation of resources that led to the crisis'.[10]

In the specific case of Thailand,[11] where the crisis was triggered on 2 July 1997 by a heavy devaluation of the *baht*, another structural weakness had made things worse, namely a seriously flawed export competitiveness strategy. In the manufacturing sector the strategy was applied primarily to lower-end value, labour-intensive exports, which were no longer price competitive, owing both to cost and quality factors. Warnings given over many years that Thailand's wages were outstripping those of its neighbours, while its productivity and investment in secondary and tertiary education, research and development were standing still, went largely unheeded. This structural crisis came to a head in the context of increasing trade liberalization and accelerating globalization, which has led more, and bigger, countries (China, India, Vietnam) to fight for the same, often more protected, labour-intensive export markets in North America, the EU and Japan.

The widening trade deficit was seen as a necessary dimension of growth and was sustained by annual export growth rates which were as high as 21 per cent in 1994 and 24 per cent in 1995. Exports then crashed, with almost no growth registered in 1996. Whilst imports also declined, the import of capital-intensive goods continued unabated, resulting in a record trade deficit of 426 billion *baht*, or $16 billion in 1996, that is approximately 8 per cent of the Thai GDP.

In addition to this structural weakness, two other factors significantly contributed to the crisis: First, speculative attacks on the *baht*, which triggered the crisis, were caused by the preservation of fixed exchange rates and the currency's peg to the US dollar – the inadequacy of financial supervision in almost all Asian countries was no doubt a factor, but such shortcomings were largely attributable to the 'undue rapidity of financial deregulation and capital-account liberalization'.[12] Secondly, the heavy devaluation of the *baht* triggered, and in its turn was triggered by, the Asian crisis. This was a necessary measure to stop export stagnation, but it inflicted enormous hardship on the population of these countries. While the drastic currency devaluations (see Table 6.2) were conceived as one of

Table 6.2 Rates of depreciation of selected Asian currencies

Currency	Exchange rate to $		Depreciation rate to $ (%)
	1 July 1997	24 January 1998	
Indonesian *rupiah*	2,432.00	14,800.00	−83.6
Thai *baht*	24.53	54.00	−54.6
Korean *won*	888.00	1,744.00	−49.1
Malaysian *ringgit*	2.52	4.58	−44.9
Philippine *peso*	26.37	43.50	−39.4
Singapore dollar	1.43	1.76	−18.8

Source: M.F. Montes, *The Currency Crisis in Southeast Asia* (Singapore: Institute of Southeast Asian Studies, 1998).

a number of measures (the others being heavy cuts in public-sector expenditures) needed to reverse the significant current-account deficits that had been testing these economies during the previous five years,[13] they wreaked social havoc on these societies and their purchasing power.

Who lost and who gained

The crisis that struck Thailand, Indonesia, South Korea and much of South-east Asia in the second half of 1997 was, above all, a social crisis. Whereas most of the attention in the immediate aftermath of the crisis was given to those sectors of society that played a direct and active role in its outbreak, inadequate notice was taken of its real victims: the weak, the poor and those who lost their jobs because of the crisis. When the human costs of the crisis were initially considered, the tendency was to focus on CEOs whose companies had gone bankrupt, or on investors who had lost their money in the stock markets. The suffering of those thrown out of work or experiencing food insecurity was neglected.

With few exceptions, those most affected by the crisis were those who had least benefited from the financial boom. Measures taken by most South-east Asian governments, including significant public expenditure reductions and increases in regressive indirect taxes, compounded the economic and social vulnerability of large sections of society. The IMF shares a heavy responsibility for the severity of the crisis because of the hard conditionalities imposed by its rescue programmes.[14]

In the case of Thailand, unemployment between February 1997 and February 1998 increased from a pre-crisis level of 2.2 per cent to 4.6 per cent. The rise becomes even more striking if seasonal unemployment is included. With this inclusion, the rates become 5.4 per cent and 8.5 per cent respectively. The National Economic and Social Development Board (NESDB) estimated that the total number of unemployed in Thailand would reach three, or even three and a half million people in 1999.[15] While this figure proved overly pessimistic,[16] it was indicative of the magnitude of the impact on Thai unemployment of the crisis, which is conservatively estimated to have directly cost at least one million workers their jobs by 1999. Moreover, additional cuts in family incomes resulted from a reduction in the working hours and wages of a significant number of people.[17]

Another group which paid heavily for its vulnerable status in society was migrant workers throughout the region. At the onset of the crisis, they were the first to be targeted by governments anxious to deal with unemployment. Malaysia and Thailand took the lead in the widespread process of indiscriminate expulsions. Both countries had huge reservoirs of migrants, with nearly two million foreign workers in Malaysia – 800,000 of them illegal – and 986,000 illegal workers in Thailand.

The large flows of displaced unemployed workers created extensive social dislocation. Efforts to divert these flows towards rural areas, as encouraged by the King in Thailand, often disrupted the alimentary and social equilibrium of those areas. People returning to the villages after years spent working in urban areas soon realized that they had lost their skills, and sometimes even the willingness necessary to perform useful tasks in the rural production system. They became a burden on their families.

Crime rates also increased. Thailand, for example, where the number of poor people was expected to grow from seven to 12 million by 1999, experienced a 10 per cent increase in crimes against property in the Bangkok metropolitan area during 1998. The total number of convicts detained in national prisons increased from 65,916 in 1988, to about 170,000 in 1998, and was predicted to reach approximately 220,000 in 1999.[18]

Another major impact of the crisis was on children. Citing Thailand again, the number of children enrolling for primary education missed the 1998 government target by 17.3 per cent, that is, by about 500,000 children. This was substantially higher than the 6.8 per cent, or some 200,000 children, that the authorities had expected would miss school that year.[19] Domestic violence against children and child labour also increased, the latter both in absolute terms and in the number of working hours per week. There were now many more street children begging for their survival.[20]

The evidence also suggests that women had to endure a disproportionate share of the load imposed by the crisis. A record of job termination circulated by the Thai Ministry of Labour and Social Welfare, covering a period between 1 January and 30 November 1998, showed that a significant proportion of retrenched workers (57.29 per cent) were women.[21]

Finally, mention should be made of the dramatic surge in suicide rates in the crisis-stricken countries. In the case of Thailand, the director of the government's Mental Health Institute indicated that the numbers of suicides during 1998 had increased from 1 per 10,000 persons in 1997, to 1.4/1.5 per 10,000.[22] The situation in South Korea was comparable.

The crisis did not leave only debris and the wounded behind. A substantial group of 'winners' can also be identified. Though many TNCs saw previously commissioned works abruptly terminated in the wake of the financial crisis, it is also the case that as a consequence of the sharp depreciation of many Southeast Asian currencies, TNCs suddenly found themselves in a quite favourable position. They were able to increase profit margins partly through cheaper labour costs in dollar terms and partly through the decline in asset prices, which gave them unprecedented basement sale prices under changed equity and ownership terms. The IMF's conditions, which included pressure for deregulation and liberalization, were proposed in the name of efficiency, but their net effect was to favour foreign ownership and provide the basis for TNC gains.

Furthermore, during the formulation of the bail-out programmes for Southeast Asia, a marked convergence of interests and objectives between the IMF, the US Treasury, and the international institutional investors and international banks became evident. That requests to deregulate the Korean financial markets and to open up bond markets to foreign banks were incorporated in IMF bail-out packages cannot be considered entirely coincidental. Banks such as Chase Manhattan, Bank of America, Citicorp and J.P. Morgan were, it seems, involved in extensive consultations with the Federal Reserve Bank of New York on the Korean bail-out programmes.[23] Robert Hormat, Vice-Chairman of Goldman Sachs International, is reported to have said: 'Thanks in part to the Asian crisis, we are in the midst of the most competitive environment in world history'.[24] Set against this backdrop, that view is more readily understandable.

Proposed adjustments: the right remedies?

The first to react to the crisis were the large IFIs and among them specifically the Bretton Woods institutions. While national governments were still trying to understand where and how the crisis had started, those institutions had already a number of rescue packages on the drawing board. Formulae for rehabilitating ailing economies were quickly presented as infallible ways out of the crisis.

The IMF found compliant executors for its policy recommendations (attached as conditionalities to the rescue packages) in South Korea's President Kim Dae Jung and Thailand's Prime Minister Chuan Leekpai,[25] 'whose own liberal democratic aspirations largely fitted the Fund's liberalization agenda'. On the other hand, it had to endure a resolute refusal by Malaysia, which rejected interference in its domestic economic policies, and a troublesome negotiation process with the defiant Suharto government.[26]

Indonesia first applied for IMF assistance on 8 October 1997, after having been faced by an unsustainable devaluation of the *rupiah*, declining reserves, collapsing financial institutions, and capital haemorrhaging from the country. By 31 October, a loan agreement of approximately $40 billion had been approved. That first agreement involved primarily macroeconomic policy measures, including high interest rates in pursuit of a tight monetary policy, closure of unhealthy banks,[27] trade and investment liberalization, dismantling of domestic monopolies, and expansion of the privatization programme.

On 6 January 1998, probably in a last desperate attempt to revive his own and his family's political and economic fortunes, Suharto made a defiant announcement in which he proclaimed substantial increases in the subsidies for petrol and staples, and a 32 per cent increase in government spending. That move brought a swift response. Enormous pressures were immediately exerted by the IMF and western and Japanese governments for Jakarta to revise the announced measures and stick to IMF conditionality. On 15 January 1998, Suharto eventually yielded and appended his signature to a second IMF agreement.

By contrast with the first agreement, the second was more specific in its targets. In addition to macroeconomic policy initiatives, it called for measures aimed directly at the heart of the Suharto clan's vested interests. It demanded full-scale abolition, or marked reduction, in the level of subsidies for the main staples. The IMF-dictated increases in energy prices, implemented on 4 May 1998, were the prime factor triggering riots and social unrest throughout the country, eventually paving the way for Suharto's own political demise.

Notwithstanding this and other instances of domestic conflict ignited by the application of IMF policies, which dates back to Thailand's request for financial assistance in August 1997, a large volume of resources flowed into the region (see Table 6.3). The problem, however, with these apparently generous funds was that they were made available essentially on 'non-concessional terms' and at market interest rates. They could hardly be considered 'foreign aid'. Their costs were borne not by the taxpayers in the source countries, but by the citizens at the receiving end of these flows, who would eventually be required, through their own governments, to repay the funds.[28]

Not surprisingly, the IMF-sponsored stabilization programmes would be subjected to widespread criticism.[29] What follows is a brief summary of that critique.

The IMF had prescribed public-sector medicine (based on budget cuts, and interest rate and indirect tax increases), which was inappropriate for this ailment, namely a private debt crisis of the kind East Asia was experiencing. Rather, the forced public sector austerity measures deepened and accelerated the economic contraction that they were supposed to ameliorate, and in the process produced a crisis in both the private and public sectors.

The IMF's macroeconomic prescriptions, based mainly on reduced public expenditures, excise duties, value-added tax (VAT) increases, and maintenance of high interest rates, accentuated the impact of the crisis on the poorest and most vulnerable sections of society. Despite a dramatic rise in unemployment rates, the 1998 budget of the Thai Ministry of Labour and Social Welfare was cut by 15.4 per cent, and that of the Ministry of Interior, in charge of community development programmes, was subjected to an even more substantial reduction of 25 per cent.[30]

The nature of IMF structural reform conditions directly interfered with domestic policy and political processes through the conditionality packages that were imposed in a host of areas normally the preserve of domestic legislatures and the executive branch of government. The shift of the institution's role to that of 'global economic policeman' has been another source of criticism. Even Martin Feldstein, an arch conservative, was moved to comment: 'a nation's desperate need for short-term financial help does not give the IMF the moral right to substitute its technical judgments for the outcomes of the nation's political process'.[31]

Table 6.3 Committed financial assistance to Asian crisis-stricken countries (as of January 1998 – in billion $)

Country	IMF	World Bank	ADB	Bilateral[a]	Total
Korea	21.0	10.0	4.0	32.0	67.0
Indonesia	10.0	4.5	3.5	22.0	40.0
Thailand	4.0	1.5	1.2	10.5	17.2
Total	35.0	16.0	8.7	64.5	124.2

[a] In the case of Korea – Australia, Belgium, Britain, Canada, France, Germany, Italy, Japan, the Netherlands, Sweden, Switzerland and the United States; in the case of Indonesia – Indonesia itself (from contingency reserves), Japan, Singapore, Australia, Malaysia, China, Hong Kong and the United States; and in the case of Thailand: Japan, Australia, China, Hong Kong, Malaysia, Singapore, Indonesia, Korea and Brunei.

Source: IMF Factsheet – 'Bail Outs, Truth or Fiction?'

The negative impact of the IMF's intervention was compounded by its timing and direction. Fundamental structural reforms were proposed in the middle of the crisis, adding to the existing panic in the financial sector and contributing to an intensified outflow of capital.[32] A certain intellectual arrogance on the part of the IMF technocracy resulted in uniform application of policy recommendations, regardless of the specific circumstances of each economy. In the words of Joseph Stiglitz, the IMF's approach was deeply flawed in that 'political recommendations could be administered by economists using little more than simple accounting frameworks'.[33]

Furthermore, the structural solution to the problem was sought in further financial and capital-account liberalization, yet the timeframe allowed for the implementation of the recommended policies was much shorter than that which had applied in the industrialized world. The latter's historical experience had, in fact, featured long periods of capital controls and only a rather gradual process of liberalization of capital accounts in more recent decades. In this sense, the Fund's persistent advocacy of greater capital-account liberalization as a panacea merely added insult to injury.

The accelerated liberalization process meant in practice a loss of economic autonomy and erosion of political sovereignty for the affected countries. Financial restructuring packages stimulated 'amazing distress sales', through which foreign investors were given 'enhanced rights to ownership, the possibility to convert debt to equity in struggling Asian enterprises and the chance of picking up other local firms at bargain basement prices'.[34]

The perception that 'double standards' were maintained by the IMF in the treatment of the domestic and foreign financial sectors had become widespread. While foreign firms enjoyed a kind of preferential bail-out therapy in the name of maintaining global financial stability, domestic companies were often abandoned to the mercy of the market. The view rapidly gained ground that IMF packages and conditionalities had encouraged the 'socialization' of the costs associated with the crisis, with Asian governments and their taxpayers carrying the ultimate burden.

The IMF's preferences and priorities also strengthened the conclusion that 'moral hazard' situations would continue to be created, whereby 'both creditors and debtors who make unwise investment choices are saved from the consequences of their bad decisions', thus making it more likely that they will undertake the same risks and commit the same mistakes in the future.[35]

There was also the 'well-founded concern about the policy and power nexus between the IMF and its major shareholder', the United States. A number of analysts viewed the IMF as a Trojan Horse, through which the US Administration, and its Treasury in particular, would 'in the face of increasing resistance at home', push through 'its free-wheeling liberalization agenda' at the international level. This strategy tended to intensify especially in crisis situations, not least during the Asian economic crisis. As a consequence, the United States was increasingly viewed as the 'instrument of western neo-liberalism'.[36]

The IMF's mismanagement of the crisis made clear its incapacity to play the twin roles of surveillance and stabilization of the international monetary system.

Its interventions in recent crises pointed to a reactive rather than proactive and preventive approach.

Finally, the IMF attracted a good deal of criticism by virtue of its repeated emphasis on the need for transparency at the domestic political level, at the very time that the institution itself continued to operate in a highly secretive manner. The Fund was inevitably subjected to the accusation of double standards. Its decision-making processes and its use of public monies were questioned precisely because they lacked transparency. IMF negotiations with individual governments were invariably covered by conditions of confidentiality. Essential documents, including Letters of Intent or Policy Framework Papers, were seldom publicly disclosed.

The Asian financial crisis and the IMF's response to it resulted in unprecedented public scrutiny of the institution's policy packages and governance mechanisms. The ensuing impetus for reform of the Bretton Woods institutions was fuelled by both conservatives and progressives around the world. While this momentum persists to some extent, it has yet to be matched by substantial change in the policy prescriptions or governance of either the IMF or World Bank.

Notes

1. C.P. Kindleberger, *Manias, Panics and Crashes: a History of Financial Crises*, 3rd edn (New York: John Wiley & Sons, 1996), p.2.
2. W. Bello, *Addicted to Capital: the Ten-Year High and Present-Day Withdrawal Trauma of Southeast Asia's Economies* (Bangkok: Focus on the Global South, 1997), p.10.
3. Kindleberger, p.186.
4. For a specific analysis of the role played by institutional investors in the Asian crisis, see Chapter 7.
5. Bello, p.3.
6. Ibid., p.5.
7. World Bank, *Private Capital Flows to Developing Countries: the Road to Financial Integration* (New York: Oxford University Press, 1997).
8. World Bank, *Global Development Finance* (Washington DC: World Bank, 1998).
9. For a more detailed discussion of the issues, see the section of Chapter 5 related to Table 5.2.
10. G-22. *Reports on the International Financial Architecture*, available online at: <http://www.ustreas.gov/press/releases/docs/g22-ltr.htm> (1998), p.11.
11. For a further elaboration of the onset of the Asian crisis in Thailand, see Chapter 7.
12. R. Culpeper, *Systemic Instability or Global Growing Pains? Implications of the Asian Financial Crisis* (Briefing B-41, Ottawa: North–South Institute, 1998), p.5.
13. M.F. Montes, *The Currency Crisis in Southeast Asia* (Singapore: Institute of Southeast Asian Studies, 1998), p.1.
14. For a more detailed analysis of the role played by the IMF in the Asian financial crisis, see later sections of this chapter.
15. In comparison with a February 1998 level of 2,730,000 unemployed.
16. According to the National Statistical Office there were 1.383 million unemployed in February–August 1999.
17. J. Chomthongdi, *Overview of Social Impacts of the Economic Crisis* (Paper prepared for the Thai Development Support Committee and Focus on the Global South, Bangkok, 1998), p.5.
18. S. Pruksakasemsuk, *Labor Situation in Thailand 1999: Thai Workers in IMF Era* (Bangkok: Center for Labor Information Service and Training, 1999), passim.

19. Ibid.
20. For a comprehensive study of the impact of the Asian financial crisis on Philippine women and children, see J.J. Chavez, *The Asian Financial Crisis and Filipino Households: Impact on Women and Children* (Manila: Focus on the Global South and Save the Children UK, 2001).
21. See Pruksakasemsuk.
22. Ibid.
23. K. Singh, *A Citizen's Guide to the Globalization of Finance* (Delhi: Madhyam Books, 1998), pp.107–8.
24. Ibid., p.108.
25. Only by 1999 did various sectors of the Thai administration begin to question the efficacy of these programmes in helping society as a whole to recover from the crisis. There was a widespread perception among politicians that the suggested remedies were poorly disguised attempts to secure foreign ownership of collapsing national companies. The animated debates that characterized parliamentary discussions of the Bankruptcy Bill in Thailand during the first months of 1999 showed some of these reactive tensions, although they also revealed the close linkages that existed between policy-makers and the corporate world. A number of powerful Thai families were fearful of being forced to admit their bankruptcy status and thus to have to repay the huge debts accumulated before and during the crisis.
26. N. Bullard, W. Bello and K. Malhotra, *Taming the Tigers: the IMF and the Asian Crisis* (Focus Paper, Bangkok: Focus on the Global South, 1998), p.68.
27. During the following month, November, the government liquidated 16 private banks, to which, in August 1998, it added the closure of another three private banks and the nationalization of another two. This policy, aimed at healing the ailing Indonesian banking system, seems to have been the only IMF recommendation to have survived and was pushed through despite the strong objections of the Indonesian government. In January 1998, after consultations with the IMF, the Indonesian government set up the Indonesian Bank Restructuring Agency to strengthen the process of reform of the banking system and to create a line of credit for banks in need. By 22 March 1999, 38 banks had been closed down (of the total 164 local banks), and the retrenchment of thousands of employees was beginning to create considerable social unrest.
28. Culpeper, p.8.
29. Among them we may include the 'former IMF employee and director of the Harvard Institute for International Development Jeffrey Sachs; previous World Bank Chief Economist Joseph Stiglitz; influential, conservative journals such as the *Economist* and the *Financial Times*; Republicans and Democrats in the US Congress; and even bone-dry neo-liberals such as former US President Ronald Reagan's chief economic adviser Martin Feldstein and Milton Friedman of the Chicago School'; see Bullard et al., p.57.
30. J. Chomthongdi, *Overview of Social Impacts of the Economic Crisis*, p.14.
31. M. Feldstein, 'Refocusing the IMF', *Foreign Affairs*, 77, 2(1998).
32. See, for example, Culpeper.
33. See 'Bank Admits HIPC Conditions Wrong', in J. Hanlon, *Debt Update*, March 1998.
34. Bullard et al., pp.58–9.
35. Ibid., p.58.
36. Ibid., pp.61–3.

7
The Role of Portfolio Investors in the Asian Financial Crisis[1]

Adam Harmes

Whereas the previous chapter examines the multiple factors which contributed to the onset of the Asian financial crisis, this chapter aims to highlight and expand on the role of western portfolio investment and its contribution to the speculative mania which preceded the crisis. At present, most explanations of the 1997 East Asian crisis focus on either weaknesses in Asian financial structures (the so-called 'crony capitalism-moral hazard' explanation) or on imprudent lending and panicked over-reaction by foreign banks, particularly commercial and investment banks (the 'financial panic' explanation). In doing so, both camps have downplayed the role played by western portfolio investment.

However, while portfolio inflows by overseas mutual and pension funds did pale in comparison with inflows from banks, this chapter argues that, by contributing to a boom-bust cycle in Asian asset markets which preceded the currency crisis, herd behaviour among institutional investors played a significant role in causing the collapse of East Asian currencies. Specifically, it argues that portfolio inflows from foreign mutual and pension funds led to a boom in asset prices which created the incentive, and provided the collateral, for debt-driven speculation and, hence, for increased bank lending. It further argues that the withdrawal of these funds prior to the devaluation in Thailand led to a collapse in asset prices which, subsequently, undermined the collateral of borrowers and led to a financial panic among creditors. Before proceeding to the argument directly, the chapter begins with an examination of how institutional investors are reducing the efficiency of international financial markets.

Institutional investors and the financial markets

As a 1997 report by the OECD notes, '[t]he emergence of institutional investors as the dominant holders of financial assets ... is one of the distinguishing features of the present financial landscape'.[2] However, despite being characterized by professional management and long-term retirement commitments, institutional investors such as mutual and pension funds are serving to increase the short-term and herd behaviour of international financial markets in three broad ways. First, institutional investors are contributing to herd behaviour by creating a concentration of investment decision-making within disintermediated capital markets. In other words, because of the rise of institutional investors, decisions related to capital allocation are becoming increasingly centralized as more and more individuals delegate control over their savings to professional fund managers. Further reinforcing this trend towards centralization is the growing concentration within the money-management industry itself. One example here is Fidelity Investments, the largest of all the mutual fund companies, whose assets under management were valued at over $650 billion dollars in 1999. Because of this trend towards centralization, capital is now being allocated collectively in an extremely direct fashion by fund managers and not, as neo-classical theory assumes, by millions of unconnected individuals.

The second way that institutional investors are contributing to herd behaviour is in the way that they seem to increase the tendency of investors to ignore economic fundamentals and, instead, to observe and follow the behaviour of others. Important here is the fact that most fund managers are evaluated primarily on the basis of 'relative performance'; that is, they are penalized for under-performance in relation to the median fund while, at the same time, are not proportionately rewarded for over-performance. According to a 1997 report by the World Bank, this leads to trend-chasing behaviour because 'fund managers will follow the investment decisions of other fund managers in order to show clients that they know what they are doing. If they follow other fund managers' decisions and the investment turns out to be unprofitable, they are more likely to be thought of as unlucky than as unskilled, since other fund managers will have made the same mistake'.[3] Also important to the tendency of fund managers to ignore fundamentals are the costs and difficulties associated with the collection and analysis of fundamental information. As a result, observing the choices of others is often a cheap and helpful alternative to analysing economic fundamentals. The key here for fund managers is to buy and sell securities on the basis of price movements without assessing whether or not they are in response to underlying fundamentals.

Finally, institutional investors may also be increasing herd behaviour within the financial markets by contributing to the emergence of a professional investment community which more easily facilitates the diffusion and use of similar frameworks for evaluating economic fundamentals. As a 1993 report by the IMF argues, 'when fund managers share homogeneous perceptions about both the evolution of financial variables and the impact of news, the potential exists for new information to produce massive purchases and/or sales and sharp movements in prices'.[4] Two frameworks for evaluating fundamentals are important here. First, like much of the financial community, institutional investors seem to adhere to the 'Washington consensus' belief in the absolute virtues of free markets and sound money. This is despite the fact, as Krugman argues, that 'the empirical evidence for huge gains from free market policies is, at best, fuzzy'.[5] As a result, they tend to allocate their capital, collectively, towards those countries which are seen to be pursuing policies of free-market restructuring.

Second, institutional investors have a number of characteristics which cause them to evaluate fundamentals on the basis of short-term investment criteria.

Chief among these characteristics is the growing competition within the money-management industry and the pressures upon fund managers to attract and retain customers by ensuring that their funds perform strongly in the short term. As a recent report by the IMF notes, 'mutual funds need to meet performance standards over a very short time horizon, and open-ended funds face the risk of sizeable net redemptions if their quarterly performance lags behind the competition'.[6] Within the funds themselves, these competitive pressures have become formalized in institutional structures which, in turn, reinforce a short-term mentality among managers. The performance of most fund managers is evaluated on a quarterly basis, and some are even employed under 30–60 day contracts.

Overall, because of their promotion of centralization, herd instincts and the use of similar frameworks for evaluating economic fundamentals, the rise of institutional investors has served to increase short-term and herd behaviour within international financial markets. Short-term horizons mean that fund managers are much more prone to ignore economic fundamentals when deciding where to invest. And when they do, herd behaviour means that investors can all be moving in the same direction. Add these together and it becomes much more likely that financial markets will over-react to economic news and that asset prices will 'overshoot' the value that is justified by their underlying economic fundamentals.

The building of Thailand's bubble economy

After a decade of high growth based on large inflows of Japanese FDI, East Asian officials implemented a number of neo-liberal reforms designed to attract foreign portfolio and banking flows. In Thailand, exchange controls were abandoned and the domestic financial system was deregulated to reduce constraints on domestic banks (by loosening capital adequacy and 'fire-wall' regulations) and to open up the stock exchange to foreign investors. To attract banking flows, Thailand maintained higher interest rates (about 4–5 percentage points higher than US rates) and set up the Bangkok International Banking Facility (BIBF) to facilitate offshore borrowing by domestic corporations and finance companies. Finally, Thai officials adopted a 'dirty-float' pegged rate regime where the value of the *baht* was fixed to the US dollar within a very narrow band. As Walden Bello argues, the pegged rate was implemented in direct response to the demands of foreign institutional investors who, unlike foreign banks which made their loans in dollars, wanted guarantees to limit their exchange rate risk.[7]

Taken together, the combination of low interest rates in the developed countries and neo-liberal reforms and strong macroeconomic fundamentals in East Asian emerging markets led to large capital inflows from overseas institutional investors. As Yung Chul Park observed at the time, '[g]iven these sound economic fundamentals and the region's commitment to liberalization, bond market dealers, fund managers, and other institutional investors have seen enormous opportunities to make money and have been purchasing East Asian assets in large quantities'.[8] Following reforms to the Stock Exchange of Thailand (SET), net portfolio inflows rose from an average of $646 million between 1985 and 1989 to $5.5 billion in 1993, with net equity flows rising from $4 million in 1992 to over $3 billion in 1993. In fact, by 1993, foreign investors became the largest purchasers of shares on the SET with over half of net foreign equity investments coming from the USA.[9] Of further importance here is the rapid rise in the capitalization of the SET from $58 billion at the end of 1992 to over $130 billion by the end of 1993.

Large capital inflows contributed to the emergence of a speculative 'bubble', as rapidly rising asset prices sent inefficient signals to Thai corporations. Rising asset prices created the incentive for domestic companies to borrow in order to generate short-term profits through stock-market and real-estate speculation. As Bello notes, 'the promise of easy profits via speculation subverted the real economy as manufacturers in Thailand and the Philippines, instead of plowing their profits into upgrading their technology or skills of their workforce, gambled much of them in real estate and the stock market'.[10] Moreover, to take advantage of rising asset prices, companies borrowed money abroad either directly or via domestic banks and finance companies. Funnelled through the newly established BIBF, increasing bank inflows led to a rise in Thailand's external debt from $21 billion in 1988 to $89 billion ($66.2 billion of which was private debt) in 1996 in what became known as the 'carry trade'. By borrowing in Japan at 6–8 per cent interest rates and re-lending in Thailand at 14–20 per cent rates, foreign and Thai commercial banks were able to make enormous profits by arbitraging interest rate differentials. Through loans to domestic corporations and direct speculation by finance companies such as Finance One, banking inflows were channelled into stock-market and property speculation and this, in turn, served to further increase asset prices.

For proponents of the Washington consensus, East Asia's rapid build-up of dollar-denominated debt is explained by 'crony capitalism', that is, the implicit guarantees that governments extended to their domestic banks and to the way that this created a situation of 'moral hazard' which encouraged excessive lending by foreign banks.[11] According to this argument, the 'Asian model' of development was one where governments pursued state-directed industrial strategies by using commercial banks to channel high domestic savings to industry. In return for keeping interest rates low, governments made implicit guarantees to the banks that they would not be allowed to fail and it was these guarantees which altered the risk assessments of foreign lenders. However, despite being one of the early proponents of the 'crony capitalism-moral hazard' view, MIT economist Paul Krugman has since argued that:

> If one really takes [the moral hazard] argument seriously, it implies not only that there should be over-investment and excessive risk-taking by entrepreneurs with access to guaranteed finance, but also that the availability of implicit guarantees should tend to crowd out 'legitimate' investment that bears the full burden of risk. Yet as Radelet and Sachs point out, in the runup to the crisis all forms of investment in the emerging Asian economies were

booming, including direct foreign purchases of equity and real estate, investments that clearly were *not* protected by any form of implicit guarantee.[12]

In other words, the moral hazard argument is not supported by the evidence, as it fails to account for the large inflows of portfolio investment that were not covered by any implicit guarantees.[13]

If moral hazard is not the answer, how, then, can we explain the excessive accumulation of debt by East Asian companies? The argument suggested here is that large capital inflows by institutional investors in 1993 led to a positive overshooting of asset prices which initiated, and appeared to justify, a large increase in debt accumulation. Initial support for this view is found in balance-of-payments data provided by the IMF which shows that portfolio inflows into Thailand peaked in 1993, one year *before* the peak of banking inflows. Of further importance is the fact that between 1992 and 1993, when equity inflows rose from $4 million to a peak of over $3 billion, the capitalization of the SET more than doubled and the market-to-book value (an approximation of Tobin's q)[14] of Thai companies' assets rose from 141 per cent to a peak of 249 per cent. Therefore, as Michael Pomerleano at the World Bank argues, 'a possible implication is that the "exuberant" valuations in East Asia were associated with large portfolio equity inflows in an illiquid market. In such a situation, marginal flows might have had a disproportionate impact on valuations'.[15]

Following the rise in asset prices, Thai corporations began to borrow extensively and banking inflows more than doubled in 1994. Thus, it would seem that Thai corporations were willing to borrow so much because artificially rising asset prices increased the incentives to engage in stock and property speculation. They were also willing to borrow in dollars because a rapidly growing economy made Thailand's pegged exchange rate appear sustainable. Foreign banks were willing to lend because of the enormous profits offered by the 'carry trade' and because rising asset prices and high growth made borrowers' underlying fundamentals seem sounder than they actually were. In terms of rising asset prices, Pomerleano suggests that:

> The findings finally offer a plausible explanation for the rapid capital expenditures in Asian economies. They suggest that there were dominant market signals stimulating rapid capital formation in the Asian economies, and a possible exit strategy through the equity market. In this context, it is notable as well that the peak of Tobin's q in Asia occurs around 1993–94, a period associated with large portfolio equity inflows.[16]

As bank loans flowed into Thailand, they were channelled by corporations and finance companies into the real-estate and stock markets in the hope of realizing quick returns. Banking inflows led to further rises in asset prices which then justified further loans in the manner of a speculative bubble. As Krugman notes, the 'overpricing of assets was sustained in part by a sort of circular process, in which the proliferation of risky lending drove up the prices of risky assets, making the financial condition of the intermediaries seem sounder than it was'.[17] As a result, as Bello notes, the 'fundamentals of borrowers were often ignored in favour of what many investors and lenders saw as the real collateral or guarantee that they would eventually get a high rate of return from their investments, which was the 8–10 per cent growth rate of the country'.[18]

1996 not 1997: the onset of the Asian crisis

To the extent that rising asset prices seemed to justify rising debt loads, proponents of the 'financial panic' explanation argue that the crisis which began in mid-1997 was not the result of any fundamental imbalances but rather was caused by a self-fulfilling panic by creditors. As evidence for this view, Radelet and Sachs argue that leading macroeconomic indicators did not lead market participants to expect a crisis. To demonstrate this point, they note that '[o]ne of the most unusual aspects of the Asian crisis is the extent to which it was unpredicted by market participants and markets analysts ... [and, as a result] ... capital inflows remained strong through 1996, and in most cases till mid 1997'.[19] While fundamentals did not seem to point to the onset of a crisis, Radelet and Sachs agree that they did show an emerging zone of vulnerability. Important here was the appreciation of the US dollar following a 1995 agreement between Japan and the USA to boost Japanese exports. As the dollar appreciated, it constituted a negative shock for Thailand's pegged, and now rising, exchange rate, which began to produce a number of dislocations for domestic companies. First, as the *baht* rose with the dollar, Thai exports declined to the extent that, in 1996, there was zero growth, down from 21 per cent in 1994 and 24 per cent in 1995. With exports declining, the current-account deficit rose sharply by 5 per cent in 1996 to 8.2 per cent of GDP.

For Radelet and Sachs, 'these signs seemed merely to suggest growing imbalances and the need for a modest adjustment, but not an impending major crisis'.[20] Instead, they argue that the crisis occurred because of certain 'triggering events' which led short-term creditors to expect the flight of other short-term creditors. In the case of Thailand, both Finance One and the Samprasong Land Company defaulted on interest payments to foreign borrowers in early 1997. As creditors became aware of growing financial fragility, they worried that if the government devalued the currency there would be an explosion in the size of Thailand's dollar-denominated debt. When the devaluation did occur, so the argument goes, it created a self-fulfilling crisis as creditors pulled out, the currency continued to depreciate and this, in turn, led to a further deterioration in the balance sheets of companies and financial institutions.

The key problem with the 'financial panic' explanation is that it ignores the role played by institutional investors and the fact that leading indicators did point to the onset of a crisis. As Radelet and Sachs themselves note: 'Stock prices provide the only indication of growing concern among market participants in the months preceding the crisis. The Thai stock market fell continuously after January 1996, a full 18 months before the crisis began.'[21] Specifically, when the appreciation of the *baht* led to a sharp rise in the current-account deficit, fund managers began to sense the potential for a devaluation. Again, Radelet and Sachs themselves note that the 'biggest warnings came in Thailand, where the expectations of currency depreciation grew markedly in 1996 and early 1997'.[22] For foreign creditors who had made loans in dollars, the small potential for a currency depreciation was not much to worry about as long as Thai corporations continued to appear solvent – and the point is, they did continue to look solvent until fund managers, who were subject to exchange rate risk, reallocated their portfolios and precipitated a sharp fall in the SET and the property market.

As asset prices began to decline, so too did the balance sheets of companies with large investments in the stock and real-estate markets, and this, in turn, led to a vicious circle of asset depreciation. Commenting on these developments, Krugman notes that the collapse of the Thai asset bubble 'involved the same circular process in reverse: falling asset prices made the insolvency of intermediaries visible, forcing them to cease operations, leading to further asset deflation'.[23] With the default announcements by Finance One and Samprasong Land in January of 1997, devaluation expectations increased further and set in motion the chain of events that led to the devaluation in July. With asset prices declining (leading to a rise in debt/equity ratios), foreign banks began to worry about the ability of borrowers to repay their loans. Then, as Bello notes, '[t]he scent of panic attracted speculators who sought to make profits...on the baht's eventual devaluation'.[24] Hedge funds, such as George Soros' Quantum Fund, began to sell the *baht* short in large quantities.[25] While the Bank of Thailand managed to temporarily defend the currency by running down its foreign-exchange reserves, it was forced to throw in the towel and let the *baht* float in the face of renewed speculative pressures in late June. The devaluation of the *baht* then initiated a run on the currency as foreign creditors pulled out *en masse*.

Just as a pull-out by institutional investors helped to initiate the devaluation in Thailand, so too did they seem to play a role in transmitting the crisis throughout the region. While circumstances varied across countries, the fundamental dynamics of high debt supported by a bubble in asset prices do seem to have been present in most of the other affected countries. As Krugman reveals, 'in all of the afflicted countries there was a boom-bust cycle in the asset markets that *preceded* the currency crisis: stock and land prices soared, then plunged'.[26] In a similar fashion to Thailand, Malaysian equity markets began to fall sharply in March 1997 with banking inflows remaining strong until the devaluation in Thailand. Moreover, as the IMF reports, '[t]he initial pressure on the [Malaysian *ringgit*] appears to have emanated from institutional investors closing out long equity positions, reflecting their concern that the stock market was overvalued'.[27]

Policy implications

Taken as whole, institutional investors do seem to have played a greater role in the 1997 East Asian crisis than the current literature would suggest. As Krugman has concluded, 'the Asian story is really about a bubble in and subsequent collapse of asset values in general, with the currency crises more a symptom than a cause of this underlying real ... malady'.[28] Therefore, if herding by foreign institutional investors, rather than moral hazard and/or financial panic among banks, was the key cause of the crisis, what are the implications for governance and policy at the national, regional and global levels?

Given that mainstream explanations of currency crises tend to focus primarily upon policy blunders by individual governments, it is not surprising that their recommendations for preventing crises focus primarily on the need for domestic-level reforms. At the national level, the key preventive measures being discussed focus on efforts to improve the quality of credit allocation. Important here are proposals for improved balance sheet transparency by Asian corporations and domestic banks as well as improved capital adequacy standards and bank supervision.

While all of these proposals are necessary, they may not be sufficient to prevent crises which are characterized by the emergence of asset price bubbles. Improving transparency rests on the assumption that for market discipline to work, investors and creditors must have accurate information. Proponents of this approach argue that improving balance-sheet transparency combined with greater capital-adequacy standards and bank supervision would prevent the build-up of excessive debt as lenders would know the true balance-sheet picture of their borrowers and would ration credit when it became excessive. Improved transparency, it is believed, would also remove the information asymmetries which give rise to herding behaviour among creditors and investors.

There are two problems with this view. First, in the case of a speculative bubble, for example, the problem is not that lenders are unaware of borrowers' debt/equity ratios but rather that these ratios are artificially lowered as a bubble in asset prices emerges. Second, herd behaviour is not solely due to a lack of transparency and information about relevant economic fundamentals. In fact, the problem is not that investors and creditors are without the relevant information about economic fundamentals but rather that they often tend to ignore it given their need to meet short-term performance pressures. In other words, herd behaviour is intrinsic to institutional investors themselves and not solely due to any lack of available information.

Recognizing that herd behaviour has more to do with international investors and creditors than with domestic borrowers implies a need for international regulation to reduce herd behaviour as well as domestic and regional measures to insulate countries from this behaviour. It is useful here for countries and regional institutions to recognize that, in times of crisis, capital controls may be necessary to impose a calming period on investors, to prevent the kind of herd behaviour that can lead to financial contagion. But an even better option than restrictions on capital outflows may be restrictions on inflows, particularly of short-term capital, in order to prevent the emergence of speculative bubbles in the first place. Possibly the best example here is the capital inflow tax imposed by Chile.[29] For many years, Chile has required that all non-equity capital inflows must be accompanied by a one-year, non-interest-bearing deposit where the costs of withdrawal decrease over time. The effect of these taxes is to discourage a reliance upon short-term inflows which, in turn, limits the potential for massive out-flows. The fact that Chile remained relatively unscathed in the aftermath of the 1994 Mexican *peso* crisis would seem to lend support to this option.

A further national and regional-level mechanism to reduce the potential for massive, herd-like, capital outflows is for governments to encourage investors to insure themselves (or hedge) against exchange-rate risk and, thus, to reduce the potential for herd behaviour when currencies come under downward pressure. Floating, rather than fixed, exchange rates are one way to encourage hedging. As Eichengreen notes, '[e]xchange rate flexibility will encourage banks and corpora-tions to hedge their foreign exposure, enhancing their ability to withstand unex-pectedly large exchange rate changes'.[30] Another, more direct, method is for governments to require mandatory (static) hedging of exchange-rate risk by mak-ing hedges a term of issue for government bonds.

In addition to these measures for insulating economies from herd behaviour among investors, there is a need for action at the global level and within the devel-oped countries which are the primary source of portfolio flows for emerging mar-kets. In particular, developed country governments and the IFIs need to reform the international financial architecture so as to reduce investor herding in the first place. One important step here, proposed by Stephany Griffith-Jones, is the imple-mentation of risk-weighted cash requirements on institutional investors.[31] Similar to the international capital-adequacy standards currently applied to banks, institu-tional investors would be required to retain risk-weighted cash reserves in the form of interest-bearing deposits in commercial banks as a capital charge. Under this pro-posal, risk-weighting would be determined by new standards for risk analysis devel-oped through consultations between the industry and the regulatory authorities. Risk-weighted cash requirements would reduce the pressures on institutions to sell assets in a declining market when faced with redemptions by individual investors.

To reinforce this measure, the IFIs need to consult with the fund-management industry to find ways to limit the pressures for herd behaviour resulting from short-term and relative performance evaluations. For example, governments could make use of tax incentives and regulations to encourage investment companies to adopt longer-term evaluation periods for fund managers. Using similar methods, it would also be useful to encourage investment companies to avoid evaluating and paying their fund managers on the basis of relative performance. In fact, a case exists for governments to mandate a system where fund managers are paid solely on their ability to deliver absolute returns. In each case, reforms will be most likely and effective when government regulation is complemented by industry participa-tion. And, as always, threats of the former will help to encourage the latter.

Notes

1. This chapter draws on a larger article on the role of institutional investors in recent currency crises; see A. Harmes, 'Institutional Investors and Polanyi's Double Movement: a Model of Contemporary Currency Crises', *Review of International Political Economy*, 8, 3 (2001).

2. OECD, *Institutional Investors Statistical Yearbook 1997* (Paris: OECD, 1997), p.9.
3. World Bank, *Private Flows to Developing Countries: the Road to Financial Integration* (New York: Oxford University Press, 1997), p.126.
4. IMF, *International Capital Markets, Part I: Exchange Rate Management and International Capital Flows* (Washington DC: IMF, 1993), p.20.
5. P. Krugman, 'Dutch Tulips and Emerging Markets', *Foreign Affairs* (July–August 1995), p.32.
6. IMF, *International Capital Flows: Developments, Prospects, and Policy Issues* (Washington DC: IMF, 1994), p.18.
7. W. Bello, 'The End of a "Miracle": Speculation, Foreign Capital Dependence and the Collapse of the Southeast Asian Economies', *Multinational Monitor*, 19, 1–2(1998), pp.10–17.
8. Y.C. Park, 'East Asian Liberalization, Bubbles, and the Challenge from China', *Brookings Papers on Economic Activity*, 2 (1995), p.361.
9. M. Tang and J. Villafuerte, *Capital Flows to Asian and Pacific Developing Countries: Recent Trends and Finance Prospects* (Manila: Asian Development Bank, 1995).
10. Bello (1998), p.15.
11. On the moral hazard view of the East Asian crisis, see P. Krugman, 'What happened to Asia?' (Mimeograph, January 1998); G. Corsetti, P. Pesenti and N. Roubini, 'Paper Tigers?: a Preliminary Assessment of the Asian Crisis', (Mimeograph, 1998).
12. P. Krugman, 'Balance Sheets, the Transfer Problem, and Financial Crises', (Mimeograph, January 1999), p.6.
13. On this critique of the 'moral hazard' argument, see S. Radelet and J. Sachs, 'The Onset of the East Asian Financial Crisis', Mimeograph, Harvard Institute for International Development, 30 March 1998.
14. Tobin's q equals the market value of a firm's shares and long-term debt divided by the value of its real capital. It is a similar measure to that of market-to-book value.
15. M. Pomerleano, 'The East Asia Crisis and Corporate Finances: the Untold Micro Story', (Washington DC: World Bank Group, Mimeograph, 1999).
16. Ibid., p.22.
17. Krugman (1998).
18. W. Bello, 'Asian Financial Crisis: the Movie', *Ecologist*, 29, 1(1999), p.29.
19. Bello (1998), p.10.
20. Radelet and Sachs, p.13.
21. Ibid., p.12.
22. Ibid., p.17.
23. Krugman (1998), p.3.
24. Bello (1998), p.14.
25. G. Soros, *The Crisis of Global Capitalism: Open Society Endangered* (London: Little, Brown and Company, 1998).
26. Krugman (1998), p.3.
27. B. Eichengreen and D. Mathieson, 'Hedge Funds and Financial Market Dynamics', (Washington DC: IMF, Occasional Paper, 1998), p.19.
28. Krugman (1998), p.3.
29. See the next chapter for an account of the Chilean *encaje* system.
30. B. Eichengreen, *Towards a New International Financial Architecture: a Practical Post-Asia Agenda* (Washington DC: Institute for International Economics, 1999), p.10.
31. S. Griffith-Jones, *Global Capital Flows: Should They Be Regulated?* (London: Macmillan Press [now Palgrave Macmillan], 1998).

8
The Case for Regional and Global Financial Regulation

Marco Mezzera, Kamal Malhotra and Mümtaz Keklik

The 'pros' and 'cons' of unregulated capital flows

The conventional wisdom

The unregulated flow of capital is facilitated through capital-account convertibility at the national level. This implies the unimpeded inflow and outflow of capital and the 'freedom to convert local financial assets into foreign financial assets and vice versa at market determined rates of exchange'.[1]

The capital account, together with the current account, determines the balance of payments of a country. An essential difference between the two is that transactions on the capital account necessarily involve domestic residents either acquiring or surrendering claims on foreigners, whereas transactions on the current account do not. Capital-account transactions can therefore involve changes to the ownership of the national capital and assets of a country with far-reaching implications for its economy. Moreover, unlike trade, components of the capital account, with the exception of some FDI flows, are inherently subject to asymmetric information, agency problems and adverse selection.[2]

Capital-account liberalization (CAL) was one of the key components of IMF and World Bank structural adjustment programmes in the 1980s and 1990s,[3] despite the fact that 'convertibility of these payments is neither an immediate requirement of membership, nor an eventual objective'.[4] On the contrary, Article VI of the IMF's Articles of Agreement, with more specific references to capital transfers, permits (within limits) usage of capital controls, and gives the Fund permission to request a member country to impose capital controls in order to prevent the use of funds from its General Resources Account in the event of a large or sustained capital flight.[5] Notwithstanding this provision and the lessons of the Asian crisis, 'the IMF's policy-making Interim Committee agreed that full convertibility for capital transactions should become the ultimate objective for all Fund members' in September 1997.[6] CAL was then made 'one of the central purposes of the Fund',[7] although this remains controversial and unimplemented. (The IMF was not the only international agency promoting CAL. It is worth remembering that prior to the 1994 crisis Mexico's application for membership of the OECD in 1993 was made contingent on the elimination of all restrictions on capital movements.)[8]

In order to grasp more clearly the issues at stake in the ongoing debate on CAL, it may be useful to describe more fully both the conceptual rationale for it and the actual experience with capital and exchange controls. The case for exchange controls has repeatedly emphasized that the preservation of a country's national autonomy may well depend on them. The history of exchange controls since World War II indicates that they emerged largely in response to the inability of standard exchange-rate regimes to ensure balance-of-payments stability in countries faced with excessive deficits, debts, inflation triggered by the depreciation of the national currency, or capital flight. Neither a fixed nor a flexible exchange-rates regime had proved successful in regulating international financial markets. Controls were developed to correct these imbalances. As the post-1945 experience of the principal market economies suggests, the nature of these imbalances varied according to the exchange-rate regime. At the beginning of the 1970s, the system of fixed exchange rates was abandoned in favour of a floating regime. As outlined in the previous chapters, in a system of fixed exchange rates, the defence of parities leads central banks to making substantial use of currency reserves, which tends to stimulate private capital speculation. On the other hand, in a system of flexible exchange rates, an upward revaluation of the national currency could worsen the current-account deficit and prompt speculative capital movements. Where exchange-rate regimes permit the development of significant imbalances, restrictions on capital-account convertibility appear to be the only means at the disposal of a country intent on preserving the autonomy of its policy-making processes and institutions. This is especially true of a country whose currency does not play a significant role in the international monetary system.

Exchange controls, which also developed to promote domestic policies, were premised on the view that the state needs to assume responsibility for key decisions on the level of investment and saving, the allocation of investment among competing uses, and the general distribution of income. They were also based on widespread agreement that a reliance on the market mechanism, given its inherent imperfections, could not assure high growth rates and other societal objectives. The financial system, it was felt, should be subordinated to the needs of production in order to promote growth, and capital controls introduced to avoid the risk of capital flight and loss of national autonomy.

Responding to the experience of such regulatory policies, a number of studies in the 1970s[9] on the 'different forms of controls on foreign exchange transactions in eleven developing countries, provided the basis for arguments in favor of economic liberalization in developing countries, what has been referred to as the Washington Consensus or the neo-liberal framework'.[10] The main proponents of this view argued that free movement of capital would produce a better global allocation of resources, namely a shift of resources from capital-rich to capital-poor countries.[11] Market interventions, the argument ran, distort market equilibrium and are inefficient and ineffective in maximizing welfare. Market imperfections, the argument went on, pointed not so much to the deficiencies of the model but to the need to define the appropriate liberalization path.

This view gained wide currency during the 1980s. With structural adjustment programmes ascendant, mainstream literature argued that the problems surrounding CAL could be resolved simply by adopting an appropriate sequence of implementation measures. Given a set of ideal initial conditions, in particular stable domestic policies and a reasonably developed process of trade liberalization, the desired outcome, it was argued, could be easily attained by following a predetermined liberalization path.[12]

In theoretical terms, this analysis is a logical extension of models built to devise optimal sequencing paths. Its emphasis on correct timing and sequencing leads it to advocate fiscal prudence and consolidation, and the need to bring inflation down to single digits, maintain sustainable current-account deficits and reserve positions after complete trade liberalization, and strengthen prudential regulation and bank supervision. Transactions on the capital account are to be fully liberalized only after all the previous measures have been implemented.

The conventional vision of free capital flows rests, therefore, on a set of hypothetical advantages which expected to derive from a financially liberalized regime:

1. 'For borrowers, capital inflows to augment domestic savings to finance higher rates of investment ... thereby boosting GDP growth';[13]
2. a reduction of investor vulnerability to domestic shocks, with investment portfolios diversified by targeting international financial assets; and
3. improvements in the quality of international financial assets as a consequence of greater liquidity and increased competition in financial markets.

Other arguments highlighting the negative impact of capital controls focused on the prospects of evasion and corruption. While evasion can be considered a widespread reaction to extensive regulations and restrictions, the case of corruption was recently highlighted in the *Economist*: 'Latin America's controls in the 1980s ... helped to feed corruption, as bureaucrats were empowered to determine who would be exempted from them'.[14] The argument here is that capital controls benefit special-interest groups able to wield effective political influence and the government bureaucrats who administer them. In connecting capital controls to rent-seeking, this criticism closely resembles the case made against other forms of government intervention in the economy.

Contrary to the expectations of economic neo-liberals, the recurring financial crises that followed CAL have all been characterized by supply-led capital inflows. The Asian crisis in particular shook the foundations of the neo-liberal economic model, and even some of its theorists began to acknowledge that the financial market is far from perfect and may contain intrinsic speculative and destabilizing tendencies.

The real disadvantages of CAL have since received much greater attention, as a result of which a number of important conclusions have emerged. Capital mobility has the potential to cause financial crises when it encourages short-term, rapidly reversible flows. CAL can lead to herding behaviour by market participants, and such irrational responses can, in turn, lead to excessive inflows of capital, which far exceed an emerging market's capacity to invest them productively at reasonable risk. As a consequence, borrowing countries become highly vulnerable to shifts in market sentiment. Excessive inflows may be followed by excessive outflows which bear little relation to the economic fundamentals of the country concerned.[15]

Indeed, there is good reason to suggest that the medium- and long-term fundamentals of the economy[16] may become distorted as a result of large inflows of foreign capital. Even where economic fundamentals remain strong, the general perception of the deleterious impact of large current-account deficits makes a country highly vulnerable to speculative attacks. Finally, attempts to finance current-account deficits by reliance on foreign funds raises the question of the composition and relative volume of different kinds of capital inflows and whether or not these flows are responsive to short-term swings in market expectations.[17]

Notwithstanding the increasing recognition among mainstream analysts that corrections need to be introduced in the way financial markets operate, they remain extremely reluctant to question the overall liberalization model. For more fundamental objections to financial liberalization, one has to turn to the arguments and analytical frameworks of Keynesians and Structuralist-Marxist development economists.

Challenging mainstream views

Advocates of external financial liberalization rely on neo-classical assumptions, namely that unfettered markets work perfectly, and that economic agents are fully rational in their expectations and preferences.[18] Keynesian and Structuralist-Marxist interpretations, on the other hand, propose the empirically well-tested thesis that markets are inherently imperfect, and challenge the notion that price formation, especially in financial markets, can be adequately understood as 'outcome of actions of a multitude of individual economic agents whose [collective] behaviour is assumed to be based on … utility maximization and rational behaviour'.[19]

Financial markets have inherent imperfections, notably asymmetric information, moral hazard and adverse selection. Price formation, especially in the case of highly mobile short-term capital, driven by speculative pressures, creates additional volatility in domestic financial markets. The objection to a global CAL model rests, therefore, on the firm belief that the current international financial system is prone to substantial instability. These destabilizing tendencies, if permitted to operate freely in the system, are likely to undermine the 'degree of control governments have over national economic policy making' and 'result in asymmetric adjustment burdens'.[20] The recent Asian experience points very much in this direction.

Many Keynesian analysts appear reconciled to the inevitability of global integration of financial markets in the long run but remain committed to the need for permanent regulatory mechanisms. Given that financial markets are intrinsically prone to co-ordination failures, they conclude that integration of developing economies into the global financial system can only be gradual. The state is seen as needing to regain leadership 'over the international flow of money' which it has lost to TNCs, in order 'to achieve sustained full employment and greater equality of income and wealth'. In this context, 'capital controls can help alter the current class configuration of economic and political *power*,[21] in support of policies of full employment, public investment, credit allocation, and income redistribution. A close look at past and existing exchange and capital control regimes suggests that these are on the whole imposed by countries which wish to preserve their national autonomy but do not believe that reliance on the market mechanism can guarantee such autonomy. One of the main positive effects of capital controls is precisely that they effectively limit the capacity of investors to create financial (as well as social and political) disarray in an economy by pulling out huge amounts of short-term capital. Even more importantly, they increase a national government's policy autonomy and the range of options available to it in selecting economic instruments to deal with crisis situations.

The common objection, that by restricting capital flows developing countries are likely to deprive themselves of a vital source of development finance, does not stand up to scrutiny. From a development perspective, the quality of private capital flows to developing countries has been poor. Such flows have rarely been invested for sustainable development purposes, and their essential short-term and volatile nature has frequently caused economic instability instead of the expected long-term economic growth. Furthermore, the flow of capital is a two-way process which in the case of developing countries often results in net negative or at best marginally positive transfers.

If any package of macroeconomic policies is to counterbalance current neo-liberal orthodoxy and safeguard the ability of states to follow independent development paths, capital controls must be considered a necessary though not sufficient condition. Agrarian reform, progressive taxation, and public investment for employment creation will also play an important part.

By contrast, Structuralist-Marxist perspectives, all too cursorily summarized here, are *a priori* opposed to the global integration of trade and financial markets. They equate mainstream efforts to redesign the global financial architecture with uncritical acceptance of the same capitalist development model that has for centuries dictated the rules of the market and militated against appropriate development in both developing and industrialized countries. The only possible alternative to that model, they conclude, lies in de-linking national economies from international markets, and in their profound restructuring by the state. There is no room here for free international capital flows. In order to break the international stranglehold of 'Washington Consensus policies' the Bretton Woods and similar institutions, it is argued, must be abolished. The proposed alternative is predicated on a profound restructuring of both the global and national economies, with priority given to the interests of labour, the poor and other marginalized and socially excluded groups. Important in this context have been the contributions of Raul Prebisch, Andre Gunder Frank and other Latin American economists and 'dependency theorists' as well as the more recent work of Prabhat Patnaik, Jayati Ghosh, CP Chandrasekhar and their associates at the School of Economic Studies and Planning at Jawaharlal Nehru University in India.

To summarize, there are four key interrelated arguments against the complete liberalization of the capital account. First, some of the fundamental assumptions of CAL advocates are open to question. The relationship between economic growth and CAL is, in some cases, negative[22] and the volatility factor makes recovery difficult in times of crisis.

Secondly, CAL makes it more difficult for governments to manage the economy and design social (including poverty-reduction) policies, in both good and bad times. It encourages capital inflows into already vulnerable bond and equity markets and the banking sector, imposing serious constraints on a government's freedom of action. This, coupled with the risk of a sudden exit of footloose capital, continues to deprive national budgets of important tax revenues.[23] Capital controls and regulations, through such market-based measures as taxes or reserve requirements, can provide a useful source of government revenue. During financial booms, as Ocampo observes, tax controls on financial flows strengthen the capacity of governments to manage their economy without excessive borrowing.[24]

Thirdly, financial instability and volatility are generally caused by large capital flows from source countries, namely the most powerful industrialized countries. It follows that financial reporting, regulation and supervision in developing countries do not offer a sustainable solution. Controls on capital inflows and outflows, which complement debt standstills, are helpful and needed.[25]

Fourthly, CAL has been advocated and implemented in developing countries despite the absence of any adequate international financial safety mechanism. In these circumstances, and in the absence of fast access to adequate emergency financing, developing countries have little or nothing to gain and much to lose by surrendering the autonomy of their decision-making processes.[26] If at all accurate, the preceding analysis points to the urgency of global financial reform, to which we now turn our attention.

Reforming the global financial system: Official responses

In the wake of the Russian, Brazilian and Asian financial crises, the international community responded with a wide range of proposals to reform the global financial system. The nuances in the ideas put forward have been many, but only a few of them have addressed structural issues. What follows is a brief outline of some of the more significant reform proposals to have emerged in recent years.

The US official position

Perhaps the most influential position has been that officially advanced by the United States, which attributes the crises to a lack of transparency and the suffocating role of crony capitalism in the crisis-prone countries. The proposed solution has centred on domestic governance reform with an emphasis on transparency and information provision to financial markets. Deregulation and privatization have been advanced as necessary instruments for the creation of more efficient markets. In this context, IMF packages became the most convenient vehicles for reform, the most important element of which was strategic banking reform centred on the implementation of prudential norms, in particular the adoption by developing countries of the Basel Core Principles for Effective Banking Supervision.[27]

President Clinton called for the international financial architecture to be adapted to the needs of the twenty-first century,[28] while Treasury Secretary, Robert Rubin, elaborated the contours of such reform by reference to key areas:[29] increased openness in the international financial system; strengthened national financial systems; more soundly based capital flows in industrial nations; and new ways to respond to crises,[30] with a greater role envisioned for the private sector in the creation of rescue packages.

Despite the advocacy of reform, the US position, as presented by Robert Rubin, may best be characterized as minor plumbing, rather than substantive reorganization. Indeed, he specifically warned against broad controls on capital movements, arguing that 'short-term speculative capital flows have played a relatively small part in what happened in the current crisis'.[31] During the World Economic Forum meeting in Davos in January 1999, Rubin restated his position in favour of financial liberalization, explicitly challenging the view that hedge funds had been a significant factor in the financial crisis.[32] Federal Reserve Chairman, Alan Greenspan, also expressed his opposition to domestic controls on hedge funds, arguing during Congressional hearings in October 1998 that such restrictive measures would merely drive hedge funds offshore, thereby placing them beyond any control.

European positions

European policy-makers and officials have tended to argue more forcefully in favour of the regulation of global financial flows. Reflecting a more general European challenge to US unilateralism, the French Foreign Minister, Hubert Vedrine, in an interview with *Libération* at the end of 1998, launched an assault on American policy, which subsequently attracted the open support of Prime Minister Lionel Jospin and President Jacques Chirac. The French initiative called for strengthened multilateral structures and rules, and was openly critical of US unilateralism. Although it drew attention to all the main global power structures, IFIs were its principal focus. Vedrine advocated urgent IMF reform to bring the institution 'more directly under the political control of member governments so as to minimize what is perceived here as the organization's role as an instrument of American influence'.[33] France's position found resonance in Japan's similar calls for IFI reform.

Germany's first Finance Minister in the Social Democratic-Green alliance, Oskar Lafontaine, put forward an innovative proposal for the creation of target zones for the three major currencies: the US dollar, the *yen* and the euro. The initiative, supported by French and Japanese authorities but opposed by the United States, came to an abrupt end with Lafontaine's resignation about one month later. Germany's position thereafter became much tamer. When asked to pass judgment on US unilateralism during an appearance before the French National Assembly's Foreign Affairs Commission, Foreign Minister Joschka Fischer refused to offer any critical comment.[34]

Among the three most influential European attitudes to reform, the British position continues to be the closest to Washington's official position. It is perhaps no coincidence that Tony Blair's 'third way' approach to globalization was enthusiastically embraced by former President Bill Clinton. According to this new political doctrine, a policy framework should be created to manage recent changes in the global order and 'produce solidarity and prosperity'. The 'third way' portrayed itself as the middle point between 'the old left [that] resisted that change' and 'the new right [that] did not want to manage it'.[35] In the words of Tony Blair's intellectual guide, Anthony Giddens, the 'third way is an attempt to transcend both old-style social democracy and neo-liberalism'.[36] To many critics, however, the 'third way' had all the appearances of neo-liberalism disguised in new clothes.

The British application of 'third way' principles to the global financial system was, at best, incrementally reformist. Tony Blair's initial calls for an overhaul of the Bretton Woods institutions[37] were soon reformulated, involving little more than minor adjustments to a few regulating mechanisms. More radical solutions, including the imposition of national capital controls, were either ignored or openly criticized.

More importantly, any serious questioning of the finance and trade liberalization agenda was studiously avoided. Echoing the US Administration's proposals, New Labour, if anything, conferred an even more powerful role on the major IFIs. The Chancellor of the Exchequer, Gordon Brown, stated: 'the challenge we face is not to weaken support for the IMF and World Bank and other international institutions...but to strengthen them by building the operational rules and institutional architecture for the new global financial system'.[38] The only concession made to the predominant role of these institutions was the call 'for a new and permanent Standing Committee for Global Financial Regulation'. The proposal, however, envisaged little more than a common framework to enable 'the IMF, the World Bank, the Basel Committee, and other international regulatory groupings to focus on global financial stability and supervision'.[39] The proposed committee evolved half a year later into the Financial Stability Forum discussed later in this chapter.

In a set of new proposals, Gordon Brown called for 'agreement on codes of conduct...a new IMF surveillance unit,...and a new approach to crisis prevention'.[40] Of these, the proposal empowering the IMF 'to assess publicly how well countries are doing in implementing [the] new rules of the game'[41] fits perfectly with what Gill calls the process of 'new constitutionalism'.[42] As Gill argues, 'efforts to define appropriate "sound" policy, for example by strengthening surveillance mechanisms of international organizations', form part of the neo-liberal strategy of governments (and international institutions) to 'operate as facilitators of...market values and market discipline'.[43] The net effect of such a strategy is to entrench the forced separation of the economic from the political realm.

The G7 response

Although surrounded by an aura of international legitimacy, the initiatives undertaken by the G7 have been remarkably similar to the US reform agenda. An ironic consequence of this is that the IMF became the pivot around which every G7 initiative concerning global financial architecture reform has since revolved.

The idea of a $90 billion fund, announced by President Clinton in late October 1998, was the first tangible G7 proposal. This contingency line of credit was conceived by G7 technocrats as a way of avoiding a recurrence of financial contagion of the kind witnessed during the Asian crisis. The intention was to provide the IMF with the necessary means to perform its role of lender of last resort.

The G7 does not appear to have anticipated that an application for such credit would immediately make that country a high credit risk in the eyes of credit-rating agencies and private financial markets, and that such a fund could trigger practices of moral hazard. Various analysts could not but be struck by the initiative's apparent failure to take account of these possible ramifications. Chossudovsky described the G7 proposal as 'the biggest financial scam of the post-war era',[44] and a 'convenient safety net for the institutional speculator', or another device 'to bail out speculators'.[45]

Disappointingly, this has, thus far, been the G7's most concrete proposal. In dealing with the controversial hedge fund issue, the G7 has limited itself to calling for closer examination of the implications arising from the operations of leveraged international finance organizations, including hedge funds and off-shore institutions, and encouraging offshore centres to comply with internationally agreed standards.[46]

In June 1999, the G7 finance ministers confirmed a previous commitment to reserve for the IMF a 'central role in the international economic and financial system'.[47] The IMF was encouraged to extend its mandate to set standards in a whole range of areas: reform of IFIs; transparency and accountability; and macro-economic policies. The report also advocated a greater role for the Fund in crisis prevention. This was expected to occur mainly through the IMF's newly created Contingent Credit Line (CCL) and through the imposition of wide-ranging lending conditionalities.

The creation of the Financial Stability Forum (FSF) and the Group of 20 have so far been the main contributions of the G7 to global financial architecture reform. The FSF was first proposed by the president of Germany's Bundesbank, Hans Tietmeyer, and approved at a meeting in Bonn of G7 finance ministers on 20 February 1999. Its constituency remains primarily G7 central bankers, finance ministry officials and regulators, and representatives from the World Bank, the IMF and the Bank for International Settlements (BIS). Notwithstanding the later addition of Hong Kong's and Singapore's central bankers, a disappointing aspect of the Forum remains the complete exclusion of developing countries.

The FSF proposes 'to assess the issues and vulnerabilities affecting the global financial system and to identify and oversee the actions needed to address them'.[48] In pursuit of this ambitious agenda, it chose, during its first meeting in April 1999, to concentrate on three main issues (highly leveraged institutions, offshore centres, and short-term capital flows). It created three working groups whose task would be to: study ways to reduce the destabilizing potential of highly leveraged institutions (HLIs); evaluate measures in borrower and creditor countries aimed at reducing the volatility of capital flows; and evaluate the impact of offshore financial centres on global financial stability and the progress being made in enforcing international prudential standards.[49]

Notwithstanding the great expectations vested by the G7 in the FSF, especially in terms of providing an early warning system for future world financial crises, its means remain rather modest. To begin with, it meets infrequently and its sanction power relies exclusively on peer pressure. As of 2001 the ability of the three working groups to play a significant role in reforming the global financial architecture remained at best questionable.[50] Another major problem was clearly identified in UNCTAD's *Trade and Development Report 2001*. The various codes and standards established through institutions such as the IMF, BIS, and the FSF

> not only for the financial sector itself, but also in respect of macroeconomic policy and policy regarding disclosure ... will not contribute to financial stability, and in many cases will involve substantial initial costs. *Moreover, the programmes required of recipient countries are wide-ranging and do not always accommodate differences in levels of development and the availability of human resources.*[51]

As for international codes and standards, like all other proposals emanating from states and international institutions located in the North, they tend to generate new obligations and are premised on the assumption that the main flaws of the system lie with recipient countries. Conveniently for the North, the burden of adjustment should be borne by the South. Yet, it may well be the industrialized countries which are the major source of financial instability.[52]

Issues in control and regulation

Numerous suggestions have been made for enhancing regulation of the international financial system. We begin with a brief survey of the issues involved before examining key proposals and the debates to which they have given rise.

Banking regulation and prudential norms

Nationally, regulators typically require banks to hold a certain amount of their capital in reserve. Internationally, the Basel Capital Accord of 1988 establishes a similar principle, suggesting that international banks hold a reserve ratio of 8 per cent. A higher proportion is recommended in the case of riskier investments.

While the Accord has been continually adapting over the years to changing circumstances, serious shortcomings still exist. To give one example, financial innovations of various kinds may have made it easier during the Asian financial crisis for banks to take greater risks without being subject to greater capital charges. Similarly, more rigorous standards may have encouraged banks in industrialized countries to make short- rather than long-term loans to banks in emerging markets.

In the new global environment the Basel standards (and banking regulation in general) raise several difficult questions. The original Basel Capital Accord was designed for banks in G10 industrialized nations (comprising central bankers from the G7, the Netherlands, Sweden and Switzerland). As indicated above, the issue is whether the same standards can apply to the increasing number of banking institutions being established in emerging developing country markets. Equally troublesome is the appropriate kind of surveillance and regulation needed to deal with derivatives which have grown enormously in importance over the past few years. At issue too are the kinds of prudential standards which could help to stabilize short-term inter-bank flows, a significant element of volatile capital movements during financial crises.

The original Basel Accord was also criticized for its failure to make adequate allowance for reduced risk exposure. After the Asian crisis, the Accord's role in contributing to financial stability became the focus of sustained critique.[53] The Accord was subsequently overhauled. The first revised draft, 'A New Capital Adequacy Framework' (June 1999), incorporated the following pillars: minimum capital rules based on weights that are more closely connected to credit risk; supervisory review of capital adequacy in accordance with specified qualitative principles; and market discipline based on timely and reliable information.[54]

One of the most contentious aspects of this New Framework is its increased reliance on credit-rating agencies to gauge capital adequacy and credit risk. The track record of many of these agencies hardly inspires confidence. Several analysts have argued that their performance during the Asian crisis contributed to its severity. The problem is all the more acute to the extent that credit ratings are used to assess a country's general economic policy, not just the health of financial actors.[55] Though many questions still await resolution, it is, nevertheless, likely that new capital standards will be strengthened, internal risk management controls improved, and greater reliance placed on market discipline.[56]

Attention has also focused on monitoring and regulating hedge funds so as to avoid a recurrence of the 1997–98 debacle. The US Treasury Secretary called on the President's Working Group on Financial Markets to prepare a report on hedge funds and other HLIs in order to better understand how they function, and how best to fit them into a stable financial system. The report, released in April 1999, offered a number of suggestions, including more frequent information disclosure. The International Organization of Securities Commissions (IOSCO) Task Force on Hedge Funds and HLIs also examined the related issues of transparency and disclosure standards.

The Asian financial crisis and subsequent reverberations in other emerging markets have provoked among both scholars and policy-makers renewed soul-searching about the free movement of capital. Short-term capital flows may not necessarily be the ideal solution for countries at widely varying levels of development. The availability of funds over an extended period would seem more valuable as they can be put to a great many uses without fear of sudden removal. Some types of FDI fall into this third category.

Regulating capital inflows: The Chilean model

The main danger posed by large capital inflows is the appreciation of the domestic currency, which may in turn damage export growth. On the other hand, foreign-exchange-market intervention to maintain the currency's value has its own problems, in particular the likely rise in domestic money supply and concomitant inflationary pressures. While 'sterilization' (that is, market interventions designed to keep the value of the exchange rate unchanged) is an option, it can lead to large accumulations of foreign-exchange reserves with returns below those of the debt issued domestically as part of the sterilization operation. In addition, sterilization keeps interest rates high, encouraging further capital inflows.[57]

The dilemmas facing policy-makers in the aftermath of the Asian crisis have prompted increasing interest in the model pioneered by Chile in the 1980s and 1990s. The main objective here was to discourage short-term speculative inflows while welcoming FDI,[58] open trade and export-led growth.[59] The principal elements of the Chilean *encaje* system (see Figure 8.1) were: sterilized intervention to prevent excessive appreciation of the real exchange rate; investment regulations specifying minimum entry amounts (Law 18 657) and duration before capital can be repatriated (Decree Law 600); and reserve requirements on capital inflows in an attempt to distinguish between long-term capital investments and short-term 'non-productive' inflows. In particular, short-term inflows were subject to a one-year reserve requirement (*encaje*) of 30 per cent, with the aim of reducing speculative flows. These controls were successful in protecting Chile from the volatility of short-term speculative capital flows without endangering longer-term productive forms of FDI.

Despite the growing reputation of the Chilean model, resorting to capital controls might not always be the most effective way of reducing the inflow of speculative capital. The success of the model also depends on a wide range of pre-existing economic conditions without which the outcome may prove more detrimental than beneficial to the stabilization and strengthening of the national economy. Analysis must be carried out on a country-by-country basis to determine how and to what degree elements of the model can be applied.

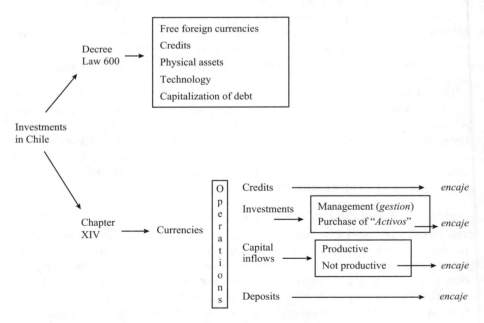

Figure 8.1   Investments in Chile and their relation to the *encaje* system

Furthermore, implementation of such measures should generally be regarded as temporary rather than permanent.

Controls on capital outflows: the Malaysian experience

UNCTAD's *Trade and Development Report 1998* argued that in the absence of a global mechanism for stabilizing capital flows, capital controls should remain part of the policy measures open to developing countries when dealing with international financial instability. This recommendation found favour in Malaysia at the time of the Asian crisis. Amid great controversy, the Mahathir government chose to ignore standard IMF prescriptions. Instead of raising interest rates and implementing austerity measures, it sought to stimulate the economy back to life. Because of the high risk of continued capital outflows, controls were introduced in September 1998, and the *ringitt* was pegged at 3.8 to the US dollar. Malaysian authorities continued to stress that the country had not isolated itself from the international financial system or abandoned the free market mechanism.[60] It was merely exercising its right to implement selective capital controls designed to protect Malaysia from a social and economic disaster.

It is now widely recognized that Malaysia did not suffer the terrible consequences that many had predicted. Economic activity resumed an upward curve, and by the time restrictions on outflows were removed in September 1999, little money had actually left Malaysia. Malaysia's crisis management having earned the respect of international policy circles, leading analysts, previously critical, now admitted that controlling capital was a feasible option in a crisis.[61] While Malaysian authorities may be credited with attaining crucial policy objectives, a note of caution is nevertheless in order. Though a plausible policy measure in times of crisis, capital controls in the Malaysian case were at least partly intended to protect powerful domestic interests which, in fact, gained disproportionately from these measures. Capital controls cannot of themselves ensure equity of outcome.

Transparency and accountability

Of three working groups set up by the G-22 in 1998 to examine ways of strengthening the international financial architecture, one had the specific task of examining issues of transparency and accountability. Its report argued that a lack of transparency and accountability had exacerbated the financial weaknesses of Asian countries, with negative impact on both individuals and the national economy, thereby making it more difficult to resolve the crisis.

The report defined transparency as 'a process by which information about existing conditions, decisions and actions is made accessible, visible and understandable', while accountability referred to 'the need to justify and accept responsibility for decisions taken'.[62] The report also distinguished between three parties – the private sector, national authorities and IFIs – all of which were called upon to become more transparent and accountable.

Increased transparency brings with it multiple advantages. It can help prevent the build-up of a country's financial and macroeconomic imbalances; it can contribute to more timely policy adjustment; and, by helping investors distinguish between sound and dubious economic policies, it can help prevent the spread of financial turmoil from one country to another.[63] At the time of writing, however, an asymmetry in expected transparency and standard-setting existed between the public and private sectors. According to Akyuz, the international community had thus far focused on the transparency of public-sector activities including fiscal, monetary and financial policies, but much '[l]ess progress has been made regarding the financial reporting of banks and other financial firms, and almost none in the case of highly leveraged institutions and offshore markets'.[64]

Transparency was by itself unlikely to ward off future crises, but the provision of greater information could in certain circumstances be of help. Leading private-sector financiers, including Julian Robertson, manager of the Tiger Fund, and George Soros, argued for more effective regulation and disclosure.[65] The IMF had assiduously encouraged more transparency from member states, but the Fund itself, despite tentative steps towards public disclosure, had yet to convince its critics of its own commitment to transparency and accountablity.

International standards

Standards are closely related to transparency. The argument has been that economies following codes and standards will inevitably contribute to a well-functioning international financial system. Standards developed by the IMF include the Special Data Dissemination Standard, the Code of Good Practices on Fiscal Transparency, the Code of Good Practices on Transparency in Monetary and Financial Policies, and guidelines concerning financial sector soundness. In addition, the Fund has prepared country case studies examining transparency practices.

Other standard-setting bodies have been active in such areas as accounting and auditing, corporate governance, and regulation of securities markets. The Basel Capital Accord has already been discussed. The Report of the Working Group on Strengthening Financial Systems highlighted the importance of the *Core Principles for Effective Banking Supervision* produced by the Basel Committee on Banking Supervision, and the *Statement of Objectives and Principles of Securities Regulation* and *International Disclosure Standards for Cross-Border Offerings and Initial Listings by Foreign Issuers* produced by IOSCO. The Financial Stability Forum Task Force on Implementation of Standards has also contributed to the process.

Tobin and other taxes on foreign-exchange transactions

In 1978, Nobel laureate James Tobin, in an address to the Eastern Economic Association, revived a proposal he had previously made about the introduction of a currency transaction tax. The proposal was, however, ignored by most mainstream economists and financial experts. In his own words, 'it did not make much of a ripple. In fact, one might say that it sank like a rock'.[66]

Recent financial crises have nevertheless given the idea of a tax on international currency transactions a new lease of life. Influential in this respect have been Europe's exchange-rate-mechanism (ERM) crises in 1992 and 1993, the Mexican crisis of 1994 and the more recent 1997–98 global financial crisis. One of the major factors contributing to renewed interest in the Tobin Tax has been its potential for raising revenue, something well understood by policy-makers, parliamentarians and civil-society representatives, concerned by current globalization and public financing trends.[67] The other main factor has been the exponential growth and volatility of foreign-exchange trading during the past two decades (see Chapter 5 for details) and the consequent desire to slow down these twin trends.

James Tobin had actually brought back to life a previous proposal made by Keynes, but while the latter emphasized the imposition of such a tax on internal financial transactions, Tobin stressed the need to widen its scope to foreign-currency transactions,[68] and recommended a tax of between 0.1 per cent and 0.25 per cent. Although the percentage might seem quite small (a tax revenue of $1000 for every $1 million traded), its impact on currency speculation was likely to be significant, while any disincentive to long-term investment was expected to be minimal.

Such a nationally implemented currency transaction tax (CTT), applied to equity and debt transactions, can be viewed positively. Its implementation might eventually be conceived in combination with specific national measures such as the introduction of capital controls. Some of the advantages of a CTT include: its efficacy in discouraging short-term speculative flows; its potential in term of revenue creation; an increase in the 'autonomy of national authorities in formulating monetary and macro-economic policy',[69] especially in times of international financial distress; its contribution to the generation of foreign-exchange reserves which can be used during periods of currency flight; its facilitation of 'the monitoring of international financial flows by providing a centralised data base on such flows';[70] and its innovative economic incentives compared to 'a command and control approach to regulating capital flows'.[71]

Such a tax remains nonetheless highly contentious, and doubts have been raised about its technical feasibility. Other concerns have included: the possibility of evasion through offshore tax havens, and of triggering a shift to new financial instruments and assets; the distortion of market behaviour; the difficulty of applying the levy globally, comprehensively and uniformly, and the likelihood that national authorities will resist the creation of a new supranational authority.

In response to the first point, Culpeper argues that the tax would be feasible if 'applied at the intermediate, netting stage of foreign exchange transactions, rather than at the initiation stage when deals are made or at the final settlement stage when payments are completed'.[72] This solution also offers a credible argument for not implementing the levy on a global basis. According to Schmidt, such a tax 'applied to the intermediate systems that net deals … is feasible and can be unilaterally imposed by any country on all foreign exchange transactions worldwide involving its own currency'.[73]

More recently, Schmidt has argued that, in the current setting, the implementation of a CTT would be easier to implement as a result of institutional change.[74] According to this newly proposed scheme, 'a CTT could now be reliably imposed and enforced on virtually the entire world's foreign exchange markets, provided at least the governments issuing the four to six main vehicle currencies agree to cooperate in imposing it'.[75] The proposed CTT would operate through the system of interbank foreign exchange netting and settlement. In the words of one analyst,

> By the device of a two-tier (two rate) CTT, with the upper penal rate applied only in objectively defined circumstances that might threaten the onset of a currency crisis, the world community acting cooperatively...could prevent rapid speculative runs on currencies, while at the same time leaving a much lower rate to be applied – and raised and lowered experimentally so as to discover the best level – as a means of raising revenue.[76]

The revenue could then be used to finance the provision of global public goods. The proposed tax would have a very low rate, and be applied, enforced and collected by national governments.[77]

As Dillon points out,[78] several countries have already developed and introduced similar taxes. Australia, Austria, Belgium, Britain, Finland, France, Germany, Hong Kong, Italy, Japan, Singapore and Sweden, among others, apply such taxes on the sale of stocks or bonds. Japan has had 'a transaction tax on securities trading as high as 55 per cent prior to April 1989', which yielded noteworthy turnover rates, even greater than in the United States.[79]

As for the second objection, it is worth noting that short-term foreign exchange transactions are highly concentrated in global financial markets. In 1992, nearly 80 per cent of such transactions occurred in just seven countries: Britain, the United States, Japan, Singapore, Switzerland, Hong Kong and Germany.[80] An agreement amongst these countries would therefore impact on the majority of transactions. It is in any case unlikely that large trading companies would compromise their good names in significant operational cost by attempting to escape from such an international levy once it becomes law. This is not to say that, to maximize its potential, such a tax would need to be implemented as comprehensively as possible. The major obstacle to its introduction is the lack of political will. The motion passed by the Canadian House of Commons in March 1999, calling on the national government to enact a tax on financial transactions in concert with the international community, might nevertheless be a sign of things to come.

Notes

1. K. Singh, *A Citizen's Guide to the Globalization of Finance* (Delhi: Madhyam Books, 1998), p.133.
2. A. Singh and A. Zammit, 'International Capital Flows: Identifying the Gender Dimension', *World Development* 28, 7 (2000).
3. As explained in previous chapters, before the displacement of pegged exchange rates by floating rates in the early 1970s, the Bretton Woods institutions had operated on the assumption that free international mobility of capital was incompatible with the preservation of reasonably free trade and full employment.
4. Oxford Analytica Brief (OAB), *International Capital Controls* (Oxford: Oxford Analytica Ltd 1998), p.1.
5. UNCTAD, *Trade and Development Report* (Geneva: UNCTAD, 2001), p.63.

6. OAB, p.1.
7. Ibid., p.1.
8. W. Bello, K. Malhotra, N. Bullard and M. Mezzera, 'Notes on the Ascendancy and Regulation of Speculative Capital', in W. Bello, N. Bullard and K. Malhotra (eds), *Global Finance: New Thinking on Regulating Speculative Capital Markets* (London: Zed Books, 2000).
9. See, for instance, I. Little, T. Scitovsky and M. Scott, *Industry and Trade in Some Developing Countries* (Oxford and New York: Oxford University Press for the OECD, 1970); J. Bhagwati, *Anatomy and Consequences of Exchange Control Regimes* (Cambridge, MA: Ballinger, 1978); A. Krueger, *Liberalization Attempts and Consequences* (Cambridge, MA: Ballinger, 1978).
10. S. Damodaran, 'Capital Account Convertibility: Theoretical Issues and Policy Options', in W. Bello, N. Bullard and K. Malhotra (eds), *Global Finance: New Thinking on Regulating Speculative Capital Markets* (London: Zed Books, 2000), p.165.
11. Singh and Zammit, pp.1254–5.
12. See Damodaran.
13. OAB, p.1.
14. 'Time to turn off the tap?', the *Economist*, 12 September 1998, pp.91–3.
15. OAB, p.1. For the role played by large capital inflows in the building of Thailand's bubble economy and the subsequent herd behaviour of investors, which stimulated contagion in the Asian financial crisis, see Chapter 7.
16. Fundamentals usually refer to magnitudes such as the current-account deficit, the rate of inflation, and so on, which need to be maintained at stable levels to preserve stability in the economy.
17. Damodaran, p.162.
18. B. Eichengreen and M. Mussa, 'Capital Account Liberalization: Theoretical and Practical Aspects' (Occasional Paper 172, Washington DC: IMF, 1998).
19. Singh and Zammit, p.1255.
20. Damodaran, p.172.
21. J. Crotty and G. Epstein, 'In Defence of Capital Controls', in L. Panitch (ed.), *The Socialist Register 1996: Are There Alternatives?* (London: Merlin Press, 1996), pp.118–21.
22. J.A. Ocampo, 'Reforming the International Financial Architecture: Consensus and Divergence', in D. Nayyar (ed.), *Governing Globalization: Issues and Institutions* (Oxford: Clarendon Press, 2001).
23. A. Cobham, 'Capital Account Liberalisation and Poverty', *Go With the Flows? Capital Account Liberalization and Poverty* (Bretton Woods Project and Oxfam, April 2001).
24. Ocampo, p.24.
25. Ibid., and Y. Akyuz, 'The Debate on the International Financial Architecture: Reforming the Reformers' (UNCTAD Discussion Papers No: 148, Geneva: UNCTAD, 2000).
26. See Ocampo.
27. These principles were issued in September 1997 by the Basel Committee on Banking Supervision, the secretariat of which is provided by the BIS. These principles serve as, and constitute, tentative guidelines for the establishment of an international banking supervisory system.
28. The *Economist*, 'Time for A Redesign? A Survey of Global Finance' (30 January 1999).
29. *Financial Times*, 'Rubin Spells Out US Ideas for Global Financial Reforms' (2 October 1998).
30. Ibid.
31. Ibid.
32. A. Friedman, 'A Proposal to Monitor World Finance System', *International Herald Tribune* (1 February 1999).
33. J. Vinocur, 'Going It Alone, U.S. Upsets France', *International Herald Tribune* (3 February 1999).
34. Ibid.

35. A. Giddens, *The Third Way: the Renewal of Social Democracy* (Cambridge: Polity Press, 1998), p.1.
36. Ibid., p.26.
37. *Financial Times* (21 September 1998).
38. G. Brown, *New Global Structures for the New Global Age* (speech by the Chancellor of the Exchequer to the Commonwealth Finance Ministers meeting in Ottawa on 30 September 1998). *HM Treasury News Release*, 158/98, available online at: <**http://www.hm-treasury.gov.uk/press/1998/p158_98.html**> (1998), p.6.
39. Ibid., p.11.
40. 'Delivering New Rules of the Game for the Global Economy'. *HM Treasury News Release*. 69/99, 21 April 1999, available online at: <**http://www.hm-treasury.gov.uk/press/1999/p69_99.html**> (1999), p.1.
41. Ibid., p.1.
42. According to Gill, 'new constitutionalism is a subtle attempt to legitimate neo-liberal globalization. It mandates a particular set of state policies geared to maintaining business confidence through the delivery of a consistent and credible climate for investment and thus for the accumulation of capital', see S. Gill 'New Constitutionalism, Democratisation and Global Political Economy', *Pacifica Review*, 10, 1 (1998), p.38.
43. Ibid., p.25–6.
44. M. Chossudovsky, *The G7 "Solution" to the Global Financial Crisis: a Marshall Plan for Creditors and Speculators* (Ottawa, document received through the mailing list 'STOP-IMF': <**stop-imf@essential.org**> (1998), p.1.
45. Chossudovsky, p.2.
46. G7, *Strengthening the International Financial Architecture*, Report of G7 Finance Ministers to the Köln Economic Summit (18–20 June 1999).
47. Ibid., p.2.
48. The *Economist*, 'World Financial Regulation: Plumb Lines' (27 February 1999).
49. *Financial Times*, 'World Financial Stability: Early Warning System Starts' (17 May 1999).
50. The FSF had its fifth meeting in March 2001.
51. UNCTAD, p.64, emphasis added.
52. Ibid.
53. Ibid.
54. According to UNCTAD (2001), a revised set of proposals was issued, including the comments by the banking industry and supervisors around the world, see p.98.
55. For a more comprehensive discussion on the New Framework, see ibid., pp.98–9.
56. US Government, *Economic Report of the President* transmitted to the Congress, Washington DC: GPO, February 1999.
57. M. Agosin and R. French-Davis, *Managing Capital Inflows in Latin America* (ODS Discussion Paper 8, New York: UNDP/ODS, 1996).
58. Ibid.
59. See OAB.
60. See, for example, M. Mohamed, *Malaysia: Measures for Economic Recovery* (Paper presented at the 1998 IMF/World Bank Annual Meetings, 1998).
61. See, for example, P. Krugman, *Capital Control Freaks*, available online at: <**http://www.slate.com/Dismal/99-09-27/Dismal.asp**> (1999).
62. G-22, *Reports on the International Financial Architecture*, available online at: <**http://www.ustreas.gov/press/releases/docs/g22-wg1.htm**> (1998), pp.3–4.
63. US Government (1999).
64. Akyuz, p.5.
65. *Financial Times* (20 October 1998).
66. M. Ul Haq, I. Kaul and I. Grunberg (eds), *The Tobin Tax: Coping with Financial Volatility* (New York: Oxford University Press, 1996), p.x.
67. Ibid.

68. A.C. Michalos, *Good Taxes: the Case for Taxing Foreign Currency Exchange and Other Financial Transactions* (Toronto: Dundurn Press, 1997).
69. Singh, K. (1998), *A Citizen's Guide to the Globalization of Finance* (Delhi: Madhyam Books), p.150.
70. Ibid., p.151.
71. R. Culpeper, *Systemic Instability or Global Growing Pains? Implications of the Asian Financial Crisis* (Briefing B-41, Ottawa: the North–South Institute, 1998), p.14.
72. Ibid., p.14.
73. R. Schmidt, *A Feasible Foreign Exchange Transaction Tax* (Ottawa: North–South Institute, 1997).
74. R. Schmidt, 'Efficient Capital Controls', *Journal of Economic Studies*, 28, 3 (2001).
75. A.C. Ross, 'A Tax on Foreign-Exchange Transactions' (Brussels: CIDSE, 2001), p.3.
76. Ibid., p.3.
77. Despite the existence of well-thought-out mechanisms for a CTT, as proposed by the above-mentioned study, a report to the UN Secretary-General, in preparation for the International Conference on Financing for Development, Monterrey, Mexico, 18–22 March 2002, indicates that more work is needed on it and recommends a carbon tax instead ('Report of the Zedillo Panel to the Secretary-General', 2001).
78. J. Dillon, *Turning the Tide: Confronting the Money Traders* (Ottawa: Canadian Centre for Policy Alternatives, 1997).
79. M.S. Scholes, *Tax Treatment of Short-Term Trading*, online, 21 March 1990, 90 TNT 63-36, Tax Analysts, pp.52–3.
80. About 55 per cent of all the foreign-exchange transactions are concentrated in just three countries: Britain, the USA and Japan; see Schmidt (1997), p.3, and also Dillon (1997), p.98.

9
Renewing the Governance of the Global Economy

Kamal Malhotra

The context and opportunity

Every cloud has a silver lining and so does every crisis. Apart from reductions in Bangkok traffic, at least on tollways, the silver lining of the East Asian crisis was the opportunity it offered to rethink the governance of the global economy – not just its financial, but also its broader economic and political aspects, which are in any case indivisible. Indeed, the East Asian crisis should have convinced even hardened skeptics of the need for such a reassessment. Despite early promising signs, it does not, however, appear to have convinced those in charge of the most advanced industrialized countries and IFIs that the institutional framework presently underpinning global economic and financial governance is in drastic need of reform. Yet the signs are clear enough. In terms of both economic growth and human development, the dominant economic and financial paradigm is unsustainable.

A fundamental shift in thinking is long overdue. Operating at many levels, such a rethink would begin by returning to first principles, namely the objectives and strategies that should inform a programme for sustainable human and social development.

Rethinking objectives and strategies for sustainable human and social development

We can no longer avoid what has for long been obvious to many outside the halls of political and economic power. If we are to achieve sustainable human and social development, the primary medium- and long-term objective cannot be economic growth or even economic growth with equity. Rather it must be development which includes but is not limited to economic growth *through* (not with) equity.

The dominant neo-liberal economic-growth paradigm, subscribed to by the World Bank, IMF and WTO along with the G7 financiers and managerial class, is strikingly different from the sustainable-human-development paradigm championed by 1998 Nobel Economics Prize Laureate Amartya Sen, or such multilateral institutions as the UNDP. The first paradigm focuses primarily on level of income as the main indicator of poverty while the second adopts a far more comprehensive view. Whereas the first paradigm views poverty as a condition, almost as a disease or a fate, the second sees it as a process, in which the poor are not passive victims but 'leading actors struggling against a process of impoverishment'.[1] Significantly, UNDP's 1997 *Human Development Report* introduced the concept of 'human poverty' as the obverse of human development. Human poverty was defined as 'the denial of opportunities and choices most basic to human development – to lead a long healthy, creative life and to enjoy a decent standard of living, freedom, self-esteem and the respect of others'.

If the second paradigm is accepted, then a primary objective over the medium to long term will be to subordinate macroeconomic and microeconomic policy-making to human development and social policy goals. This may at first sight appear to be a radical proposal, certainly if judged by neo-liberal economic orthodoxy, yet on closer inspection its theoretical justification and practical feasibility can be seen to rest on solid foundations.

Two other considerations may be crucial if governance of the global economy is to be fundamentally renewed at all levels. The first suggests that, in line with the principle of subsidiarity, global governance mechanisms ought to be subordinated to those at the local, national and regional levels. The second consideration focuses on the need to subordinate, at all four levels simultaneously, the financial 'bubble' economy to the real, productive economy (that is, the economic activities through which goods such as food, clothing and shelter, and services such as health and education are produced and delivered – in short, production geared to the satisfaction of basic needs).

The need to subordinate economic to social policy, and global governance structures to local, national and regional ones, is the main focus of this chapter. It will examine the requirements and implications of a broader notion of political governance and advance a number of concrete proposals as part of a coherent programme of renewal. First, it is necessary to explain the importance of subordinating the financial to the productive economy. The fundamental objective of all financial policy is to ensure the best possible growth, redistribution and employment outcomes in the productive economy, that is, in the arena where socially useful goods and services are produced. In this context, the 'simplistic complaint that the financial sector produces nothing by itself contains an element of truth'.[2] As Greenspan himself has clearly acknowledged, 'a global financial system, of course, is not an end in itself. It is the institutional structure that has developed over the centuries to facilitate the production of goods and services'.[3]

Financial institutions and transactions must, therefore, be judged by the contribution they make to growth, redistribution and employment in the productive economy. As John Eatwell and Lance Taylor aptly put it, 'there is no point in having a financial sector that is in some senses "efficient" on its own terms if the result is a less efficient real economy'.[4] Yet this has been the prevailing trend, with growth rates in every G7 economy in the 1980s and 1990s having slowed to around two-thirds of the corresponding rates in the 1960s.[5] If developing countries are taken as a whole, their average growth rate has experienced a comparable decline during this period. More importantly perhaps, four out of seven rapidly industrializing East and South-east Asian economies exhibited the same trend in their per capita growth rates even before the 1997–98 financial crisis.

In adopting a human development framework, it may not be enough, however, to re-subordinate the financial system to the real economy. At least as important is the identification of concrete measures whereby macroeconomic and microeconomic policy can be effectively tailored to social and human development policy objectives and strategies. In practical terms, this will require that a different approach to economic and political governance, distinct from the dominant neo-liberal model, should apply at all levels of governance – local, national, regional and global. It will also mean a significant shift in the current balance of power and initiative between the four levels in favour of the first three and away from the global.

While all four levels of governance are necessary, and the importance of local governance (for example, the role of local governments, small and medium business enterprises, and community-based and other local civil-society organizations) cannot be underestimated, this chapter focuses on national economic and political governance. This level is viewed as having strategic importance in the context of current patterns and processes of globalization.

Prospects and proposals

Economic governance implications

In terms of economic governance, a programme of renewal will necessitate a number of key policy choices. Monetary policy must respond to the needs of small- and medium-scale productive enterprises and average households in the domestic economy, not to foreign investors, hedge funds, banks and speculators who dominate the financial 'bubble' economy. Fiscal policy must involve a progressive direct taxation system instead of the largely minimalist and regressive tax regimes which hold sway in most industrialized and developing countries today. Such taxation systems must be supported by the political will and institutional capacity needed to enforce tax collection.

Only such a fiscal policy framework, coupled with significant reductions in both poverty and inequality among the general population, can provide the long-term domestic resources needed to fund the range of public and social expenditures capable of sustaining comprehensive human-development strategies over the medium and long term.

Central to such a fiscal policy direction will be national implementation of a CTT to be applied on international financial foreign-exchange transactions within the framework of an international co-operation agreement.[6] This tax ought to be sufficiently high to serve as a disincentive for speculators and should therefore be aimed principally at short-term capital flows. An incentive system will need to be devised whereby revenues generated from such a tax can be shared between the national, regional and global tiers of governance.

The tax would be levied at the national level, but a lower rate would apply to the currency transactions of residents compared to non-residents whose countries are also parties to the international taxation agreement.[7] To function effectively, such a system need not be universal, or enjoy in the first instance the participation of all major financial centres. It could be introduced in graduated fashion, with countries such as Canada, whose parliaments have voted for such a tax, and others which may choose to do so establishing in the initial phase an open but non-binding international co-operation agreement – that is, states would be free to join or not join, and if they joined, they would do so at the time of their choosing. This would be the short-term objective.

A one-third allocation of revenues to the national level would provide a strong incentive for governments to participate. The other two-thirds would be allocated to regional and global institutions on an equal basis through a new International Tax Organization created for this purpose (about which more later).

The CTT would encourage governments to refrain from substituting indiscriminate foreign financial flows for progressive domestic taxation since this is neither a desirable objective nor a sustainable development strategy. To be viable such a fiscal policy direction would require an economic policy to be firmly rooted in both domestic savings and a domestic market through the expansion of the real purchasing power of the poor and marginalized, making it not as heavily dependent on external engines of growth (for example, foreign financial flows or exports) as the current strategy of many developing countries. Additionally, it would require a world trading system based on rules which seek to maximize the development potential of the poorest nations and the poor within them rather than the market access and market share of the industrialized nations in the developing world.

A discriminatory approach to foreign financial flows may also be appropriate. Indeed, a large contributor to recent crises has been an all-too-indiscriminate approach to attracting financial flows and a vast over-rating of their real or potential contributions to people-centred economics and development. Regulations should be introduced to increase the reporting requirements of investors, especially hedge funds, which are currently exempt from these. Another measure would be the introduction of capital controls at the national level, especially on inflows. These should be phased out in a gradual manner if and when the institutional framework to manage such a phasing-out effectively is in place at national, regional and global levels as part of a coherent and comprehensive world financial framework.

In addition to countering the problems posed by short-term flows, care must also be taken to discriminate between different types of longer-term FDI. Much FDI is not developmental in the sense that it does not contribute to appropriate and genuine technology transfer, the building of research and development (R&D) capacity, or the creation of strong backward linkages and multiplier effects stimulating local production in the host economy. Moreover, given that two-thirds of FDI comprises mergers and acquisitions, its contribution to the production of useful goods and services is limited and often over-rated.[8] Worse still, given the liberal and competitive foreign investment regimes of most developing countries (for example, tax holidays, full repatriation of profit), the net impact of FDI on the balance of payments of the host country, especially over the long term, can often be negative.

As already indicated, at the national level, particularly in the absence of an appropriate global financial regulatory framework, capital controls, selectively and wisely applied, will remain essential. Such capital controls are needed to ensure a discriminatory approach not only to short-term financial flows but also to longer-term FDI. Only in this way can a country ensure that its foreign-exchange outflows are not exceeded by, or grossly mismatched with, its foreign-exchange earnings, and maintain a reasonable degree of economic and political autonomy.

Political governance implications

It has already been argued that economic and political governance issues need to be viewed as indivisible and inseparable. While this chapter is particularly concerned with renewing the governance of the global economy, this crucial interdependence and indivisibility has obvious implications for national political governance. With some modifications, the comments that follow apply equally to the regional and global levels, especially in terms of roles and responsibilities of elected parliamentarians and CSOs.

In addition to making electoral democracy more representative, legitimate and effective through the renewal of democratic parliamentary processes, the demands of better and more sustainable political governance pose at least two immediate and related challenges. The first involves moving beyond electoral to more substantive and popular forms of democracy. The second raises a more serious consideration, namely issues of process and participation.

A formidable but crucial dimension of both challenges is the need to institutionalize the input of citizens and civil society in all areas of policy-making. Economic and political governance will increasingly require an active citizenry functioning within a vibrant civil society to assume a wide range of independent watchdog roles and responsibilities.

The respective roles and responsibilities of state and civil society

The definition and elaboration of appropriate governance roles for civil society *vis-à-vis* the state must be considered against a backdrop of the diminishing efficacy of state action. Operating within the global framework of economic neo-liberalism, governments are finding it increasingly difficult to honour the social, economic, political and cultural responsibilities they have assumed and commitments they have made to their citizens, and especially the poor and the vulnerable.

None of this is to justify civil society becoming a substitute for the state in service delivery in areas (for example, health, education, water, power, roads and other public infrastructure) where in fact it is the latter which has primary and legitimate responsibility. It has become all too convenient in recent years, ideologically and practically, for states and donor organizations to transfer such roles to certain sectors of civil society. Empirical evidence suggests that this is bad practice. The strengths of CSOs do not lie in large-scale service delivery, which is nevertheless necessary if significant advances are to be made in poverty or inequality reduction, employment creation, or even social integration. Only governments and inter-governmental institutions are equipped to operate on the scale needed for these tasks.

Indeed, there is no empirically proven substitute for the state in the provision of public goods. Market failure in this area has been even greater than state failure. As for CSOs, their fragmented and small-scale character makes them unsuitable for the task. This is borne out by the historical experience of industrialized countries as much as by the current experience of the developing world. The nation-state may be weakening and international organizations may have proved relatively impotent, but as Rieff has cogently argued,

> the suggestion that civil society can cope where nations have failed is, in fact, a counsel of despair ... Without a treasury, without a legislature or an army at its disposal, civil society is less equipped to confront the challenges of globalization than nations are, and more likely to be wracked by divisions based on region and self-interest of the single-issue groups that form the nucleus of the civil society movement ... why should fragmented groups of like-minded individuals be more effective in, say, resisting the depredations of environmental despoilers than a national government?[9]

To agree with this view is not to suggest that CSOs do not have a crucial role to play in political and economic governance. Appropriate CSO roles, however, are primarily concerned with monitoring, proposing and influencing policy. This implies that if CSOs are to usefully contribute to effective governance of the global economy (that is, by playing appropriate roles in areas where they have a comparative advantage *vis-à-vis* states and governments), they will need to direct their limited resources and energies to campaigning, advocacy and other policy-influencing strategies aimed at ensuring that states fulfil their core responsibilities and national and international commitments. Such roles also imply a CSO commitment to and capacity for monitoring the performance of governments and IGOs, and pioneering process or content alternatives to the dominant mainstream policies of the IFIs, regional multilateral development banks, the WTO, BIS and other regional and global economic governance institutions.

Sadly, however, the complementary governance potential of CSOs is far from being realized. One impediment has been the unsympathetic or positively hostile approach of the state. Another derives from the fact that many NGOs, an important subset of CSOs, have operated primarily within a North–South resource transfer paradigm, not unlike the framework favoured by the much larger bilateral and multilateral donors, where the emphasis is primarily on funding. NGOs have been favoured for this role by both donors and recipient governments at least partly because this has kept the lid on simmering public discontent. As one astute commentator has observed, NGOs were 'ordained to be ladles in the global soup kitchen'[10] of the new world order.

Key future challenges and dilemmas for the state–civil society relationship

International experience suggests that there are important governance roles for both the state and civil society, which cannot be easily substituted or transferred from one to the other. To realize their full governance potential, states must reclaim many of the functions they have willingly or reluctantly abdicated to the market or CSOs. Civil society, for its part, will need to assume a multiplicity of roles. None is more important than that of effectively challenging the authoritarian attitudes and policies of governments, while simultaneously drawing attention to and strengthening the activist role played by the state in a number of cases, such as in the early stages of East Asia's industrialization.

Is it possible for the state to perform one role but not the other, or are they inseparable – in effect two sides of the same coin? While it is a formidable challenge and dilemma, civil society must endeavour to separate the enabling from the disabling functions of the state and support the former while thwarting the latter. This is because NGOs – civil society more broadly – and the market are not viable or even desirable substitutes in the performance of either economic or political governance roles. These are the responsibility of a socially activist and enabling state.

Challenging the authoritarian tendencies of governments is particularly important in non-democratic states where CSOs are precluded from working in partnership or collaboration with their governments to advance sustainable human development. Applying continuous pressure on such governments to democratize may be the primary governance role (that is, creating an enabling environment) that CSOs can perform in such circumstances.

Another important function of civil society is to help build transparent and accountable institutions with the political will and capacity to guard, regulate and enforce legislation and other appropriate action against the excesses of an unregulated market and in the interests of the poorest, most vulnerable and marginalized sections of society. In the current neo-liberal global and regional environment this has become an increasingly urgent task. It is nevertheless a task that is vital for the achievement of the core responsibilities and commitments of states, not least with respect to sustainable human development.

Civil society must at the same time devise an appropriate response to the widening service delivery gaps created by the dominance of macroeconomic neo-liberalism. These gaps have been accentuated by the steady roll-back of the state and the growing asymmetrical power of the market, especially of transnational industrial and finance capital *vis-à-vis* both governments and civil society. CSOs must find ways of doing this without themselves becoming mere 'ladles in the global soup kitchen'. While this does not imply that they should not directly be involved in direct poverty alleviation, service delivery or employment expansion programmes, it does imply that their state substitution roles in scaled-up direct service delivery should as far as possible be limited to situations of short-term crisis and humanitarian response. Their major governance role at the local community level, in addition to demonstrating innovative approaches of service delivery for replication by government, should be to strengthen the capacity of poor, powerless and marginalized communities and the population more widely to make legitimate social demands and claims on the state and governments in power – demands, which if met, will directly contribute to the achievement of sustainable human and social development. This once again implies prioritizing awareness-building, organizing and analytical capacity-building functions over direct service-delivery ones.

Finally, in this era of accelerating globalization, there is a need to support state capacity and ability with a view to constraining and regulating the power and reach of global international financial and trade institutions and transnational corporate conglomerates. The aim must be to restore the initiative to both local communities and a reformed, more activist and enabling national state. Sustainable development will be impossible to achieve without such a change in the balance of power.

The regional level

We have thus far emphasized the pre-eminence of the national level in any renewed governance of the global economy. There is, however, also a place for complementary and supportive regional institutions and mechanisms. These will assume added significance given the acceleration of globalizing tendencies and the proliferation of inter-governmental regional and sub-regional economic groupings and blocs, for example, APEC, NAFTA, EU, MERCOSUR, the Free Trade Agreement for the Americas (FTAA). Yet, the regional tier remains by far the weakest in the overall framework of governance.

Inter-governmental regional institutions and mechanisms

A number of scholars and policy-makers have emphasized the successes of such inter-governmental regional groupings as ASEAN, MERCOSUR and the EU. In the European context, reference is often made to the creation of the euro and European Monetary Union (EMU). These success stories, however, are limited in number and inspiration. More crucially, the capacity of these regional bodies and mechanisms to act as mediating or countervailing layers of economic and political governance, able to support the national and local levels and counteract the dominant role of the global level, is at best modest. More often than not, the aim has been to make regional blocs handmaidens of, or testing grounds for, standardized rules that are later intended for adoption by global multilateral institutions (for example, NAFTA and now FTAA in relation to the WTO). Conversely, a number of innovative regional proposals have been effectively aborted. For example, Japan's Asian Monetary Fund proposal was stillborn because of opposition from the IMF and US Treasury.

Regionalism's poor track record may be changing slowly with the creation of the EMU and euro. The latter has the potential to counterbalance the US dollar as a currency of international exchange. In the Asian region, too, the crisis has served as a catalyst for the creation of an 'Asian Currency System' based on a trade-weighted basket of currencies that would include the US dollar but also the Japanese *yen* and the euro.[11] The Japanese proposal for an Asian Monetary Fund or facility, which was effectively resisted when it was first mooted – under attack, the Japanese proposal was meekly withdrawn – re-emerged a year later. As the crisis deepened and the IMF came under attack from all sides, Japan produced the watered-down Miyazawa Initiative. The notion of a formal and substantial regional monetary arrangement continues to gather pace.

The governance of the global economy would certainly benefit from the creation of an appropriate regional or sub-regional monetary facility. An East Asian Monetary Fund appears the most feasible in the short term. This would not be just a new fund operating within an existing institution, but a new institution responsive to regional and country-specific realities. Its aim would be to encourage greater competition and pluralism in monetary and fiscal policy choices, especially in times of crisis.

Such an institution would be tripartite in its composition, with its membership limited to countries within the region or sub-region. Although membership would be open to governments, CSOs, parliamentary and private-sector organizations, only governments would have voting powers. Decisions would be made in accordance with democratic principles and no member would enjoy a right of veto.

While the creation of such an institution may in the short term be feasible only in East and South-east Asia – this region has the resources to underwrite such a fund (through accumulated foreign-exchange reserves) and the institutional capacity to create it – the long-term objective would be to establish such regional institutions in all continents.

Regional civil-society initiatives

Civil society initiatives at the regional level have so far been largely reactive to inter-governmental initiatives, rather than strategic and proactive, and may be regarded as the weakest link in the chain of civil-society activism. Noteworthy initiatives have included the Common Frontiers/Common Fronteras project involving Canadian–Mexican–US networks, initiated by Action Canada Network's continental free trade policy research and analysis project; the series of annual mobilizations around the APEC forums; a similar but parallel mobilization in Asia and Europe around the Asia-Europe Summits (ASEM); and the April 2000 mobilizations in Quebec City against the emerging FTAA, led by the newly created Inter-Hemispheric Social Alliance.

These initiatives, amply described in various documents,[12] need not detain us here. It is nevertheless important to emphasize that if these campaigns are to be useful, they will need to move beyond critique to the articulation of workable and sustainable alternatives with respect to the process and content of global economic and political governance. While civil-society proposals are beginning to do this, these are still few and far between and often lack the coherence and comprehensiveness they need if they are to be taken seriously.

The global level

If sustainable human development is to be effectively pursued, much attention will need to be given to the future global financial, economic and social architecture.

As in the case of regional bodies and mechanisms, the fundamental principle that should underlie the creation of global institutions is that they be enabling and supportive of national (especially) and regional initiatives, and should not attempt to dominate or supplant them.

However, in the context of a highly globalized economy and financial system, resorting merely to national or even regional regulation will not be enough. International financial liberalization poses heightened risks for both national economies and the world economy. An effective policy towards capital markets must therefore be global in nature. National capital controls, however desirable, are likely to be ineffective in dealing with either the source or scale of the problem, and are likely to be subverted by neighbouring countries intent on attracting finance capital by pursuing contrary (for example, financial liberalization) policies.

Accountability of the Bretton Woods institutions to a reformed UN system

If it is accepted (as has been argued in this chapter) that economic policy should primarily serve medium- and long-term human and social policy goals, then it follows that regional and global financial institutions, including the IMF, World Bank, ADB and WTO, should be more consistent with human and social policy objectives. Logically, then, they should play a subordinate role *vis-à-vis* regional and UN institutions that have primary responsibility for defining and promoting those policy objectives.

While this expectation is far removed from today's reality, and while such a radical change in global governance will neither be credible nor feasible unless the entire UN system is radically reformed, it is nevertheless unavoidable if the governance of the global economy is to serve human-development objectives. Indeed, a shift in the balance of power back to something approaching the original intentions of those who created the UN system in San Francisco in 1945 is more or less self-evident. The Bretton Woods institutions were simply meant to serve as the specialized arms of the UN and be accountable to it – something which has never been implemented,[13] and which the Bretton Woods twins, WTO and financial institutions such as BIS continue to resist. The centre of gravity of global economic governance needs to shift away from the current, relatively undemocratic and narrow financial and economic framework to relatively more democratic institutions centred around the notions of social and human development which are to be found in other parts of the UN system.

Despite the UN's serious shortcomings and relative impotence, there is no case for establishing new global multilateral institutions until the more fundamental issues of economic and political governance raised in this chapter have been addressed. Without first addressing the defects that contribute to the presently dysfunctional global governance system, the creation of new institutions would merely multiply existing defects and imbalances.

Similarly, eliminating the IMF, World Bank and WTO, as many have demanded over the years, will not resolve the underlying problems of global governance, because these three organizations are merely a symptom, not a cause, of the malaise that has prevailed since the demise of the Bretton Woods system in the early 1970s. Their shutdown will merely lead to the creation of 'new' mirror-image institutions to perform the specialized tasks which they were originally established to accomplish. In the area of trade, however, a shutdown of the WTO could help facilitate the revival and strengthening of a reformed UNCTAD which has historically had a much more Southern-sensitive and development-friendly approach to trade issues.

An Economic and Social Security Council[14]

Such a council should be created as a principal organ of the UN (comparable in status to the Security Council), accountable to a strengthened and more powerful General Assembly. While in the short to medium term this Council should build on ECOSOC, in the longer term it should supersede this body. The proposed People's Assembly and Consultative Assembly (see Chapter 15) should also be represented in the Economic and Social Security Council in the long term, although voting power should lie only with state members.

In the short term and as an intermediate step, the existing ECOSOC should be upgraded. Steps to assist this could include holding more frequent and more focused meetings. The Council should, for example, meet to discuss specific economic and social issues such as a financial crisis or a significant globalization trend that warrants attention. This might mean a one-day meeting every couple of months.

A strengthened role for the Bureau (the executive) could be another short-term reform. The Bureau should meet whenever the Chair judges this to be necessary to discuss both substantive and procedural issues, as do the Bureaux of other bodies such as the ECOSOC commissions. If these meetings were sufficiently frequent and substantive, they would change both the nature of ECOSOC deliberations and country representation for the better.

Such modest changes in the short term could be achieved by ambitious use of the powers already available, either by a decision of the existing bodies or through the initial leadership of the Chair. These would be significant changes in their own right, and would lay the groundwork for the more ambitious changes recommended in the medium to long term.

In the longer term, the powers and mandate of ECOSOC need to be enlarged, and its name should be changed to Economic and Social Security Council. The powers of this Council should be expanded to include: a summoning power to ensure a degree of accountability of all key actors, monitoring, research and analysis, advocacy, and a regular rapporteur responsibility. Its mandate should be expanded to include all economic, financial and systemic issues (for example, debt, trade, finance, private capital flows, ODA), which were part of the agenda of the International Conference on Financing for Development in 2002.

The specialized agencies of the UN, the Bretton Woods institutions and the WTO would all have to respond to any summons served on them by Council members, as would non-state actors such as TNCs and CSOs. This would not imply any power to direct the policy of these organizations, but Standing

Committees of the Council could be created for a number of policy areas (for example, finance and debt).

In addition, *ad hoc* sub-committees could be formed to examine specific issues arising out of particular developments (for example, a specific financial crisis). Standing and *ad hoc* committees of the Council would have the power not only to summon officials and experts, but also to issue periodic reports outlining testimony, providing research and analysis by committee staff and making non-binding policy recommendations to the UN General Assembly, IMF, World Bank, WTO and other relevant organizations, which would be expected to act on these.

While the Council, at least in the medium term, may not have any enforcement or sanction capability over the institutions to which it makes recommendations for action, it will be able to use its power of summons to call on these institutions to explain their response to its recommendations. This should provide a source of political leverage, especially if the actions or inaction of these institutions is made public after the summons. It will be necessary, therefore, for this whole process to be institutionalized and made transparent from the inception of the Council. To this end, the Council's reports should be made available to the membership of the General Assembly and the wider public.

In the longer term, the Economic and Security Council, without power of veto, should take on key decision-making roles in its areas of mandate similar to those of the reformed Security Council outlined in Chapter 15. Committee membership should be on a rotation basis with each country having an equal vote. Election to the Council should follow the same basis as this book's proposals for election to a reformed Security Council.

A reformed IMF

Apart from being made more transparent and accountable, a reformed IMF should be confined to its original narrow mandate, consistent with its original Articles of Agreement. As Martin Feldstein correctly pointed out in the context of the East Asian crisis and the IMF 'bail-out rescue' packages that followed, it is not appropriate for the IMF to impose economic changes which are not essential to address the balance-of-payments problem and which may contradict the choices of the country concerned.

Consistent with this, IMF reform should have three priorities for implementation in the short to medium term: First, IMF operations should be limited to their mandate of surveillance and stabilization. This will imply a phasing out, for example, of the Poverty Reduction and Growth Facility (PRGF, formerly the Enhanced Structural Adjustment Facility) through which the IMF influences long-term structural reform in its borrower members. Secondly, no change should be made to its Articles of Agreement mandate on capital-account convertibility. Instead the emphasis should be on strict enforcement of the current Article relating to capital-account controls. Finally, its surveillance role should be universally implemented, with particular stress on the implementation of this role *vis-à-vis* industrialized countries which are the source of the vast majority of global capital flows. In the short to medium term, the IMF should be tasked with surveillance of both the volume of capital flows and their specific composition and destination.

A reformed world trading system

The principal justification of the current world trading system and its main global institutional mechanism, the WTO, is that they promote free trade. In practice, they function primarily to facilitate negotiations and bargaining about market access on a reciprocal basis between countries. 'Free trade' is not the typical outcome of this process; nor is enhanced consumer welfare, much less development. Trade has become the lens through which development is perceived, rather than the other way around. The net result has been the confusion of ends with means. The obvious conclusion is not that trade is undesirable but that the benefits of trade openness for development have been greatly oversold. Deep trade liberalization cannot be relied upon to deliver high rates of economic growth or poverty reduction, and does not therefore deserve to be accorded the high priority it typically receives in the development strategies of leading multilateral organizations.[15] As was recently stated at UNCTAD's 2000 Raul Prebisch Lecture,

> it isn't at all obvious that further external liberalisation ('openness') is now in every country's interest and in all dimensions or that in the over-arching sweep of global economic history what the world now most requires is a set of global rules that promote or ease the path to greater freedom for global market actors, and are universal in application.[16]

A reformed world trading system will require a fundamental shift in both mindset and the structure of trade negotiations. The overarching principle should be development not 'market access'. This would have two far-reaching implications. First, it would enable developing countries to articulate their needs in an autonomous way and pursue policy choices and institutional innovations that depart from prevailing orthodoxies. Secondly, the WTO or a future global multilateral trade organization that replaces it (perhaps a reformed but strengthened UNCTAD) would have as its main function not harmonization and the reduction or elimination of national institutional differences, but the management of the complex interaction of diverse institutional arrangements.[17]

More specifically, such a world trading system would be based on the following principles: trade as a means to an end, not an end in itself; trade rules that allow for diversity in national institutions and standards; the recognized right of countries to protect their own institutions and development priorities but without the parallel right to impose these institutions and priorities on others.[18] While market access for developing-country products in industrialized-country markets will remain important, a development mindset would suggest differential market access for different countries, depending on their level of development, with the least developed economies getting full market access without any expectation of reciprocity.

Three other institutional reforms are worth noting here. Particularly useful would be the establishment of a new supranational body, an International

Taxation Organization (ITO), which would take responsibility for the allocation of revenues at the regional and global levels of the national level Currency Transaction Tax (CTT) earlier recommended. Its governing council would be made up only of representatives of tax-imposing governments who would be responsible for deciding the allocation and use[19] of the tax revenue generated at the regional and global (but not national) level. Allocations at these levels (two-thirds of the total) should be designed to facilitate the achievement of the 2015 Millennium Development Goals agreed at the 2000 UN Millennium Summit of world leaders. Allocations at the regional level should give priority to legitimate and effective multilateral organizations, while allocations at the global level should give priority to the UN system. Such a distribution of revenues would make it possible for the UN to establish greater autonomy from its richest and most powerful members.

In its formative years, the ITO would maintain its full independence from existing global governance mechanisms including the UN, both because of its non-universal character and because such independence would help it achieve its tasks more efficiently. In the medium to long term, especially as its membership expands, it should become accountable to the proposed Economic and Social Security Council. There is reason to believe that, once established, the ITO would generate the political pressure for most UN member states to join it. Where states did not join, their residents, as non-residents of tax-imposing states, would continue to pay higher taxes than residents of tax-imposing states for currency transactions in those states. Moreover, their governments would be excluded from decision-making with regard to tax allocations at both the regional and global levels.

An equally important initiative would be the creation, under the broad auspices of the UN, of an International Debt Arbitration Mechanism. Such a mechanism should address the presently invidious situation where creditors are simultaneously the arbiters of debt. Such a repay mechanism would also be tasked with identifying different categories of debt (for example, odious or illegitimate debt) and ruling on which categories should be cancelled and which should be repaid. It should also determine the conditions, priority and time frame for such repayments.

Serious consideration should be given to the creation of an International Bankruptcy Court, modelled along the lines of Chapter IX of US Bankruptcy Law.[20]

Civil-society action at the global level

Civil-society initiatives and proposals for global governance are more numerous and wide-ranging than at the regional or even national level. They cover such issues as reform of the Security Council and creation of a Global People's Assembly linked to the General Assembly. They also involve more specific campaigns, including the successful Campaign to Ban Land Mines, the campaign against the OECD's Multilateral Agreement on Investment (MAI), the campaign for an International Criminal Court, the Structural Adjustment Participatory Review Initiative (SAPRI), and Social Watch.

Since the failed WTO ministerial meeting in Seattle in late 1999, which many regard as a watershed in terms of CSO global mobilization, a succession of high-profile citizens' mobilizations have coincided with major global and regional multilateral meetings and conferences in Washington DC, Geneva, Prague, Porto Alegre, Genoa, the fourth WTO ministerial meeting in Doha, Qatar, in November 2001 and the International Conference on Financing for Development in Monterey, Mexico, in March 2002. These citizen initiatives have targeted their displeasure on the World Bank, IMF, WTO, G7 and the World Economic Forum. The critiques and proposals put forward through these campaigns have been amply documented. As in the case of regional civil-society campaigns, the challenge here is to articulate more cohesive and comprehensive alternatives for global economic and political governance and to project those alternatives in ways which gain maximum publicity. But this may not be enough. In the years ahead, civil society will need to complement advocacy with a much more sophisticated educational role that is directed to all sections of society, and resonates with their anxieties and aspirations. Critical evaluation, advocacy and education should be seen as the three indispensable pillars of a reinvigorated civil society capable of developing and sustaining the momentum and enthusiasm for the democratization of economic governance.

Notes

1. UNDP, *Overcoming Human Poverty* (New York: UNDP Poverty Report, 1998).
2. J. Eatwell and L. Taylor, *International Capital Markets and the Future of Economic Policy*, CEPA (Working Paper No.9 New York: New School for Social Research, 1998).
3. A. Greenspan, Chair, US Federal Reserve, 14 October 1997.
4. See Eatwell and Taylor.
5. Ibid.
6. For detailed work on the technical feasibility of a CTT, see particularly R. Schmidt, 'Efficient Capital Controls', *Journal of Economic Studies*, 28, 3 (2001).
7. For a more detailed version of a similar proposal, see H. Potamaki, *Democratising Globalisation: Leverage of the Tobin Tax* (London: Zed Books, 2001).
8. For a recent account of the empirical evidence of FDI and policy lessons and implications, see G. Hanson, *Should Developing Countries Promote Foreign Direct Investment?* (Group of 24, Discussion Paper No.9, February 2001).
9. D. Rieff, 'The False Dawn of Civil Society', *Nation*, 22 February 1999.
10. A. Fowler, 'Capacity Building and NGOs: a Case of Strengthening Ladles for the Global Soup Kitchen?', *Institutional Development*, 1, 1 (1994), pp.18–24.
11. *Smart Partnerships in Key Economic Sectors: Reform of the International Monetary System* (APEC Business Summit, Kuala Lumpur, 16 November 1998).
12. For the Common Fronteras campaign against NAFTA see, for example, J.W. Foster, 'Redefining Governance: the Transnationalization of Civic Participation in North America' (Mimeograph, Ottawa, 1993); and C. Thorup, 'The Politics of Free Trade and the Dynamics of Cross Border Coalitions in US-Mexico Relations', *Columbia Journal of World Business*, XXVI, 2 (1991), pp.12–26. For the civil-society mobilization around APEC see, for example, W. Bello and J. Chavez-Malaluan (eds), *APEC: Four Adjectives in Search of a Noun* (Manila: Manila People's Forum on APEC, Focus on the Global South, Institute of Popular Democracy, November 1996); and W. Bello, *Challenging the Mainstream: APEC and the Asia Pacific Development Debate* (Hong Kong: ARENA, Asia

Alliance of YMCAs, CCA, DAGA, October 1995). For civil-society contributions around ASEM I, see B. Brennan, E. Heijmans and P. Vervest (eds), *ASEM Trading New Silk Routes: Beyond Geo-Politics and Geo-Economics, Towards a New Relationship Between Asia and Europe* (Amsterdam: Transnational Institute and Focus on the Global South, 1997).

13. For an historical account of the dynamics that brought about the establishment of the Bretton Woods institutions, see Chapters 1 and 4.
14. J.A. Camilleri, K. Malhotra and M. Tehranian, *Reimagining the Future: Towards Democratic Governance* (Melbourne: Department of Politics, La Trobe University, 2000).
15. D. Rodrik, *The Global Governance of Trade as if Development Really Mattered* (New York: UNDP, September 2001).
16. G.K. Helleiner, 'Markets, Politics and the Global Economy: Can the Global Economy Be Civilized?', 10th Raul Prebisch Lecture (UNCTAD, December 2000).
17. See Rodrik (2001).
18. D. Rodrik, 'Five Simple Principles for World Trade', *American Prospect* (17 January 2000).
19. For a more detailed version of a similar proposal, see Potamaki.
20. For detailed proposals, see the work of K. Raffer, University of Vienna, presented at Global Civil Society Hearings, 'High-Level Event on Financing for Development' (New York: UN, 5–6 November 2000). See also UNCTAD's proposals for such a Court made first in 1986 and then reiterated after the Asian crisis of 1997–98.

Part III
Global Peace and Security

10
Conflict Prevention: Towards a Multidimensional Approach

Michalis S. Michael

The end of the Cold War and the subsequent void left in international relations by the collapse of superpower 'certainty' brought a sense of urgency to the search for a new world consensus, that would somehow emanate from and revolve around the UN. Indeed, the end of ideological and strategic bipolarity brought with it an unprecedented expectation that the UN would now be able to undertake the role for which it was originally intended: to resolve conflicts. Constrained by Cold War rivalries, the UN, it was thought, had for 45 years been handicapped in effectively pursuing its main objective: maintenance of international peace and security. And nowhere was peace more prevalently threatened than in intra-state conflicts which accounted for 53 out of 56 major armed conflicts between 1990 and 2000 – the majority conducted in Africa and Asia.[1]

Despite the rich intellectual reservoir of information, analysis and research on conflict resolution accumulated since the 1950s,[2] it was not until the end of the Cold War that mainstream international policy-makers and diplomats began to embrace conflict resolution as a useful tool of their trade.[3] Crucial to the success or failure of conflict resolution will be the UN's capacity to adopt and apply the ideas and strategies developed by scholars, conflict analysts and international NGOs. Our purpose here is not to exhaust the whole gamut of conflict-resolution theories and techniques but rather to project those ideas and proposals which are conceptually and practically relevant to advancing global governance reform towards the development of an integrated and multi-track approach to conflict prevention.

Conceptual framework: Conflict-management typology and definition of concepts

Before analysing existing initiatives undertaken by multilateral organizations and considering what reforms might be appropriate, we first need to have a working understanding of several concepts employed in the conflict-resolution literature, many of which overlap and are often used in different and interchangeable ways.

Peacemaking, defined by Boutros-Ghali as 'action to bring hostile parties to agreement, essentially through such peaceful means as those foreseen in Chapter VI of the Charter of the United Nations',[4] aims to limit the intensity or extent of the conflict, or alternatively to resolve it. The main elements of peacemaking are listed in Article 33 of the UN Charter: negotiation, enquiry, mediation, conciliation, arbitration, judicial settlement and resort to regional arrangements.[5] To this extent at least peacemaking appears to have a relatively clear basis in the Charter.[6]

Peacemaking efforts in the early stages of conflict, and especially when conflict is latent rather than overt, may best be designated as *preventive diplomacy*.[7] Here we have in mind a range of diplomatic and other strategies, processes and techniques designed to prevent disputes from escalating into widespread violence,[8] relapsing into protracted conflicts,[9] or proliferating to other countries. Boutros-Ghali, in *An Agenda for Peace*, pointed to five components of preventive diplomacy: confidence-building measures, fact-finding,[10] early warning, preventive deployment and demilitarized zones.[11] The first three were considered core elements of the practice, though the last two might also prove necessary.[12] His introduction of coercive elements into the notion of preventive diplomacy attracted considerable criticism, and raised doubts as to the diplomatic nature of this practice. The conception of preventive diplomacy adopted here reflects the same scepticism, and precludes any deployment or threat of force.

Confidence-building measures (CBMs) aim to create mutual confidence and build trust between disputing parties. Such measures include exchange of military missions, creation of regional and sub-regional risk-reduction centres, arrangements for free flow of information, improving trade relations, developing people's diplomacy, including educational, cultural and tourist exchanges and monitoring of arms agreements. CBMs are significant vehicles, especially in protracted ethnic conflict, for establishing a process of communication with and devilification of the 'other'.

Early warning draws its mandate from Article 34 of the Charter,[13] and entails information-gathering and analysis in order to assess a developing conflict situation. Besides utilizing data emanating from a global network that monitors evidence of potential environmental damage, nuclear accident, population movements, threat of famine and spread of diseases, such information has to be combined with historical, social, political, military and economic indicators relevant to particular disputes.[14] The development of such an information-gathering and processing system would enable early warning to forecast and prioritize potential conflict scenarios, and devise a series of relevant options for preventive action.

Peacebuilding can be seen as a more holistic approach to conflict prevention.[15] Peacebuilding activities range from the creation of frameworks of dialogue through to international regimes designed to tackle such problems as poverty, unemployment, population pressures, water scarcity or absence of telecommunications hot-lines.[16] In contrast to Boutros-Ghali, who conceives of peacebuilding as a post-conflict activity, Gareth Evans distinguishes between two types of peacebuilding: one aims to prevent security problems from arising in the first place, and the other aims to prevent their recurrence once they have arisen.[17]

Drawing on UN experience during the 1990s, Kofi Annan has further stressed the intrinsic value of *post-conflict peacebuilding*, and argued for the involvement of other relevant inter-agency teams, NGOs, and local citizens' groups engaged in such diverse tasks as emergency relief, demobilization of combatants (preventive disarmament), mine-clearing, conduct of elections, establishment of police forces, and initiation of developmental programmes. For Annan post-conflict peacebuilding depends on the implementation of peace agreements. Conversely peacebuilding must underpin their implementation, for without sustained support they are vulnerable to breakdown.[18]

Long-term prevention is a relatively recent addition to UN terminology. In expounding on this controversial strategy, Annan has emphasized the role of democracy as 'a non-violent form of internal conflict management', which envisages all major social groups becoming stakeholders in an inclusive government through participation in its major institutions. He advocates three long-term strategies: encouragement of people-centred security in conflict-prone states; development of policies that minimize the risks of conflict by conducting 'conflict impact assessments', modelled on environmental impact assessments; and involvement of TNCs in creating a climate of market and human security.[19]

Symmetric and asymmetric conflicts

An important dualism in the typology of conflict resolution is the distinction between symmetric and asymmetric conflicts – a dimension that is often neglected or underestimated.[20] The role of multilateral institutions is especially important yet highly problematic in an international system characterized by varying degrees and combinations of symmetry and asymmetry. Symmetric conflicts may be loosely defined as those where the main protagonists are more or less comparable in power (not just military but economic and organizational, as well as other forms of power) and in their general disposition to third-party intervention. Asymmetric conflicts, on the other hand, are characterized by significant inequalities of power and differences in the extent to which the disputing parties are willing to co-operate with multilateral institutions. Clearly, multilateral diplomacy, and especially outside intervention, if it is to have any prospect of success in a given conflict, will need to take into account the symmetry or asymmetry of a conflict. Neutrality is particularly appropriate in symmetric conflicts, but less so in conflicts where one party is much stronger and intent on dominating or even exploiting the other.

Third-party mediation which fails to address the power imbalance in a given conflict will sooner or later run into difficulty. As Jones notes, the Norwegian facilitation of the Oslo Accords failed because they did not factor into their strategy the disparity of power between the two parties.[21] Once the accumulated goodwill was exhausted, the mediation process became vulnerable to collapse.

Time continuum

The foregoing observations suggest that peace and security are relative concepts, not only in the obvious sense that they are not all-or-nothing propositions (that is, total peace versus total violence), but in the more complex sense that violence and peace unfold over time. To measure success or failure (of any conflict-management initiative or of the institution which has authorized it), it is imperative to trace, as carefully as possible, the consequences of actions and deliberations (including inaction) over the short, medium and longer terms. Obviously, different situations and contexts will imply short, medium and long terms of different duration, but for the purpose of our analysis it may be useful to describe the period covering the short term as anything between a few months to two years, the medium term anything between two and ten years, and the longer term anything up to a generation or more.

From the above discussion of concepts, a few principles emerge that will guide our analysis and recommendations.

1. We are concerned with non-coercive means and strategies of conflict management.
2. We place the stress on prevention rather than cure, on building conditions of peace not just after the conflict has subsided but before it has crossed the threshold into violence (pre-conflict process).
3. We understand conflict prevention and management to be inseparable not only from security as traditionally understood but also from socioeconomic, psychological and cultural arrangements.
4. Finally while acknowledging the distinction between intra-state and inter-state conflict, we are mindful of the fact that the domestic/external divide is often at best blurred and at worst misleading.

A survey of the UN and other multilateral prevention initiatives

Here we examine three facets of multilateral conflict prevention and management: the attempts of Secretaries-General to create the necessary political will within the international community; institutional reforms in the formulation of conflict prevention strategies; and the performance of UN and other missions in the field.

Political will

Conflict prevention is fraught with conceptual and political difficulties that render states reluctant to embrace a course of action which they fear might encroach on their sovereignty.[22] Moreover, the urgency of a crisis is not always immediately apparent to national governments, international media or world public opinion. Several important questions suggest themselves: By which criteria does the UN determine which conflict or crisis is to be targeted for a conflict prevention response? Should European conflicts such as the Northern Ireland and Basque disputes also be subjected to conflict-prevention monitoring? Or are they to be assigned 'low' priority status, given restricted UN resources and the EU's potential role? Might there not be in that instance a legitimate suspicion that UN-sponsored conflict prevention is simply a mechanism at the disposal of the major western powers to pursue their own interests?

Boutros-Ghali in his *Supplement to An Agenda for Peace* declared that the biggest obstacle to the UN's pursuit of preventive diplomacy was the reluctance of parties in a dispute to accept UN involvement. He saw the solution to this state-centric mentality as lying in the long-term development of a new ethos amongst member states more receptive to UN assistance at critical moments.[23] Both Boutros-Ghali and his successor, Annan, have emphasized the intrinsic humanitarian and cost-saving value of conflict prevention. To establish conflict management and prevention firmly on the international agenda, both Secretaries-General have consistently devoted a sizeable section of their annual reports to this issue.[24] In recent years, several other reports by the Secretary-General provided added momentum to this campaign.[25]

Perhaps most significant was the Millennium Summit of September 2000, which Annan used to generate debate amongst heads of government on conflict prevention. The report may be said to have articulated the 'Annan doctrine'. Any viable prevention strategy, it was argued, must address the root causes of conflict which would involve: reduction of world poverty; promotion and protection of human and minority rights by both vertical and horizontal inclusion; and 'naming and shaming' those individuals, states and private sector actors who profit from conflict and war. [26]

By redefining conflict to incorporate long-term socioeconomic and political as well as ethno-religious factors, the Boutros-Ghali/Annan approach has introduced into the debate such key issues as globalization, environmental degradation, unequal economic and resource distribution, development and growth, and the contested question of individual versus minority rights. Placed in the wider context, it is perhaps not altogether surprising that the new conflict-prevention rhetoric should have been misinterpreted, at least in some quarters, as part of a design to reinforce the anti-state processes of globalization and internal fragmentation.

Organizational reform

The Department of Political Affairs (DPA), established in 1992 to handle political functions previously managed by other UN entities,[27] has since focused on a wide range of inter-related areas ranging from preventive action and peacemaking to background research for the purposes of the Security Council and General Assembly. With regard to preventive diplomacy the DPA developed a five-pronged policy:

1. information- and intelligence-gathering to identify potential crisis areas through early warning and fact-finding;
2. provision of advice and political guidance to the Secretariat;
3. third-party preventive action, including mediation/negotiation, goodwill and political missions;
4. application of international pressure through public statements and reports by the Secretary-General as well as through Security Council and General Assembly initiatives;
5. introduction of both positive and negative measures (carrot-and-stick approach), including allocation of funds in association with relevant UN agencies, targeted sanctions, and support for track-two initiatives.[28]

The DPA has nevertheless been restricted in fulfilling its mandate by limited resources and personnel, confusion over inter-departmental jurisdiction, and an in-house propensity to accumulate and assess information, hence subsequent proposals for 'sharing' arrangements, especially with the Department of Peace-keeping Operations (DPKO). For its part, the *Brahimi Report* supported more 'fre-quent use of fact-finding missions to areas of tensions' and recommended the establishment of an Executive Committee on Peace and Security (ECPS) and therein an Information and Strategic Analysis Secretariat (EISAS) to be jointly administered by the DPA and DPKO.[29]

Several observers recommended the creation of a 'lessons learned unit' within the DPA, similar to that of the DPKO, to utilize outside experts and encourage information-sharing with other UN departments.[30] Given the problems associated with fund allocation and bureaucratic duplication, a more realistic proposal might be to expand the already-existing unit in DPKO in order to incorporate both pre- and post-conflict prevention and link it administratively to the DPA. Such a reformed unit could invite input – depending on the area and issue in question – from relevant regional organizations, NGOs and outside experts/scholars.

For Ismat Kittani, Under-Secretary-General for Peacekeeping, the problem is not that the DPA 'suffers from a lack of information,' nor that it needs its own 'intelli-gence service'[31] but that it cannot effectively manage such information. To address this problem, the DPA put together a policy analysis team, but with modest results. The other two restraints have impinged on the DPA's conflict-prevention capabili-ties, namely, difficulty in finding eminent persons to act as special envoys and the financial limitations of its budget.[32] The Norwegian government has set up a Fund for Preventive Action, which it has placed at the disposal of the UN Secretary-General. The fund, which is earmarked specifically for special envoys, provides a partial solution.[33] Similar funding arrangements have been instigated in the area of education and training, as exemplified by the UN Institute for Training and Research (UNITAR) which runs a programme on peacemaking and preventive diplomacy funded exclusively by governments and foundations.[34]

As for regional organizations, the EU and the OSCE represent the most advanced attempts to integrate conflict prevention and management into organizational structures. In a recent communication on conflict prevention the European Commission explained how the EU and its instrumentalities could best aid inter-national effort to prevent conflict. Essentially, the Commission draws on Europe's post-1945 reconstruction experience. The emphasis is on achieving stability and prosperity through regional integration and expansion of trade. It advocates European policies linking aid with political progress (democratization) and the development of conflict-prevention measures to deal with transnational issues, including smuggling of drugs and small-arms, depletion of natural resources, env-ironmental degradation, slavery, population flows and unethical TNC practices.[35]

As far back as 1990 the OSCE (then CSCE) had established a Conflict Prevention Centre to monitor 'unusual' and 'hazardous' military activities.[36] Two years later, the Helsinki Summit introduced a new model for conflict prevention by setting up on a case-by-case basis *ad hoc* groups with specified mandates.[37]

The CSCE restructured its whole institutional hierarchy by recasting conflict prevention and management as one of its priorities. This cultural change has permeated throughout the CSCE's organizational structure, incorporating early warning (Office for High Commissioner on National Minorities, Office for Democratic Institutions and Human Rights, Representative on Freedom of the Media), mediation (Court of Conciliation and Arbitration), and mid/post-conflict peacebuilding in its field missions.[38]

However, confusion persisted over the respective roles of the EU and the OSCE, not to mention NATO. The question arises as to how overlapping and duplicating activities can be reduced or transformed into a complementary symbiosis. What, in any case, is their relationship to the UN, which both organizations acknowledge as having the 'lead role' when it comes to co-ordinating conflict responses? The International Crisis Group has recommended in this context a series of policy, organizational and procedural reforms.[39] Especially worthy of consideration is the proposal that the EU, given its membership and capabilities, concentrate on pre-conflict prevention by tackling the long-term socioeconomic and environmental conditions conducive to conflict whereas the OSCE might deal more effectively with post-conflict peacebuilding.

Successes and failures

During the Cold War the UN's response to international crises was distinguished by two characteristics: it was remedial rather than preventive; and it intervened predominantly in inter-state conflicts. The Nigerian civil war (1967–70) over the secession of Biafra offered a striking example of the difficulties posed for the UN and the OAU by sovereignty. So did Britain's rejection of U Thant's offer to act as mediator during the Northern Ireland crisis of 1970. The UN's record during this period also suggests at best limited success in such inter-state disputes as Indonesia and Netherlands over West New Guinea (1962), Saudi Arabia and Yemen (1962), Guinea and Ivory Coast (1967), Britain and Iran over Bahrain (1970), and Iran and Iraq (1974). Perhaps the most dramatic mediation effort of this period came during the Cuban missile crisis of 1962 when the Secretary-General visited Havana and offered the UN as a neutral venue for direct communications between the superpowers.[40]

Since the end of the Cold War, the UN has been unable, thus far, to translate effectively its rhetoric and institutional reforms into tangible outcomes, especially when it comes to early conflict prevention. UN responses to crisis management are still largely reactive and over-reliant on first-track traditional diplomacy in late pre-conflict situations. This approach was successfully applied in November 1998 when Annan averted a last minute American/British all-out air strike against Iraq over weapons inspections.[41] But this episode has proved to be the exception rather than the rule.[42]

The UN's more general failure is clearly illustrated in the first post-Cold War inter-state armed conflict, where both early and late preventive diplomacy failed to resolve the Iraq–Kuwait border dispute before it escalated into the Gulf War. As Evans argues, despite knowledge of the issues in the Iraq–Kuwait dispute (oil pricing, the Rumaila oil field, the Warba and Bubilya Islands and debt), the UN and others failed to appreciate the underlying cause of Iraq's desperation, namely the disastrous economic effects of its eight-year war with Iran. Even when it came to late prevention, a month before Iraq invaded Kuwait (August 1990), the international community failed to take Iraqi threats seriously, to appreciate its troubled financial situation, or to activate an effective early warning system.[43]

Whilst in 1990 international attention was focused on South Africa, it was in fact in the Balkans and the Central Africa/Great Lakes Region that violent conflicts erupted in devastating proportions. In particular Rwanda revealed the weaknesses of the UN's early-warning capacity and the breakdown of communication throughout the UN system.[44] The UN, it seems, had completely misunderstood the conflict and allowed exogenous factors unrelated to the situation to prevail in its policy formulation and response.[45]

Similarly, European regional organizations proved incapable of coping with the Yugoslav crisis of 1990, failing either to prevent or to manage the conflict that was to ensue. Complacent over the relatively non-violent transition of ex-communist states in Eastern-Central Europe and the Baltic, the EU/OSCE failed to comprehend the distinctiveness of the Yugoslav federated model and underestimated the potent force of competing ethno-religious nationalisms in a region heavily populated by national minorities. The political damage done to the reputations of the CSCE/OSCE and EU paved the way for other actors (NATO and United States) to take the initiative in responding to the unfolding Yugoslav conflict.[46]

Finally, Cambodia and East Timor constitute interesting cases not only for redefining peacekeeping but also for their comparative treatment by the UN and regional organizations during and after the Cold War. For example, although the UN deplored Indonesia's invasion of 1975 and supported the East Timorese right to self-determination,[47] it did not expedite the process until the late 1990s. More importantly, both cases illustrate the important role that regional organizations (ASEAN between Cambodian factions) and powers (Australia between Indonesia and the UN) can play as third parties.[48]

A number of key lessons emerge from the above examples: first, the intrinsic importance of an effective early-warning system; secondly, the need to understand the intricate socio-political dynamics of individual cases and the capacity to forecast potential changes; thirdly, regional actors and organizations (who share common language, culture/identity, history, association and networks) are often more effective in resolving local conflicts than great powers or international organizations.[49]

Future possibilities

Enough has been said to indicate the pressing need for a global and comprehensive preventive action plan with the UN at its epicentre. To this end the UN needs to develop a multi-track approach, engaging and consulting with a wide range of actors at all tiers of governance. Central to this approach is the attempt to integrate different strategies (political settlement, problem-solving, rapprochement and reconciliation), different methods (mediation, peacekeeping, CBMs) and different third-party agents (UN, regional and sub-regional organizations, governments, IFIs, NGOs, academic institutions, think-tanks, individual experts, private business, journalists). Such an integrated approach needs to take into account the circumstances prevailing at any given time in the conflict cycle and the various levels of the social conflict pyramid (political and military elites, middle-level policy-makers, non-government opinion-makers and local urban or rural community groups).

First-track diplomacy cannot encompass the full range of conflict-transformation processes, techniques or strategies any more than second- or third-track diplomacy can. As Clements argues, several tracks and approaches have each a role to play. Beginning with the more obvious ones the list would include:

- 'inter-governmental diplomacy' at the UN;
- 'governmental peacemaking' through bilateral negotiations;
- 'second track diplomacy using unofficial forums' (for instance Norwegian mediations which led to the 1993 Oslo Accords);
- 'citizen diplomacy through private means', including use of traditional networks;
- 'economic diplomacy', including packages by donor agencies designed to sustain peace;
- mediatory or other third-party intervention by CSOs (for example, religious groups such as the Quakers) with an established reputation for impartiality and conflict-resolution skills;
- women's diplomacy, utilizing women's movements, at both the local and international level, to mobilize women in conflict-transformation processes;
- 'communications diplomacy', with media-generated information and analysis helping to rally public opinion and shape perceptions of policy-makers and decision-makers;[50]
- other forms of citizen diplomacy, including establishment of 'peace zones', 'peace corridors' and 'co-operation zones';
- 'peace education' and training programmes which address the root causes of conflict and promote a culture of peace and understanding, especially amongst young people and students;
- 'creative' or 'celebrity diplomacy' using as intermediaries well-known artists, entertainers, sports personalities and athletes.[51]

But such a multi-track approach raises, at least conceptually, a series of questions regarding its management, co-ordination and implementation. How is a coherent, flexible and effective multi-track conflict-prevention strategy to be pursued? Although it is not our intention to answer these highly pertinent questions in any definitive sense, we can begin by articulating them in a more specific way. How do we know which track to use and when in any given situation? Who should take the lead in initiating a preventive strategy? Who will co-ordinate this strategy? Is such co-ordination possible given the polycentric character of international politics? What are the implications of all this for the UN system as a whole?

Early warning offers at least part of the answer to several, though by no means all, of these questions. From the very beginning of conflict resolution as an intellectual discipline, early warning has been proposed as an essential component in any model of conflict prevention. However, it was the Rwanda and Yugoslavia débâcles that convinced even sceptics of the potential contribution of early warning to conflict prevention.

Any serious attempt to construct an effective early-warning system is immediately confronted with two broad problems: one is methodological and the other deontological. Both concern the quality, accuracy and speed of information in any given conflict situation. There is first the need to construct a centralized network of intelligence-gathering, or information data-system, that monitors events and developments throughout the world and constantly ranks and prioritizes them according to a risk pendulum.

Such information could be derived from a broad range of sources and resources: national governments, NGOs – both those dealing with conflicts generally (such as International Alert, INCORE) and those with a more specific brief (for instance, Amnesty International, Human Rights Watch) – the media, academics and experts, UN specialized agencies and regional organizations. For both monitoring and evaluation purposes, the UN could establish its own network on the ground by setting up UN information posts in every country – the scale of operation and allocation of resources and staff could be rationalized (that is, increased or decreased) with changing circumstances (see below). To retain the UN's legitimacy it is imperative that this information be made public, and transparency and accountability be maintained. The open dissemination of information would help to expose any political attempt at misinformation or misrepresentation designed to produce a certain course of action – or inaction – on the part of the UN. Another advantage in the transparency of information is that it could act as a warning signal by exposing prospective aggressors to international public scrutiny.

Independent experts, think-tanks and research centres can develop sound analysis of the origins and dynamics of different conflicts, while second-track conflict-resolution practitioners might be able to design appropriate responses that will not unduly alarm national leaders by raising the spectre of UN interference in their domestic affairs. The aim here must be to combine early warning and early responses to conflict in a flexible blend of strategies.

If it is agreed that the UN should play a leading role in identifying useful sources of analysis and information and integrating these into coherent strategies, then a strong case can be made for the establishment of a UN-sponsored *International Crisis Prevention and Response Centre* (ICPRC). Directly accountable to the Secretariat, such a Centre would co-ordinate and gather all relevant information, drawing on a broad range of UN and external sources, such as NGOs, think-tanks, universities and research institutes, media outlets, local UN national offices (see below), even co-opting the intelligence services of member states and regional organizations. Except in matters of vital national security, states would be expected to co-operate with the UN in maintaining an extensive information bank. The Centre would provide regular public reports, serve as an early-warning system, and make assessments and recommendations for the Secretary-General's consideration. Where possible the ICPRC would be supported by regional crisis centres and link into the network of UN national offices. One important component of each office's activities would be to contribute to the UN's early-warning, fact-finding and conflict-analysis capacity. Conflict prevention and management would be made an integral part of its brief.[52]

A second and closely related initiative would be to encourage UN agencies and instrumentalities which deal with the causes and consequences of conflict to develop, in close collaboration with the ICPRC, more sophisticated early-warning, information-gathering and assessment capabilities, and where appropriate, to use their programmes for low-level third-party intervention. In particular, the UNHCR should undertake a more critical role in encouraging and monitoring lasting agreements, especially in conflicts involving large numbers of displaced persons or refugees. In different settings, the 'good offices' of the ICJ could be used more frequently and in more sustained fashion to bring warring parties together for purposes of reconciliation. Specialized agencies could play a more active part in mediation and conciliation by judiciously integrating these processes into their development, environment and human-rights programmes.

Such an integrated strategy would also facilitate the more direct and co-ordinated involvement of CSOs and regional organizations in preventive diplomacy and peacebuilding programmes, including mediation and fact-finding missions to diverse conflict zones. Such closer co-operation could be diversified and appropriately institutionalized. For example, the EU, APEC, or even the G7 in conjunction with the World Bank and IMF, could form task forces to assist the UN in the areas of conflict-prevention-oriented development and aid-programmes. The OSCE, OAS and OAU, on the other hand, could concentrate on post-conflict peacebuilding tasks. Such an arrangement could also enable financial and technical assistance to be extended to those regional organizations which confront multiple and complex conflicts, notably the OAU and ASEAN which lack the resources and financial capacity of more developed actors such as EU or OSCE.

Even at the national level, governments should be encouraged to develop and integrate early warning and preventive action in their foreign-policy formulation. Aid, development and environmental programmes, human-rights initiatives, diplomatic efforts and membership of multilateral organizations could be integrated into a coherent conflict-prevention strategy.[53]

One of the most common and debilitating limitations on a conflict-prevention capability is closely linked to the financial and budgetary constraints. To address this problem at all effectively a radical approach is needed. It may now be time to apply the principle that a levy be made on affluent OECD countries and TNCs in accordance with a formula agreed to by the UN General Assembly, for the express purpose of funding operations, programmes, missions and institutions endowed with conflict-prevention functions. The underlying logic of such a proposal is that conflict prevention is a sound investment which will yield a direct and often tangible benefit to these countries and corporations, given that enhanced political stability and military security are necessary conditions for expanding trade and economic activity more generally.

There is, moreover a clear correlation between conflict prevention as a cost-saving measure and costs incurred in conflict.[54] In addition to the costs directly associated with the development and deployment of military capabilities are the costs of rebuilding damaged economies, and the flow-on effects in terms of refugees and asylum seekers and the measures undertaken by way of border surveillance, deterrence, coercion and administrative processing occasioned by these large and often unpredictable population movements. Within such a context, there is a strong argument for a larger and more sharply focused contribution by IFIs to long-term conflict prevention and peacebuilding, including conflict impact assessments for all major international economic and social development programmes.

Conclusion

Sooner or later any transformative project committed to a human security model of conflict resolution will have to deal with the prevailing state-centric outlook that permeates the UN and other multilateral organizations. Many observers remain sceptical of this possibility, given that the UN itself institutionalizes power politics and does not – perhaps cannot by virtue of its Charter – provide an alternative model to traditional geopolitics.[55] Yet it seems an unavoidable conclusion that the UN system, if it is to become actively engaged in conflict resolution – especially pre-conflict prevention and post-conflict peacebuilding – will from time to time need to intervene in ways which challenge the principle of absolute state sovereignty as encapsulated in the UN Charter and constantly reaffirmed by the Security Council.[56]

In addition to the lingering impact of the theory and practice of state sovereignty, two other roadblocks have impeded the development of a global, multi-layered, and multidimensional conflict-prevention strategy. First, great power dominance of international relations – and the asymmetry which it implies – has often put a brake on the application of effective conflict-prevention and conflict-resolution strategies. As the Gulf War and Kosovo conflicts indicate, a great power, and especially a superpower, is likely to expect a different set of rules to apply when its own interests are involved. The second fundamental obstacle has to do with socioeconomic inequality, with the disparities of wealth, status, income and leverage. These conditions constitute a breeding ground for conflict creation and highly inhospitable terrain for conflict prevention. An effective, long-term conflict-management strategy must therefore meet the three-pronged challenge posed by the sovereignty discourse, great-power dominance and the disparities of wealth and income. In that deeper sense, conflict prevention is inseparable from the wider political and economic reform agenda canvassed in previous and subsequent chapters of this book.

Conceptually at least, the answer may lie in the democratization of conflict prevention, since it is only such a strategy which offers a plausible response to all three roadblocks. As the argument developed in this book will elaborate, approaches to conflict management must themselves be consistent with the democratization of global governance. Conflict prevention must, in other words, proceed with the active participation of all relevant parties (states and non-state actors) at all levels of the decision-making process.

The Boutros-Ghali/Annan campaign to raise the international profile of conflict prevention has neither been matched by appropriate institutional reform nor translated on the ground into effective or timely preventive strategies and initiatives. Judging from the available evidence, the UN's recent track record is only marginally distinguishable from its pre-Cold War achievements. The UN and other multilateral organizations will need to develop the intellectual and institutional capacity to differentiate between, and at the same time integrate, conflict prevention, peacekeeping and peacebuilding. They will also need to devise strategies and decision-making processes that operate simultaneously in – and interact between – the short, medium and long term on the one hand, and the local, national, regional and global tiers of governance on the other.

Notes

1. For the relevant SIPRI survey, see
   <http://editors.sipri.se/pubs/yearb.html> (14 September 2001).
2. In the late 1960s Johan Galtung unsuccessfully attempted to label the study of conflict as 'conflictology': see J. Galtung, 'Conflict as a Way of Life', in H. Freedman (ed.), *Progress in Mental Health: Proceedings of the Seventh International Congress on Mental Health* (New York: Grune & Stratton, 1969), pp.26–8.
3. For a comprehensive historical and theoretical survey of conflict resolution, see C.R. Mitchell, *The Structure of International Conflict* (London: Macmillan, 1981); for more up-to-date treatment, see H. Miall, O. Ramsbotham and T. Woodhouse, *Contemporary Conflict Resolution: the Prevention, Management and Transformation of Deadly Conflicts* (Cambridge: Polity Press, 1999).
4. B. Boutros-Ghali, *An Agenda for Peace: Preventive Diplomacy, Peacemaking and Peace-keeping*, A/47/277-S/24111, 17 June 1992, para.20.
5. L.M Goodrich and E. Hambro, *Charter of the United Nations: Commentary and Documents*, 2nd edn (London: London Institute of World Affairs/Stevens & Sons, 1949), pp.591–2.
6. Peacemaking techniques are further detailed in United Nations, *Handbook on the Peaceful Settlement of Disputes between States* (New York: UNDPI, 1992).
7. Kofi Annan prefers to refer to 'preventive action' rather than 'preventive diplomacy' as there are several forms of action that can have preventive effect. This attitude is more in keeping with our overall approach. Suffice it to say here that 'preventive diplomacy' has a solid place in the generally accepted UN lexicon; for the UN Secretariat's view, see 'Preventive Action and Peacemaking', available online at:
   <http://www.un.org/Depts/dpa/docs/peacemak.htm> (13 April 2001).
8. Evans also distinguishes between 'early preventative diplomacy' (also referred to as 'crisis diplomacy') which involves third-party intervention at the beginning of a conflict and 'late preventative diplomacy' when armed conflict is imminent and the intention is to dissuade the parties from becoming involved in it: see G. Evans, *Cooperating for Peace: the Global Agenda for the 1990s and Beyond* (Sydney: Allen & Unwin, 1993), p.10. Furthermore, 'early' preventative diplomacy should deploy low-profile, non-coercive and non-military measures; whereupon resorting to more visible and coercive methods of 'late' preventative diplomacy is a clear indication that 'early' attempts have failed: see J. Leatherman, W. DeMars, P. Gaffney and R. Varyrynen, *Breaking Cycles of*

Violence: Conflict Prevention in Intrastate Crises (West Hartford, CT: Kumarian Press, 1999), pp.42, 99.

9. These conflicts have been variously described also as 'deep-rooted conflicts', 'intractable conflicts', and 'protracted social conflicts'. See, respectively, J. Burton, *Resolving Deep-Rooted Conflict: a Handbook* (Lanham, MD: University Press of America, 1987), L. Kriesberg, A. Northrup and S. Thorson (eds), *Intractable Conflicts and Their Transformation* (Syracuse, New York: Syracuse University Press, 1989), E. Azar, 'Protracted International Conflicts', in E. Azar and J. Burton (eds), *International Conflict Resolution: Theory and Practice* (Sussex: Wheatsheaf, 1986), pp.28–39, E. Azar, *The Management of Protracted Social Conflict: Theory and Cases*, (Aldershot: Dartmouth, 1990).

10. Boutros-Ghali (1992) expanded the conventional meaning of fact-finding to incorporate, in addition to information provided by governments, supplementary informal sources, see para.25(c).

11. Ibid., para.24–33.

12. Kofi Annan considers both preventive deployment and preventive disarmament as complementary measures of preventive diplomacy. *Preventive deployment*, according to UN definition, provides a 'thin blue line' with the aim of containing conflicts at the early stage of violent conflicts, to act as a circuit-breaker in the circle of tension-ridden areas or between highly polarized communities (for example, UNPREDEP in Macedonia, 1995–99). Harder measures are entailed in *preventive disarmament*, which overall aims to reduce the small-arms and light weaponry and/or prevent weapon-trafficking into conflict-prone regions (as exemplified by ONUMOZ in Mozambique, 1992–94), see 'Report of the Secretary-General on the Work of the Organization', A/54/1, 31 August 1999, para.42–4. The difference between these two preventive actions is that preventive disarmament is mandated as part of or following a settlement agreement between the conflicting parties and will include monitoring a ceasefire, and the separation and demobilization of forces. In this context preventive disarmament should be considered as comprising a component of post-conflict peacebuilding.

13. Goodrich and Hambro, p.592.

14. International Peace Academy, OAU/IPA Joint Task Force on Peacemaking and Peacekeeping, 'Report on Africa', January 1998, available online at: <http://ipacademy.org/publications/Report/Africa/PubliRepoAfriPP98> (19 April 2001).

15. James Sutterlin regards peacebuilding as the 'macro approach' to conflict prevention; see J.S. Sutterlin, *The United Nations and the Maintenance of International Security: a Challenge to Be Met* (Westport, CT: Praeger, 1995), p.71.

16. Evans, pp.9–10.

17. Evans, p.9.

18. A/54/1, para.45–6.

19. Ibid., para.47–52.

20. See Miall, Rambotham and Woodhouse, pp.12–4. For further information on the transformation of assymetric conflicts and the dynamics of relationship structures between uneven conflicting parties, see A. Curle, *Making Peace* (London: Tavistock, 1971) and J.P. Lederach, *Preparing for Peace: Conflict Transformation Across Cultures* (New York: Syracuse University Press, 1995).

21. D.L. Jones, 'Mediation, Conflict Resolution and Critical Theory', *Review of International Studies*, 26, 4 (October 2000), pp.659–61.

22. 'The UN's Power Failure: Nation States Stifle its Freedom to Act', the *Guardian*, 7 September 2000.

23. B. Boutros-Ghali, *Supplement to An Agenda for Peace: Position Paper of the Secretary-General on the Occasion of the Fiftieth Anniversary of the United Nations*, A/50/60-S/1995/1, 3 January 1995, paras 27–8.

24. See, for example, A/55/1, 30 August 2000, paras 29–39; A/54/1, paras 68–88, 31 August 1999; A/53/1, 27 August 1998, ch.1.a, paras 25–55; A/52/1, 3 September 1997, ch.2(d),

paras 78–94, A/51/1, October 1996, ch.4, paras 643–1127, A/50/405, 18 October 1995, ch.4, paras 581–988.

25. See A/55/985-S/2001/574, 7 June 2001; S/1998/318, 13 April 1998, and S/1998/833, 22 September 1998. The latter two led to SC resolutions 1265 (1999) and 1296 (2000).

26. K.A. Annan, *We the Peoples: the Role of the United Nations in the 21st Century* (New York: UNDPI, 2000), pp.44–6.

27. S/23500, 31 January 1992.

28. See
    <http://www.un.org/Depts/dpa/normal.htm> and
    <http://www.un.org/Depts/dpa/docs/peacemak.htm> (31 August 2001).

29. 'Report of the Panel on United Nations Operations', A/55/305-S/2000/809, 21 August 2000, paras 65–75.

30. K. Clements, 'International Peace Institutions', in J. Lampen (ed.), *No Alternative? Nonviolent Response to Repressive Regimes* (York, UK: William Sessions, 2000), pp.23–4.

31. The proposition that the UN needs to establish an intelligence capability, albeit for its peacekeeping operations, was put forward by H. Smith, 'Intelligence and UN Peacekeeping', *Survival*, 36, 3 (Autumn 1994), pp.174–92.

32. I. Kittani, 'Preventive Diplomacy and Peacemaking: the UN Experience', in O.A. Otunnu and M.V. Doyle (eds), *Peacemaking and Peacekeeping for the New Century* (Lanham: Rowman & Littlefields, 1998), pp.99–101.

33. See Fund for Preventive Action, European Platform for Conflict Prevention and Transformation, online at:
    <http://www.euroconflict.org/euroconflict/guides/orgs/un/92.htm> (24 September 2001).

34. This programme targets non-military staff from the UN, regional organizations and foreign ministries, to train them in conflict analysis, mediation and negotiation: see UNDPA, 'Programme in Peacemaking and Preventive Diplomacy', at:
    <http://www.unitar.org/peacemaking> (29 July 2001).

35. European Commission, *Communication from the Commission on Conflict Prevention*, COM(2001), 211 final, Brussels, 11 April 2001.

36. CSCE, Summit of Heads of State or Government (19–21 November 1990), *Charter of Paris for a New Europe* (Paris 1990), p.17.

37. CSCE, Summit of Heads of State or Government (9–10 July 1992), *Helkinski Document 1992: the Challenges of Change*, paras 16–21.

38. See
    <http://www.osce.org> (18 September 2001).

39. See International Crisis Group (ICG), *EU Crisis Response Capability: Institutional and Processes for Conflict Prevention and Management*, ICG Issues Report No.2, Brussels, 26 June 2001.

40. See U Thant, *View for the UN* (New York: Doubleday, 1978), pp.48–56, for Cuban missile crisis, pp.154–94; also see K. Waldheim, *The Challenge of Peace* (London: Weidenfeld & Nicolson, 1980), pp.47–8.

41. The *Guardian*, 23 November 1998.

42. Annan's intervention, however, has not prevented British-American air raids against Iraq altogether (such as the one that took place on 9 September 2001 which resulted in eight Iraqi fatalities), *BBC News*, 10 September 2001, available online at:
    <http://news.bbc.co.uk/hi/english/world/middle_east/newsid_1534000/1534916.stm> (4 October 2001).

43. Evans, pp.68–9.

44. 'Report of the Independent Inquiry into the Actions of the United Nations During the 1994 Genocide in Rwanda', 15 December 1999, available online at:
    <www.un.org/news/ossg/rwanda_report.htm> (24 September 2001).

45. 'Comprehensive Report on Lessons Learned from United Nations Assistance Mission for Rwanda (UNAMIR)', October 1993–April 1996, available online at:
    <www.un.org/depts/dpko/lessons/rwanda.htm> (25 September 2001).

46. By the mid-1990s the role of the OSCE had been restricted to monitoring the elections in Bosnia as stipulated by the 1995 Dayton Peace Agreement. Even at this juncture the various parties preferred the OSCE over the UN in monitoring the elections, see R. Holbrooke, *To End a War* (New York: Random House, 1998), pp.290–1, 319, 341.

47. SCR 384, 22 December 1975.

48. For Evans UNTAC vindicated the role of middle power diplomacy (Australia), in conjunction with 'like minded countries' (Indonesia and Vietnam), regional organizations (ASEAN), the local political Cambodian factions and the Security Council, proving that local regional initiatives can succeed, see G. Evans, 'The Comprehensive Settlement to the Cambodian Conflict: an Exercise in Cooperating for Peace', in H. Smith (ed.), *International Peacekeeping: Building on the Cambodian Experience* (Canberra: Australian Defence Force Academy, 1994), pp.10–11.

49. See B. Frederking, A. Pyatt and S. Randol, 'Who You Gonna Call? Third Parties, Conflict Resolution, and the End of the Cold War', *Online Journal of Peace and Conflict Resolution*, 3, 2 (June 2000):
    <www.trinstitute.org/ojpcr/p3_2fredpr.htm> (18 July 2001).

50. For further information see M.J. O'Neill, 'Developing Preventive Journalism', in K.M. Cahill (ed.), *Preventive Diplomacy: Stopping Wars before They Start* (New York: Routledge/Centre for International Health and Cooperation, 2000), pp.67–79, and E. Gardner, 'The Role of Media in Conflicts', in L. Reychler and T. Paffenholz (eds), *Peacebuilding: a Field Guide* (Boulder/London: Lynne Rienner, 2001), pp.301–11.

51. Clements, pp.36–7.

52. For the rationale for and detailed description of these offices, see Chapter 15.

53. Such a strategy was recommended by the Australian Parliament's Joint Standing Committee on Foreign Affairs, Defence and Trade, *Australia's Role in the United Nations* (Canberra: Parliament of the Commonwealth of Australia, 2001), pp.110–18.

54. World Vision Australia estimated that if conflict prevention had been applied to the actual conflicts of Bosnia, Rwanda, Somalia, Haiti, Gulf War, Cambodia and El Salvador, the outside powers would have saved approximately $128.7 billion, see World Vision Australia, Submission No.99 cf. ibid., p.114.

55. A.C. Tingel, *Conflict Resolved? A Critical Assessment of Conflict Resolution* (London: Pinter, 1998), p.12.

56. Recently, the Security Council has clearly reaffirmed 'its commitment to the principle of sovereign equality, national sovereignty, territorial integrity and political independence of all States', see S/RES/1318 (2000), para.1.

11
The UN and Disarmament: a Global and Regional Action Plan

Michael Hamel-Green

Despite the increased threats posed by the development and increasing availability of technologies of mass destruction (nuclear, chemical, biological and missile delivery systems), and the pattern of recurring deadly conflicts during the twentieth century, the world is beginning the new millennium in the context of a dangerous deadlock over disarmament.

The five major nuclear powers, while paying lip service to the objective of total elimination of nuclear weapons – most recently at the Non Proliferation Treaty 2000 Review Conference – have so far refused to agree to a definite timetable of nuclear disarmament, or even a substantive process for discussing such disarmament.[1] In 1998, the previous 'threshold' states of India and Pakistan conducted nuclear tests and announced their intention of developing nuclear weapons.[2] Israel, while not openly declaring its nuclear weapon status, is also known to have acquired a nuclear weapons capability.[3] In the case of other WMDs, that is, chemical and biological weapons, substantial progress has been made on negotiating conventions to outlaw such weapons (Chemical Weapons Convention: CWC, and Biological Weapons Convention: BWC) but less agreement has been reached on the detail of the necessary verification and control mechanisms for implementing them.[4] In the case of missile proliferation, there are few restraints at all, except for the non-universal and increasingly ineffective Missile Technology Control Regime.[5] Countries with medium- or long-range missile capabilities in addition to the five major nuclear powers now include Iran, Iraq, Syria, Libya, Israel, India, Pakistan, Japan and North Korea.[6] The new Bush Administration threatens to turn the current deadlock in arms control and disarmament into an actual roll-back of existing agreements and an unravelling of the whole multilateral non-proliferation regime. The Administration has indicated that it will pursue National Missile Defence and Theatre Missile Defence systems even if this means abandoning the ABM Treaty with Russia; that it will not ratify the newly negotiated Comprehensive Test Ban Treaty (CTBT); and that it will not support the proposed verification and control protocol to the BWC.[7]

The 2001 terrorist suicide attacks on the World Trade Centre and Pentagon have further heightened awareness of the need for global controls over nuclear and other WMDs. Some experts have long been concerned that non-state actors, such as terrorist groups, may begin using nuclear, chemical or biological weapons.[8] The 2001 terrorist attacks on America certainly demonstrated that terrorist groups are rapidly acquiring the organizational skills and resources necessary to mount biological and chemical attacks, if not a nuclear attack in the form of a 'suitcase' bomb or an attack on a nuclear power station.

The next ten years are likely to prove a watershed in deciding whether the governments of the world develop the collective political will to agree on global and regional disarmament objectives and processes, or whether they return to an anarchic, and ultimately suicidal, pursuit of national 'security' strategies based on new technologies of mass destruction that will make the atrocities of the twentieth century seem like mere peccadillos.

Despite its inherent limitations as an organization of sovereign states, the UN will be pivotal in determining which path the countries of the world choose to take. It is the primary global organization with the capacity to mobilize international opinion and co-ordinate collective action to achieve disarmament.

An overview of the UN's disarmament role

Historically, the UN has played a crucial role in both regional and global disarmament processes and initiatives, either directly as the forum for debate and negotiation of disarmament and arms control treaties, such as the Partial Test Ban Treaty (PTBT, 1963) and the Non Proliferation Treaty (NPT, 1968), or indirectly as the channel for international pressure on relevant states to negotiate bilateral or regional disarmament treaties, such as the US-Russia START I and START II treaties, and regional treaties, such as the Tlatelolco Latin American Nuclear Weapon-Free Zone Treaty (LANWFZ, 1967).[9]

More specifically, the UN's First Committee and General Assembly have served to provide regular and continuing forums for member states to debate and initiate disarmament initiatives, and the annual sessions of the Disarmament Commission and Conference on Disarmament (CD), particularly the latter, have provide forums for multilateral negotiations. The UN has held three Special Sessions on Disarmament, in 1978, 1982 and 1986, to seek agreement on a global disarmament agenda. To a lesser extent, the Security Council has also provided a forum for arms-control debates, particularly in relation to crises with proliferation implications, such as Iraqi and North Korean breaches of the NPT. At a regional level, the UN has regularly sponsored regional conferences on security, disarmament and arms-control matters, created several regional centres on these issues, and begun to work more closely with regional bodies on disarmament measures.[10]

Even during the Cold War, when so many UN initiatives were frustrated by the exercise of ideologically motivated vetoes, the UN was still successful in promoting a degree of incremental progress on disarmament and arms control. It is a remarkable paradox that at the height of the Cold War, the UN was still able to bring the world community together in the first three Special Sessions on Disarmament, but in the post-Cold War Period – when supposedly new 'windows of opportunity' were opened up for disarmament dialogue – the efforts to convene a fourth Special Session have repeatedly failed. Further, some of the most important multilateral treaties that remain at the heart of controlling nuclear weapons proliferation were negotiated during this period, including the already mentioned NPT and PTBT, the Outer Space Treaty and the Seabed Treaty. In the same period, the UN fostered, supported and gave its *imprimatur* to a number of important regional denucleariza- tion initiatives, including the LANWFZ mentioned above and the 1985 South Pacific Nuclear Free Zone, and proposals for establishing NWFZs in other regions, such as South Asia, Africa and the Middle East.[11] Admittedly, the progress consisted mainly of partial measures, and, in the case of the NPT, was seriously flawed by its discriminatory character (legitimizing the possession of nuclear weapons by the Permanent Five on condition that they move towards disarmament), but collect- ively the above treaties remain the most important steps to disarmament so far taken by the world community.

In the post-Cold War period the most dramatic progress was in the initial bi- lateral agreements between the United States and Russia to reduce their nuclear arsenals and cease active deployment of tactical nuclear weapons. However, this initial bilateral progress was not followed up by the consistent progress towards complete disarmament envisaged in Article VI of the NPT. The UN, for its part, continues to promote multilateral initiatives, focusing particularly on the CTBT, a Fissile Materials Cut-Off Treaty (FMCT), bans on landmines, confidence-building and transparency measures, and regional NWFZs.

The most notable achievement was the negotiation of a draft CTBT in the CD, finally approved by the General Assemby in late 1996; however, the entry into force of the Treaty could well be blocked or indefinitely delayed by the 1999 refusal of the US Congress to ratify it.[12] Other achievements during this period were the negotiation and successful establishment of the African NWFZ Treaty, which the UN directly facilitated through its joint auspicing of the negotiations with the OAU, and support for ASEAN's establishment of a South East Asian NWFZ.[13] The UN also sought to foster similar zones in the Middle East and Central Asia, commissioning expert studies of the feasibility of such a zone or a Weapons of Mass Destruction Free Zone (WMDFZ) in the Middle East, and directly assisting the Central Asian states in negotiating a draft treaty on a Central Asian NWFZ.[14] Finally, the ICJ, following an international citizens' cam- paign and requests from both the WHO and the General Assembly, made a land- mark 1996 judgement that the use and possession of nuclear weapons was illegal in almost all conceivable circumstances and called for member states to negotiate in good faith for the complete elimination of such weapons.[15]

Strengths and weaknesses in UN disarmament approaches

Since the end of the Cold War the UN has continued to pursue partial and lim- ited disarmament and arms-control measures. It has also continued to play the crucial role of establishing international norms and expectations concerning dis- armament and non-proliferation. Its strengths have included:

- sustaining annual debates over arms control and disarmament even when major players appeared reluctant to entertain further initiatives;

- functioning as one of the few international channels for non-nuclear countries to network and exert collective pressure on the nuclear 'hold-outs';
- developing co-ordinated global/regional policy approaches to arms control and disarmament;
- using its expertise and resources to assist in conducting regional and global studies on disarmament; and
- providing the international legal, moral and political authority to contest trends in some member states towards the use or threat of use of WMDs as an instrument of national policy.

While the UN has continued to make progress on a number of fronts, it continues to have a number of weaknesses in dealing with disarmament and arms control. The most salient weaknesses are associated with its inherent organizational character as an association of sovereign states, and the historically determined procedures that have failed to keep pace with the changes in the world environment. Many important disarmament proposals and initiatives are aborted at their very inception by a few countries exercising their veto – in the Security Council or in such consensus-procedure forums as the CD. India, for many years, successfully blocked discussion of regional NWFZs in the Disarmament Commission. China and Russia blocked a total landmines ban in the Conference on the CWC. The United States has consistently blocked a consensus on the convening of a Fourth Special Session on Disarmament.

A second weakness has been the meagre resources allocated to the UN. As the Under-Secretary for Disarmament Affairs has noted, the UN Department for Disarmament and Arms Regulation (UNDDAR) has an annual budget that is approximately half the size of the cost of a single new fighter plane.[16] For an organization charged with global responsibility for implementing disarmament policies and strategies, the resources allocated under present funding arrangements are ludicrously inadequate.

Thirdly, the UN has failed to mobilize the world community and NGO networks beyond the governments directly involved. It has not been able to live up to the expectations raised by the 1992 Earth Summit where a great many NGOs were mobilized alongside governments. Without the kind of pressure that various CSOs can exert on their respective governments, there is little prospect that the 'problem' governments can be induced to take disarmament issues more seriously.

In what follows, current UN disarmament proposals and strategies will first be surveyed, and then a new UN disarmament action plan will be proposed, based upon an integrated and phased approach at both global and regional levels of action.

Current UN disarmament proposals and initiatives

Galvanized by the sense of urgency created by the Indian and Pakistani nuclear tests, and the failure of the eight nuclear states to agree on a definite and substantive process for eliminating their nuclear arsenals, eight middle-level states came together in June 1998 to form a coalition for a 'new agenda' focused on creating a 'nuclear-weapon-free world'.[17] Drawing upon some of the ideas and approaches of the earlier Canberra and Global Governance Commissions, Brazil, Egypt, Ireland, Mexico, New Zealand, Slovenia, South Africa and Sweden proposed a new disarmament agenda that specifically called upon the nuclear weapon states to 'give an unequivocal commitment to the speedy and total elimination of their respective nuclear weapons' and 'bring to a conclusion' the negotiations for elimination required under Article VI of the NPT. In a series of subsidiary strategies, the agenda also calls for:

- the immediate bringing into force of START II and the commencement of START III negotiations, coupled with the integration of the other nuclear states into the disarmament process;
- negotiations to reduce reliance on and eliminate all non-strategic nuclear weapons;
- de-alerting and removal of nuclear warheads from delivery vehicles;
- review of strategic doctrines (for example, 'first-use');
- negotiation of legally binding negative security guarantees to non-nuclear members of the NPT;
- further establishment of regional NWFZs, particularly in the Middle East and South Asia;
- a moratorium on production of fissile materials pending the negotiations of a FMCT in the CD;
- restraint by the three nuclear-capable nations (Israel, India and Pakistan) who have not acceded to the NPT;
- establishment, through CD mechanisms, of an appropriate body to deal with nuclear disarmament; and
- the convening of an international conference on nuclear disarmament and proliferation.[18]

The original eight members of the New Agenda Coalition were joined by a further 26 sponsors and the core 'new agenda' was adopted in the form of a General Assembly resolution by a vote of 97 to 19, with 32 abstentions.[19] All of the nuclear or nuclear-capable states except for China voted against. By the time of the 2000 Millennium General Assembly, support for a revised version of the New Agenda resolution had substantially increased to 154 with 3 against (India, Israel and Pakistan) and eight abstentions (including France and Russia).[20]

Outside the UN forums, a number of influential independent commissions on disarmament have been supported or sponsored by individual states, including the 1982 Olaf Palme Commission that pioneered the concept of 'common security',[21] the 1996 Canberra Commission on the Elimination of Nuclear Weapons,[22] many of whose recommendations were incorporated into the New Agenda Group's resolutions already discussed, and most recently the 1999 Tokyo Forum which advanced 16 key recommendations for immediate and longer-term action on nuclear proliferation and disarmament.[23] The Tokyo Forum rejected the notion that nuclear weapons, pending their final elimination, could have any function other than to deter the use of other nuclear weapons, thereby dismissing the currently fashionable rationales in some nuclear policy quarters (especially the United States) that nuclear weapons need to be retained to counter biological and chemical weapon threats.

Both the 'New Agenda Group' and the Tokyo Forum proposals for a new disarmament agenda, while important and constructive, have limitations that, in the present global and regional context, may well mean that they will be rendered irrelevant by a downward spiral into mutual distrust and collapse of international agreements.

One key limitation is that they fail to identify target dates for securing progress and identifying phases in the nuclear elimination process. No doubt this omission was motivated by a wish to propitiate the Permanent Five nuclear powers. The latter already exercise their power of veto in the Security Council; they should not also be granted the right to veto the international community's whole disarmament agenda. The Tokyo Report purports to be advancing a disarmament 'Action Plan for the 21st Century', but any realistic and credible action plan must include some notion of target dates and duration of phases or stages in the implementation process.

Another limitation, as Jurgen Scheffran observes, is that 'ballistic missiles and other delivery systems have been largely ignored in international arms control and disarmament' and unilateralist approaches to defend against missile attack, such as the American National Missile Defence and Theatre Missile Defence are beset with technical viability, financial and political difficulties.[24] In Scheffran's view, the international community needs to consider a range of new measures, including moratoriums on ballistic missile testing and development, regional MFZs, freezes on current missile levels, and an eventual global treaty on elimination of all ballistic missiles.

A further limitation is that both sets of agenda proposals are solely directed at governments. Yet many past disarmament successes, such as the 1963 PTBT, the INF Agreement, the 1996 ICJ judgement on the legality of nuclear weapons, and some regional NWFZ proposals, have been linked closely to the mobilization of CSOs in favour of disarmament initiatives. The increasingly urgent need to address the present impasse in disarmament will depend not only on the goodwill and determination of the non-nuclear nations spearheading the 'New Agenda' proposal but also on regional and global pressure and mobilization of CSOs. Organizational and procedural changes in the UN's disarmament negotiation machinery would need to incorporate both government and CSO roles and inputs.

Proposed new UN disarmament policies, strategies and initiatives

Given the urgency of finally eliminating nuclear and other WMDs as a precondition for securing the common future of humanity, and to address some of the limitations that have so far prevented turning this principle into practice, it is vitally necessary that UN member states adopt an agreed policy of identifying phases and time lines of negotiation, treaty conclusion, and treaty implementation and enforcement as steps towards the elimination of all WMDs. Despite the present impasse in disarmament diplomacy, it is not unreasonable, on the basis of the minimum periods necessary to develop the political will and actually conduct the required negotiations, to propose that the UN should consider setting a target date around 2020 for the final verified and enforced elimination of all classes of WMDs.

This proposed deadline allows for an initial five-year period of arresting the present increasingly dangerous slide towards national reliance on WMDs. This initial period would be aimed at strengthening existing arms control measures, introducing new measures designed to 'cap' or 'freeze' current WMD capabilities, and mobilizing the international community (at governmental and civil-society levels) behind the new disarmament action plan. This period would culminate with a formal commitment to actively negotiate a treaty for the phased elimination of nuclear weapons, and strengthened verification and enforcement agreements to back up the existing CWC and BWC. The ensuing five years would involve the signing and progressive ratification and development of implementing machinery for the nuclear weapons elimination treaty. The third period would involve an initial stage of nuclear weapons reductions by treaty parties, further phases in verified nuclear weapon reduction, and the elimination of all remaining WMDs by the target year of 2020.

At a regional level, the above three phases would involve a UN-regional organization partnership in developing complementary or facilitating regional measures to serve as stepping-stones or rungs on a ladder towards the final 2020 target date of WMD elimination. One of the principal strategies at a regional level would be UN-regional organization co-operation in exploring, developing, negotiating, and implementing regional NWFZs and WMDFZs for specific regions, particularly in the Northern Hemisphere.

UN member states should work towards adopting an agreed phased action policy and strategy which might be called 'An Action Plan for a Nuclear Weapon-Free World, 2003–2020'. The first short-term 'mobilization, commitment and consolidation' phase from 2003 to 2007 would involve the mobilization of the international community at all levels in support of new global and regional WMD elimination agreements, and strengthening and extending existing nonproliferation and arms control measures. The second medium-term 'negotiation and treaty establishment' phase from 2008 to 2012 would entail the negotiation and ratification of new elimination agreements, creating the necessary verification and enforcement machinery. The third longer-term 'step-by-step implementation and enforcement' phase from 2013 to 2020 would begin the staged implementation of the treaties and associated verification machinery with the aim of achieving the total elimination of nuclear weapons by the end of the period.

Short term (2003–7): UN mobilization, commitment and consolidation strategies

The UN strategy in the short term should have four interrelated elements:

1. a multi-track mobilization process involving all levels of the international community to generate the necessary political will for agreement on substantive disarmament measures;
2. facilitation of the fora and avenues for securing collective commitment to these measures;
3. a consolidation process to resist the current slide away from existing non-proliferation and arms agreements; and
4. a process to enlist regional organization capabilities for creating 'stepping stone' and confidence-building measures towards global disarmament objectives, with particular emphasis on creating new regional NWFZs and/or WMDFZs.

This phase would have the global objective of a culminating agreement to negotiate a phased nuclear weapon elimination agreement in the CD; and regional objectives of securing the establishment of further NWFZ establishment in the Northern Hemisphere, including a zone in Central Asia, and establishment of linkages between existing zones.

UN multi-track mobilization for a nuclear-free world

Following such global fora as the UN Millennium Assembly and the Year 2000 NPT Review Conference, the time is ripe for the UN General Assembly and Secretariat to undertake a multi-track mobilization of governmental, NGO and academic organizations, and popular constituencies, in a concerted global campaign to lock states which possess nuclear weapons into binding schedules for the freezing, reduction and elimination of their nuclear arsenals and related WMDs.

Such a multi-track mobilization would involve UNDDAR, the Secretary-General, and the relevant subsidiary organs of the General Assembly, which would embark on ongoing consultations with both governmental and non-governmental institutions to maximize pressure on the nuclear and WMD 'hold-out' states over the ensuing five years.

This multi-track mobilization should involve UN consultations at the earliest possible opportunity between sympathetic governments, concerned NGOs and relevant academic institutions, on the strategies and phasing of an integrated campaign. One way of achieving this would be for UNDDAR to establish an Advisory Panel on the UN Disarmament Action Plan, which would bring together accredited governmental, NGO and academic representatives on a regular ongoing basis, say four times a year, until the agreed plan is implemented.

As in the case of the anti-landmines campaign, one effective strategy is the simultaneous use of NGO and governmental pressure at crucial decision-making conferences, accompanied by parallel action-oriented multi-track conferences convened and hosted by a sympathetic government. For example, one of the New Agenda initiators, Sweden and Ireland, could themselves host nuclear weapon-elimination conferences in a manner analogous to the role played by Canada during the 1996 Geneva Conference on landmines. During the conference itself, Canada hosted meetings of sympathetic anti-mine governments, and, assisted by the lobbying efforts of NGOs, was able to expand quite rapidly the number of supporting governments. Then, after the unsuccessful compromise outcome of the conference, Canada pressed home its initiative by convening further meetings of supporting governments outside the formal UN structures. This process culminated in the internationally recognized 1997 Ottawa Convention.[25]

Such a multi-track mobilization would need to win over progressively those governments holding out over nuclear weapons, through a combination of grassroots pressure, direct lobbying and pressures on governments, disarmament research, and negotiation at bilateral and multilateral levels.

Facilitation of fora and processes for securing commitment

The existing UN disarmament fora have inherent limitations. The Disarmament Commission and the CD both have consensus requirements which have allowed single member states to frustrate or block disarmament initiatives; the General Assembly has a vast agenda that often does not permit detailed consideration of disarmament issues; and the Security Council tends to be preoccupied with immediate crises and is limited by the veto.

A number of new initiatives and reforms will be necessary to facilitate the processes of securing member states' commitments to substantive disarmament. One of the most obvious and urgent is the convening of a further (fourth) Special Session on Disarmament to update the already agreed 1978 disarmament agenda and seek to build in additional commitments to the phased elimination of all WMDs. An associated initiative would be to seek agreement to continue scheduling Special Sessions on Disarmament at three-yearly intervals until the final verified and enforced elimination of such weapons is achieved. There is still no consensus on the proposal for a Fourth Special Session, mainly due to US resistance to setting a date, and the earliest possible date for such a session would seem to be 2004. The Special Sessions, together with the five-yearly NPT Review Conferences, are crucial to developing and crystallizing the impetus to pursue negotiations in the CD, or in other multilateral or bilateral fora. As the Tokyo Forum recommended, the NPT should also be restructured to create a permanent secretariat and consultative committee to enable the commitment of all parties, nuclear and non-nuclear, to be more closely monitored and encouraged. At both the NPT Review Conferences and further Special Sessions on Disarmament, there should also be full scope for the convening of parallel NGO conferences, and mechanisms for allowing NGO consultative input to the conference proceedings.

As further recommended by the Tokyo Forum, the present procedural arrangements that allow blocking of disarmament negotiations in the Committee on Disarmament and Disarmament Commission should be reformed by replacing the consensus requirement with a two-thirds majority vote, and by making better use of *ad hoc* working groups not bound by the consensus requirement. During the 2000 deliberations of the CD, the outgoing Canadian President,

Christopher Westdal, made a number of concrete suggestions for reforming the forum, which deserve close attention: raising the question of the Conference having a more direct 'public, informational and educational role', making better use of its function of 'assembling and cross-germinating a unique concentration of NACD (non-proliferation, arms control and disarmament) expertise', and increasing its transparency.[26]

Consolidation measures

In the present disarmament impasse, a vital component of short-term UN strategy is to seek to strengthen existing non-proliferation and arms-control measures (for instance, the NPT, ABM Treaty, CTBT), to further negotiate 'freezing' or 'capping' measures (for example, the proposed FMCT), and to strengthen the verification and enforcement machinery for the CWC and BWC. The principal consolidation and strengthening measures needed are already contained in the New Agenda resolution, but – as in the case of more far-reaching elimination initiatives – need to include target dates for implementation.

Regional strategies

The short-term focus here would be to work closely with regional organizations in encouraging the negotiation and implementation of regional NWFZs, WMDFZs and MFZs. The UN and some regional organizations have already had considerable success in promoting and negotiating regional NWFZs, particularly in the Southern Hemisphere. In at least one of the regions, Africa, nuclear weapons had already been developed by one regional state, South Africa during the Apartheid era, and the treaty serves to prevent the reintroduction of such weapons. In another, South America, a potential nuclear rivalry between Brazil and Argentina was averted by their adherence to LANWFZ, coupled with bilateral verification agreements between the two countries.

While the UN has played both a political role in supporting the establishment of all the existing NWFZs, and a direct role in negotiations on the African and Central Asian NWFZs, UN co-operation and organizational linkages with regional organizations in other regions have been relatively weak, consisting only of occasional *ad hoc* meetings and discussions between the UN Secretariat and the regional organizations.

As an integral part of the short-term strategies proposed, the UN should pursue a partnerships initiative with regional organizations, aimed at supporting the establishment of new regional NWFZs and WMDFZs and assisting the member states and secretariats associated with such zones to co-operate with each other and function more effectively as a lobby group for both extension of the zones and global elimination agreements.

The processes and structures of this UN-regional organization partnership would vary according to the characteristics of the regional body, the region's current arms-control agendas, and its specific history and conditions. In some regions, initial discussion might focus on confidence-building measures until sufficient trust was developed to tackle more far-reaching disarmament measures.

Further, in accord with the multi-track initiative already proposed, a UN-regional organization partnership would seek to involve NGOs, academics and wider popular constituencies in the region, and promote direct citizen-to-citizen contact and meeting on disarmament issues.

In the short term, some specific regional disarmament initiatives that should be pursued by the UN and regional organizations as an integral part of the broader WMD-elimination campaign include such initiatives as: conducting a comprehensive experts' study of regional NWFZs, WMDFZs, and MFZs; conclusion and ratification of a Central Asian NWFZ; convening of a regional forum on WMD control initiatives in the Middle East; co-operation with the OSCE, and with sub-regional groupings such as the Nordic Council, on regional NWFZ and WMDFZ possibilities in Central and Northern Europe; and the establishment of a permanent secretariat linking all NWFZ organizations.

Medium term (2008–12): Negotiation and ratification of elimination measures

Assuming successful outcomes in the first phase and a consequent increased pressure on member states to enter into serious disarmament negotiations, the medium-term (2008–12) phase would commence with an agreement to begin substantive multilateral negotiations in the CD on a phased nuclear-weapons-elimination treaty; together with parallel regional efforts to secure commencement of similar negotiations on NWFZs, WMDFZs, and MFZs in the Middle East, South Asia, North-east Asia and Europe.

As in the case of the preceding phase, a multi-track mobilization process would be needed to discourage governments from retreating from or seeking to evade their elimination commitments. This would be achieved through direct monitoring and lobbying of governments at a national level, the new UN consultative and advisory structures established in the earlier phase, the concerted efforts of sympathetic governments (such as the expanding New Agenda group), and the use of parallel NGO conferences at the key disarmament-related conferences.

The principal UN disarmament fora during this period would be a further (fifth) UN Special Session on Disarmament in 2007 (assuming previous agreement on a three-yearly cycle of such sessions). This would be the key target forum for achieving a consensus or near-consensus commitment on proceeding with substantive negotiations on a phased nuclear weapons elimination agreement; and for reviewing progress on parallel commitments to achieve regional NWFZs or WMDFZs. It would need to include as a lead-up both general preparatory meetings and regional preparatory meetings.

Over the ensuing three years, there would be intensive negotiations on the elements, modalities, phasing and verification/enforcement machinery of a nuclear weapons elimination agreement analogous to the universal BWC and CWC. At a regional level, there would be parallel negotiations on NWFZs or WMDFZs in such regions as the Middle East, South Asia, North-east Asia, Central Europe and Northern Europe.

Towards the middle of this period, in 2010, there would be a sixth UN Special Session on Disarmament that would become the target forum for a signed global nuclear weapons agreement, and international recognition of new regional agreements. The 2010 NPT Review would also serve to apply pressure on member states for signature of the global agreement, and enable continued input from parallel NGO conferences under a sustained multi-track mobilization strategy.

Long term (2013–20): Implementation and enforcement stages

This phase would commence with the process of ratification and entry into force of a global nuclear weapons elimination treaty. The target date for entry into force and establishment of operational verification and enforcement machinery could be at a further UN Special Session on Disarmament in 2013.

Depending on the negotiated stages for moving towards complete elimination, the target date for complete elimination and placing all remaining weapons under international control might occur in the period beginning 2020. This period would necessarily be one of consolidating the machinery of verification and enforcement to ensure there was no possibility of breaches and break-outs.

At a regional level, there would be parallel processes of ratification and implementation of regional agreements. If, as envisaged in the previous phase, regional NWFZs, WMDFZs and MFZs were successfully negotiated for such regions as the Middle East, South Asia, North-east Asia and sub-regions of Europe, building on prior strategies of regional confidence-building and conflict resolution, then the period 2013 to 2020 would involve the progressive implementation, verification and enforcement of these zones.

Such zones would serve to strengthen the global elimination processes through complementary regional NWFZ or WMDFZ arrangements and other bilateral-multilateral agreements that take account of regional conditions and requirements. In some regions, this may mean an overlay of regional verification and inspection arrangements in addition to global arrangements.

Summary of the proposed new UN disarmament approach

Table 11.1 shows in summary form the proposed UN Disarmament Action Plan phases and objectives, globally and regionally.

The implementation of this plan would require a number of procedural and structural changes. One of the most important would be an agreement to convene Special Sessions on Disarmament on a three-yearly basis to plan and oversee the disarmament process over an extended period; and the creation of a permanent NPT secretariat and consultative committee to monitor progress on the disarmament plan.

To address the need for civil-society involvement, there would need to be new multi-track structural arrangements to ensure input from CSOs, parallel NGO conferences at NPT Review Conferences and at the CD, and establishment of a UNDDAR Advisory Panel on the UN Disarmament Action Plan. At a regional

Table 11.1 Proposed UN Disarmament Action Plan (2003–20)

Year	Fora	Global measures	Regional measures
Short term (2003–7) (mobilization, commitment and consolidation)			
2003	Bilateral; regional organizations; UN Security Council	START II ratification START III negotiations	NWFZ links
2004	UNSSD4 + parallel NGO conferences	Consolidation measures Missile controls FMCT signed	NWFZ/WMDFZ study Regional CBMs
2005		CTBT ratified/in force	Multi-track diplomacy
2007	UNSSD5 NPT Review Conference	FMCT ratified/in force Commitment to begin elimination treaty Negotiations in CD START III in force	Commitment to start NWFZ, WMDFZ negotiations in regions of South Asia, Central Asia, North-east Asia, Europe
Medium term (2008–12) (negotiation and treaty establishment)			
2008		Elimination treaty negotiations	NWFZ/WMDFZ negotiations
2010	UNSSD6 NPT Review Conference	Treaty signed Progressive ratification	New regional treaties signed
2011–12		Progressive ratification	
Long term (2013–20) (staged implementation and enforcement)			
2013–14	UNSSD7	Treaty ratified, in force Initial reductions stage Establishment of verification/enforcement machinery	Ratification of new NWFZs Implementation of new regional treaties
2015	UNSSD8 NPT Review Conference	Review of initial stage Review of progress	
2018–20	UNSSD9	Confirmation of total elimination Consolidation of enforcement machinery	

level, the UN-affiliated Dag Hammarskjold Foundation, in co-operation with other NGOs, made a promising start with its September 2000 International Seminar in Uppsala, Sweden. This brought together regional NGOs and government representatives as part of a longer-term project to promote and facilitate the negotiation of regional NWFZs, particularly in North-east Asia, South Asia, the Middle East and Central Europe.[27]

To overcome the problem of single states successfully blocking negotiations, there would need to be a revision to CD procedures to change the consensus principle to two-thirds majority approval; and agreement of the Security Council to restrict veto rights so that at least two vetos are required to block any decision.[28]

Finally, there would need to be ways of creating new funding sources to pay for disarmament machinery and nuclear weapon destruction costs, possibly including a 'disarmament levy' generated through a small tax on all military transactions and transfers between states; or, as has been recently proposed as a more general method of increasing UN resources, the imposition of a small tax on all international currency transactions and/or international air travel.[29]

Conclusion

The present impasse in the international community's efforts to control and eliminate nuclear and other WMDs could lead either to a progressive breakdown in the present non-proliferation regime, or to a heightened awareness of the catastrophic dangers associated with such weapons and a new international political will to outlaw them forever.

There are both constraints and opportunities in the present context. Many longstanding elements of the previous UN disarmament agenda have been delayed or frustrated by conservative-nationalist forces currently dominating the governments of a number of major powers. At the same time, an increasingly large number of middle-level and small countries, including both non-aligned and western-aligned states, have come together to promote a new UN Disarmament Agenda that has the potential of developing international momentum towards the control and phasing out of nuclear and other WMDs.

This New Agenda involves, as a critical first step, unilateral or multilateral agreements to de-target, de-alert, and physically separate from means of delivery, all nuclear weapons. This is essential because of both the existence of serious regional conflicts and the dangers of accidental nuclear war. Further steps include bilateral negotiations between America and Russia on START III reductions; commencement of plurilateral negotiations amongst all the nuclear states to reduce their nuclear arsenals; and a serious commitment from all the nuclear powers to negotiate the 'speedy and total elimination' of all nuclear weapons.

Despite the importance of the New Agenda as a set of first steps to consolidate the non-proliferation regime and catalyse new progress on disarmament, and the significance of a new and expanding core of states prepared to work together to put pressure on the nuclear and 'hold-out' states, the New Agenda proposals have some gaps. The Agenda fails to identify the phases and target dates necessary to achieve substantive nuclear disarmament. It does not sufficiently address the need for new measures to deal with ballistic-missile and unconventional (terrorist) delivery systems. Finally, it does not address the need for the international mobilization of civil society to put the necessary pressure on governments and leaders.

As envisaged in the above proposed plan, the UN will need to greatly enhance its role in disarmament at both a central level and a regional level, and to adopt a multi-track strategy of enlisting the support, commitment and follow-through of both sympathetic governments and academic, NGO and popular constituencies.

Centrally, it will need to seek agreement on the regular three-yearly scheduling of Special Sessions on Disarmament to oversee the disarmament process, with accompanying parallel NGO conferences; institute a Peoples' Assembly[30] that would also involve a Peoples' Disarmament Committee; improve the monitoring capacities of the regular five-yearly NPT Review Conferences; convene an Advisory Panel on a UN Disarmament Action Plan; and use a 'snowballing' approach of involving progressively more countries, both within and outside the UN's own fora, in applying co-ordinated political pressure on the nuclear and WMD 'hold-out' states.

Regionally, the UN will need to embark on a new level of partnership with regional organizations involving joint sponsorship of disarmament fora, studies and negotiation processes. In the proposed plan, there would be a particular focus on establishing new regional NWFZs, WMDFZs and MFZs, and linking up existing NWFZS. Where such regional organizations do not yet exist, the UN can potentially contribute through supporting or actually convening *ad hoc* bodies. The nature of the UN partnership with regional organizations and bodies will vary according to the specific regional structures and the relative stage of development in regional dialogue and co-operation in arms-control and security issues.

The particular significance of regional conflicts in the post-Cold War environment and the increasing probability of state and non-state actors involved in such conflicts resorting to WMDs mean that it will be vital for the UN to pursue the new disarmament agenda at both global and regional levels simultaneously. Each is integrally linked to the other, and failure to achieve progress on one level will potentially unravel progress on the other. One of the few hopeful developments that might be expected to emerge from the 2001 terrorist attacks on the United States is a renewed awareness that the kind of regional and global security problems now confronting us demand multilateral co-operation and negotiation, preferably through the UN, rather than counter-productive unilateralist approaches.

Notes

1. R. Johnson, 'NPT2000: Implementing the Disarmament Pledges', *Disarmament Diplomacy*, No.48, July 2000, p.3; J. Rissanen, 'CD Concludes First Part of 2001 Session Empty-Handed', *Disarmament Diplomacy*, 55 (March 2001), pp.30–3.
2. E. Arnett, 'Nuclear Tests by India and Pakistan', *SIPRI Yearbook 1999* (Oxford: OUP, 1999), pp.371–86; P. Bidwai and A. Vanaik, *New Nukes: India, Pakistan and Global Nuclear Disarmament* (New York: Olive Branch Press/Interlink Books, 2000); R. Azizian (ed.), *Nuclear Developments in South Asia and the Future of Global Arms Control*

(Wellington: Centre for Strategic Studies/Department of Political Studies, University of Auckland, 2001).

3. R.S. Norris and W.M. Arkin, 'Appendix 8A: Table of Nuclear Forces', *SIPRI Yearbook 2000* (Oxford: OUP, 2000), p.491; A. Cohen and M. Miller, 'How To Think About and Implement Nuclear Arms Control in the Middle East', in B. Roberts (ed.), *Weapons Proliferation in the 1990s* (Cambridge, MA: MIT Press, 1995), pp.366–70.

4. J. Rissanen, 'BWC Update', *Disarmament Diplomacy*, 54 (February 2001), pp.30–5; A. Kelle, 'CWC Update', *Disarmament Diplomacy*, 57 (May 2001), pp.18–22.

5. M. Smith, 'The MTCR and the Future of Ballistic Missile Non-Proliferation', *Disarmament Diplomacy*, 54 (February 2001), pp.19–25.

6. Norris and Arkin, pp.478–95; I. Anthony, 'Appendix 11A', *SIPRI Yearbook 2000*, pp.670–1; M. Smith, 'European Perspectives on Ballistic Missile Proliferation and Missile Defences', in K. McCloud (ed.), *Missile Proliferation and Defences: Problems and Prospects* (Monterey: Occasional Paper No.7, Special Joint Series on Missile Issues, Monterey Institute of International Studies/Mountbatten Centre for International Studies, June 2001).

7. F. Jishe, 'Nagging Uncertainty and Growing Concern: the Bush Administration's Arm Control Policy', *Disarmament Diplomacy*, 55 (March 2001), pp.3–7; J. Rissanen, 'US Jeopardises BWC Protocol', *Disarmament Diplomacy*, 57 (May 2001), pp.23–5.

8. See, for example, J.P. Zanders, E.M. French and N. Pauwels, 'Chemical and Biological Weapon Developments and Arms Control', *SIPRI Yearbook 1998* (Oxford: OUP, 1998), pp.593–4; J.B. Tucker (ed.), *Toxic Terror: Assessing Terrorist Use of Biological and Chemical Weapons* (Cambridge, MA: Belfer Centre for Science and International Affairs, MIT Press, 2000).

9. United Nations, *The United Nations and Disarmament: a Short History* (New York: UN, 1988), pp.1–6, 34–44, 55–6, 69; United Nations, *The United Nations and Disarmament 1945–85* (New York: UN, 1985); D. Whittaker, *United Nations in the Contemporary World* (London: Routledge, 1997), pp.57–67.

10. J. Dhanapala (ed.), *The United Nations, Disarmament and Security: Evolution and Prospects* (New York: UN, 1991), pp.105–26.

11. Ibid., pp.72–7.

12. J. Mendelsohn, 'The Bush Presidency: Reconsidering the CTBT', *Disarmament Diplomacy*, 53 (December 2000/January 2001), p.5.

13. A. Acharya and S. Ogunbanwo, 'The Nuclear Weapon-Free Zones in Southeast Asia and Africa', *SIPRI Yearbook 1998*, pp.443–56.

14. J. Prawitz and J.F. Leonard, 'A Zone Free of Weapons of Mass Destruction in the Middle East: A Political Project', *Pacifica Review*, 11, 3 (October 1999), pp.258–9; J. Goldblat, 'Central Asia: a Nuclear-Weapon-Free-Zone in Statu Nascendi', *Pacifica Review*, 11, 3 (October 1999), pp.325–8.

15. International Court of Justice, *Legality of the Threat or Use of Nuclear Weapons* (Advisory Opinion of July 8 1996), A/51/218, 1996.

16. J. Dhanapala, Address to International Seminar on Nuclear Weapon-Free Zones, Dag Hammarskjold Foundation, Uppsala, Sweden, 2 September 2000.

17. Foreign Affairs Ministers of Brazil, Egypt, Ireland, Mexico, New Zealand, Slovenia, South Africa, and Sweden, *Towards a Nuclear-Weapon-Free World: the Need for a New Agenda*, Joint Statement, 9 June 1998, Nuclear Age Peace Foundation website: <http://www.nuclearfiles.com/docs/1998/980609-new-agenda.html>

18. General Assembly First Committee Resolution A/C.1/53/L.48/REV.1, 13 November 1998.

19. R. Johnson, *First Committee Report 1998, Disarmament Diplomacy*, No.23 (November 1998) pp.11–14.

20. *UN Press Release*, GA/9829, 29 November 2000.

21. Independent Commission on Disarmament and Security Issues, *Common Security: a Programme for Disarmament* (London: Pan Books, 1982).

22. Canberra Commission on the Elimination of Nuclear Weapons, *Report* (Canberra: Commonwealth of Australia, August 1996).

23. Tokyo Forum for Nuclear Non-Proliferation and Disarmament, *Facing Nuclear Dangers: an Action Plan for the 21st Century* (Tokyo: Japanese Ministry of Foreign Affairs, 25 July 1999).
24. J. Scheffran, 'Moving Beyond Missile Defence: the Search for Alternatives to the Missile Race', *Disarmament Diplomacy*, 55 (March 2001), pp.21–6.
25. Z. Lachowski, 'The Ban on Anti Personnel Mines', *SIPRI Yearbook 1998*, pp.545–76.
26. Cited in J. Rissanen, 'Geneva Update', *Disarmament Diplomacy*, 54 (February 2001), p.28.
27. See M. Hamel-Green, 'The Uppsala Declaration on Nuclear Free Zones', *Pacific News Bulletin*, 15, 10 (October 2000), p.2.
28. For a possible parallel Security Council reform see Chapter 15.
29. See Chapter 15; see also C. Peck, *Sustainable Peace: the Role of the UN and Regional Organizations in Preventing Conflict* (Lanham, MD: Rowman & Littlefield, 1998), p.257.
30. See Chapter 15.

12
The Politics of Biological and Chemical Disarmament[1]

Susan Wright

A strong western orthodoxy concerning the problem of biological warfare has gripped western governments and arms-control organizations alike. Since the end of the Cold War, western, particularly American, perceptions of security threats have shifted from the intense focus on the Soviet nuclear threat to a fear of 'proliferation' of weapons of mass destruction in the Third World. The threat of biological weaponry (often in tandem with chemical weaponry) is a prominent and particularly emotive element of this fear, justified by claims that biotechnology can overcome previous deficiencies of biological weapons and that the low cost and relative ease of production make them attractive to Third World countries. The sources of this threat are typically portrayed as 'rogue' states and 'terrorists' that are by definition beyond the reach of 'civilized' regimes of prohibition. The attacks on the World Trade Centre and the Pentagon of 11 September 2001, in which a powerful form of civil technology – jet aircraft – was turned into a ferocious weapon, has intensified fears that the power of biomedical and chemical technology could be similarly perverted.

The aim of this chapter is to go beyond the immediate security responses provoked by the events of 11 September and to address the conditions of war, extreme deprivation and radical insecurity which have provided fertile ground for anti-western forms of terrorism to develop since the end of the Cold War. In examining the history of western attitudes to chemical and biological warfare (CBW), the focus is on identifying national, regional and international responses that would promote human and environmental security rather than negative security based on deterrence and technology denial.

The evolution of the 'rogue doctrine'

The dominant western assumption that the problem of chemical and biological warfare since the end of the Cold War is posed by rogue states and terrorists has its origins in the non-proliferation policies which began during the Cold War, and which expressed the interest of both superpowers to prevent the spread of the technologies of mass destruction that they themselves were pursuing.[2] The United States abandoned its own biological weapons programme in 1969 and endorsed an international treaty to ban these weapons, because it believed that their spread would 'not act as much to strengthen the big powers as it would to endow dozens of relatively weak countries with great destructive capability'.[3] As Han Swyter, a Defence Department adviser explained in 1969: 'The proliferation of chemical and biological capability would tend to reduce the world's balance of power, reducing ours. We would lose some of the advantages of nuclear and conventional capability which wealth gives to us and to the Soviets'.[4] A second motive, of equal geopolitical significance, was that the United States could rely for its defence on nuclear weapons, thereby ensuring that the BWC completed in 1972 would be marked by the division of its parties into nuclear-possessor and non-possessor states.[5]

During the Cold War, official concerns about a Third World biological weapons threat, which were in any case hypothetical, disappeared as tensions between the two superpowers escalated and the threat of a nuclear confrontation consumed attention. However, as superpower relations improved in the 1980s, official interest turned once again to the question of proliferation in the Third World. In 1985, a secret report of the US Defence Science Board concluded that 'the chemical and biological threats are increasing, Third World proliferation is getting worse, and the possible consequences are extremely serious'.[6] Such warnings were aired with increasing regularity in the late 1980s, eventually paving the way for what Michael Klare has called 'the rogue doctrine'.[7]

This view was foreshadowed in *Discriminate Deterrence*,[8] the report of a Reagan Administration commission charged with developing a long-term security strategy for the United States. While the Commission still saw the power of the Soviet Union as an 'extreme' threat, it also introduced the view that rising regional powers in the Third World, armed with nuclear or chemical weapons and ballistic missiles, could pose new threats to American security – a view that was soon taken up by Washington think tanks and various members of Congress.

The Commission did not specifically mention biological weapons but by the following year, these weapons also began to figure in security scenarios, along with the related notion of a special category of countries deemed sufficiently immoral to use such things. 'Maverick', 'rogue', 'backlash' and 'outlaw' began to enter the security lexicon to denote countries that had, in President George H.W. Bush's words, 'contempt for civilized norms'.[9] US estimates of the numbers of states pursuing development of chemical and biological weapons increased. CIA Director William Webster claimed, ominously, that '20 nations may be developing chemical weapons... At least 10 countries are working to produce both previously known and futuristic biological weapons'.[10]

Iraq under Saddam Hussein invaded Kuwait on 2 August 1990 and instantly became the leading symbol of the 'rogue' state, a concrete embodiment of the post-Cold War threat. The Gulf War itself quickly became seen as the first experience of combat against such a threat, and a model for future combat. As former Secretary of Defence Dick Cheney told Congress in March 1991: 'The Gulf War presaged very much the type of conflict we are most likely to confront again in this new era – major regional contingencies against foes well-armed with advanced conventional and unconventional munitions'.[11]

Such appraisals both of the threat and of the military preparations needed to confront it were almost seamlessly transmitted to the incoming Clinton Administration. As President Clinton told the opening session of the UN in 1993:

> One of our most urgent priorities must be attacking the proliferation of weapons of mass destruction, whether they are nuclear, chemical, or biological... [W]e know that many nations still believe that it is in their interest to develop weapons of mass destruction... More than a score of nations likely possess such weapons and their number threatens to grow. These weapons could destabilize entire regions. They could turn a local conflict into a global human and environmental catastrophe.[12]

The attribution of rogue status varied, depending on context, sometimes extending as far as Israel, but regularly figuring on virtually all such lists were a group of 'core rogues', all deemed hostile to US interests and all claimed to possess chemical and biological weapons or, at least, 'capabilities' to produce them: Iran, Iraq, Libya, North Korea and Syria.[13]

By the mid-1990s, the 'rogue doctrine' was fully entrenched in Washington and London policy circles, as well as elsewhere in the west. Moreover, as evidence that Saddam Hussein had acquired a biological arsenal was uncovered by the UN Special Commission (UNSCOM) in 1991–95 and as defectors revealed that the former Soviet Union had pursued a huge bioweapons programme that dwarfed the Iraqi one, the threat posed by potential rogue use of biological weapons came to the fore. Reinforced by claims that the techniques of the new biogenetics would produce even more alarming forms of biological warfare that would overcome past problems of control, biological warfare began to loom as a new threat, deemed comparable in power to that of nuclear weapons.[14]

The nerve gas attack on the Tokyo subway by the Aum Shinrikio cult in 1995, and the discovery that the cult had also attempted, unsuccessfully, to produce botulinum toxin and a strain of anthrax, was used to justify an expanded definition of the threat of biological and other weapons of mass destruction that included terrorist use and that also blurred differences between threats posed by 'terrorists' and 'rogue regimes'. According to former Defence Secretary William Perry in 1996:

> Terrorists operate in a shadowy world in which they can detonate a device and disappear, as the poison gas attack in Tokyo illustrates. Rogue regimes may try to use these devastating weapons as blackmail, or as a relatively inexpensive way to sidestep the U.S. military's overwhelming conventional military superiority... The bottom line is, unlike during the Cold War, those who possess nuclear, chemical, and biological weapons may actually come to use them.[15]

For the remaining years of the century, government agencies, congressional committees, defence intellectuals, journalists, and even fiction writers continued to fan fears of the use of biological and other weapons of mass destruction by unruly aggressors.[16] In his 1998 state of the union address, Clinton promised to address the dangers of biological weapons deployed by 'outlaw states, terrorists, and organized criminals'.[17] Amidst escalating claims, a bipartisan congressional commission headed by former CIA director John Deutch released a massive report that portrayed 'a dangerous world where hostile forces will seek to exploit WMDs to their advantage and to threaten us'.[18] By the late 1990s official fear of WMDs in the hands of rogues and terrorists had reached cataclysmic levels, in which biological weapons in particular were portrayed as playing an especially insidious role.[19] The concept of terrorists converting powerful non-military technologies into weapons was beyond the imaginations of defence planners.

Implementation of the 'rogue doctrine'

In Washington, the 'rogue doctrine' shaped arms-control and technology-denial regimes on the one hand and military strategy on the other. The Bush and Clinton administrations adapted the Cold War practice of technology denial to the rogue threat through export controls aimed at stemming the flow of dual-purpose materials to states suspected of biological, chemical or nuclear proliferation. The United States also actively supported the Australia Group, a group of some 30 industrialized countries that meets in private to share intelligence data and to co-ordinate export controls on countries deemed to be proliferators.[20] An Enhanced Proliferation Control Initiative that placed strict controls on exports of a variety of biological agents and equipment to 28 states suspected of biological proliferation was adopted by the Bush Administration in November 1990 and by the Australia Group in 1992. Clinton in 1994 continued the controls, justifying them by declaring a national emergency 'in light of the dangers of the proliferation of nuclear, biological, and chemical weapons'.[21]

But in pursuing a policy of 'discriminate non-proliferation' the United States attempted to use these international regimes to impose restrictions on states considered hostile, while avoiding the same restrictions on its own behaviour. When the United States ratified the CWC in 1997, it did so only on condition that it could impose three major restrictions on on-site inspections that did not apply to any other party. A close observer of CWC developments has concluded that these conditions and the conduct of the United States during on-site inspections radically undermined the integrity of the treaty.[23] While requiring a higher level of transparency for other states, the United States was intent on maintaining a relatively high level of opacity for its own vast industrial and military operations.[24] The administration of George W. Bush went even further when, in July 2001,

Both administrations were involved in negotiations related to the international legal regimes banning chemical and biological weapons. The Bush Administration was actively engaged in the negotiation of the CWC, completed in 1992 during Bush's term of office. In 1997 Clinton stated: 'The U.S. ... continues to play a leading role in the international effort to reduce the threat from biological weapons. We are an active participant in the Ad Hoc Group striving to create a legally binding protocol to strengthen and enhance compliance with the [BWC]'.[22]

it rejected the draft BWC protocol partly because 'it would do little to deter those countries seeking to develop biological weapons' but also because 'it would put national security and confidential business information at risk'.[25]

Furthermore, the United States and its western allies insisted on retaining the Australia Group (AG) and applying export controls even against non-western countries that are parties to the BWC and the CWC in good standing. While states such as Iran, India, Pakistan and China (all parties to the BWC and the CWC) were targeted as 'proliferators', Israel, which is often listed as a state with strong interests in biological and chemical weaponry and is not a party to either treaty, was described in an authoritative account of the AG as having 'working relations' with individual AG members.[26] Israeli scientists have also received contracts from the US biological defence programme.

Despite an understanding achieved late in the CWC negotiations that the need for the AG would be reviewed once the CWC entered into force, the group and its operations continued, which served as a serious source of North-South friction. 'With the CWC already in force, the AG is absolutely redundant, discriminating, and politically unacceptable', claimed Ambassador Sha Zukang of China in 1997.[27] Most fundamentally, the arrangement perpetuated the western view that informs non-proliferation policy generally: that the real BW danger is associated with countries in the South, especially those seen as hostile to the west, which are made subject to controls that are seen as unnecessary for countries in the North.

By far the most ruthless form of technology denial was that practised by the UNSCOM against Iraq. The UN Security Council ceasefire resolution 687 gave UNSCOM extraordinary powers to investigate Iraq's WMDs and to ensure that they were destroyed. This authority was reinforced by economic sanctions that held the entire Iraqi population captive throughout the 1990s and was estimated to have been responsible for over a million civilian deaths. US policy documents show that the US government accurately anticipated that denying Iraq the means to purify its water supply would cause an increased incidence of disease, with a major impact on children. When former Secretary of State Madeleine Albright was asked how she justified the deaths of half-a-million Iraqi children, she responded that 'it was a very hard choice' but that 'we think the price was worth it'.[28]

Throughout the 1990s and beyond, the rogue doctrine framed public discussion on post-Cold War military planning and spending.[29] As Dick Cheney noted in 1991, the Gulf War was used as a precedent for future wars against rogue states, both for its military successes and for its failures: first, pre-emption of 'rogue' use of WMDs through bombing designed to demolish WMD facilities; second, development of defensive measures for fighting in a combat environment contaminated by WMDs; finally, should it be necessary, the ability to threaten massive retaliation if WMDs were used.[30] The Defence Department's 'Counter-Proliferation Initiative', launched by former Secretary of Defence Les Aspin in December 1993, incorporated all of these dimensions.[31]

In the background of these plans, there is the third dimension noted above: the threat of massive retaliation should a rogue state turn to use of WMDs. Despite official denials that the Department of Defence contemplates retaliation with nuclear weapons for use of chemical or biological weapons by rogue regimes, the evidence suggests otherwise. Former Secretary of State James Baker acknowledged that the possibility of nuclear weapons being used against Iraq if the latter used chemical or biological weapons had been conveyed to the Iraqi foreign minister during the Gulf War.[32] Former President Bill Clinton acknowledged the role of nuclear weapons in deterring adversaries from using WMDs,[33] and the United States retains the option of first use of nuclear weapons – a position consistent with Washington's longstanding refusal to adopt the principle of no first use of nuclear weapons.

With the heightened perception of a biological and chemical threat in the 1990s, funding for biological and chemical defence increased steeply. Congressional appropriations for chemical and biological defence (including procurement) during the decade doubled between financial year (FY) 1996 and FY2000, from almost $400 million to $800 million.[34] Spending on biological defence over the decade rose from $75.3 million in FY1990 to over $470 million in FY2000 – an increase in real terms of more than 400 per cent.[35] With such a large increase in numbers of projects combined with a marked decrease in detailed information about them provided to the US Congress, it became difficult for the public to track the lines of development pursued by these programmes.

The erosion of public knowledge of the chemical and biological defence programmes had a marked effect on the nature of projects pursued under these programmes in the 1990s and beyond. NGOs and journalists uncovered projects that, if subjected to public scrutiny, would have provoked serious misgivings – anthrax bacteria engineered to tolerate antibiotics, bacteria that degrade components of weapons systems, chemical substances with non-lethal but highly unpleasant effects, to name a few examples.[36] In September 2001, three reporters for the *New York Times* noted that one reason for President George W. Bush's rejection of the draft BWC inspection regime was a desire to shroud further biological warfare projects in secrecy.[37] These projects, including a plan to genetically engineer a strain of anthrax capable of overcoming the protection provided by vaccination, were especially troubling. They threatened the BWC, both directly and indirectly, by stimulating research elsewhere aimed at constructing novel biological weapons or testing the means for production and dissemination.

Appraisal

To question the 'rogue doctrine' is not to deny the serious security risks posed by biological and other WMDs. It is not to belittle the dangers posed by the huge, secret, Soviet bioweapons programme, the smaller programme pursued by Iraq, the attempted production of biological agents by the Aum Shinrikio, or the prospects of civil technologies which use hazardous chemical or biological agents being transformed into weapons.[38] It *is* to call into question the wisdom of the dominant western approach, in which major western powers portray themselves as acting responsibly, even while retaining a huge arsenal of nuclear weapons, while deeming others to be hostile and irresponsible.

In the first place, there are obvious asymmetries in the western response. The highly secret Soviet programme, with some 50,000 employees, vast facilities, huge stockpiles, and deliberate efforts to produce novel pathogens for which there is no treatment, constitutes by far the most egregious violation of the BWC. There are serious charges that these continued in secret with the demise of the Soviet Union, and certainly Russia, in maintaining some closed biological facilities, has not yet provided adequate reassurance.[39] Yet Russia figures far less frequently on lists of 'proliferators' or 'rogues'. Perhaps even more important, the primary approach to its previous transgressions is a set of co-operative measures funded by western states that aim to keep former bioweaponeers usefully employed on civilian projects.[40] By contrast, the UN response to Iraq's chemical and biological weapons programmes has been purely punitive and coercive. Under strong western influence, the Security Council decided that there would be no economic carrots for the 'rogue' state.[41] A similar double standard has been applied in the case of export controls, as noted earlier.

Second, claims of proliferation are far less specific than they might appear at first glance. A report issued in 1991 by the US Office of Technology Assessment defined biological 'proliferants' as 'countries reported as having undeclared offensive biological warfare programs' and went on to explain that such programmes might 'include anything from research on offensive biological weapons to actual stockpiles of munitions'.[42] Such a broad definition poses several problems, given the overlap between defensive and offensive activities, at least until large-scale activities are reached, and the fact that virtually all work with micro-organisms is dual purpose: it can be pursued for both peaceful and military purposes.

Even if clear evidence of WMD programmes were to be established, this does not mean that such programmes threaten the West. For example, in the Middle East, where there is a clear pattern of non-adherence both to the BWC and the CWC, it is impossible to address state interests in chemical and biological weapons without also addressing the presence of nuclear weapons in the region. This is not to condone attempts to acquire WMD but rather to argue that anti-proliferation efforts are unlikely to be effective because they do not address the fundamental causes of the problem.

Of course, the term, 'rogue', has been all along an almost exclusively Anglo-American construction, a generalization that served to justify the continuing high military budgets for defences against rogues. It had never been accepted universally, even in the West. The French foreign minister, Hubert Vedrine, commented in 2000: 'It's not a geopolitical category we use. It is difficult for Europeans to imagine one of these rogue states attacking the United States'.[43] By 2000, the Clinton Administration had begun to back away from assigning rogue status. On 19 June 2000, Madeleine Albright announced that 'rogue states' would be renamed 'states of concern'.[44] However, early in his presidency, George W. Bush reversed that trend.[45] After all, the existence of rogue states was essential for providing the rationale for national missile defence. The fluidity of the concept underscores its artificial character.

Third, experienced terrorism experts have questioned worst-case, catastrophic scenarios depicting mass casualty attacks with biological or chemical weapons on the grounds that the technical difficulties involved are more serious than these scenarios indicated. They have argued that the lesson to be learned from the Aum Shinrikio's attempted development of biological and chemical weapons and its use of the latter is not the *ease* of a terrorist attack with such weapons but the major technical *difficulties* they presented.[46] While the attacks on the World Trade Centre and the Pentagon showed that the unthinkable can happen, they did not change the basic argument that a massive attack with chemical or biological agents is dangerous for those who develop them, depends on access to skilled personnel, requires the technological capacity to produce lethal chemical or biological agents, and poses significant difficulties for dissemination of the chemical or biological agent.

The diplomatic and military dimensions of US counter-proliferation policy have had the effect of widening the 'North–South' gap. The negotiations for the BWC compliance protocol from 1995 to 2001 demonstrated American self-interest, especially in not burdening its pharmaceutical and biotechnology industries or its military establishments with intrusive inspections.

Moreover, the unilateral character of American counter-proliferation preparations, which made reference only to NATO, not to the Security Council, suggested that the United States might take a military response to a proliferation concern into its own hands. The Anglo-American bombing raids on Iraqi defences throughout the 1990s and on or close to Baghdad in 1996, 1998 and 2001, which were not approved by the Security Council, US use of UNSCOM for espionage, and the bombing of a Sudanese factory, claimed (without any substantial evidence) to be making chemical weapons have given particular weight to such criticisms.[47]

One final dimension of US international policy with a bearing on access to biological technologies by developing countries under the BWC should be noted: the need for rich countries to recognize the importance of working to increase the 'positive security' of developing countries by supporting their efforts to improve medical, public health and agricultural services and technologies. Arguably, the strengthening of the intellectual-property regime during the Uruguay Round of the GATT undermines the implementation of Article X of the BWC, under which parties to the convention undertake to facilitate the fullest possible exchange of biological science and technology for peaceful purposes.[48] Generally, the forms of international intellectual-property protection for pharmaceutical drugs and living things established in the 1990s are seen as working against the interests of most people in developing countries by increasing the cost of medical and agricultural products, driving peasant farmers from their land, and consequently exacerbating levels of poverty and disease that already define a state of acute crisis.

At the beginning of the twenty-first century, the deep asymmetries in the US response to the problem of chemical and biological warfare produced a series of dead ends. The UN investigation of Iraq's WMDs under strong US influence resulted in one of the worst possible outcomes: a discredited inspection agency unable to complete its responsibilities; a low-intensity, undeclared war against Iraq that has not been approved by the Security Council; and sanctions that have devastated the Iraqi people. The treatment of international regimes as extensions of western non-proliferation policy united non-western and developing countries in their sense that the western alliance is not even-handed in arms-control arenas, denying access to advanced technologies that it holds close and insisting on lopsided inspection regimes. Above all, there was the illegitimacy of western retention of nuclear weapons while attempting to deny biological, chemical and nuclear weapons to selected others, and even using the threat of nuclear weaponry to back this denial.[49]

Concluding proposals

For long-term efforts to address the CBW problem, it is especially important for the United States to discard the brash and often destructive unilateralism that has guided its post-Cold War posture towards other states, especially those seen as hostile, and to seek to nurture instead a co-operative internationalism that treats all states, whether viewed as close or distant, as having equal status under international law. More generally, co-operative internationalism means western commitment to do no harm to innocent civilians in hostile states and to use the great wealth of the West to address the poverty and disease endemic in developing countries. The proposals below are intended to further these general goals.

International level

If the United States and its western allies are serious about achieving strong and universal commitments to chemical and biological disarmament, the counter- and anti-proliferation policies of the last decade, which ultimately rely on nuclear weapons, are not the way to go. Rather than seeing the BWC and the CWC as anti-proliferation instruments, these international agreements should become part of a global effort to abolish *all* WMDs and move towards general and complete disarmament.[50]

Furthermore, international arms-control and disarmament treaties need to be developed and implemented in ways that ensure an equitable balance of rights and obligations so that these treaties do not benefit the richer, industrialized states at the expense of poorer, less industrialized states. This principle can be realized in three major ways in connection with the BWC and the CWC. First, all states should develop rigorous implementing legislation without self-serving qualifications that dilute the transparency and effectiveness of these treaties. Second, states that are in compliance with the BWC and the CWC should receive equal treatment with respect to trade in the dual-purpose agents and equipment covered by these treaties. The present export controls co-ordinated by the Australia Group should be replaced by international export-control standards established and implemented within the frameworks of the CWC and the BWC. Third, the sacrifices made by developing countries to join and implement the

CWC and the BWC should be recognized and compensated through measures developed under the provisions of Articles XI and X respectively, which require states to share relevant knowledge, materials and technologies for peaceful purposes. Such arrangements should recognize the needs of developing countries to develop indigenous forms of technology under their own intellectual-property regimes.[51]

The BWC, which at present amounts to little more than an exhortation to abandon biological weapons, needs to be strengthened. As many parties to the convention recognized during the negotiations for a compliance protocol from 1995 to 2001, transparency of biological activities is an essential feature. To ensure the effectiveness of the CWC and the BWC Protocol, all states and relevant sub-state organizations should support high levels of transparency through declarations and inspections. In particular, the biotechnology, pharmaceutical and agrichemical industries should acknowledge that transparency for verification purposes should override interests in maintaining secrecy for commercial reasons. Furthermore, it is important that states which have pursued biological weapons programmes in the past should acknowledge and declare them and explain the steps they took to dismantle the programmes and to destroy stockpiles.

Beyond verification of compliance, the basic prohibitions of the BWC and the CWC also need to be strengthened in order to prohibit activities which threaten to undermine these treaties. In particular, the development of novel biological and chemical agents that do not have unambiguously peaceful purposes should be prohibited, even if these activities are promoted for defensive purposes. Oversight to ensure that both military and civil organizations comply would be required.

Regional level

While the development and strengthening of the international prohibition of chemical and biological weapons is essential, the Middle East is a special case where a regional approach to weapons of mass destruction is needed as a first step towards adherence to the NPT, CWC, and BWC. The outstanding territorial disputes between Israel and Lebanon, Syria and the Palestinians must be settled before substantial progress on arms control can be made. Furthermore, arms-control talks will need to involve all relevant states, including Syria, Iran and Iraq, and they will need to address *all* weapons of mass destruction. It is unrealistic to expect major states in the region to agree to one form of disarmament if other major weapons systems (conventional as well as unconventional) are not addressed.[52]

Iraq is a further special case. It is the only state in the region which has been subjected to a coercive process of disarmament and the effects on the civil infrastructures of Iraq have been devastating, effectively returning Iraq to a pre-industrial economy and causing over one million civilian deaths. This crisis calls for drastic change in policies based on sanctions. The most urgent need is to rebuild basic public-health, medical, agricultural and educational infrastructures. This should be coupled with restoration of normal trade relations, with export controls co-ordinated by the UN and designed to ensure peaceful end-uses for imports of chemical and biological dual-purpose agents and equipment. Until regional disarmament of WMDs becomes possible, Iraq should be encouraged to engage in confidence-building measures with the Gulf states and with Iran.[53]

Roles of non-governmental organizations

Finally, citizens can play essential roles in strengthening government commitments to chemical and biological disarmament. Professional societies, research organizations, corporations, institutions of higher education and individual scientists and engineers should pledge not to engage knowingly in research or teaching that furthers the development or use of biological and chemical weapons and should be involved in creating institutions, such as protection for whistle blowers, that support these commitments. Industrial and educational organizations also need to encourage high levels of transparency as a major form of support for the BWC and CWC. Given that such conditions have not yet been effectively developed, the path ahead for citizens is indeed challenging.

Notes

1. This chapter draws on my contributions to a forthcoming book, *The Biological Warfare Question: an Appraisal for the 21st Century*. I thank Romica Singh, Hazel Tamano and Joseph Brunner for their creative assistance with research, and P.R. Chari, Stephen Endicott, Richard Falk, Edward Hagerman, Margaret Melkonian, Amin Saikal and Victor Sidel for generative discussion of the proposals, many of which were presented at the Hague Appeal for Peace Conference, The Hague, 12–15 May 1999. I would also like to acknowledge the hospitality of the United Nations Institute for Disarmament Research, Geneva, where a draft of this chapter was written, and the generous support of the Ford, MacArthur, and New England Biolabs foundations and of the University of Michigan.
2. T. Rauf, 'Defining the Proliferation Problem' (Paper presented at a conference, 'Biological Warfare and Disarmament: Problems, Perspectives, Possible Solutions', UN Institute for Disarmament Research, Geneva, 5–8 July 1998); B. Roberts, *Weapons Proliferation and World Order* (The Hague: Kluwer International, 1996).
3. M. Meselson, Review of *Tomorrow's Weapons, Chemical and Biological* by Jacques Hirshon Rothschild, *Bulletin of the Atomic Scientists*, 20 (October 1964), pp.35–6.
4. H. Swyter, 'Political Considerations and Analysis of Military Requirements for Chemical and Biological Weapons', *Procedures of the National Academy of Sciences*, 65 (1970), p.266.
5. For evidence of strategic thinking about the importance of nuclear weapons in relation to biological weapons, see S. Wright, 'The Geopolitical Origins of the 1972 Biological Weapons Convention', in S. Wright (forthcoming).
6. Defence Science Board Task Force, *Report on Chemical Warfare/Biological Defence* (1985), quoted in US Department of the Army, Army Science Board, *Final Report of the Ad Hoc Group on Army Biological Defence Research Program* (July 1987), p.6.
7. M. Klare, *Rogue States and Nuclear Outlaws: America's Search for a New Foreign Policy* (New York: Hill and Wang, 1995), p.26.
8. US Commission on Integrated Long-Term Strategy, *Discriminate Deterrence* (Washington DC: USGPO, January 1988).
9. President George Bush, speech before the Commonwealth Club of San Francisco, 7 February 1990, quoted in M. Klare, p.237, n.54.
10. US Senate Committee on Governmental Affairs and Permanent Subcommittee on Investigations, Hearings: *Global Spread of Chemical and Biological Weapons*, 100th Cong., 1st Session, 8 February–17 May 1989, p.10.
11. Secretary of Defence Dick Cheney, statement before the House Foreign Affairs Committee, Washington DC (March 1991) quoted in M. Klare, p.63.

12. US White House, Office of the Press Secretary, Address by the President to the 48th Session of the UN General Assembly, 27 September 1993. See also A. Lake, 'Confronting Backlash States', *Foreign Affairs*, 73, 2 (1974), p.46.
13. See, for instance, US Office of Technology Assessment, *Proliferation of Weapons of Mass Destruction: Assessing the Risks* (Washington DC: USGPO, August 1993), p.15.
14. For example, R. Latter, 'Biological Weapons: the Growing Threat' (Wilton Park Paper 124, January 1997), p.1.
15. US Department of Defence, Office of the Secretary of Defence, *Proliferation: Threat and Response* (Washington DC: USGPO, April 1996), p.iii.
16. See, for instance, R. Preston, *The Cobra Event* (New York: Ballantine Books, 1997); J. Miller, S. Engelberg and W. Broad, *Germs: Biological Weapons and America's Secret War* (New York: Simon & Schuster, 2001), pp.225–6.
17. US White House, Office of the Press Secretary, 27 January 1998.
18. US Commission to Assess the Organization of the Federal Government to Combat the Proliferation of Weapons of Mass Destruction, *Combating Proliferation of Weapons of Mass Destruction* (14 July 2000), pp.v–vi.
19. A. Carter, J. Deutch and P. Zelikow, 'Catastrophic Terrorism', *Foreign Affairs*, 77, 6 (November–December 1998), pp.80–94.
20. A. Smithson, 'Separating Fact from Fiction: the Australia Group and the Chemical Weapons Convention' (Occasional Paper No.34, Washington DC: Henry L. Stimson Center, March 1997).
21. Executive Order 12735, *Federal Register* 55 (1990), 48,587; Executive Order 12938 (14 November 1994); W.J. Clinton, 'Message to Congress on Weapons of Mass Destruction', *Weekly Comp. Pres. Doc.* 33 (12 November 1997), 1786.
22. W.J. Clinton, 'Message to the Congress on Weapons of Mass Destruction', 1786.
23. A. Smithson, 'Still Rudderless: the Chemical Weapons Convention at Two', in O. Thranert (ed.), *Preventing the Proliferation of Weapons of Mass Destruction: What Role for Arms-Control?* (Bonn: Friedrich-Ebert-Stiftung, 1999), p.67. The three conditions were (a) allowing the President to refuse a challenge inspection; (b) refusing to allow samples to leave US territory; and (c) restricting the list of industry facilities subject to declaration and inspection.
24. O. Thranert, 'The Positions of the Three Depositary Nations – the United States, Russia, and the United Kingdom – on Verifying Compliance with the Biological Weapons Convention', in S. Wright (forthcoming); S. Wright and D. Wallace, 'Varieties of Secrets and Secret Varieties: the Case of Biotechnology', *Politics and the Life Sciences*, 19, 1 (March 2000), pp.33–45.
25. E. Olson, 'U.S. Rejects New Accord Covering Germ Warfare', *New York Times* (26 July 2001), A7.
26. J.P. Robinson, 'The Australia Group: a Description and Assessment', in H.B. Brauch et al. (eds), *Controlling the Development and Spread of Military Technologies: Lessons from the Past and Challenges for the 1990s* (Amsterdam: VU University Press, 1991).
27. P. O'Sullivan, Statement on Behalf of the Australia Group, 629th Plenary Session of the UN Conference on Disarmament, UN Document CD/1164, pp.1–2; S. Wright, 'Bioweapons: Cuba Case Tests Treaty', *Bulletin of the Atomic Scientists* (November/December 1997), pp.18–19.
28. T. Nagy, 'The Secret Behind the Sanctions', *Progressive* (September 2001); L. Stahl, 'Punishing Saddam', produced by Catherine Olian, CBS, *60 Minutes*, 12 May 1996.
29. See Klare, pp.97–168 for details.
30. S. Carus, 'Prevention Through Counterproliferation', in R. Zilinskas (ed.), *Biological Warfare: Modern Offense and Defence* (Boulder, CO: Lynne Rienner, 1999), pp.194–96.
31. Ibid, pp.200–3.
32. J.A. Baker, with T.M. DeFrank, *The Politics of Diplomacy: Revolution, War, and Peace, 1989–1992* (New York: G.P. Putnam, 1995).
33. US Commission to Assess the Organization of the Federal Government to Combat Proliferation of Weapons of Mass Destruction, *Combating Proliferation of Weapons of Mass Destruction* (14 July 2000), pp.57–8.

34. US Commission to Assess the Organization of the Federal Government to Combat the Proliferation of Weapons of Mass Destruction (2000), Appendix E-3.

35. US Department of Defence, Annual Report on Chemical Warfare and Chemical/Biological Defence Research Program Obligations, 1 October 1989 to 30 September 1990; Monterey Institute of International Studies, Center for Nonproliferation Studies, *Federal Funding to Combat Terrorism, Including Defence against Weapons of Mass Destruction, FY 1998–2001*, available online at: <**http://cns/miis.edu/research/cbw/terfund.htm**>; US Department of Defence, Chemical and Biological Defence Program Annual Report to Congress, March 2000, Annex E.

36. S. Aftergood, 'The Soft-Kill Fallacy', *Bulletin of the Atomic Scientists* (September/October 1994), pp.40–5; B. Rosenberg, '"Non-lethal" Weapons May Violate Treaties', *Bulletin of the Atomic Scientists* (September/October 1994), pp.44–5. For accounts of recent developments, see the Sunshine Project, 'Tinkering with the Genes of Biological Weapons' (13 July 2000) and 'Non-Lethal Weapons Research in the US: Calmatives and Malodorants' (July 2001), available online at: <**www.sunshine-project.org**>.

37. J. Miller, S. Engelberg and W.J. Broad, 'U.S. Germ Warfare Research Pushes Treaty Limits', *New York Times* (4 September 2001), A1, A6; J. Miller, 'Next to Old Rec Hall, A "Germ-Making Plant"', *New York Times* (4 September 2001), A6; Miller, Engelberg and Broad, *Germs*.

38. On speculation concerning terrorist interests in crop-duster planes, see J. Blum and D. Eggen, 'Airborne Poison via Crop Duster?', *International Herald Tribune* (25 September 2001), pp.1, 4; on dangers posed by transportation of hazardous cargo, see A. Revkin, 'States Are Asked to Pull Over Any Truck Allowed to Carry Hazardous Cargo', *New York Times* (27 September 2001), B5.

39. A. Rimmington, 'Invisible Weapons of Mass Destruction: the Soviet Union's BW Program and its Implications for Contemporary Arms-Control', in S. Wright (forthcoming).

40. A. Smithson, 'Toxic Archipelago: Preventing Proliferation from the Former Soviet Chemical and Biological Weapons Complexes' (Report No.32, Washington DC: Henry L. Stimson Center, December 1999).

41. A. Saikal, 'The Coercive Disarmament of Iraq', in S. Wright (forthcoming); T.Y. Ismael and J.S. Ismael, 'Cowboy Warfare, Biological Diplomacy: Disarming Metaphors as Weapons of Mass Destruction', *Politics and the Life Sciences*, 18, 1 (March 1999), pp.70–8.

42. US Office of Technology Assessment (1993), p.65.

43. See, for example, S. Mufson, 'Threat of "Rogue" States: Is It Reality or Rhetoric?', *Washington Post* (29 May 2000), A01.

44. C. Marquis, 'U.S. Declares "Rogue Nations" Are Now "States of Concern"', *New York Times* (20 June 2000), A8; S. Mufson, 'A "Rogue" is a "Rogue" is a "State of Concern"', *Washington Post* (20 June 2000), A16.

45. 'Rogue States of America: Why Bush Needs the Bad Guys', the *Guardian* (12 March 2001), p.21.

46. See, for instance, US House of Representatives, Committee on Government Reform, Subcommittee on National Security, Veterans Affairs, and International Relations – Hearing: Combating Terrorism (20 October 1999), testimony of B. Jenkins; B. Hoffman, 'Change and Continuity in Terrorism', Address to the Conference on Terrorism and Beyond: the 21st Century (Oklahoma City National Memorial Institute for the Prevention of Terrorism and the RAND Corporation, 17 April 2000); M. Leitenberg, 'Aum Shinrikio's Efforts to Produce Biological Weapons: a Case Study in the Serial Propagation of Misinformation', *Terrorism and Political Violence* (Winter 1999), pp.149–58.

47. S. Wright, 'The Hijacking of UNSCOM', *Bulletin of the Atomic Scientists*, 55, 3 (May/June 1999), pp.23–5; T. Weiner and J. Risen, 'Decision to Strike Factory in Sudan based on Surmise Inferred from Evidence', *New York Times* (21 September 1998), p.1.

48. B. Dhar and S. Chaturvedi, 'The Patent Regime and Implementing Article X of the BTWC: Some Reflections', *Politics and the Life Sciences* (March 1999), pp.103–8; B. Dhar, 'The Global Patent Regime and Implementing Article X of the BWC', in S. Wright (forthcoming).

49. R. Falk, 'The Illegitimacy of the Non-Proliferation Regime', the *Brown Journal of World Affairs*, IV, 1 (Winter/Spring 1997), pp.73–82.
50. See the previous chapter.
51. Such a requirement would entail major changes in the current intellectual-property regime administered by the WTO.
52. For further discussion of these issues, see S. Wright and R. Falk, 'Conclusions', in S. Wright (forthcoming).
53. For further discussion, see A. Saikal in S. Wright (forthcoming).

13
Reforming Multilateral Peace Operations: a Survey

Eşref Aksu

The post-Cold War period has witnessed a proliferation of 'multilateral peace operations' – a term that is used here to refer to two crucial notions which have been in wide circulation for decades: peacekeeping and peace enforcement. The former is usually thought to involve deployment and non-coercive activities of multinational personnel authorized by IGOs with the specific purpose of handling violent conflict. The latter can be said to cover coercive multilateral operations ranging from limited-scope sanctions to full-scale collective security action.

This chapter surveys major policy-oriented studies of multilateral peace operations (hereafter: peace operations) in the post-Cold War period. Inescapably, such a survey also entails an indirect examination of the peace operations conducted to date. Identifying the strengths and weaknesses of peace operations, however, is not as important for our purposes as the reform proposals which have arisen from consideration of these strengths and weaknesses. The twin aims of the chapter are to discern the general tenor and orientation of major proposals and to point to possible drawbacks in the way 'reform' has been conceptualized, and in so doing pave the way for the next chapter.

Two points need to be clarified in advance. First, in the post-Cold War period success and failure in peace operations have been the subject of numerous studies. While several of these may have implications for future reform, we focus attention on a smaller number of explicit and representative *reform* studies which are among the most 'notable' in terms of their source, authorship and/or potential audience. While subjective and restrictive, this approach is necessary for the sake of manageability. Secondly, this chapter displays no more than a few characteristic, influential and compatible proposals advanced by selected studies. It puts the emphasis on the 'basic' ideas that underlie and connect those proposals, trying to minimize the injustice it inevitably does to the actual richness and nuances of the studies under examination.

Reform studies: Detecting common denominators

Since the publication of Boutros-Ghali's *An Agenda for Peace*[1] an increasing number of reform studies have addressed peace operations. As one would expect, the main preoccupations, concepts and internal structures of these studies are not consistent with each other. Moreover they cannot be easily put into the same basket because they enjoy radically different degrees of 'specificity'. At one end of the spectrum are highly specific studies which examine nothing more than one strategically selected aspect of peace operations within the UN system.[2] At the other are comprehensive reports which put forth a wide range of reform proposals in a number of large policy areas – not only in the context of the UN, but in the broader context of global governance.[3] Understandably, limited-scope studies cannot be expected, nor do they intend, to be as critical of the 'bigger picture' as broader-scope studies. What further complicates our account is the time factor. It is difficult, and arguably even methodologically suspect, to examine *An Agenda for Peace* and the *Brahimi Report*[4] as if both were the product of the same time and context.

Despite their significant temporal and thematic differences, however, important similarities and commonalities exist between the various assessments of peace operations. In other words, the 'evolution' of the global reform agenda (that is, the changes in ideas that occur from one study to the next) does not overshadow the 'cumulative' effect of similar/compatible points stemming from the different studies. To begin with, it is possible to find a number of observations which recur in several studies, including our own volume. Not only are these observations uncontested but they are frequently alluded to, if not always prominently highlighted. We begin our survey with a brief synopsis of these observations.

Consensus 1: The end of the Cold War proved a critical threshold

The transition from the Cold War to the post-Cold War period is believed to have been crucial for peace operations in two respects. First, the removal of strategic and ideological bipolarity, which had been the most important global ordering principle since 1945, resulted in the eruption of a great many more violent conflicts world wide, including ethno-cultural and religious rivalries. Peace operations became increasingly necessary. Secondly, this necessity was met with increasing willingness on the part of the international community to conduct peace operations. Crucial in this regard was the *rapprochement* between major world powers, especially the Permanent Five. The first half of the 1990s witnessed the rapid proliferation of peace operations. Even though the difficulties encountered in this period led to the slowing down of authorizations in the second half of the decade, the idea and practice of active multilateral response to crises remained very much alive.

The growing number of peace operations was accompanied by a change in their *modus operandi*. Put differently, the post-Cold War period brought along qualitative as well as quantitative change. Qualitative change was in part a by-product of the kinds of conflict in response to which peace operations were authorized. With the eruption of new forms of violence, many of which took shape within rather than between states, the international community began to authorize peace operations not so much in response to inter-state conflicts as to the radically different challenges posed by intra-state violence. In the process, the discrepancy between the doctrine and the practice of 'peacekeeping' drastically widened, and the distinction between 'peacekeeping' and 'peace enforcement' became blurred. The practice of peacekeeping expanded both in terms of *breadth* and *depth*.[5] On the one hand, the spectrum of activities associated with peacekeeping became ever 'broader'. On the other, peacekeeping entailed 'deeper' levels of involvement in the performance of various tasks.

Consensus 2: Multilateral responses to a number of catastrophes ended in failure

Several reform studies are in agreement that such post-Cold War cases as Bosnia, Somalia and Rwanda qualify as clear-cut 'failures'. Almost any discussion of failure, at least by implication, makes reference to these cases. Interestingly, what exactly is considered here as failure is not made clear, let alone the causes of failure. Aside from the conduct of field operations, 'inaction', 'timing', aims' and 'results' also constitute grounds for criticism depending on the study's perspective. Nevertheless, agreement on the label 'failure' seems broad-based simply because the cases in question appear to qualify as failure by any number of criteria. In a sense, they signify *complete* failures and offer a consensual reference point from which generalizations are derived.[6]

There is also a tendency in several studies to see the bright side of peace operations. In order to point to the potential for future improvement, reference is made to a number of agreed-upon 'successful aspects' of such individual cases as Namibia, Cambodia and Mozambique. Several notable reform studies in the post-Cold War period predate such controversial operations as those in Kosovo, East Timor and Sierra Leone. It is possible to argue, as we do below, that some of these cases demonstrate vividly striking weaknesses in the way reform has been conceptualized. An examination of these cases becomes even more instructive when taken together with a number of earlier peace operations (for instance, UN operations in Iraq and Haiti, and non-UN operations in Chad and Sinai) the assessments of which are by no means consensual.

Consensus 3: Various kinds of 'interconnectedness' should be confronted

There appears to be at least tacit agreement that *both* the conflicts and the multilateral responses take shape in an environment of 'interconnectedness'. The design of peace operations must therefore reflect awareness of various kinds of interconnectedness and take their implications into account. The complex relationship between different broad policy areas (for instance, economic, social, political) is a recurrent theme, albeit an insufficiently developed one.[7] Better developed is the notion of the inseparability of different peace and security problems, including disarmament, civil unrest, refugees and terrorism.

The interrelatedness between different 'methods' used in handling violent conflict is by far the most consensual point arising out of the various reform studies, regardless of their differing emphases.[8] The methods in question may be visualized in terms of such generic activities as 'peacekeeping', 'peacemaking', and 'peacebuilding'. They can also be visualized with reference to more 'basic' tasks which are the ingredients of those generic activities, such as monitoring, negotiation and technical assistance. It should be noted, though, that the importance assigned to interconnectedness varies significantly from one study to the other. Disagreements exist, furthermore, as to which issues are more interconnected than, and which should have greater priority than, others.

Consensus 4: There are significant 'political' barriers to success

The last major point of agreement is that success – regardless of how it is defined – is hindered by a lack of political will, especially on the part of major powers. However, this realization usually leads to wishful thinking rather than concrete 'proposals'. For the sake of adopting a more realistic stance, several studies make just passing reference to the critical problem of lack of political will,[9] and choose to concentrate on technical and operational problems instead, such as the need to improve the quality and quantity of material, financial and human resources. The enormity of the political barriers to success (and to reform) is frequently hinted at, but rarely systematically addressed.[10]

Discerning the global 'reform project'

While agreement on a number of points does not necessarily lead reform studies to develop entirely similar proposals, it does suggest a degree of consistency in their overall approach. Not infrequently we find quite comparable or compatible ideas despite the fact that each major study is the product of a different time period and/or a different context. Such consistency enables us to draw a framework within which we can usefully summarize several of the most sophisticated and/or influential reform proposals that were in circulation at the dawn of the twenty-first century.

The present section synthesizes major compatible points arising from selected reform studies dealing with peace operations, and narrates them as if they were all part of one and the same large and continuous global 'reform project'. Special care is taken to avoid 'careless' eclecticism, and to cite the common denominators of comparable proposals. Although some of these proposals have already materialized, at least in part, our account does not exclude them, for to do so would lead to an incomplete representation of the larger international reform agenda. Drawing on this integrated narrative, then, the last section goes on to suggest some major weaknesses in the way reform has been conceptualized. It should be readily apparent that not all the proposals reviewed in this section are compatible with the reforms advocated in this volume. It is nevertheless crucial for any serious reform study to digest and come to grips with the range of noteworthy proposals that preceded it, which is precisely the function of the present chapter.

Given the organizational incongruence between various studies, this section draws a special framework for summarizing their main points. The majority of proposals are assigned here to three groups which relate to the major temporal phases of any given UN operation: assessment, authorization/early planning, and implementation. Those proposals which clearly cut across these three phases constitute our last group. Crucially, implicit in this categorization is also our overarching argument: that the success or otherwise of peace operations is often considered to be a function of relatively secondary issues, such as the quality of assessment, authorization, planning, implementation, and cross-cutting organizational and financial arrangements.

Assessment phase

The first ingredient of success is usually thought to be a thorough assessment of actual and potential crises. Here the emphasis is put on early-warning mechanisms and the selection of the most appropriate methods of dealing with a given conflict. The main ideas in circulation revolve around the following items.

Mechanisms to bring conflicts to the attention of the international community

Identification of dangerous conflicts is a challenge. Arrangements are proposed through which information from issue-specific sources can be synthesized, and political indicators developed to assess potential threats to peace. In general, the early-warning responsibility is placed with the UN Secretariat. It is also noted, however, that the problem is perhaps less one of early warning than of early action. An early-warning system should be combined with consistently updated contingency plans for preventive action.[11]

More fact-finding, we are told, should be initiated by the UN. The Security Council should consider appropriate preventive action in response to reports from the relevant departments in the Secretariat. ECOSOC should not hesitate to advise the Security Council of potential emergencies arising out of economic and social conditions. The creation of regional 'peace and security response centres' to help carry out preventive diplomacy has obvious relevance for early-warning capabilities. The establishment of an 'operational-level headquarters' may facilitate generic contingency-planning, triggering early-warning mechanisms as well as liaison with regional arrangements.[12]

A number of studies stress the need to distinguish between the general conditions of poverty, inequality and environmental degradation that may generate instability in the long term and the specific developments, policies or abuses that may precipitate violent conflict. The former would need to be addressed as part of a larger effort to promote sustainable development.[13]

Options and methods to be considered

Once a conflict has been identified, the next step is to determine how it should be approached. Available options, other than peace operations, for resolving conflicts include such preventive measures as making use of Article 33; the ICJ; good offices; and 'preventive development'. Certain circumstances may warrant preventive deployment of peacekeeping troops, which should generally be considered as a last resort in the prevention phase. Such deployment, it is argued, would signal the need for further Security Council action should conflict erupt. It could be a vital measure for avoiding both conflict and the need for more forceful action.[14]

A case may be made that the use of active force should *not* be regarded only as a last resort in desperate circumstances. Nevertheless, when employing force for preventive purposes, states should do so only with a clear Security Council authorization that details the arrangements under which force will be used and the agencies that will be involved in the action. Secondly, for preventive action, a multilateral response should be the norm – a norm that should apply to large as well as small states.[15]

Types/stages of conflict and forms/methods of intervention

When all else fails, intervention, it is argued, may become necessary. The choice of method should be related to the type or stage of the conflict in question. One option is that of sanctions which usually begin with the imposition of an arms embargo. Hitherto, the second step normally favoured has been comprehensive economic sanctions. A more suitable second step would be to apply measures that are better focused on target groups. The Security Council would ensure, when sanctions are introduced, that humanitarian programmes are available to help the most vulnerable groups, and multilateral aid is available to those countries which suffer from the effects of sanctions.[16]

When sanctions are imposed, care should be taken to define objective criteria for determining that their purpose has been achieved. The criteria for evaluating the effectiveness of sanctions would not be changed to serve purposes other than those which motivated the original decision. The aim of sanctions would be modification of political behaviour rather than punishment. Nevertheless, sanctions may need to be accompanied by a blockade and by a range of controls over commercial, financial and trading mechanisms from the outset. Signals should be clear on the behaviour required for sanctions to be lifted and, where possible, accompanied by an incentive package to encourage compliance. Sanctions would need to be considered in the context of a broader strategy to influence the country on which sanctions are applied. The costs involved in the application of sanctions would be borne equitably by all members. Mechanisms would be established within the UN Secretariat to assess matters related to the imposition of sanctions.[17]

As for military options, a distinction has been drawn since *An Agenda for Peace* between three kinds of forces that the UN may use in different situations: forces which would be committed to UN service on a permanent basis to respond to inter-state aggression; 'peacekeeping' forces; and 'peace enforcement' units to be deployed to enable peacekeepers to carry out their mandate. While coercive action should be taken normally as a last resort, retaining the option has been deemed essential to the UN's credibility. Enforcement action in support of peacekeeping proved an especially sensitive issue. This type of action, it has been argued, should be based on a short-term mandate, and before its expiry the Security Council should review whether its objectives are still attainable. The enforcement action would be fully and clearly explained to the public. The force commander would have to report regularly to the Security Council. UN forces, it is sometimes stressed, should not be introduced unless it is agreed that they will remain *as long as* is necessary for the establishment of conditions allowing for sustained relief.[18]

In the wake of the changing (geo)political realities, stress has also been placed on the need to address 'complex emergencies' in general, and the issue of 'humanitarian intervention' in particular. The UN would set out principles and benchmarks for specific responses to violent conflicts, including those undertaken under Chapter VII of the Charter. Military strategies, such as systematic rape, would be specifically cited as violations of international humanitarian law to which the Security Council would need to respond. The UN Charter would be amended to permit intervention on humanitarian grounds, but such intervention would be restricted to cases involving extreme violations of human security. A set of criteria would be applied to determine whether humanitarian intervention should be authorized in a given crisis, and another set of criteria as to how UN humanitarian intervention should be conducted.[19]

Authorization/early planning phase

Meticulous assessment, while necessary, is not sufficient for peace operations to be successful. Several reform studies have proposed measures which would impact on the overall orientation of peace operations from the authorization/early planning stage. Proposed reforms relate to the establishment of consultative mechanisms, improvement of mandates, advance contingency planning, and allocation of adequate resources. A representative set of major ideas advocated is outlined below.

Consultative mechanisms

Once intervention is considered appropriate, the main task, according to several studies, becomes that of planning and completing the proposed mission. This task, it is stressed, should not be undertaken without invoking relevant consultative mechanisms. For each operation, a consultative committee could be formed, including representatives of troop-contributing countries. More generally, those countries would be consulted as part of the Security Council's decision-making on peace operations. To increase the likelihood of success, civilian and military senior staff would be chosen early and involved with the planning of the operation.[20]

Frequent reference has been made to the utility of permanent consultative mechanisms. The UN Secretariat would establish/strengthen planning units for specific mission components (police, human rights, electoral), and achieve greater integration between planning and operations. One measure would be the creation of a UN general staff for peace operations with a 'surge' capacity at times of greater demand. A multinational group of professionals with expertise in intelligence and reconnaissance could be recruited to serve as a source of independent analysis for the Security Council. Other ideas advanced have included a revitalized Military Staff Committee and a troop-contributors forum, comprised of major troop-contributing states, which would meet periodically to review peacekeeping issues.[21]

Formal mandate

The goals and methods of peace operations, many studies insist, should be the subject of clear agreement translated into precise mandates. When the Security Council finally authorized deployment, it would make clear whether the deployed personnel would be used for peacekeeping, for peace enforcement under Article 40, or for collective security action under Article 42. Forces would not be allowed to exceed the Council's mandate. Any change to the original mandate would have to be approved by the Security Council and explained to participating member states. Guidelines for the protection of peacekeepers would be incorporated in the rules of engagement rather than invoking Chapter VII on a case-by-case basis. The Security Council, in establishing a peacekeeping operation, would prescribe a time frame for the conclusion of the Status of Forces Agreement. If the UN contemplated despatching missions to conflicts where the use of force might be required to avert major violence, it would have to determine from the outset its source of authority in the Charter, specifically mandate the mission accordingly, and provide the necessary resources. It would be the Security Council's responsibility, and not the force commander's, to determine whether there was some acceptable principle, in international law and practice, on which to rely when applying force. Every peacekeeping mandate, furthermore, would have a clearly designated set of termination criteria.[22]

Facing potential problems in advance

Problems which may arise from changes to the nature of peace operations during the course of incidents on the ground, it has been suggested, should be addressed in the preparation of formal mandates and complementary instruments. When sanctions are imposed, for instance, other affected states should have a realistic possibility of having their difficulties addressed. Remedies might include compensation from levies on the target country after the sanctions have achieved their goal, and compensation from special funds. Violations of an imposed sanction should automatically result in a flow-on of the sanctions to the violator.[23]

As to peacekeeping, demonstrable will and capacity to deploy sufficient peacekeepers in strength would be a precondition of any new peacekeeping operation. It would be helpful to bring hostile acts against UN personnel under universal jurisdiction. It would also help, albeit indirectly, if UN peacekeepers made an effort both to be and be seen to be impartial. Countries with special interests in, or close historical association with, a conflict should not contribute troops to a peacekeeping operation. On the other hand, the principle that the Permanent Five should refrain from any active part in peacekeeping might need to be discarded for the sake of effectiveness. Considerations of 'will' and 'effectiveness' might also require the UN to give serious thought to pulling out in certain situations. Conversely, should it decide to stay, it would have to be prepared to deal with the aftermath of enforcement operations, including subsequent internal crises. Special consideration would be given to operations which have 'transitional administration' mandates.[24]

Human and material resources for the envisaged intervention

Any decision on intervention must be based on careful assessment of the availability of human and material resources. Keeping precise records of available or committed resources for future operations is often advanced as a must. Proposals have been made for expanded databases to be developed on national capacities for contributions to peacekeeping in such areas as civilian police, senior military commanders, human rights monitors, and potential special representatives or envoys.[25]

The UN's staff resources in peacekeeping and logistical support have been deemed in need of significant strengthening. Standby units could be organized into task-specific multinational 'capability components' (such as an observation force or humanitarian assistance force). Member states would ensure the availability – perhaps through standby arrangement systems – of qualified civilian as well as military personnel to serve in peace operations. Arrangements under Article 43 for committing military forces to the UN on a permanent basis are considered long overdue. A number of recommendations have stressed the need for police components in peacekeeping. The Secretary-General has been called upon to establish a permanent civilian police capability within the Secretariat, capable of rapid deployment. The creation of specialized UN 'humanitarian security' police and UN 'fiscal' police has also been advocated.[26]

The question of training has attracted special attention. Arrangements for training peacekeepers need reviewing and improvement. Actual training, it has been suggested, could be left to member states, with the main responsibility for training assigned to states which have the greatest military capacity and expertise. The UN for its part would encourage the establishment of training centres, and develop standard training materials. An international staff college or a UN 'system' staff college would train the trainers.[27]

With regard to material resources, a pre-positioned stock of basic equipment could be established in the UN, so that it can be made available at the start of an operation. The UN would work towards the acquisition, lease and pre-positioning of such equipment, or enter into a services agreement with member states for the provision of this equipment from national reserves. Governments could commit themselves to keeping certain equipment on standby for immediate sale, loan or donation to the UN. Member states in a position to do so would make air- and sea-lift capacity available to the UN free of cost or at lower than commercial rates. Furthermore, partnerships could be established between governments that need equipment and those ready to provide it. Standard items such as motor vehicles and field accommodation could be held in stock in key regional centres.[28]

Implementation phase

While careful assessment and design may pave the way for effective peace operations, proper implementation has its own set of requirements. The weaknesses of peace operations at the implementation stage have been judged equally important obstacles to their success. Numerous studies have consequently addressed the crucial questions of deployment, command/control and review.

Initial/rapid deployment

Many reports have recommended swift action once a mission is authorized, hence the emphasis on measures to enhance the UN's rapid-reaction capacity. Special procedures could be instituted to permit the rapid transfer of Secretariat staff to serve with peace operations. A rapidly deployable small, multi-disciplinary group could be established for immediate despatch to the field with a view to getting the operation under way.[29]

Reference is also made to 'early deployment contingents', which would not only assist in planning and rapid deployment, but also provide a force commander, headquarters staff and forces familiar with command and control procedures. The standby arrangements system could be refined and strengthened, with special emphasis on the ability of member states to meet specific readiness targets for potential service in rapid-reaction operations. A rapid-reaction force would be the Security Council's strategic reserve to be deployed in emergency situations. The Secretary-General has been encouraged to use such techniques as the 'peacekeeping services agreement' concept to facilitate rapid deployment and effective support. The establishment of regionally based operational-level headquarters might also prove helpful.[30]

Command and control

A key contention has been that the chain of command must be clear, unified and legitimate. The basis for the operational control of UN enforcement operations should always lie, it is usually stressed, in a Security Council authorization. Overall UN control and unity of command should be respected, even when particular missions have been delegated to a coalition command. The political direction of UN peacekeeping operations would be the responsibility of the Security Council, with executive direction and command being that of the Secretary-General. Command in the field should be entrusted to the chief of mission who would have authority over all UN entities. Governments would not attempt to provide guidance to their contingents on operational matters.[31]

Monitoring, reporting and reviewing the intervention

It is considered vitally important for the international community to know exactly what is happening in the field. In particular, the Security Council has been strongly urged to consider upgrading its reporting requirements from force commanders. Communication between forces and the UN Secretariat needs to be strengthened, with the latter responding quickly to force recommendations or requests. An enhanced capacity within the Secretariat to gather, receive, analyse and disseminate information has also been stressed. This suggests greater reliance on such new technologies as satellite imagery. More issue-specific proposals have included the call for the establishment of a field monitoring system for assessing the impact of sanctions, and the introduction of an ombudsman to monitor the performance of large-scale peace missions with regard to human rights.[32]

Cutting across the three phases: Organizational and financial arrangements

Cross-cutting organizational and financial weaknesses are believed to have substantial bearing on the success of peace operations. As a consequence numerous proposals have been advanced with a view to improving the quality of assessment, authorization and implementation through appropriate organizational and financial rearrangements.

Reorganizing the UN

Much emphasis has been placed on augmenting the strength and capability of an international civil service, with particular attention paid to such units in the UN Secretariat as the DPKO and the Office of the Military Adviser. In addition, the establishment of a number of new units has been advocated (for example, 'operational-level headquarters', 'security assessment staff', and/or 'information and strategic analysis secretariat'). Such an entity would be drawn from existing departments and through secondment from functional organizations. It would draw heavily on data and expertise available in the various arms of the UN system, and perform an early-warning and threat-assessment function.[33]

The restructuring of the wider UN 'system' would have implications for the conduct of peace operations. Relevant proposals which would require substantial 'organizational' change have included the appointment of a number of Deputy Secretaries-General, one of whom would be in charge of the combined relief functions; integration of conflict prevention activities across the whole UN system; better co-ordination between relevant units; decentralization; reorganization of UN regional commissions; establishment of UN system offices in developing countries; and the various proposals which call for adaptation of the UN's principal organs to changing realities.[34]

The most notable and relevant idea which would require a more fundamental 'structural' rather than 'organizational' change is the expansion of the Security Council. This principle has been generally accepted, but questions of 'how and how many' have remained the subject of intensive debate. The performance of peace operations would also be positively, though indirectly, affected by the establishment of a permanent International Criminal Court and of a Council for Petitions in which non-state actors could exercise the right of petition.[35]

(Re)organizing relevant actors

The relationship between the UN and various types of actors have implications for peace operations. Several improvements depend on the tacit if not explicit approval of member states. Two proposals deserve mention here: first, the idea that states might try to develop frameworks for effective participation in international humanitarian efforts and peace initiatives (for instance, as per the 'Norwegian Model'), and secondly, the notion of 'friends of the Secretary-General' who might prove helpful, provided that they act only upon the Secretary-General's specific request.[36]

Attention has also been drawn to the under-utilized potential of regional arrangements. They could establish means, linked to the UN, to monitor circumstances of incipient violence. It may also be politically more feasible for the bulk of future missions to be composed of troops from the region concerned. The method of delegating implementation of UN-authorized operations to regional organizations could be further developed, although Security Council control over the operations would be retained.[37] As for non-governmental actors, they could perform an early-warning function and be more systematically integrated into the UN's peace and security function. Not only NGOs, but a range of other CSOs could clearly contribute to the shaping of peace operations.[38]

Financing peace operations

The international community, it has been repeatedly stated, must be prepared to make significantly greater funds available for peace operations. Changes are thought necessary in the scale of assessments, but in any case governments must pay swiftly their assessed contributions, and fully fund humanitarian consolidated appeals. While the funding of peacekeeping continues to be viewed as the collective responsibility of all member states, the case has been made that as long as permanent members seek to retain their special privileges in the Security Council, they should continue to pay a higher assessment rate. States are invited to finance their peacekeeping contributions from their defence, rather than foreign affairs, budgets. Other proposals to strengthen the financial basis of peace operations include the adoption of the Tobin Tax, the introduction of a mechanism to draw upon the income of arms-exporting countries, and the charging of interest for affluent member states which enter into arrears on their dues. Finally, as regards the actual spending of money, new financial regulations have been advocated, which would involve the delegation of responsibility and commensurate authority to appropriate senior UN officials to facilitate the effective implementation of peace operations.[39]

Reflections on the global 'reform project'

Thus far we have suggested that the post-Cold War period has produced successive reform proposals which, despite their many differences, are to a considerable degree comparable or compatible. The cumulative impact of these proposals was perhaps nowhere more visible than in Boutros-Ghali's and Annan's incremental improvements in the UN Secretariat. Meaningful reform, however, requires that more fundamental challenges are met. The global reform agenda needs to be complemented by, if not restructured on the basis of, a number of more primary considerations.

Losing sight of objectives in the judgement of success

The idea of 'reform' inevitably rests on notions of success and failure which are not easy to determine in the context of peace operations. While some commentators argue that the determination of success should be strictly confined to the mandate of an operation, others raise a number of problems with this approach. First, owing to vague wording, the evaluation of the mandate's content, let alone its implementation, is often problematic. Secondly, the success or failure of individual missions is of course important, but not more so than the overall success or failure of the peace operations mechanism as a whole. Perhaps equally important is the relative nature of any evaluation. As William Durch asks:

> Is a mission that keeps foes apart for ten years, but whose involuntary departure is followed by war, a success for what it sustained for a decade, or a failure for what happened afterward? Is a mission that keeps foes apart indefinitely

a success for having spared them new bloodshed, or a failure for having made them dependent on its presence, for having removed the need to settle old grievances?[40]

Difficult though this may be, any serious reform programme must establish a clear set of yardsticks by which the peace operations can be assessed and, where necessary, improved. Criteria offered by reform studies – usually implicitly – against which peace operations should be judged include, for instance, 'quick response' and 'cost effectiveness'. While these and similar criteria may spell success in some limited sense, they are certainly not enough to drive meaningful reform. Despite the proliferation of innovative ideas, which has enhanced the debate, the importance of a critical factor remains strikingly under-emphasized in many reform studies: namely, objectives. What peace operations should accomplish, whether individually or collectively, for them to be considered successful has been a neglected question.

Success has not been directly associated with the attainment of clearly identified objectives. As a result, the illusion is often created of success, and therefore reform, being linked to what might be labelled 'operational' targets. To give but one striking example, there is a significant subset of reform proposals which call for an expansion in the financial basis of peace operations. Unless accompanied by a convincing explanation of what exactly the money would be used for, such proposals cannot contribute to meaningful change. The objectives of peace operations and of related reform are frequently treated as if they were clearly understood and universally accepted. This may be a profoundly mistaken assumption.

Arguably, the foremost problem with peace operations has been the ambiguity of their objectives. This problem transcends the question of ambiguous wording of formal mandates, and touches the ambiguity surrounding the overall conceptualization of peace missions. The more interesting question is not whether a given formal mandate is clear enough, but what any peace mission should be designed to do. Was it, for instance, appropriate for the UN to authorize a peace operation to 'restore democracy' as it did in Haiti? The answer to this and similar questions are far from obvious, and merit closer attention.

Success and failure are relative judgements which may need to be governed by two considerations: first, how closely outcomes match objectives that have been set; secondly, how adequate the chosen instruments are for the attainment of the objectives. The former consideration immediately raises a critical question: Does success imply the matching of *any* objectives that may have been set? In other words, if there are problems with the objectives, what does it matter if the outcomes coincide with them or not? This question still awaits systematic scrutiny.

Underestimating the question of consistency

As our survey has demonstrated, a number of studies either develop standards as to what kind of crisis deserves what kind of multilateral response, or encourage the development of such standards. There is, however, a notable silence on the consistent application of comparable measures to comparable cases. Peace operations may need to be judged in part by the degree of consistency in applying standards. Reformers may need to insist that similar diseases should be treated with similar determination, subject to periodic and systematic review of the agreed-upon treatment methods.

It is well established that each conflict has its own unique dynamics and circumstances. Consequently the appropriate response may need to be tailored to the case in hand. Nevertheless, if, for instance, particular types of 'threats to peace' are deemed to warrant peace operations, as in Somalia or Haiti, the assessment may need to take into account whether there were similar cases to which the international community failed to respond. From this perspective, the inaction in such cases as Sudan or Burma may impinge on the question of success, and should therefore be addressed. If emphasis is to be put on the ultimate objective, a simplistic argument that the conditions in the latter cases were not favourable to peace operations will not do.

Neglecting the time factor

Assessment of peace operations does not systematically take account of the time factor. In the first place, 'time-sensitive evaluation of success' has not been made an integral part of the global reform agenda. Whether the designated objectives have been met can usually be appreciated only with the passage of time. There is little indication in several reform studies that assessment of success is considered a continuous process rather than a one-time endeavour. On the other hand, assessment is rarely considered a matter of *both* retrospective and prospective reflection. In other words, evaluation of peace operations is not necessarily understood in terms of focused examination of whether the designated objectives *were, are* or *will be* achieved.

A second manifestation of the time factor is that different objectives have different time implications. The crucial question here is whether (due to political, technical or financial considerations) the objectives of peace operations are to be kept deliberately short term. It should be admitted that such objectives as conflict transformation or democratization (leaving aside, for the moment, the question of whether these are 'appropriate' objectives for peace operations) cannot be achieved in the short run. Any open-ended objective – for instance, 'prevention of a recurrence of fighting' as in Cyprus – would also need to be assessed from a time perspective. If peace operations are to be authorized merely to put an immediate stop to the fighting (again leaving aside whether this would be an 'appropriate' objective), withdrawal may need to follow as soon as the objective is met.

Ambivalence as to the UN's place in the 'hierarchy' of authority

There seems to be no alternative to the UN in the co-ordination of global peace efforts. For this reason, the UN remains at the centre of several reform studies, including the present volume. However, as the Korean, Gulf and Kosovo crises have aptly demonstrated, the UN's authority and competence are highly problematic.

The relationship between the UN and the peace operations that have taken place so far, or that are yet to take place, needs careful scrutiny.[41] Even if the UN were believed to be simply a 'policy instrument' of states, the question would need to be asked: What should be the UN's role in relation to peace operations?

Both during and after the Cold War the UN's authority over peace operations has been continuously challenged. In the Cold War environment, the UN was effectively marginalized in peace and security issues. The Organization was rendered ineffectual through such means as exclusion of items from its agenda, use of the veto, or refusal to make payments. On the other hand, the UN's authority over such extra-UN peace operations as in Chad, Sinai (MFO) and Lebanon (MNF) was at best ambiguous.

In the post-Cold War period, at first, the proliferation of UN peace operations created the impression that the Cold War challenges to the UN's authority were over. The decades-old complex of Namibia-Angola crises, for instance, was finally addressed by respective UN operations. The western enforcement against Iraq (1991) received a previously unlikely moral support from the Soviet Union. China consented to negotiations over Cambodia's destiny. Yet before long it was understood that the challenge to the UN's authority over peace operations would continue.

Most strikingly, the UN was not only sidestepped, but its 'normative' authority over peace operations openly questioned. The most visible example of this challenge was perhaps the 1999 Kosovo crisis, where a Cold War defence alliance (NATO) took almost independent enforcement action despite strong international reservations. No matter how legitimate the cause, there was little reference to the UN during the planning, authorization and implementation of the operation. At the time of writing, NATO, rather than the UN, was mobilized in connection with the crisis in Macedonia and the World Trade Centre disaster in New York. Does the UN enjoy a supreme normative authority as far as the authorization, conduct and/or evaluation of peace operations are concerned? This question is seldom addressed by major reform studies – certainly not in systematic and persistent fashion.[42]

Conclusion

The numerous reform proposals in circulation perform a useful task in that they provoke further reflection on the way peace operations are contemplated and conducted. At the beginning of the new century, several promising notions are on the international agenda. What is largely missing, however, is a focused attempt to identify the 'first principles'. It is quite possible that different studies, or for that matter different actors, have different priorities. Be that as it may, it is our contention that meaningful reform is necessarily a function of first principles. If the international community intends to go beyond palliative measures and sporadic improvements, it may need to engage in serious debate about such challenging issues as objectives, consistency, time and authority, while persistently addressing the fundamental problem of lack of political will.

Notes

1. B. Boutros-Ghali, *An Agenda for Peace: Preventive Diplomacy, Peacemaking and Peace-keeping* (New York: UN, 1992).
2. For example, Canada, *Towards a Rapid Reaction Capability for the United Nations* (Ottawa: Government of Canada, September 1995).
3. A leading example is Commission on Global Governance, *Our Global Neighbourhood* (Oxford: OUP, 1995).
4. 'Report of the Panel on United Nations Peace Operations', A/55/305-S/2000/809, 21 August 2000.
5. See S.R. Ratner, *The New Peacekeeping: Building Peace in Lands of Conflict After the Cold War* (New York: St. Martin's Press [now Palgrave Macmillan], 1995), pp.42–3.
6. The nature of the Rwanda case as 'complete' failure is well encapsulated in the 19-point 'Conclusions' of the 'Report of the Independent Inquiry into the Actions of the United Nations during the 1994 Genocide in Rwanda', S/1999/1257, 15 December 1999.
7. The Commission on Global Governance emphasizes, for instance, that for the UN to be effective in complex emergencies, its different roles (military, political, humanitarian, development) must be performed simultaneously; see p.106.
8. The *Brahimi Report*, for example, deliberately pursues a combined examination of conflict prevention, peacemaking, peacekeeping and peacebuilding; see paras 10–14.
9. See, for instance, the quick reference to the role of 'leadership' in Carnegie Commission on Preventing Deadly Conflict, *Final Report* (December 1997), pp.29–30, 40–1.
10. A striking example is the *Brahimi Report* which explicitly gives weight to operational problems and pragmatism; see pp.viii, 1.
11. Boutros-Ghali (1992), para.26; Commission on Global Governance, p.98; Canada, pp.43–4; Carnegie Commission, pp.44–8; B. Boutros-Ghali, *Supplement to An Agenda for Peace: Position Paper of the Secretary-General on the Occasion of the Fiftieth Anniversary of the United Nations* (New York: United Nations, 1995), para.56; Oxfam International, *Improving the UN's Response to Complex Emergencies* (Position Paper, November 1997), p.10; K.A. Annan, *Renewing the United Nations: a Programme for Reform* (New York: United Nations, 1997), paras 65, 111; Independent Working Group on the Future of the United Nations, *The United Nations in its Second Half-Century* (New York: Ford Foundation, 1995), available online at: <http://www.library.yale.edu//un/unhome.htm> (10 March 1999), paras 11–13 under Part 3a.
12. Boutros-Ghali (1992), para.25; Canada, p.51; Commission on Global Governance, p.99; Annan, para.110; *Brahimi Report*, para.32; G. Evans, *Cooperating for Peace: the Global Agenda for the 1990s and Beyond* (NSW: Allen & Unwin, 1993), pp.178, 181.
13. Commission on Global Governance, pp.94–7; Carnegie Commission, chs.3–4; *Brahimi Report*, para.29; the South Centre, *For A Strong and Democratic United Nations: a South Perspective on UN Reform* (Geneva: the South Centre, 1996), p.20.
14. Commission on Global Governance, pp.92, 100–1; Boutros-Ghali (1992), paras 23–38; Boutros-Ghali (1995), paras 26–8; Carnegie Commission, pp.136–8; Oxfam, p.11; South Centre, p.228.
15. Carnegie Commission, pp.62–3.
16. Commission on Global Governance, p.107; Independent Working Group, para.31 under Part 3a.
17. Boutros-Ghali (1995), paras 66–76; Evans, pp.138–40; Commission on Global Governance, p.108; Carnegie Commission, pp.54–6, 139; Annan, para.108.
18. Boutros-Ghali (1992), paras 42–4; Evans, pp.145–54.
19. Oxfam, p.8; Commission on Global Governance, pp.89–91; Evans, pp.154–8; Carnegie Commission, pp.59–62.
20. Independent Working Group, para.23 under Part 3a; Evans, pp.108, 116, 122, 181; Commission on Global Governance, pp.102–3; Canada, p.38; *Brahimi Report*, paras 97, 101(b); United Nations Association of the United States of America (UNA-USA),

The Preparedness Gap: Making Peace Operations Work in the 21st Century (January 2001), pp.31–2.

21. Evans, p.124; Commission on Global Governance, p.109; Canada, p.38.
22. Evans, pp.109, 113, 127, 150–2; Annan, para.115; Boutros-Ghali (1992), para.68; *Brahimi Report*, paras 51, 55, 64; Independent Working Group, para.22 under Part 3a; Carnegie Commission, pp.59–62.
23. Boutros-Ghali (1992), para.41; Boutros-Ghali (1995), para.101; Evans, pp.140–2.
24. Evans, pp.110–12, 128, 148; Commission on Global Governance, p.104; *Brahimi Report*, paras 39–40, 83.
25. Evans, pp.125–6; Canada, pp.46, 49; Oxfam, p.10; *Brahimi Report*, paras 96, 101, 130–2; UNA-USA, p.27.
26. E. Childers and B. Urquhart, *Renewing the United Nations System* (Uppsala, Sweden: Dag Hammarskjold Foundation, 1994), pp.204–5, 209; Canada, pp.52, 59; Boutros-Ghali (1992), paras 43–4, 51; Boutros-Ghali (1995), paras 30–1; Oxfam, pp.12–13; *Brahimi Report*, paras 118–26, 135–45; 219–25; UNA-USA, pp.17–18, 25–6.
27. Boutros-Ghali (1992), para.52; Evans, p.126; Childers and Urquhart, p.210; Canada, p.54; Oxfam, p.13; *Brahimi Report*, para.136.; UNA-USA, pp.21–2.
28. Boutros-Ghali (1992), paras 53–4; Boutros-Ghali (1995), para.45; Canada, p.47; Evans, p.126; *Brahimi Report*, paras 151–69.
29. Boutros-Ghali (1992), para.52; Annan, paras 64, 112, 115; Canada, p.63.
30. Evans, p.125; Boutros-Ghali (1995), para.44; Canada, p.48. For differing versions of the idea of a rapid-reaction force, see Independent Working Group, paras 24–9 under 3a; Commission on Global Governance, pp.110–12; Carnegie Commission, pp.66–7; Oxfam, pp.12–13; Annan, para.113; *Brahimi Report*, paras 84–91, 110–17; and the Military Working Group on a Multinational United Nations Stand-by Forces High Readiness Brigade, *Non-Paper* (A/51/75-S/1996/166, 5 March 1996). For sceptical views on a 'standing' rapid-reaction force, see Evans, pp.163–5; UNA-USA, pp.23–5.
31. Boutros-Ghali (1995), paras 38, 41; Evans, pp.148–49, 160–61; Carnegie Commission, p.66; UNA-USA, pp.29–31; Commission on Global Governance, pp.102, 109; Canada, p.52; Annan, para.119.
32. Independent Working Group, para.31 under 3a; Evans, pp.127–8, 149; Childers and Urquhart, p.203.
33. Boutros-Ghali (1992), para.52; Evans, pp.120–4, 170–4; Canada, p.46; Independent Working Group, paras 11–13 under Part 3a; Annan, paras 117–18; *Brahimi Report*, paras 68–75, Part IV.
34. Evans, pp.121, 158–9, 171, 174, 179–81; Childers and Urquhart, pp.198–9, 203–4; Carnegie Commission, p.139; Boutros-Ghali (1992), para.81; Boutros-Ghali (1995), paras 90–4; Annan, paras 37–8, 121. Concerning the last point, see Boutros-Ghali (1992) (on ECOSOC and the Security Council), paras 26, 71; Independent Working Group (on Security Council), para.9 under Part 3a; and South Centre (on General Assembly), pp.20–1.
35. Evans, pp.180–1; Independent Working Group, paras 8–9 under Part 3a; Carnegie Commission, pp.140–2; Oxfam, p.9; Commission on Global Governance, p.92, 233–41, 260–3.
36. Carnegie Commission, pp.108, 134, 138; Boutros-Ghali (1995), paras 83–4; *Brahimi Report*, paras 266–7, 274–6.
37. Boutros-Ghali (1992), paras 64–5; Commission on Global Governance, pp.104–5; Carnegie Commission, pp.146–9; Oxfam, pp.13–14. With regard to possible *modes* of co-ordination between the UN and regional organizations, see Boutros-Ghali (1995), paras 86–8.
38. Commission on Global Governance, pp.98–100; Canada, pp.47, 51; Boutros-Ghali (1995), para.89; Carnegie Commission, pp.49, 110–27.
39. Commission on Global Governance, pp.112–13; Boutros-Ghali (1992), paras 47–8, 69–74; Oxfam, p.16; Evans, pp.117–120; the South Centre, pp.77, 97–8; Canada, p.42; Annan, para.114; *Brahimi Report*, paras 172–8, 195–6; UNA-USA, pp.33–7.

40. W.J. Durch (ed.), *The Evolution of UN Peacekeeping: Case Studies and Comparative Analysis* (London: Macmillan, 1994), p.12.
41. This is especially important given such problematic remarks as '[t]he problem, not the institutions or their mandates, should be the prime concern'; see Commission on Global Governance, p.102.
42. A typical case is the UN's own *Brahimi Report* which is notably silent on this issue; see especially the uncritical account in pp.17–18, paras 104–6. An important exception in this regard is Boutros-Ghali (1995), see paras 85–8.

14
Peace Operations: the Road Ahead

Joseph A. Camilleri

This chapter aims to identify the norms which must guide a programme of serious reform in the development of peacekeeping and peace enforcement. Without such conceptual underpinning the reform agenda will yield at best half-baked solutions with pragmatic politics as their only rationale. We examine both inter-state and intra-state conflicts as well as the problems posed by humanitarian intervention.

First a preliminary observation. Contrary to earlier assessments, the enormous demands placed by peace operations on the UN's skills and resources have not been an aberration confined to the immediate post-Cold War period. Peacekeeping personnel declined sharply in 1995. As of January 1996, the total deployment of military and civilian police personnel stood at approximately 29,000, less than half of its previous levels. These numbers continued to decline right through to 1999 when they dropped to approximately 12,000, but the decline has since been reversed, and by the end of 2000 the total military and civilian police strength stood at about 38,000 to which must be added some 3,500 international civilian staff serving in peacekeeping operations.[1] As recent developments indicate (the large-scale operation in Kosovo, the new mission in the Democratic Republic of the Congo and in East Timor, the expansion of the mission in Sierra Leone), the introduction of a substantial UN presence in a range of conflict situations is a trend that is likely to be with us for some time to come.

Key principles that should govern peace operations

One of the most difficult questions facing any multilateral approach to security is whether or not to use force, and if so, in what circumstances. Even when a decision has been made to use or just to deploy force, a number of subsidiary questions have still to be addressed: How much force? In what form? With what specific objectives in mind? On whose authority? With whose resources? Any decision therefore made by a multilateral institution to deploy, threaten or use force must be subjected to close and continuing scrutiny.

Reliance on force by states has become increasingly problematic, and its consequences, intended and unintended, increasingly damaging, if for no other reason than the destructiveness of military technology. Reliance on force by a multilateral institution may be more legitimate but no less problematic, and its consequences no less damaging. It follows, then, that in performing its security function the UN should refrain from using or threatening military force, except as a last resort, unless, that is, the ensuing injury to life is estimated to be greater than if force were not used or threatened (the conditions implicit in the notion of last resort are spelt out below under 'Use of Force'). The use or threat of force cannot be central to the achievement of the UN's objectives. Otherwise 'establishing' or 'maintaining' the peace risks becoming another name for war, eventually bringing the multilateral institution into disrepute and severely eroding its legitimacy.

Force cannot be justified as an instrument of policy, unless it is to achieve desirable outcomes. Such outcomes then become the primary objectives, the ultimate yardstick by which success or failure should be measured. Four *primary objectives* apply in varying degrees to the use, threat and deployment of military force.

(1) The first objective must be to prevent the outbreak of hostilities or, where armed conflict has already erupted, to minimize the level of violence. Preventing or minimizing the accumulation [hence threat] of force in conditions of conflict must also be treated as a high priority, since it is likely to accentuate mutual suspicion and mistrust. The accumulation of force, particularly in underdeveloped economies, is likely to militate against the satisfaction of basic human needs (for example, food, shelter, clothing, health). In other words, it kills by other means.

(2) An often more difficult objective is to resolve the conflict (that is, eliminate the sources or perceptions of conflict) or at least produce conditions favourable to the long-term co-existence of the conflicting parties (that is, to significantly displace the use or threat of force as the determining influence on the relationship of those parties in favour of a range of co-operative activities).

(3) A closely related objective is to bring quick and preferably lasting relief to unacceptable levels of human suffering arising directly or indirectly from the actual use or threat of force. UN intervention, even where this is not formally part of the mandate, must be so conceived and executed as to enhance the prospects of long-term social and economic rehabilitation.

(4) A fourth objective is to detect any early signs of genocidal activity,[2] and, as the UN's report on the 1994 genocide in Rwanda makes clear, in the event of detection to engage in timely preventive action.[3]

Although in particular conflicts one objective may dominate, invariably the strategies pursued and actions taken will involve some mix of two or more objectives.

These primary objectives are just as valid for intra-state as for inter-state conflicts. A great many conflicts have in any case both a domestic and an external dimension (for instance, Cyprus, Kashmir, Northern Ireland). Multiple outside actors are often implicated, including political patrons, arms vendors, buyers of illicit commodity exports, regional powers which become militarily involved, and neighbouring states which host fleeing refugees.[4] The boundaries separating states are often highly porous, and at times virtually meaningless. There is certainly a strong case for reviewing boundaries imposed by colonial, imperial or otherwise oppressive policies (for instance, the former Soviet Union, North/South Korea, Indonesia/East Timor, Papua New Guinea/Bougainville). Maintaining the territorial status quo in rigid fashion may simply accentuate tensions, and increase the probability of hostilities.

In certain circumstances the settlement of the dispute may not be possible within existing political arrangements or existing demarcations between 'sovereign' jurisdictions. The restoration of peace may require more sustainable constitutional arrangements which may or may not accord with existing boundaries or even with prevailing notions of sovereignty. They may involve the pooling of sovereignty, or alternatively the development of numerous overlapping and intersecting layers of authority, which may bear little resemblance to the existing demarcation of territorially distinct spheres of sovereign jurisdiction.[5] A wide range of federal, confederal and consociational arrangements may need to be considered in tandem with various forms of regional or international involvement, protection, association or trusteeship.

In addition to the four primary objectives, consideration must also be given to a number of *secondary objectives*. These are secondary not in the sense of being less important but in that their value to the conduct of peace operations may be less direct.

(1) *Enhancing the UN's legitimacy* is perhaps the most important of these secondary objectives. The aim here is to strengthen the confidence of the international community generally in the UN's capacity to act justly and impartially – that is, with greater transparency in its decision-making processes. As the UN's own inquiry into the Rwanda genocide graphically demonstrates, the failure to avert the catastrophe had a great deal to do with hidden agendas, secretive decision-making, and primitive impact-assessment procedures.[6] In Rwanda, as in Burundi and Somalia, both Security Council members and the UN bureaucracy tended to base their decisions on whether or not to intervene on the basis of state and bureaucratic interests, and to obscure these either by withholding or distorting available information.[7]

(2) *Democratizing the UN* is another obvious and closely related objective. Member states, the world's peoples (not just nations) and the international community generally must be given greater ownership of the UN's decision-making processes. This means first and foremost higher levels of accountability, that is, more effective mechanisms for subjecting decisions to detailed and on-going scrutiny. Particularly useful here would be more vigorous and adequately resourced procedures of impact assessment. For example, any major decision to act or not to act in a given conflict should normally be accompanied by an evaluation of the likely consequences, and that evaluation subjected to international scrutiny.

(3) *Enhancing the UN's effectiveness*: the choice of strategies should closely dovetail with the specified objectives. Wise strategic choices will in turn depend on accurate diagnosis of the conflict, resolution of complex dilemmas arising from competing priorities or even conflicting objectives, appropriate choice of therapies, and properly functioning institutions (which emphasizes once again the importance of legitimacy and democratic participation).

(4) The fourth objective relates to *efficiency*, which may be defined as the capacity to achieve the desired outcomes in a given conflict with the least human and financial resources. Efficiency is not just an economic but a social requirement. This has two implications: the UN must bring into play *only* those resources that are necessary for the achievement of a given objective. Conversely, the UN must be prepared to deploy *all* the resources that are necessary for success, but strictly within the limits set by the four primary objectives.

It remains to say a word about the confused and highly contested issue of humanitarian intervention.[8] Perhaps the clearest rationale for such intervention has been given by Kofi Annan:

> ... surely no legal principle – not even sovereignty – can ever shield crimes against humanity. Where such crimes occur and peaceful attempts to halt them have been exhausted, the Security Council has a moral duty to act on behalf of the international community.[9]

The notion implicit in this passage is that intervention is in certain circumstances appropriate even in the absence of the host state's consent.[10] Such action however must fulfil a number of conditions:

1. Grave and large-scale violations of human rights must have occurred or be imminent.
2. Clear and objective evidence must exist of such occurrence or threat.
3. No effective remedial action by the government of the state in question is in sight.
4. Other peaceful attempts to end the violations have been exhausted.

To these should be added a number of criteria alluded to in the earlier discussion:

1. The use of force is limited to stopping human rights abuses.
2. The action is supported by those for whom it is intended.
3. There is a high probability of success.
4. International humanitarian law is adhered to during the course of the intervention.
5. The action and its purposes are clearly explained to the local population and to the international community.[11]

For these complex criteria to apply, one other condition must also be met: the UN's authority must serve as the final arbiter. The language of humanitarianism cannot be allowed to mask the pursuit of naked self-interest. NATO's decision to intervene without UN authorization, as in Kosovo, should not therefore constitute a precedent.[12] In the event of one or other permanent member preventing the Security Council from taking action, it should be possible for the General Assembly to apprise itself of the question, and for intervention to proceed if it is supported by a two-thirds majority. This procedure would prevent the rigidity which the power of veto imposes on Security Council deliberations, yet at the same time ensure the legitimacy of any intervention.[13]

A word on method

On the basis of the conceptual framework outlined above, this chapter sets out a number of proposals. Some are new, others are under discussion, and a few are in the early stages of implementation. Here they are integrated as part of a larger reform package aimed at the achievement of both primary and secondary objectives.

Most of the proposals outlined here could be implemented over the medium term (over two to ten years). A number of more radical recommendations, however, may take longer to implement (anywhere between 10 and 25 years). By the end of this longer period, progress in disarmament and arms-control negotiations should pave the way for substantial global and regional, quantitative and qualitative reductions in the main elements of military power (force components, inventories of weapons systems, military personnel and spending), and place clearly defined, verifiable and carefully monitored limits on arms production and trade. In Chapters 11 and 12 respectively Hamel-Green and Wright have set out a number of insightful proposals for nuclear, chemical and biological disarmament. On the assumption of slow but steady progress in this direction, a substantial shift should gradually unfold from national to multilateral strategies for preserving or restoring peace. During this second phase member states would be expected to honour their obligations under Articles 43 and 45 of the UN Charter by making available to the UN pre-designated ground, air and naval personnel, ships and planes. At the same time, peacekeeping and peace enforcement units would undergo a transition from national contingents earmarked for use by UN or regional organizations to an all-volunteer force at the command of the Security Council. This phase would see the establishment in stages of a permanent global security system. The proposals contained in this chapter, though they are consistent with, and are meant to facilitate, such a scenario, do not specifically address the organizational or policy changes required for this longer-term transformation.

For purposes of analytical convenience, we begin with a series of short- to medium-term proposals, most of which would not require substantive amendment of the UN Charter. In line with the analysis in the previous chapter, they are grouped under three headings, each corresponding to a key stage in UN decision-making. These stages represent a logical as much as a temporal sequence. The aim is to clarify what options, strategies and methodologies are available to the UN as it attempts to respond to the actuality or possibility of armed conflict.

The three phases may be designated as follows:

Assessment phase.   This refers to the period preceding any decision to intervene. The key questions to be resolved during this phase include: Should the UN intervene? In what circumstances and at what moment? What form should the intervention take? What are the options and likely consequences of each option?

Authorization/early planning phase.   It is during this period that the decision is made to intervene. Questions to be considered include: what strategies should be pursued by the UN operation; what resources are required; how these can be most effectively harnessed; which are the most appropriate administrative and command arrangements; what consultative and decision-making mechanisms should be instituted; and how the mandate should be formulated.

Implementation phase.   This is by far the longest phase because it involves implementation, review and evaluation. Throughout the period of deployment, important decisions will have to be made about duration, size and composition of the operation. Other issues will include the establishment of appropriate monitoring processes, and the review and possible revision of the mandate in the light of new knowledge or new circumstances.

Assessment phase

UN intervention in armed conflict to a large extent depends for its validity on the quality and timeliness of the information on which it is based, hence the importance attached to early warning systems, adequate fact-finding resources, and extensive conflict analysis capabilities. In its assessment of the UN's failure the *Rwanda Report* stressed 'the lack of correct analysis, both in UNAMIR and within the Secretariat, but also by Member States'.[14] A number of improvements have since been made to the UN's analytical capacity, but much still needs to be done.

To this end several initiatives seem feasible and desirable. First, as indicated in Chapter 10, a strong case can be made for a UN national office to be established in *every* member state. One important, but by no means the only, function of this office (the equivalent of a diplomatic mission) would be to contribute to the UN's early-warning, fact-finding and conflict-analysis capacity with respect to the host country. The UN office would also help to reinforce and rationalize the UN's other functions, whether it be in health, education, environment or human rights. It would, in other words, provide a point of co-ordination for all UN agencies and programmes in that country. In this sense, a UN office should be seen as a natural development, building on what already exists. Such offices could be established where governments are sympathetic, and the list expanded as time goes on. Although the size and responsibilities of each office might be the subject of consultation with each government, the latter could not exercise a veto over its activities or its size. Every office would have a skeletal staff which could be expanded or reduced with changing circumstances. Such an office would report directly to the Secretary-General and indirectly to the Security Council.

A second, much discussed, initiative which would appreciably enhance the UN's capacity for conflict resolution is the establishment of a UN-sponsored International Crisis Prevention and Response Centre (hereafter: Crisis Centre). One of the UN's own recent publications stressed the need for expanding the sources of information available to the Security Council by tapping into the knowledge resources of a great many actors, internal and external to the UN system.[15] For its part, the *Brahimi Report* recommended that the Executive Committee on Peace and Security (ECPS) formed by Kofi Annan to improve inter-departmental co-ordination create an Information and Strategic Analysis Secretariat (EISAS). The bulk of EISAS would be formed by consolidating the various units to which are assigned policy and information-analysis roles related to peace and security.[16] This is clearly the desired direction, but a case can be made for a more ambitious initiative.

Accountable to the Secretary-General, the Crisis Centre envisaged here would have direct access to the resources available to different arms of the UN system, member states, regional and other international organizations, accredited independent think-tanks, universities and research institutes, and to labour and non-governmental organizations with consultative status at the UN. Each member state would be expected to co-operate with the UN in maintaining a high-quality information bank, except where it can establish that withholding the required information is vital to its national security. The Centre would be expected to: (a) prepare regular reports for widespread public dissemination (to the UN system, to governments, and to research, educational and advocacy organizations); (b) serve as an early-warning alert system, drawing potential crises to the attention of the Secretary-General and the Security Council; and (c) make assessments and recommendations for the Secretary-General's consideration, either at his request or its own initiative. In both instances such assessments and recommendations would be made automatically available to all member states of the Security Council.

A third initiative, modest at first sight but with far-reaching possibilities, readily suggests itself. The Security Council could convene periodic public meetings (perhaps twice a year) to review actual or potential conflict situations around the world. These meetings, some of which might be convened in the vicinity of these conflicts, would attempt to identify gaps in the UN's knowledge of the relevant situations and set directions for further work in the formulation of effective responses. Consideration would be given to any situation which might lead to the outbreak of armed hostilities some time over the ensuing five years. In cases requiring either immediate attention or further review within the following three to six months, the Security Council might opt for a fact-finding mission to be despatched to the conflict.

Any UN department, agency or programme should be required to apprise the Secretary-General as soon as it is in possession of information suggesting an actual or potential emergency. Once early-warning processes indicate the emergence of a crisis, initial contingency-planning should begin under the Secretary-General's initiative and with the assistance of the Crisis Centre and other relevant UN bodies.

Preventive deployment

Once an actual or potential conflict is identified, the Security Council should carefully consider how to approach the case. The initial response should be to prevent the outbreak of hostilities, or, where that has already occurred, to prevent any deterioration of the conflict. Preventive measures of a diplomatic kind, which should normally be assigned the highest priority, are examined in Chapter 10. Attention here is directed to the possibilities for preventive deployment.[17]

The UN's Preventive Deployment Force in Macedonia offers one of the few practical applications of this concept. Lessons drawn from that experience suggest that the concept has much potential but also severe limitations. The preventive deployment of a UN force may be useful if it conveys a clear message that recourse to violence by any of the parties would trigger even more forceful action. Such deployment, however, should occur only in cases where there is a high probability of deterring conflict, and only with the consent of the host country. The Council would need to specify the objectives of the mission, and establish that the proposed deployment is fully consistent with the above conditions.

As a general rule, preventive deployment should encourage co-operative behaviour through inducements rather than threats. It should normally proceed in a demilitarized zone (preferably one created by the agreement of the parties), and should, if at all possible, be used as the basis for the establishment of a co-operative zone (an area in which the parties undertake to engage in some mutually beneficial activity, low-key though that activity may be, at least initially). Preventive deployment should not be seen as a substitute for preventive diplomacy, but as helping to create a climate within which preventive diplomacy is more likely to succeed. Preventive deployment should be accompanied by pre-conflict peacebuilding,[18] including a range of sustainable development programmes organized in close collaboration with other UN agencies and programmes, as well as NGOs.

Sanctions

Sanctions have over the last ten years become one of the most contentious policy instruments at the UN's disposal.[19] In April 2000 the Security Council established an informal committee to explore ways of enhancing the effectiveness of sanctions. There was, however, already enough evidence to suggest that for sanctions to be effective they would need to be applied in a more systematic yet flexible fashion. While comprehensiveness (for instance, targeting a state's entire trade as was the case with Iraq) may in some cases contribute to effectiveness, it offers no guarantee of success.[20] According to one study, swift, forceful sanctions tend to be more effective than slow, incremental measures. The critical factor here is the degree to which neighbouring states, trading partners and regional organizations comply with Security Council resolutions.[21]

There is, nevertheless, a danger that preoccupation with the effectiveness of sanctions may obscure consideration of the soundness of the overall policy. Experience suggests that sanctions should be used sparingly and selectively, and as one instrument among others. The aim should be to apply pressure on the offending government rather than the civilian population, unless wider sanctions are strongly supported by a wide cross-section of the population. Targeted sanctions are preferable to a comprehensive programme precisely because the punishment is concentrated on the party that is guilty of breaching the peace or violating human rights.

Targeted sanctions can encompass a wide range of instruments, including embargoes on military sales, sensitive or dual-use technologies, and communications equipment; international travel restrictions; and financial sanctions. The latter can be highly effective if they freeze the financial assets not so much of governments generally, but of targeted decision-making elites, their families, friends and supporters.[22] But whichever instrument or combination of instruments is used, the desired outcome will not eventuate unless the Security Council, the Chairs of its Sanctions Committees and the Secretariat are able to enhance the transparency of their work, improve the quality of communication and collaboration with member states, CSOs[23] inside the targeted country, and international research, advocacy, humanitarian and aid agencies.

It is also worth stressing that swiftness may not guarantee success any more than comprehensiveness does. Depending on circumstances, the Security Council may need to punish the offending party in a graduated fashion to signal to the offending party that unpleasant consequences will follow continued defiance. Conversely, there should be a promise of the phased lifting of sanctions should the offending party progressively comply with the Council's directives. Sanctions should be extended to states, corporations or other actors who are acting in contravention of the sanctions. Though such powers are implicit in the language of the UN Charter, it is preferable that they should be made explicit.

Where innocent civilians are hurt by the application of sanctions, whether willingly or otherwise, effective humanitarian programmes should be instituted to assist the most vulnerable groups. Such programmes could be financed by specific or permanent funds established for the purpose. Where the deprivation to the society as a whole is not severe, compensation could be offered after sanctions have been lifted, with funding derived from levies applied on the target government. For humanitarian relief to succeed, the UN must have a capacity to assess the likely impact of sanctions before they are imposed, and most importantly to monitor their impact during the course of sanctions and for some considerable time after they have been lifted. Such assessment, particularly with respect to public health, economic well-being and governance, is necessary if the relief and rehabilitation offered by the UN is to prove timely, commensurate and effective.[24]

Use of force

Here we consider the actual use of military force. Such intervention should be authorized only when a clear case can be made that the benefits outweigh the costs. *The use of force should be entertained as a last resort.* Less coercive strategies must be given a chance to work, and, as Michael is at pains to show in Chapter 10, the emphasis in the initial stages of a crisis should be placed on preventive diplomacy. Where prevention is not successful, other approaches to peacemaking (conciliation, mediation, adjudication) should first be tried. Where the severity of the conflict leads the UN to deploy military force, and in extreme circumstances to resort to its actual use, the Security Council should specify what noncoercive strategies have been pursued and with what results.

The use of force should normally preclude civilian casualties. The likely impact on civilian life should be clearly outlined in an impact assessment which will have been prepared as part of the decision to intervene. Injury to civilian life and property should be carefully monitored throughout the operation, and, in the event that it exceeds the expectations set out in the impact assessment, the entire operation should be subjected to immediate review.

Where intervention is contemplated on humanitarian grounds, advice should be sought from a standing Independent Review Tribunal, specifically established to weigh up the arguments for and against intervention. The tribunal would be asked to determine whether the available evidence points to 'gross violations of the security of people'. For this purpose indiscriminate killings, genocidal policies, ethnic cleansing, and large-scale premeditated destruction of physical and social infrastructure could all be said to constitute gross violations. The composition and procedures of such a tribunal should be such that it can be convened at short notice, and that its examination of the issues can be quickly completed so as not to delay an appropriate UN response to urgent situations.

Should it be resolved that UN intervention is necessary, the aim must be to use the minimum force necessary to achieve key objectives, ideally in quick and enduring fashion. In opting for a peace-enforcement strategy, priority should be given to one or more of the following security outcomes: (a) establishment and monitoring of a cease-fire; (b) creation and monitoring of special demilitarised or co-operation zones; (c) demobilization of armed forces; (d) restoration of law and order, particularly in intra-state conflicts; and (e) removal of landmines and other weapons and toxic substances posing a danger to civilian life. As soon as conditions permit, a careful transition should occur from peace enforcement to peace-keeping. The military presence may need to be complemented by civilian and police personnel of sufficient number and skill to enable a further transition to peacemaking and peacebuilding.

Authorization/early planning phase

The degree to which any peace operation will achieve the primary and secondary objectives previously outlined will greatly depend on the processes and mechanisms used during the authorization and early-planning phase of UN intervention. We propose to discuss these under the following headings: *impact assessment, formulation of mandate, deployment of human and material resources, general mechanisms* and *operation-specific mechanisms*.

Impact assessment

Given the considerable human, organizational, financial and political implications of any intervention, the costs and benefits must be carefully evaluated. The UN's varied experience in the post-Cold War period suggests that, if the potential of UN peacekeeping is to be realized, enthusiasm may have to be tempered by caution. Each peace operation must be fine-tuned to respond to local circumstances. To this end the overall assessment of the conflict conducted during the previous phase must be made operational, and analytical tools developed to guide the ensuing stages of the decision-making process.

Of critical importance are the functions of the impact-assessment process. First, it should provide the Security Council with a reasonable information base on which to form a judgment on the pluses and minuses of intervention, and on the consequences likely to accompany different forms and different scales of intervention (essential for the effectiveness of UN decisions). Secondly, it should provide the wider international community with the information base it needs to subject the Council's decision to probing scrutiny (essential for purposes of transparency and accountability). Thirdly, it should enable both the Security Council and the wider international community to judge whether the peace operation is proceeding as originally intended, or whether its mandate should be modified, or even altogether terminated.

In assessing the impact of any intervention, several key questions are especially pertinent. The first set of questions revolves around the actual conditions on the ground (social, economic and political as well as military) and how these are likely to be affected by the proposed peace operation. The second set of questions relates to the degree of local support there is for UN intervention (from the main political groupings involved in the conflict but also from the public at large). What is the likelihood that one or more parties to ceasefire or peace agreements will renege on their commitments and even challenge their implementation? Will the UN operation have to contend with 'spoilers'?[25] The third set of questions focuses on the issue of resources: What resources (military and financial) are necessary for the proposed operation? Are they readily available? What would the implications be should one or more contributing states decide to withdraw their support, and the resources needed for the operation fall short of the optimum or minimum level, whether in quantitative or qualitative terms?

Given the complexity of the issues to be considered, the impact-assessment process should be conducted by an independent, adequately staffed and well-resourced Impact Assessment Office located in the Department of Peace Operations (the new name for a revamped DPKO) and accountable to the Secretary-General. Its conclusions should be presented to the Security Council both before any decision is made, and periodically thereafter to assist an ongoing review of the operation. These conclusions should also be made public to facilitate international scrutiny and better-informed public debate. The Impact Assessment Office should be able to draw on the information available to relevant UN Offices, other UN agencies, government departments of member states, NGOs and independent research institutes with expertise in the particular conflict.

Formulation of mandate and complementary instruments

Numerous commentaries on the UN's recent performance have insisted on the need for carefully defined mandates. If lack of clarity is intended to conceal lack of agreement on the objectives of the peace operation either among members of the Security Council or among states contributing forces, or for that matter between the Security Council and the parties to the conflict, it may be preferable for the UN not to intervene in the first place.

An initially transparent and specific mandate may not be enough. Where, for example, a peacekeeping operation assumes peace enforcement – let alone collective security – functions (whether under Article 40 or Article 42), such modification should proceed only after the mandate itself has been duly revised. The mandate should at all times specify the purposes for which force is to be used, the amount of force to be expended, the targets against which it is to be used, and the chain of political and military authority governing its use. Where one or more countries are requested to deploy their military capabilities on its behalf, the UN must specify in some detail, via the mandate, the authorization, monitoring and accountability procedures which are to apply for the entire duration of the operation.

The mandate, which should enshrine the principle of impartiality, would thus become an important CBM in its own right, most importantly among the local population. Even in conflicts where the Security Council does not propose to adopt a neutral stance – it may take action against an offending party, including spoilers who renege on undertakings they have given – its actions must nevertheless be impartial in the sense that they are clearly consistent with the Charter and other agreed principles and procedures. The way these are interpreted and applied cannot be seen to privilege one state against another, one permanent member against another, or permanent members against the rest of the membership. In the interests of transparency the mandate should, wherever possible, specify the social, political, legal or military conditions which would prompt the UN operation to be withdrawn or scaled down.

Deployment of human and material resources

Peace operations are by their very nature resource-intensive, which explains why member states may be reticent to contribute troops or other resources. They may be nervous about risking lives for the sake of uncertain or unachievable objectives; or they may be unconvinced that the operation has sufficient support either from the parties to the conflict or from the international community. All of this merely underscores the need for caution and careful planning on the part of the UN system, which is not to say that global and regional peacekeeping capabilities should not be improved. Limitations of size and capacity contributed greatly to UNAMIR's inadequate response to the unfolding crisis after 6 April, although the failure to act in timely fashion was also a crucial factor.[26]

Resources must also be of the right kind and available when needed. As Kofi Annan has aptly remarked, '[e]very time there is a fire, we must find fire engines and the funds to run them before we can start dousing the flames. The present system relies almost entirely on last minute, ad hoc arrangements that guarantee delay...'[27] Clearly, the UN's access to military and civilian personnel and to logistic support should be greatly strengthened.

With the expansion of functions performed by peace operations, the need for access to well-qualified civilian staff has inevitably increased. Civilian tasks relating to the political aspects of a peace mission include administration and logistics, human rights and public information. Other civilian functions relate to governance at the local and national levels, including administration and services, budgetary and fiscal systems, public utilities, the health and education sectors, judiciary systems, demobilization and de-mining. By mid-2000 some 12,500 local and international civilian personnel were engaged in multidimensional peacekeeping.[28]

Timely access to the necessary resources, military and civilian, may occur in one of two ways: either by the UN itself developing its own staff and equipment resources, or by member states placing more of their national capacities at the disposal of UN peacekeeping operations. The problem with the latter approach is that it makes the UN's activities and decision-making processes vulnerable to the vagaries of national priorities. By the same token, the development of the UN's own military and civilian capabilities is itself likely to prove difficult and controversial. For some time to come the UN will have to rely on a combination of the two approaches. Mechanisms must therefore be devised whereby national contributions of personnel and equipment are increasingly formalized and made routine. Where a country is unwilling to contribute on such a basis (that is, without strings attached), it may be preferable for the UN to do without this kind of assistance.

It is, of course, feasible, even in the short term, for the UN to develop its own resources. A number of small but important first steps readily suggest themselves. First, the UN could acquire a substantial pre-positioned stock of basic military equipment for use at short notice in the early stages of a peace operation. Secondly, packages of equipment could be made available for different types of operation, including equipment specifically designed to support humanitarian and disaster relief missions. Thirdly, a permanent civilian police capability could be placed at the disposal of the Secretary-General for rapid deployment in peacekeeping operations or immediately after the withdrawal of military personnel. Police training and practices are normally better suited to assisting with a wide range of law and order functions, including low-level protection for UNHCR convoys and other UN and NGO personnel engaged in humanitarian operations, their transport and their supplies; training and support for local police units; and supervision of the electoral system. Increasingly, both military and police units will need to be trained to perform complementary and even mutually reinforcing roles. In the short term, however, access to such human resources will depend on national contributions to UN capabilities. The UN's recent Standby Arrangements System and Rapidly Deployable Mission Headquarters are promising attempts in this direction, and are discussed further under *Implementation Phase* on page 244.

There is also much to be gained from the establishment of pools or rosters of different types of military and civilian personnel, who will have been provided with adequate and standardized training and can be enlisted in UN operations at short notice. Several categories of personnel are envisaged here, including senior military commanders who might serve as force commanders in UN operations; experienced diplomats, judges or civil servants who could act as special representatives (SRSGs) or special envoys; national police officers, especially those with expertise in law and order functions; other experts (usually but not exclusively civilian), with particular knowledge of the countries hosting UN operations, or with special skills in such areas as monitoring of human rights and supervision of elections.

Contributing states should be required to provide training for peace operations that conforms to UN standards. Following the recommendations in the *Brahimi Report* a number of changes have been implemented by the DPKO, including the establishment of a Standardization and Evaluation Section in the newly named Training and Evaluation Service. The aim is to provide member states with standardized training guidance and advice through the preparation of packages of training materials.[29] Another useful step has been the establishment of UN Training Assistance Teams comprised of selected experts who are 'on call' to give guidance and advice to new troop-contributing countries.[30] It may be necessary, however, to go beyond this by creating a well-resourced International Peace Operations Centre that recommends international training standards to the Secretary-General, develops training materials, mounts training programmes for designated military and civilian personnel, and keeps a detailed record of the training activities of all contributing states.

Mechanisms

How successfully the UN performs the three functions we have just described (that is, impact assessment, formulation of mandate, deployment of resources) will to a considerable extent depend on the adequacy of the available mechanisms. Here we examine two types of mechanism: *conflict-specific mechanisms* (that is, those that have been established to deal with the unique features of a given conflict, hence a particular peace operation); and *general mechanisms* (that is, those that have applicability across the board). Both types of mechanism are in need of considerable reform.

As a generalization, the UN's peace operations should rest on institutions that are inclusive, transparent and accountable. Decision-making processes should enable competing interests or priorities to be identified, and an acceptable balance struck between them. As dramatically illustrated in the cases of Iraq, Somalia and even Bosnia, the UN may choose military effectiveness but in the process erode its legitimacy. Alternatively, it can opt for a more inclusive or democratic approach, which could, however, prolong the conflict, or fail to gain the necessary support of one or more of the great powers. The proposals that follow do not offer a complete solution to these dilemmas, but they indicate the general direction which organizational reform should take.

General mechanisms

Peace operations would benefit greatly from the oversight of a Strategic Committee which would report to the Secretary-General, and through him to the Security Council. The Strategic Committee would have many of the functions envisaged for the UN's Military Staff Committee (MSC), originally sanctioned by Article 47 but effectively moribund since 1948. To revitalize the MSC is likely to prove extremely difficult, and possibly counterproductive.[31] Apart from remedying the MSC's limited membership, a broader politico-military structure would help to co-ordinate the political and military components of each operation, reconcile the needs of humanitarian action with the strategies and techniques of peacekeeping or peace enforcement, and more generally strike a balance between military effectiveness and political legitimacy. To this end a minor amendment to the UN Charter will be necessary.

The Strategic Committee would retain military oversight of all peace operations, including those dealing with peace enforcement, and even on those occasions when a competent state, group of states, or regional organization has been asked to perform certain strategic functions, or supply crucial personnel, equipment, or other resources. It would also need to consult with the parties to the dispute, the contributing member states, independent military experts and academics, concerned media representatives, and NGOs with first-hand knowledge of the conflict. One of the virtues of such wide-ranging consultation is that it would strengthen the Committee's authority, and substantially expand its access to information and analysis.

The Strategic Committee would be serviced by the Department of Peace Operations, in particular by the Peace Operations Adviser and the UN General Staff for Peace Operations, and advised by the Force Contributors Committee (for more details see below).

Conflict-specific mechanisms

Given the vastly different interests and priorities of the parties to the dispute, not to mention the great powers or the states contributing forces, maintaining the integrity and independence of the UN command must be regarded a high priority. To this end the Secretary-General should appoint, on the advice of the Strategic Committee, an Integrated Task Force for each peace operation, to be headed by the SRSG. The task force would not be unlike the Integrated Mission Task Force envisaged in the *Brahimi Report*,[32] except that the emphasis here is on integrating all the key players on the ground. Closely connected with a planning and support cell in the Department of Peace Operations, the Task Force would co-ordinate the military and civilian activities of the peace operation, and ensure timely response, particularly to fast-moving, life-threatening situations. In addition to the SRSG, the Task Force would include the force commander and the officers in charge of intelligence, operations, logistics, civil affairs and liaison staff. Representatives of UN entities (for instance, UNHCR, WHO, UNICEF) and NGOs (for example, ICRC, OXFAM) working in the field could be co-opted as members of the Task Force.

In November 2000, the Security Council underlined the importance of an improved system of consultation between the troop-contributing countries, the Secretary-General and the Security Council.[33] There may be a case, however, for institutionalizing this process, and establishing a Contributing Forces Panel to act in close liaison with the Integrated Task Force. The Panel, which would comprise one representative from each of the contributing countries, would meet regularly to be briefed on the progress of the peace operation, the performance of the various contributing forces, and in particular future requirements in terms of personnel and equipment.

Implementation phase

We use this third phase of peace operations to discuss issues of rapid deployment of military and civilian personnel, and also the institutional and financial requirements needed to ensure accountability, transparency and legitimacy.

Initial/rapid deployment

If the UN is to be able to respond to urgent humanitarian situations, a strong case can be made for the speedy deployment of initial contingents. Such a Rapid Reaction Force would be deployed by authorization of the Security Council, and be under the effective control of the Secretary-General (through the Strategic Committee). In the first instance such a force might be small (approximately 10,000 strong), but multi-disciplinary in skills and functions, and capable of modest expansion (perhaps to 30,000) over a five-to-ten-year period. It could be used for purposes of preventive deployment, peacekeeping and peace enforcement. Made up of volunteer civilian and military personnel, it would be recruited and trained by the International Peace Operations Centre established for the purpose.

In line with this thinking, the Danish government proposed in August 1995 the establishment of a multinational peace force. From that proposal emerged the concept of a Multinational UN Standby Forces High Readiness Brigade, which could be brought together from a number of national contributions at between 15 and 30 days' notice. Once fully developed, the high-readiness brigade could form the core of the more ambitious Rapid Reaction Force outlined above.

Standby arrangements

The Secretary-General's Standby Arrangements System was explicitly designed to provide the Security Council with such a much larger, longer-term capacity. As of the end of 1999, 87 countries had committed a total of 147,500 personnel.[34] These arrangements represent a step in the right direction, but serious doubts remain as to their adequacy.

For the UN's standby capacity to be effective, services agreements with national governments would need to specify:

1. the specialized personnel (both military and civilian), equipment and services that could be made available to deal with a range of contingencies;
2. the political, cultural and other considerations which would determine whether or not a request can be met;
3. the time frame within which requests for contributions would be met;
4. the standards of training that would have been provided and the quality of the equipment to be made available;
5. the partnerships, if any, concluded with other member states, enabling a more appropriate match between personnel and equipment. In line with this last suggestion the *Brahimi Report* recommended that partnerships be encouraged with a view to forming coherent brigade-size forces, ready for effective deployment within 30 days of a Security Council decision establishing a traditional peacekeeping force, and within 90 days for complex peacekeeping operations.[35] Encouragement, however, may not be enough. The UN Secretariat may need to perform a more proactive role, and ensure that an expanded standby system can over time meet as many as three large concurrent peace operations.

Monitoring and reporting

The mechanisms and procedures outlined under *Authorization/Early Planning Phase* above are just as relevant to monitoring and reporting during this third phase. A few key points are worth noting here.

1. For an effective command-and-control structure, and for political decision-making to be closely reflected on the ground, the lines of communication between the Secretary-General and the peace operation must at all times be open. In particular there must be the closest possible liaison between UN Headquarters and the Integrated Task Force.
2. The Secretary-General, acting through the Strategic Committee, should be able to respond quickly to requests and recommendations from the SRSG (acting through the Integrated Task Force).
3. Gross violations of human rights, the almost inevitable result of armed conflicts, are often one of the primary justifications for intervention. It is vital therefore that every peace operation contribute to improved human rights conditions in the host country. To this end two separate measures are proposed. First, the peace operation should, in collaboration with UN's human rights agencies and relevant NGOs, perform a monitoring role, reporting regularly to the Secretary-General, who may then authorize further action, or, where the situation warrants it, bring it before the Security Council and the International Criminal Court. Secondly, and as proposed by Childers and Urquhart, every major UN field mission, comprising military or police units, should be accompanied by an ombudsman,[36] who would monitor the conduct of operation itself, and provide regular and public reports to the Secretary-General, and, where serious violations are detected, reports on individual incidents.

The Secretary-General's directive of August 1999, though not binding on states, requires UN forces, whether acting as combatants or in self-defence, to apply the fundamental principles and rules of international humanitarian law. Contributing states, for their part, are expected to prosecute in their respective national courts any personnel accused of breaches of the Geneva Conventions and Protocols.[37] In years to come it will be necessary to codify the principle that contributing states are parties to all relevant agreements and conventions that make up the body of international humanitarian law.

Organizational arrangements

In our discussion of the *Authorization/Early Planning Phase* above (pages 243–4) we have already referred to several new or revamped mechanisms, namely the Strategic Committee, the Peace Operations Adviser, the General Staff of Peace Operations, and the Force Contributors Committee. What follows is a brief elaboration of the structure and function of these bodies.

The main tasks of the Strategic Committee have already been outlined. Its membership would consist of one nominee from each of the members of the Security Council, normally a senior military adviser. It would be advised and supported by sub-committees or working groups comprised of other officials and independent experts. Resolutions of the Strategic Committee would need to carry an absolute majority of the membership of the Security Council, with each member entitled to one vote, and none able to exercise a veto.

The principal function of the Peace Operations Adviser, whose office would be located within the Department of Peace Operations, would be to act as Chief of Staff for the Strategic Committee. He would advise the Secretary-General and the Strategic Committee, and through them the Security Council, on the military implications of the use of force in a given situation, and on the size and structure of the force (including the appropriate mix of military, police and other personnel) that would be necessary for any given operation. He would also propose appropriate command structures and rules of engagement, and regularly report on the overall progress of the peace operation.

The General Staff for Peace Operations, again located within the Department of Peace Operations, would comprise a fully professional permanent military and civilian staff with linkages to other relevant UN agencies and NGOs. Its responsibilities would include: servicing the Rapid Reaction Force; monitoring the peace-operations services agreements and the readiness of national forces available for assignment to peace operations; gathering, analysing and distributing operational-level military information; preparing and maintaining contingency plans; developing standard operating procedures; establishing training standards and training facilities both for the Rapid Reaction Force and the national military and civilian personnel assigned to UN operations; and co-ordinating logistic, financial and administrative functions.

The Force Contributors Committee, as distinct from the Force Contributors Panel, would function as a standing committee comprising one representative from each of the leading contributing nations. To determine which countries are entitled to representation, a formula would be devised, which takes account of the size of a country's population, and the scale and frequency of its personnel, equipment and financial contributions. Any country that falls below the agreed benchmark would lose its entitlement to membership of the Committee, while other countries that attained the benchmark would be invited to join it. The Committee would meet periodically to review the objectives, operational conduct and changing requirements of peace operations, and through the Strategic Committee would periodically report to the wider UN system.

Peacebuilding

Peace operations are meant to restore peace. There is more to this, however, than the silencing of guns. The task is to create the necessary psychological, social, economic and political conditions for peace. As many have forcefully argued, peacebuilding must be made an integral part of all UN activities, including peace operations.[38] Kofi Annan identified the key elements of peacebuilding as national reconciliation and justice, respect for human rights, the rule of law, democratic politics, and sustainable economic growth.[39] While the precise mix is open to debate, these are the very ingredients which have also featured prominently in discussions of 'comprehensive' and 'human' security.[40] To this formulation, however, must be added two elements critical to the success of post-conflict peacebuilding.[41] The first involves disarmament, reintegration of soldiers and militias, and reform of police and judicial structures. Success on this front is, as the experience in El Salvador, Haiti and Cambodia has shown, vital to fostering societal trust in the institutions of the state, and in its capacity to deliver both individual and societal security. The second refers to the closely connected but often elusive need of post-conflict societies to construct a new sense of identity, and a vision of the past and of the future capable of sustaining a culture of legitimacy and participation.

The foregoing formulation aptly reminds us that peacebuilding has as much to do with process as with outcome. In this context three elements have been advanced as central to the peacebuilding process: capacity for dialogue and compromise among societal actors; public security that allows for diversity of expression and debate among these actors; and participation by all key actors in the management of conflict.[42]

The *Brahimi Report* has emphasized that governments, non-governmental parties and the UN's developmental agencies must all play a part in the peacebuilding effort.[43] As of June 2001 the UN had created 13 political and peacebuilding missions involving the deployment of just under 600 civilian and military personnel. But peacebuilding in fact constituted the most critical and resource-intensive dimension of the UN's largest peacekeeping operations, notably in Bosnia and Herzegovina (UNMBIH), Kosovo (UNMIK) and East Timor (UNTAET).[44]

An important principle should inform the approach to operation-specific organizational change. External actors, the UN included, do not hold all the keys to the restoration of peace. The active involvement of international NGOs, though useful and necessary, can only complement those of local actors. Account must be taken of local culture, local needs and local modes of regulation. While it makes several valuable recommendations, the *Brahimi Report* is insufficiently sensitive to this principle.

With this principle firmly in mind, however, there is much to be gained from bringing the UN's diverse activities in the host country under one overarching umbrella. While remaining relatively autonomous, these agencies and programmes should form part of an overall peacebuilding strategy devised in consultation with civil-society groups which are active in development, public security, human rights and environment. The aim should be effective pooling of information, timely responses to emergency situations, and better use of resources. Such an arrangement would also allow UN agencies involved in peacebuilding to have their services more closely integrated, especially after UN forces have been withdrawn.

At the generic level, there is an equally strong case for the systematic co-ordination of UN departments and agencies with a stake in peacebuilding (for instance, UNICEF, UNIFEM, UNHCR, UNDP, the World Bank). The Executive Committee on Peace and Security is well placed to take this initiative, and to this end oversee the establishment and functioning of an inter-departmental peacebuilding unit with suitable NGO representation. Such a unit would see to it that each peace operation was provided with an early peacebuilding capacity, and prepare the ground for a more concerted peacebuilding effort once the operation itself has ended. The rationale for this proposal, as for the larger reform strategy, is that successful peacekeeping, let alone peace enforcement, ultimately depends on how effectively the selective and highly measured use of force has been integrated into a coherent programme of peacemaking and peacebuilding.

Notes

1. See UN Peacekeeping from 1991 to 2000, available online at: <**http://www.un.org/ Depts/dpko/dpko/pub/pko.htm**> (13 July 2001).
2. See E.A. Kolodziej, 'The Great Powers and Genocide: Lessons from Rwanda', *Pacifica Review: Peace, Security and Global Change*, 12, 2 (June 2000), pp.121–45.
3. See 'Report of the Independent Inquiry into the Actions of the United Nations during the 1994 Genocide in Rwanda' (hereafter: the *Rwanda Report*), 15 December 1999, p.44, available online at: <**http://www.un.org/News/ossg/rwanda_report.htm**> (13 April 2001).
4. The transnational dimension of internal conflicts is clearly recognized by the 'Report of the Panel on UN Peace Operations' (hereafter: the *Brahimi Report*), 17 August 2000, p.2, available online at: <**http://www.un.org/peace/reports/peace_operations/docs/ part2.htm**> (13 April 2001).
5. See J.A. Camilleri and J. Falk, *The End of Sovereignty: the Politics of a Shrinking and Fragmenting World* (Aldershot, UK: Edward Elgar, 1992), pp.250–1.
6. *Rwanda Report*, pp.23–5.
7. Reflecting on his own experience at the UN at the time of the Rwanda crisis, Michael Barnett concluded that the UN began 'to evaluate strategies and actions according to the needs of the bureaucracy and…to frame discussions and policies in a different manner'; see M.N. Barnett, 'The UN Security Council, Indifference and Genocide in Rwanda', *Cultural Anthropology*, 12, 4 (1997), p.575.
8. The moral and political complexities that bedevil the notion of humanitarian intervention are examined in R. Falk, 'Hard Choices and Tragic Dilemmas', *Nation* (20 December 1993), pp.755–64.
9. See *Millenium Report* of the Secretary-General, 3 April 2000, available online at: <**http://un.org/millenium/sg/report/ch3.htm**> (7 July 2001).
10. This principle appears to have acquired increasing international support; see A. Cassese, '*Ex Iniuria Ius Oritur:* Are We Moving towards International Legitimation of Forcible Humanitarian Countermeasures in World Community?', *European Journal of International Law*, 10, 1 (1999), pp.23–30.
11. A very useful set of criteria for humanitarian intervention is offered in 'Humanitarian Intervention: Definitions and Criteria', *CSS Strategic Briefing Papers*, 3, 1 (June 2000), p.2.
12. Subsequent NATO utterances provide disturbing evidence of future possibilities. See O. Bring, 'Should NATO Take the Lead in Formulating a Doctrine on Humanitarian Intervention?', *NATO Review*, 47, 3 (Autumn 1999), pp.24–7.
13. The contrary view – that intervention may be appropriate even in the absence of a two-thirds majority in the General Assembly – raises difficult and ultimately insoluble questions as to the legitimacy of the decision-making authority. Such a view is advanced by P.V. Jakobsen and T.B. Knudsen, 'The Kosovo Question: Humanitarian Intervention without the UN?' (Paper presented to the ISA 41st Annual Convention, 14–19 March 2000, Los Angeles, CA).
14. *Rwanda Report*, p.34.

15. UN DPKO Lessons Learned Unit, 'Multidisciplinary Peacekeeping: Lessons from Recent Experience', p.3, available online at: <**http://www.un.org/Depts/dpko/lessons/ handbuk.htm**> (13 July 2001).
16. *Brahimi Report*, Part 2, pp.11–12.
17. These possibilities are canvassed in B. Boutros-Ghali, *An Agenda for Peace: Preventive Diplomacy, Peacemaking and Peace-keeping* (New York: United Nations, 1992), ch.3.
18. For a fuller discussion of the role of pre-conflict peacebuilding, see Chapter 10.
19. Numerous official and scholarly analyses have contributed to the on-going debate. Particularly useful recommendations have emerged from: Boutros-Ghali's *Supplement to An Agenda for Peace* (1995); UN Security Council, Chairs of the Sanctions Committees, *Issue Paper Concerning the Sanctions Imposed by the Security Council*, 30 October 1998; John Stremlau, 'Sharpening International Sanctions: Towards a Stronger Role for the United Nations', a report to the Carnegie Commission on Preventing Deadly Conflict (New York: Carnegie Corporation, November 1996); T.G. Weiss, D. Cortright, G.A. Lopez and L. Minear (eds), *Political Gain and Civilian Pain: Humanitarian Impact of Economic Sanctions* (Lanham, MD: Rowman & Littlefield, 1997).
20. See D. Cortright and G.A. Lopez, *The Sanctions Decade: Assessing UN Strategies in the 1990s* (Boulder, CO: Lynne Rienner, 2000), pp.222–3.
21. Ibid., p.215.
22. See S.D. Porteous, 'Targeted Financial Sanctions', in M. Berdal and D.M. Malone (eds), *Greed and Grievance: Economic Agendas in Civil Wars* (Boulder, CO: Lynne Rienner, 2000), pp.173–88.
23. See Chapter 15.
24. Cortright and Lopez, pp.224–30.
25. The need to grapple with the challenge posed by spoilers or would-be spoilers is succinctly articulated in the *Brahimi Report*, Part 2, p.2.
26. A.J. Kuperman argues that, 'had UNAMIR been reinforced several months prior to the outbreak of violence … genocide might have been averted … Such reinforcement would have required 3,500 additional high-quality troops in Kigali, armored personnel carriers, helicopters, adequate logistics, and the authorization to use force … without consulting'; see 'Rwanda in Retrospect', *Foreign Affairs*, 79, 1 (January/February 2000), p.116.
27. *Millennium Report*, p.7.
28. See note prepared by the UNDPI at: <**http://www.un.org/Depts/dpko/dpko/ intro/civ.htm**> (13 July 2001).
29. See UN DPKO Mil. Div. Training and Evaluation Service News Bulletin, 1(2001), p.5.
30. See 'Organization of UNTAT' at: <**http://www/un.org/Depts/dpko/dpko/training/ untatorg.htm**> (13 July 2001).
31. The argument for a new structure is clearly developed by J. Whitman and I. Bartholomew, 'Collective Control of UN Peace Support Operations: a Policy Proposal', *Security Dialogue*, 25, 1 (1994), pp.77–92.
32. See *Brahimi Report*, Part 4, pp.6–8.
33. SCR 1327, 13 November 2000, p.3.
34. Progress Report of the Secretary-General on Standby Arrangements for Peacekeeping, prepared by DPKO, 1 May 2000, p.1, available online at: <**http://www.un.org/Depts/ dpko/rapid/anr.htm**> (10 July 2001).
35. *Brahimi Report*, Part 3, p.6.
36. E. Childers and B. Urquhart, *Renewing the United Nations System* (Uppsala, Sweden: Dag Hammarskjold Foundation, 1994), p.203.
37. A. Coles and H. Durham, 'Applicability of International Humanitarian Law to United Nations Peacekeepers', *International Humanitarian Law* (November 1999), pp.12–13.
38. G. Evans, *Cooperating for Peace: the Global Agenda for the 1990s and Beyond* (NSW: Allen & Unwin, 1993), pp.10–11.
39. *Millenium Report*, p.12.

40. For a useful outline of these and related notions of security, see Carnegie Commission on Preventing Deadly Conflict, *Final Report* (Washington DC: Carnegie Corporation, 1997).
41. See B. Pouligny, 'Multinational UN Peacekeeping Missions and the Promotion of the Rule of Law: the Interactions between Peacekeepers, International and Local NGOs' (Paper presented to the ISA, 41st Annual Convention, Los Angeles, CA, 14–18 March 2000).
42. C. Kumar, 'Conclusion', in E.M. Cousens and C. Kumar (eds), *Peacebuilding as Politics: Cultivating Peace in Fragile Societies* (Boulder, CO: Lynne Rienner, 2001), p.186.
43. *Brahimi Report*, Part 2, p.5.
44. See 'Report of the Secretary-General on the Work of the Organization', General Assembly Official Records, 55th Session, Supplement No.1 (A/55/1), pp.11–12.

Part IV
Reimagining the Future

15
Major Structural Reform

Joseph A. Camilleri

Previous chapters have analysed a number of intractable problems which have severely handicapped the UN's capacity to act and weakened its legitimacy. Tehranian's diagnosis of the contemporary human predicament has articulated the need to rethink the larger framework of global governance, of which the UN is the largest, most complex, perhaps most authoritative, but still only one, of its many constituent parts. What follows is a preliminary attempt to think through the institutional implications of the analysis and recommendations offered thus far.

Though the UN clearly remains the centrepiece, the intention is to integrate into the reform agenda several other key actors, not least transnational corporations, international and regional governmental organizations, and the multiple and varied groups independent of the state that comprise civil society, all of which have as of now at best limited or sporadic connection with the UN system. Expressed a little differently, the aim is to situate global governance at the juncture that links the world polity, the world economy and what may loosely be referred to as 'global civil society'.[1]

The call for renewal of global institutions is not, of course, new.[2] With a few notable exceptions, however, the emphasis has been on geopolitics. Many have rightly attributed the UN's newly found activism in the late 1980s and early 1990s to the demise of the Soviet Union and the unchallenged capacity of the United States to project power on a global scale. More sophisticated interpretations have emphasized the dominance of the West, and the increasing dependence of the entire UN system on the West's military, economic, ideological and organizational strength.[3] Yet western power is itself subject to limitations and contradictions. Western powers, the United States included, have had enormous difficulty in managing problems of order in weak, fragmenting states. To this must be added a number of transnational issues, notably transboundary pollution, transnational crime, piracy, the global spread of disease, large-scale population movements, and terrorism. As the events of 11 September 2001 have so dramatically brought home to the United States, this macropolitical agenda palpably exceeds the problem-solving capacities of territorially bound states.[4]

Precisely because of the intractability of these problems, the West has generally supported – notwithstanding Washington's periodic unilateralist and isolationist tantrums – the deepening and broadening of international institutions. The modern state system, understood as 'the division of the globe's surface into fixed, mutually exclusive, geographically defined jurisdictions enclosed by discrete and meaningful borders',[5] corresponds less and less with actual, let alone potential, reality. Even if one did not go as far as Jeremy Kobrin and others, who argue that we are already witnessing the birth of a new medievalism,[6] there can be little doubt that the last few decades have seen the steady diffusion of power and authority.

The rise of multiple and overlapping political sites and juridical authorities poses a critical question, which lies at the core of this project: How can the presently hierarchical yet polycentric world order be reconciled with the democratic idea? One of the most helpful responses thus far to this question has come from David Held who advocates the construction of 'a cosmopolitan democracy with global reach'.[7] For Held, a cosmopolitan democratic legal framework would be one in which the duties and functions traditionally centred on the state would be shared across different political levels – local, national, regional and international. Such a framework would require an overarching system of laws and institutions capable of sustaining the complex forms of interdependence in the era of globalization. One of the distinguishing features of the Held formulation is the principle of subsidiarity, namely the notion that local, micro-regional, national, macro-regional, or even transnational entities would remain autonomous and act within their own sphere of competence. Decisions would be made at a higher level only if the issues to be determined involved degrees of interconnectedness and interdependence which made them unresolvable at lower levels. As a consequence, sovereignty, understood as autonomy, would no longer be the exclusive prerogative of the state, but *'could be entrenched and drawn upon in diverse self-regulating associations, from states to cities and corporations'.*[8]

Held's conception of cosmopolitan democracy suggests fruitful and far-reaching possibilities for normative and institutional change. One caveat, however, may be necessary at this point. Held is surely right to argue that the democratic idea, though originally conceived largely in the context of city-state and then nation-state, is applicable to every level of human organization. He is also right to suggest that the ideal system would be one in which all its constituent parts and all tiers of governance are founded on respect for democratic laws and principles. Yet within the global order no one tier of governance need have primacy over the others, or arrogate to itself the right to define for others what constitutes acceptable democratic practice. A more feasible but also more desirable process would be one which encourages the democratic ethic simultaneously in all tiers of governance, remembering that democratic practice within and between tiers will always be subject to renegotiation and renewal.

The proposals that follow, though they focus on global governance reform, are in fact premised on – and designed to cultivate – this more nuanced and expanded notion of cosmopolitan democracy. They seek to privilege a notion of legitimacy, which is premised on more extensive and mutually reinforcing forms of participation at every level of decision-making. Using the existing UN system as the institutional point of departure, it proposes a programme of relatively radical yet by no means unimaginable reform. Such restructuring would have four related aims: (a) to circumscribe the dominance of the major centres of power and wealth within global multilateral institutions; (b) to empower all member states to play a more active role in the fulfilment of the UN's major objectives; (c) to enable the UN system to serve as a more effective mechanism capable of co-ordinating all the world's multilateral institutions in the economic as much as the security domain; and (d) to open up the global multilateral system to the voices and insights of non-state actors and make it more responsive to an emerging global consciousness and rapidly developing notions of global citizenship.

General Assembly

The most immediate and perhaps most easily achievable goal of global governance reform is the revitalization of the General Assembly. As a part of this process the Commission on Global Governance recommended in 1995 'regular theme sessions, effective exercise of budgetary authority, and the streamlining of its agenda'.[9] Though much of this has yet to be implemented, a more radical step would seem timely and necessary. A reformed Security Council and a newly established Economic and Social Security Council (see below) should present detailed annual reports, including recommendations for future initiatives. Member states would then have the opportunity to review, and comment on, the performance of both Councils. At the completion of its deliberations, the General Assembly would formulate a number of broad policy guidelines for the following year with respect to global security and the world economy.

In between annual meetings, should either Council be deemed to have given insufficient attention to the guidelines of the preceding year, a mechanism could be introduced for emergency meetings of the General Assembly – perhaps at the request of at least one-third of its membership. If a majority of member states were dissatisfied with the actions of either Council, the General Assembly would have the power to require that council to reconvene and review its handling of the relevant issues, in the light of advice received from the General Assembly. While the General Assembly would not be empowered to override the Security Council, and would not wish to interfere with the day-to-day running of the Economic and Social Security Council, it should be able to place the decisions and deliberations of both Councils under the international spotlight and compel them to justify or reconsider their positions.

Peoples' Assembly

The question immediately arises: can the international community be adequately represented through the intermediary of states, particularly as many of them do not have the kind of institutions which could even remotely be described as democratic? Often, governments pay scant regard to the wishes of their citizenry, let alone to the rights of minorities. There is therefore a strong case to be made for the establishment of a second chamber, a Peoples' Assembly,[10] which would inject into

UN debates a more realistic appreciation of the insecurity experienced by a large fraction of humanity, and a greater degree of independence *vis-à-vis* the major centres of power and wealth.

The Peoples' Assembly would, much like the European Parliament, function as a house of review, carefully monitoring the decisions and deliberations of the General Assembly, the Security Council, the Economic and Social Security Council, as well as the performance of the Secretary-General and of the various departments and agencies of the UN system. The Assembly, although it would not have legislative functions, would receive reports and seek information from, as well as offer advice to, the General Assembly, the two councils and the Secretary-General. Members of the Peoples' Assembly would be directly elected (perhaps every five years) by their constituencies on the basis of universal suffrage, a secret ballot and the principle of one vote one value (with each constituency having an approximate population of six million, that is an electorate of between three and four million). The boundaries of each constituency would be proposed by an Electoral Commission located within the UN Secretariat and jointly approved by the General Assembly and Peoples' Assembly.

Elections, which would be preceded by widespread public debate and free media coverage, would be organized by the relevant national government, but closely monitored by an international inspection team established by the Electoral Commission and accountable to the Peoples' Assembly. Each state's membership of the UN would be conditional on compliance with these requirements. One of the positive spin-offs of such an arrangement is that it would exert significant pressure on authoritarian governments to apply over time the same democratic procedures, or some version of them, to their own national political system. It would also encourage local populations to devote more attention to international affairs, offering them another vehicle for applying pressure on their respective governments, and slowly but steadily fostering the articulation of world public opinion.

Consultative Assembly

As is now well understood, global insecurity is at least as much economic as military in its origins, hence the notion of 'human security' which seeks to move beyond a state-centric view of the world and gives due consideration to such issues as environment, population movements, food and energy security, marine resources, trade, financial flows, human rights, transnational crime, gender issues and much else.[11] The Peoples' Assembly would be one useful step in this direction. Economic and social wellbeing is shaped by the conduct, whether through omission or commission, of a great many actors other than states. It is only prudent, therefore, that these non-state actors be brought into the decision-making process and made more accountable for their actions. The question then becomes: What would such a forum look like, and what might be its relationship to the other main organs of the UN?

The forum would obviously need to represent all relevant actors, that is all actors with an important contribution to make by virtue of their expertise, resources and membership, and the international scope of their activities. This third chamber, to be known as the Consultative Assembly, would have a membership of approximately 1,000. Three main types of organization would be represented: transnational firms (industrial, commercial and financial) through the intermediary of their respective international (or regional) umbrella associations; trade unions and professional associations (again through the intermediary of international or regional associations), and a range of educational, scientific, cultural, religious and public-interest organizations active around issues central to the UN's agenda (for example, peace, environment, development, human rights, social welfare, education). On the basis of the above criteria – which would need to be further elaborated and refined – the UN Secretariat would prepare a list of organizations to be accorded consultative status. The list would then be submitted for consideration, possible modification, and approval by the General Assembly. Once the Peoples' Assembly and the Consultative Assembly have been established, both chambers would have the right to offer advice about future changes to the composition of the Consultative Assembly, but the ultimate decision would remain solely that of the General Assembly. The Consultative Assembly would closely interact with the Peoples' Assembly and exercise roughly similar powers and functions. These arrangements would remain in force for a period of ten years, at the end of which a general review should be conducted of the membership, functions and powers of both chambers.

The proposal to give the world's largest corporate institutions a direct voice within the UN system may at first sight appear incongruous. Why give these enormously powerful economic players an added opportunity to pursue their interests, given that they already have highly effective platforms for this purpose (for example, the World Economic Forum), and enjoy privileged access to national governments and multilateral institutions (for example, IMF, World Bank, ADB, APEC). The answer is essentially twofold. The most powerful players in the market place must over time become more transparent and more accountable for their decisions. This will be one of the few arenas in which their views, priorities and actions can be subjected to international public scrutiny, where they will need to interact and negotiate on a continuing basis with other parties wedded to vastly different objectives and perspectives. While Kofi Annan's 'Global Compact' initiative may be seen as a step in the same direction, it does not even begin to satisfy the requirements of transparency and legitimacy.[12] The membership dues which these organizations would be expected to pay in accordance with an agreed assessment formula would make a welcome contribution to the UN's budgetary needs.

Security Council

Established primarily with a view to perpetuating the geopolitical status quo of 1945, the Security Council has found it extraordinarily difficult to adapt to changing geopolitical circumstances, let alone to more holistic conceptions of security.[13] Permanent membership and the power of veto have, if anything, tended to obstruct the path to collective security.[14] With the passage of time these organizational principles have become increasingly anachronistic and debilitating.

Many have questioned whether the Permanent Five would ever contemplate such devolution of power and authority. On the other hand, it cannot be assumed that US primacy, or even that of a concert of powers, would long escape criticism and resistance from a wide range of state and non-state actors. Though the obstacles are both obvious and daunting, the elimination of the veto is nevertheless essential to any programme of structural reform.[15] On the other hand, the change need not be accomplished overnight. A phased approach might begin with relatively modest modifications to the power of veto, then proceed to more substantial ones, and eventually eliminate it altogether. Initially, permanent members would retain the veto, but limitations would be placed on the frequency with which it was used, and the issues in relation to which it was exercised. In cases where the veto could no longer be exercised, resolutions would still have to be carried by a two-thirds majority. Even after the veto has been phased out, perhaps over a 15-year period, great powers could still enjoy permanent membership, but such membership would have to be periodically reviewed, for example every ten years, to ensure that it accurately reflects changing power realities. Over the next five to ten years, depending on the speed of geopolitical and institutional change, permanent membership might be extended to Germany, Japan, India and possibly Brazil. By the end of the ten-year period, it may be appropriate for Britain, France and Germany to relinquish their permanent membership in favour of the EU.

Changes to the composition and status of permanent membership should be accompanied by changes to the rotating membership. To ensure greater representation the membership of the Security Council could be expanded from 15 to between 23 and 25, depending on the number of permanent members. Two rotating members, each serving a term of two years, would be elected by all states within appropriately designated regions. Though ultimately an arbitrary exercise, the demarcation of regions can nevertheless have a degree of political coherence and maintain at least rough parity in terms of population, wealth and other capabilities. One possible classification might consist of Western Europe, Eastern Europe and Russia; Africa; the Middle East, West Asia and Central Asia; South Asia; East Asia and Oceania; North and Central America; and South America.

An enlarged and more democratically constituted Security Council would need to adopt a more systematic approach to the management of global security. To this end, member states could hold a biennial summit meeting – each time in a different but strategic location – at which they review recent trends, set out the broad parameters of the emerging security agenda, and map out future strategies. The prestige and authority accruing to a reinvigorated Security Council cannot obscure the fact that at any one time it will represent no more than the views and interests of a limited number of states, many of which may be unrepresentative even of the views or interests of their respective populations. The Council's functions and powers must therefore be set within the larger and more representative framework of the General Assembly and the other two proposed assemblies. While the Security Council would remain the authoritative body with day-to-day responsibility for the maintenance of global peace and security, it should function as the international equivalent of a modern national cabinet ultimately account-able to the national legislature.

Economic and Social Security Council

In its 1995 report the Commission for Global Governance proposed the estab-lishment of an Economic Security Council that would 'provide a long-term strategic policy framework in order to promote stable, balanced and sustained development'.[16] Separate recommendations covered the need for a stronger mul-tilateral trade system committed to free trade and an enhanced capacity for the IMF to exercise oversight of the international monetary system and provide balance-of-payments support for developing economies. Following a series of world conferences, notably the 1995 World Summit for Social Development, the UN system committed itself to the eradication of poverty and to this end agreed to pursue a co-ordinated strategy involving the various elements of the UN system, including the Bretton Woods institutions.

These and subsequent proposals and initiatives, well-intentioned though they may be, fail to address the most fundamental problems posed by the inequalities of power and wealth. In line with the principle of subsidiarity, national institu-tions should be sufficiently robust to be able to set their own economic priorities and develop their own economic resources without undue external interference (by which is meant the actions of powerful players in the market place, not just governments). As Malhotra has argued at length in Chapter 9, national institu-tions should be able to apply, when circumstances require, a range of national controls over trade, capital flows, technology transfers, and other transactions which impede the achievement of key social and economic objectives. This notional capacity, however, is severely restricted by the vast inequalities within and between national societies on the one hand, and the degree to which global markets can penetrate deep inside national economies. Global and regional institutions are therefore required to perform two key functions: (a) to provide resources and institutional support to the world's weaker economies; and (b) to establish a more democratic framework of international decision-making which sets standards for the functioning of the world economy and develops the mech-anisms needed to monitor and enforce those standards.

To this end the UN system must provide far more effective and authoritative leadership than has thus far been the case. Perhaps the single most important step would be to establish a broadly based Social and Economic Security Council to replace the existing Economic and Social Council. As Malhotra proposes, the new Council would serve as the apex of all economic multilateral organizations. It would over a period of years reorganize the international financial framework, create an International Taxation Organization, and assume overall responsibility for debt relief for developing economies, and in particular debt cancellation for low-income heavily indebted countries. Its most important institutional task, however, would be to bring under effective oversight the World Bank, IMF and WTO, and establish and supervise a strict code of conduct for the operations of transnational corporations, international banks and other IFIs.

The Council's membership, structure and relationship to the other major organs of the UN would parallel the proposed arrangements for the Security Council. All major centres of economic power would enjoy permanent membership but without the power of veto. The rest of the membership would be drawn on a rotational basis from the designated regions, but in the interests of representing a wide range of economies with different needs and at different stages of development the total membership would be larger than that of the Security Council (perhaps six to eight permanent members and four members from each region). The Economic and Social Security Council would be accountable to the General Assembly, but would also closely interact with the Peoples' Assembly and the Consultative Assembly. It would be serviced by functional and regional commissions, standing committees and expert working groups which would include representatives of states not currently represented on the Council, other relevant units of the UN system, global and regional IGOs, industry, and labour and civil-society groups, as well as individuals known for their integrity, independence and expertise. The proposed architecture would become the primary site in which the complex processes of economic globalization and transnationalization would be subjected to scrutiny and guidance by various 'local, national and transnational political publics'.[17]

Secretary-General/Secretariat

The UN's legitimacy and effectiveness will depend in part on the stature and authority, and the administrative and financial resources at the command of the Secretary-General and his staff. Choosing people who possess the necessary skills, insights and independence to fill the office of Secretary-General and other senior positions is therefore of prime importance. The Secretary-General must assist the UN's deliberative organs to discharge their responsibilities more effectively by regularly presenting them with clearly defined options and proposals.

The Secretary-General must also use the structures of the UN system and other fora, including national parliaments, national and international conferences, and the media, to articulate a vision of the UN system which is faithful to its fundamental principles yet sensitive to rapidly changing economic, political and cultural conditions. In other words, the Secretary-General is uniquely placed to anticipate and crystallize the UN's ongoing reform agenda.

A more transparent and representative selection process would help to enhance the legitimacy of the office and the co-operative ethos of the institution. To this end an advisory committee could be created to consult widely with governments and the two new assemblies before proposing a short-list of no more than five for the consideration of both the Security Council and the Economic and Social Security Council. The Councils would have the power to remove names from the short-list or to add new ones, so long as the resulting list included at least three but no more than five names. That list would then be submitted to the General Assembly, which would then make the appointment through an exhaustive ballot such that the appointee would have secured in the last ballot the vote of at least two-thirds of the membership of the Assembly.

To enhance co-ordination within the Secretariat, and between the Secretariat and the rest of the UN system, it would be useful to consolidate reforms already under way. For example, the functions of the recently established Senior Management Group could be expanded and formalized. To reconcile efficiency and inclusiveness, it may be worth experimenting with a smaller and a larger cabinet, each having the necessary status but serving different functions. The smaller cabinet would be chaired by the Secretary-General and include all Deputy Secretaries-General (each department and major office would be headed by a Deputy Secretary-General). It would aim to improve inter-departmental communication and co-ordination, especially in the short term. It would not entail any derogation of the ultimate authority invested in the Secretary-General. The larger cabinet, comprising the Secretary-General, all Deputies and the heads of UN agencies and programmes not directly administered through the Secretariat, would have a long-term planning function for the UN system as whole. Its purpose would be to rationalize functions and activities, improve the flow of communication, and identify longer-term administrative problems. The Secretary-General would have primary responsibility for setting the agenda and periodically reviewing the effectiveness of administrative arrangements.

Financial arrangements

The inadequacy of the UN's financial arrangements has been the subject of extensive discussion and numerous proposals.[18] The meagreness of the UN's overall financial resources is clear when set against the demands imposed by the range and complexity of its functions. While the UN Secretariat staff, which serves 189 countries and over six billion people, has been reduced by more than 20 per cent over the last decade, the Bretton Woods agencies have more than doubled in size. Its annual budget in the mid- and late-1990s averaged $1.3 billion, estimated to be less than 4 per cent of New York City's budget.[19] If to this were added the budgets of all the UN's major social and development programmes, including the UNDP and the WFP, the total budget would still be well under $8 billion. Recurring cashflow problems have often resulted in peace, humanitarian and other operations starting later, finishing earlier, or proceeding with less preparation, equipment or personnel, than necessary. Moreover, the UN is uncomfortably dependent on the contributions of a handful of member states, notably the United States.

To place the UN on a sounder financial basis the General Assembly should form a high-level independent Financial Advisory Committee[20] to investigate the future funding of the entire UN system. Unlike previous attempts this advisory committee would from the outset be given the necessary status and authority and a clear framework established for its report to be brought to some finality within a fixed time frame. The Committee would comprise eminent financial experts but also senior government representatives from the North and the South, noted for their longstanding association with the UN system. Having consulted widely, the Committee would within 12 months prepare a report for consideration by the General Assembly, setting out a few key options, each encompassing a ten-year time frame. Over a six-month period the General Assembly would identify its preferred option and any necessary modifications. The General Assembly's Fifth Committee, in collaboration with the Advisory Committee and with input from a wide range of UN bodies and governmental and non-governmental agencies, would resubmit to the General Assembly a revised and detailed proposal for debate, possible amendment and final adoption through an exhaustive ballot procedure within a three-month period. After this two-year period the Advisory Committee would remain in existence for another three years to provide advice and support for the implementation of the new financial structure.

While the Financial Advisory Committee would be given a wide brief, its mandate could nevertheless specify a number of key requirements or ideas to be considered. The resources available to the UN system to meet its peace/security, economic, social, environmental and human-rights responsibilities need to be substantially increased over ten-year period and beyond. A possible target might be an average annual increase in the UN system's total budget of 10 per cent over the next ten years. In December 2000, the General Assembly agreed to lower the ceiling of the amount to be paid by any single country to the UN's regular budget from 25 to 22 per cent of the total.[21] Another target worth considering might be for the contribution of any single country to the UN system's total budget (including social and economic programmes) to be progressively scaled down to 10 per cent of the total amount over a specified time period (perhaps 10–15 years). The diminishing US contribution could be offset by a corresponding increase by the other industrialized and emerging economies (notably Western Europe and East Asia), and to a lesser extent the rich oil-exporting countries.

There is a case for reviewing the provisions of Article 19 regarding financial assessments.[22] Member states falling in arrears should, perhaps six months after payment falls due, be required to provide an explanation. Should the General Assembly not be satisfied with the explanation, the offending state would have another six months in which to meet its arrears and do so with interest. Should the state in question fail to comply with these requirements, it would forfeit its vote in the General Assembly, unless a two-thirds majority of the General Assembly is prepared to waive this requirement. Should the same state fail to pay its dues for a second consecutive year, it would also forfeit its vote on the Security Council, if it is a member of that body. If not, it might forfeit its vote in a number of other UN agencies, committees and programmes (the details to be determined by the General Assembly on the advice of the Fifth Committee).

The proposed inquiry should also consider various international taxes or licensing fees proposed in recent years, notably a foreign-currency transaction tax, a foreign-exchange-currency licensing fee, a tax on international trade, taxes on military expenditures or the production of any number of toxic or polluting substances, and fees for use of the global commons, notably the oceans, international airspace and space outside the earth's atmosphere, including parking geostationary satellites.[23] To apply and administer these taxes and fees would require the co-operation of member states, and a degree of global regulation.

Once the Consultative Assembly has been formed all member organizations would have to pay dues according to a formula that reflects the capacity of each organization to pay, with a ceiling on the proportion to be contributed by any one organization. Donations from groups and individuals should be considered only if stringent procedures can ensure that no donor, or cluster of donors, is able to exercise undue influence over UN activities and priorities.

Other possibilities might include: a large Peace and Security Reserve Fund (to help finance urgently needed conflict-prevention, peacekeeping, peacemaking and peacebuilding activities); retention of budgetary surpluses from one year to the next; a provision enabling the Secretary-General in the event of emergencies to borrow at very low interest rates from the UN's financial institutions; and the introduction of IMF special drawing rights linked to UN peacekeeping or peacebuilding activities.

Regional organizations

Regional organizations are likely to play an increasingly important role in the evolution of the global multilateral system. Because of its multifaceted and universal responsibilities the UN is in permanent danger of living beyond its means – not only financially but politically and institutionally. Both economic and geopolitical factors have favoured the uneven, often slow but steady integration of regions,[24] although with a few notable exceptions regions have yet to connect in systematic fashion with the UN system or, more generally, with the emerging 'macropolitical' agenda.

While maintaining their autonomy and distinctiveness, regional and global institutions could co-operate more effectively, mutually reinforce their legitimacy, mitigate in each case the constraints imposed by limited resources, and in appropriate circumstances pave the way for concerted action. Such collaboration, envisaged in Chapter VIII of the UN Charter, can span the whole gamut of governance functions, including economy, environment, education, health and human rights. While the EU and to a lesser extent such groupings as ASEAN and MERCOSUR may be considered, as Malhotra indicates, 'mediating or countervailing layers of governance',[25] they have yet to develop adequate mechanisms which can on the one hand support local and national levels of governance against intrusive, often highly damaging forms of globalization, and on the other facilitate beneficial linkages with global multilateral institutions.

By way of illustration, the emphasis here is on the peace and security function, partly because it is the most sensitive, and perhaps least-developed area of potential co-operation.[26] Several recent attempts at regional involvement in peace operations are indicative of the pitfalls that lie ahead. In this context three highly controversial episodes are worth recalling:

1. the decision to place responsibility for the implementation of the military aspects of the General Framework Agreement for Peace in Bosnia and Herzegovina with NATO and create the multinational Implementation Force (IFOR);[27]
2. the decision to establish the Stabilization Force to succeed IFOR;[28]

3. the decision approving the Kosovo force (KFOR) to establish and maintain a secure environment in Kosovo.[29]

Even more troublesome was the earlier decision taken by the US-led coalition to launch Desert Storm on the basis of what it regarded as the Security Council's enabling resolution.[30] Similarly, NATO's military campaign against Serbia launched in March 1999 in response to the breakdown of the Rambouillet Agreement had as its only legal basis the failure of an opposing draft resolution put to the Security Council by Russia and China. The attack on the Chinese Embassy in Belgrade, unintended or not, and the substantial loss of Serbian civilian life and infrastructure resulting from NATO's aerial campaign, merely compounded the problem. Less problematic, but not entirely devoid of ambiguity, was the decision to authorize the establishment of an Australian-led multinational force (INTERFET) to restore peace and security in East Timor, protect and support UNAMET in carrying out its tasks, and facilitate humanitarian assistance.[31]

The obvious question is: what is an appropriate division of labour between global and regional multilateralism? To this there is no simple or single answer. In the area of peace operations, Boutros-Ghali suggested five categories of possible co-operation: consultation, diplomatic support, operational support, co-deployment and joint operations.[32] Here, we prefer to consider not so much the division of *labour* as the division of *authority* between the global and the regional. Conceptually, we can identify three main possibilities. The first assigns the regional organization a relatively minor and at best supportive role, whether it be pooling the collective resources of its member states or encouraging them to assist on an individual basis. The second option envisages a reversal of roles, with the regional organization acting as the prime mover at all stages of the peace operation (that is, assessment, planning/early authorization and implementation), and the UN playing a minor or supporting role, helping to give the operation a legitimacy it might not otherwise enjoy. The third option involves shared responsibility for the peace operation, with both the UN and the regional organization contributing the necessary personnel and equipment, and an agreement between the two organizations regarding general lines of authority and the chain of command on the ground.

The second option carries considerable risks. Most obviously, the regional organization may be unable to act impartially in relation to the warring parties, or alternatively its actions may come to reflect the interests of its most powerful member. By closely associating itself with such an operation, the UN may damage its own credibility and legitimacy.

This brief analysis suggests several important rules-of-thumb. At the most general level, and in line with the philosophy that states should progressively relinquish the use of force in settling international and even national disputes, it is preferable that the authorization to apply force in particular instances (whether in the context of peacekeeping, peace enforcement or collective action against aggression) should be the preserve of the UN. Once the UN has made such a decision and established a clear mandate for the operation, a small or even large part of the operation could be devolved to a regional organization. Such an arrangement should normally satisfy a number of conditions.

First, the UN should conclude a formal agreement with the regional organization setting out the respective functions and powers of the two bodies. Secondly, the Security Council should at all times retain ultimate authority over the decision to initiate, expand, curtail or terminate the operation. The will of the Security Council with respect to these matters should require an affirmative vote consistent with accepted procedural requirements. Thirdly, the regional organization should provide the Strategic Committee with regular reports on the conduct of the operation, and furnish without delay such additional information as it might require from time to time.

For collaboration to be effective, a regional organization would need to subscribe to the same principles as the UN, and be firmly committed to the peaceful settlement of disputes. It should be constituted as an *inclusive* regional security mechanism, open to all states in the region or sub-region (for example, the OSCE, ASEAN), rather than an exclusive collective-defence organization more akin to a military alliance (for example, NATO), which is likely to exert a polarizing rather than a moderating influence on inter-state relations, or serve as a vehicle for the exercise of great-power influence. The regional organization should have an established infrastructure, a well-developed framework of decision-making, and a high level of credibility with its members. Its personnel must be trained to the required UN standards, and comply with accepted UN procedures.

Regional organizations can, of course, collaborate with the UN in non-military ways, particularly in peacebuilding. They can contribute to economic reconstruction, restoration of educational and health services, diplomatic mediation, supervision of elections, monitoring of human-rights practices, and various forms of humanitarian assistance. They can facilitate, through early-warning and other mechanisms, the prevention of violence, and, where serious crimes have occurred, encourage member states to co-operate with relevant tribunals or the International Criminal Court.

Regional organizations, precisely because they have different histories, mandates, structures, degrees of internal cohesion, and capabilities, cannot be expected to perform similar functions, or the same function to the same standard. Much could be gained therefore if the UN were to oversee a thorough review of existing regional organizations. Such a review might suggest a more viable delineation of regions, remembering, however, that this process is subject to periodic reassessment in the light of changing circumstances. More importantly, such a review could evaluate the needs of different regions, and ways of enhancing their capabilities and performance. Concrete possibilities worth exploring include the establishment of regional security dialogue mechanisms, crisis-prevention centres and peacekeeping centres, and more effective linkages between regional organizations and regional arms of the UN system (for instance, UN Standing Advisory Committee on Security Questions in Central Africa, UN Regional Centre for Peace and Disarmament in Kathmandu).

Regional organizations can perform a multiplicity of economic, financial, cultural and technical functions conducive to human security. In the economic arena, Chapter 9 has highlighted the value of establishing regional monetary funds responsive to regional and country-specific needs. Quite apart from issues of trade, investment and finance, the regional tier of governance can play a use-ful role in mobilizing resources and developing more effective strategies to deal with such challenges as piracy, organized crime, population movements, the AIDS pandemic, and human-rights violations. But as with the other tiers of gov-ernance so with the regional tier, the emphasis must be on fostering democratic impulses and institutions. Regional parliaments, courts and commissions can in different ways promote greater accountability in decision-making, more effective protection of human rights and a stronger culture of participation.

The robustness of regional organizations and their contribution to democratic practice are likely to be substantially enhanced through denser networks of inter-action between different tiers of governance, not least between the regional and global tiers. A useful step in this direction might be the creation in each region of a forum which brings together the directors of UN centres in the region and the representatives of regional UN commissions (for example, Economic Commission for Africa, Economic and Social Commission for Asia and the Pacific) and agencies on the one hand, and regional IGOs and NGOs on the other. Such a regional forum, provided its deliberations and decisions are themselves transparent, would make for a more efficient division of labour, greater awareness of the potential for institutional collaboration, and greater capacity to subject all levels of decision-making to more rigorous public scrutiny.

Emerging global civil society

Civil society is not a new concept. Its meaning, however, has over time become the subject of contestation, spawning multiple and at times sharply contrasting interpretations.[33] Previous chapters have implicitly and explicitly pointed to the pivotal role which an enhanced notion of civil society can make to the theory and practice of global governance reform. It cannot be stressed enough, however, that civil society cannot be reduced to that amalgam of social movements and organizations of progressive or liberal disposition.[34] For both analytical and policy purposes, it is preferable to use the term 'civil society' to denote the entire range of associations, other than those operating for profit in the market place, that have their own distinctive identity and sense of belonging, are independent of the state, yet help to shape community and public discourse.[35] Included in this notion are local communities of various kinds, groups for leisure and charity, labour unions and professional associations, and scientific, intellectual, religious, cultural and sporting organizations. Civil-society organizations (CSOs) are to be distinguished therefore from non-governmental organizations (NGOs), a nar-rower term often used to refer to associations active around such issues as devel-opment, human rights, gender, environment or peace.[36] In this sense, NGOs should be seen as a distinctive subset of CSOs.

Our central contention here is that global institutions – and the way they con-nect with national, regional and sub-regional tiers of governance – must become the catalyst for a new culture of participation at every level of decision-making. To this end, the UN system must actively incorporate the insights and resources of civil society understood in its wider sense. The involvement of CSOs, operating globally, regionally and sub-regionally, would also give a deeper meaning and content to the idea of human security. To illustrate, many of the conflicts in which the UN intervenes, or considers intervention, are indicative of societies experiencing ethnic, religious and cultural frictions, often the by-product of far-reaching economic and social transformations, with obvious implications for personal security, disparities of income and wealth, environmental quality, and political stability. There is an important corollary to this proposition, namely the need for a holistic approach to the prevention and resolution of conflict.

Effective strategies must pay attention to the close interconnections not only between states, or between them and multilateral institutions, but between governance and civil society functioning in a variety of spaces – national, international and transnational. The institutional innovations proposed here – Peoples' Assembly, Consultative Assembly, and numerous other mechanisms – are specifically designed to facilitate such strategies. A few other possibilities merit particular attention. Civil-society groups, selected for their expertise, legitimacy, and extensive public support, could be given substantive consultative status with regional organizations and their various organs and agencies (the EU, ASEAN, OAU, OSCE, Islamic Conference and so on), as well as with UN regional agencies and forums. Civil-society umbrella organizations known for their expertise or grassroots connections (for instance, Council for Security and Cooperation in Asia Pacific, Asia Pacific Civil Society Forum, Pacific Conference of Churches) could be given the right to make submissions to regional IGOs, to comment on preliminary drafts of agreements and other documents, to have regular consultations with the Secretary-General's Special Representatives or Special Envoys, and to nominate representatives to the Consultative Assembly. In the case of specific operations or activities, civil-society organizations and networks could be given full or, where more appropriate, consultative membership of relevant UN bodies (including agencies, standing committees, functional and regional commissions, and integrated task forces established for individual peace operations), and boards and working groups of such international organizations as the World Bank, the OECD or the IAEA.[37]

These and other linkages are no doubt feasible, perhaps desirable. Yet a note of caution may be helpful. Too close a connection with the apparatus of governance may deprive civil society of its independence of action and the critical edge of its analysis. While civil society can perform useful organizational and even co-ordinating tasks, its unique contribution is to help set the standards of humane governance, and vigilantly to observe the application and enforcement of those standards. In addition, CSOs, especially large international structures, are themselves subject to the twin temptations of centralization and closed decision-making. The democratization of civil society should be treated as an end in itself, although it could also greatly facilitate the democratization of regional and global governance. The most pressing challenge posed by globalization is to build institutions and reform existing ones in ways which allow people in all facets of human organization a part to play in resolving the issues which affect their common future.

Notes

1. J.A. Camilleri, 'Impoverishment and the Nation State', in F.O. Hampson and J. Reppy (eds), *Earthly Goods: Environmental Change and Social Justice* (Ithaca, NY: Cornell University Press, 1996), pp.122–53.
2. Among the scholarly studies, a few are worth noting: R. Falk, *On Humane Governance: Toward a New Global Politics* (Cambridge: Polity Press, 1995); D. Held and D. Archibugi (eds), *Cosmopolitan Democracy* (Cambridge: Polity Press, 1995); A.J. Paolini, A.P. Jarvis and C. Reus-Smit (eds), *Between Sovereignty and Global Governance: the United Nations, the State, and Civil Society* (New York: St. Martin's Press [now Palgrave Macmillan], 1998). More policy-oriented reports have included: *The Challenge to the South: the Report of the South Commission* (Oxford: OUP, 1990); Common Responsibility in the 1990s, 'The Stockholm Initiative' (Stockholm: Prime Minister's Office, 1992); Commission on Global Governance, *Our Global Neighbourhood* (Oxford: OUP, 1995).
3. M. Shaw, *Theory of the Global State: Globality as an Unfinished Revolution* (Cambridge: CUP, 2000), p.253.
4. The notion is elaborated in J.A. Camilleri and J. Falk, *The End of Sovereignty? Politics in a Shrinking and Fragmenting World* (Aldershot, UK: Edward Elgar, 1992), pp.148–51.
5. S.J. Kobrin, 'Back to the Future: Neomedievalism and the Postmodern Digital Economy', in A. Prakash and J.A. Hart (eds), *Globalization and Governance* (London: Routledge, 1999), p.167.
6. See, for example, P. Hirst and G. Thompson, 'Globalisation and the Future of the Nation-State', *Economy and Society*, 24, 3, pp.408–42; S.J. Kobrin, 'The Architecture of Globalization: Sovereignty in a Networked Global Economy', in J.H. Dunning (ed), *Governments, Globalization and International Business* (Oxford: OUP, 1997); A-M. Slaughter, 'The Real World Order', *Foreign Affairs*, 76 (5) 1997, pp.183–7.
7. D. Held, *Democracy and the Global Order: From the Modern State to Cosmopolitan Governance* (Cambridge: Polity Press, 1995), p.232.
8. Ibid., p.234; emphasis in the original.
9. Commission on Global Governance, p.345.
10. This is not an entirely new idea. See J. Segall, 'A Second UN Assembly', in F. Barnaby (ed.), *Building a more Democratic United Nations* (London: Cass, 1991); also E. Childers, 'The United Nations and Global Institutional Discourse and Reality', *Global Governance*, 3, 3 (September–December 1997), p.375. For an exposition of some of the difficulties surrounding the concept of a popular assembly, see D. Archibugi, 'The Reform of the UN and Cosmopolitan Democracy', *Journal of Peace Research*, 30, 2 (1993).
11. See M. Renner, *Fighting for Survival: Environmental Decline, Social Conflict and the New Age of Insecurity* (New York: W.W. Norton & Co, 1996), pp.135–53.
12. The 'Global Compact' concept was first proposed by Secretary-General Kofi Annan in January 1999, and the first high-level meeting took place in June 2000. But it was made clear from the outset that the purpose of the exercise was not to develop a regulatory instrument or code of conduct, but simply to promote institutional learning; see 'The Global Compact: What It Is and Isn't', available online at: <**http://www.unglobal-compact.org/gc/unweb.nsf/content/whatitis.htm**> (13 July 2001).
13. For a detailed assessment of the performance of the Security Council during the 1990s, see J. Dedring, 'The Role of the UN Security Council in Peace and Security in the Post-Cold War Era; First Steps in the Exploration of a Misunderstood Organ of Global Governance' (Paper presented at the 2000 ISA Convention, 14–18 March 2000).
14. For a sharply critical analysis of the organizational principles on which the Security Council rests, see H. Köchler, *Democracy and the International Rule of Law* (Wien/Vienna: Springer-Verlag, 1995), pp.85–116.
15. See P. Wallensteen, 'Representing the World: a Security Council for the 21st Century', *Security Dialogue*, 25, 1 (1994), pp.63–75.
16. Commission on Global Governance, p.342.

17. See P.G. Cerny, 'Globalization, Governance, and Complexity', in Prakash and Hart, p.189.
18. See P. Taylor, 'The United Nations System under Stress: Financial Pressures and their Consequences', *Review of International Studies*, 17, 4 (October 1991), pp.365–82; H. D'Orville and D. Najman, 'A New System to Finance the United Nations', *Security Dialogue*, 25, 2 (1994), pp.135–44; J.P. Walker, 'Alternative Financing for the United Nations: an Idea whose Time Has Finally Come?', *Economic and Trade Policy*, Policy Staff Commentary, No.10 (December 1995).
19. R.P. Mendez, 'Financing the United Nations and the International Public Sector: Problems and Reform', *Global Governance*, 3, 3 (September–December 1997), p.285.
20. Several official and unofficial expert groups have met and made a number of thoughtful and moderate recommendations, few of which have thus far been adopted; see 'Financing an Effective United Nations: Report of the Independent Advisory Group on United Nations Financing' (the *Ogata-Volcker Report*), annexed to document A/48/460, Note by the Secretary-General, 11 October 1993.
21. UN Press Release GA/9850, 23 December 2000, p.1.
22. Mendez, pp.290–1.
23. Ibid., pp.298–303.
24. See L. Fawcett and A. Hurrell (eds), *Regionalism in World Politics* (Oxford: OUP, 1995); G. Fry, 'A Coming Age of Regionalism?', in G. Fry and J. O'Hagan (eds), *Contending Images of World Politics* (London: Macmillan, 2000), pp.117–31; E.D. Mansfield and H.V. Milner, 'The New Wave of Regionalism', *International Organization*, 53, 3 (Summer 1999), pp.589–627.
25. See Chapter 9, under Inter-governmental regional institutions and mechanisms, page 153.
26. See B. Rivlin, 'Regional Arrangements and the UN System for Collective Security and Conflict Resolution: a New Road Ahead?', *International Relations*, XI, 2 (August 1992), pp.95–110.
27. SCR 1035, 21 December 1995.
28. SCR 1088, 12 December 1996.
29. SCR 1244, 10 June 1999.
30. SCR 678, 29 November 1990.
31. SCR 1264, 15 September 1999.
32. B. Boutros-Ghali, *Supplement to An Agenda for Peace: Position Paper of the Secretary-General on the Occasion of the Fiftieth Anniversary of the United Nations* (New York: United Nations, 1995), para.86.
33. See J. Ehrenberg, *Civil Society: the Critical History of an Idea* (New York: New York University Press, 1999).
34. The argument is developed more fully in J.A. Camilleri, *States, Markets and Civil Society in Asia Pacific* (Cheltenham, UK: Edward Elgar, 2000), pp.354–9.
35. A very similar representation of civil society is offered by R.W. Cox, 'Civil Society at the Turn of the Millenium: Prospects for an Alternative World Order', in R. Higgott and A. Payne (eds), *The New Political Economy of Globalisation*, Vol.II (Cheltenham, UK: Edward Elgar, 2000), pp.453–9.
36. The growing importance of CSOs is now widely recognized in the literature, although there is still a tendency to equate global civil society with international NGOs; see, for example, R. Devetak and R. Higgott, 'Justice Unbound? Globalization, States and the Transformation of the Social Bond', in Higgott and Payne (eds), p.580; also T.G. Weiss and L. Gordenker (eds), *NGOs, the UN, & Global Governance* (Boulder, CO: Lynne Rienner, 1996).
37. Thus far, only a few tentative steps have been made in this directions. See, for example, R. O'Brien, A-M. Goetz, J.A. Scholte and M. Williams, *Contesting Global Governance: Multilateral Economic Institutions and Global Social Movements* (Cambridge: CUP, 2000).

16
The Politics of Reform

Joseph A. Camilleri

The preceding chapters have addressed from different perspectives a common set of questions: What is the most plausible diagnosis for the multifaceted predicament afflicting contemporary international society?; What are the institutional obstacles to an appropriate response?; most importantly, What normative and institutional remedies might be available to us at this historical juncture? The three-layered approach to global governance which animates this study rests on two key assumptions: first, that institutional reform must be driven by an overarching notion of human security; and second, that in order to achieve this goal decision-making structures and processes must be consistent with the idea of 'normative democracy'.[1]

The idea of human security has been criticized – not entirely without justification – on the grounds that it is definitionally elusive and so all-encompassing as to lack analytical rigour. Sustainable development, human rights and fundamental freedoms, the rule of law, good governance, protection of the environment, and social equity have all been proposed as integral to human security. Can a concept made up of such disparate elements command serious attention among either scholars or policy-makers? One can rightly draw attention to the 'universal, interdependent and people-centred' quality of human security. But that is not enough. What gives the concept its analytical and programmatic coherence is the premise that each of its constituent elements plays a part in sustaining a social order which resonates sufficiently with its members to inspire in them confidence in the future.[2] It is precisely the idea of a 'legitimated social order' which informs the proposed programme of political and economic reform.

Such a programme must of necessity come to terms with a rapidly globalizing world, marked by increasing sensitivity of one geographical area to another, and of one sector, be it military, economic or environmental, to another. Trade rivalries, international debt, destabilizing financial flows, transborder pollution, drug-trafficking, large population movements, human-rights abuses, piracy and terrorism all point to the interconnectedness of the international system. This study has critically evaluated the performance of existing institutions, and detected not merely inefficiency or inefficacy, but a paralysing crisis of legitimacy. It is not simply that institutions, be they national, regional or global, lack the organizational capacity and resources needed to meet the multiple challenges of globalization. It is that institutional practice does not adequately reflect the normative framework which the international community has progressively enunciated, and more to the point, that it does not inspire sufficient confidence or respect to mobilize human energies on anything like the scale needed for the task.

In the light of this inescapable conclusion, a series of proposals are here advanced for far-reaching institutional reform. Building on the insights of previous studies, a model of cosmopolitan democracy is advocated, which seeks to develop and entrench democratic institutions at every level of human organization. Given that states are enmeshed today in a complex system of overlapping and intersecting spheres of activity, the principles of transparency and accountability, it is argued, must be enshrined in all global institutions, not just the UN. Indeed, the broadening and strengthening of institutional capacity cannot be limited to the global arena. Regionalism, a trend which has already gained considerable momentum and which can serve as a useful antidote to the excesses of globalization, must itself be subjected to the test of democratic legitimacy. In any case, the democratization of regional and global institutions, essential though it may be, cannot be a substitute for local and national autonomy. Such democratization will better approximate its full potential to the extent that it breathes new life into the political and administrative organs of both local and national communities.

Taking the argument to its logical conclusion, the approach taken in this volume calls for civic participation to be introduced at all levels of governance, and for participation at one level to mirror, facilitate and connect with participation at other levels. A closely related but distinct implication is worth stressing here. While giving effect to notions of global responsibility, emerging international rules, procedures and organizations must not allow the ideology of global governance to be used as a weapon by core actors, that is, states and economic interests located predominantly in the West, to impose their preferences and priorities on the periphery. The aim of structural reform must be to avoid both the politics of domination ('one-worldism') and the politics of paralysis and fragmentation ('statism').

The programmatic approach of this volume, intellectually coherent and normatively appealing though it may be, must nevertheless grapple with the substantial gap that separates the preferred future from political actuality. We must somehow confront the problem of power. To visualize in some detail what this preferred future might look like – through a multiplicity of scenarios, possibilities and proposals for change – helps to make the project more feasible and compelling. Yet there is more to political reform than scholarly analysis or institutional advocacy. One of the notable missing links in much of global governance discourse is precisely how to bridge actual and potential reality. This concluding chapter seeks to address this gap.

It begins by examining the dynamic of social and institutional change and the historical context within which it unfolds. Change, as we know, is not synonymous with reform. Some features of the evolving economic and political landscape may constitute serious impediments to the democratization of global governance. Other features may perform a countervailing role more in keeping with the proposed reform agenda. The task then is to discern on the one hand the embedded material, ideational and institutional influences inimical to that agenda, and on the other those political, economic and cultural trends most likely to give it added impetus. We should then be better placed to identify key agents of change and develop a typology of the actual and possible strategies which can sustain their action.

Governance and global social change

The puzzle of reform has thus far been described in terms of the gap separating political actuality from the preferred future. Yet the actual is never static. The steady development of multilateralism over the last hundred years is itself evidence of change. The decisions to create the League of Nations and later the UN can only be understood as reactions to the perception of change. Policy-makers, no doubt mirroring shifts in public sentiment, had concluded that in the vastly altered conditions of the twentieth century the ravages of war required an altogether different approach to the management of inter-state conflict. Since 1945 the UN system itself has undergone considerable change, as may be gauged from the steady enlargement of its functions, activities and organizational complexity. In peacekeeping, environment, economic development, human rights, international humanitarian law, health, drug-trafficking, indigenous affairs, and other areas of policy, the UN and its agencies have assumed a co-ordinating role in, and at times even direct responsibility for, setting standards, and to a lesser extent monitoring and enforcing the application of those standards.

It is useful, then, before proceeding to an analysis of future prospects, to reflect, however briefly, on the recent advocacy and practice of institutional change. Andy Knight's analytical framework merits particular attention because it helps to contextualize much of the discourse on multilateral reform. He posits three main approaches to UN reform, which he labels respectively 'incremental', 'adaptive', and 'radical'.[3] According to the incrementalists, the original structural and constitutional framework of the UN remains basically sound, and only improvements to the functioning of various organs need be contemplated. The emphasis here is very much on efficiency, and on administrative and financial rationalization of a kind that will not disturb the interests of the dominant coalition within the UN.

Adaptive reformists, on the other hand, while they remain wedded to the spirit and letter of the UN Charter, acknowledge that a measure of adaptation to a changing international environment may be necessary. However, they do not question the ends that the UN has set itself – merely the means by which they are to be achieved. Existing functions, activities and organizational arrangements may be abandoned or modified, and new ones introduced, with only limited reference to overall coherence or to the deeper intellectual or structural currents bearing upon the international system. Radical reformists are divided into two groups: the 'dissolutionists' primarily identified with the political right in US foreign policy, which sees relatively little use for the UN, except as a limited instrument for the maintenance of US hegemony; and the 'successionists' who, struck by the irrelevance of the UN to current global conditions, advocate a completely new conception of international society, making way for new constitutional and organizational arrangements.

Though highly instructive as an account of the competing views and underlying interests reflected in recent discourse, Knight's typology is nevertheless limiting because of its emphasis on the degree of change that is proposed – from retention to abandonment or wholesale reconstruction of the existing edifice – and on the constitutional or organizational dimensions of change. Several other dimensions are, it is arguable, at least as relevant to the analysis of institutional change. Three are especially noteworthy. The first relates to the normative framework which endows any institution with its fundamental objectives and the ultimate benchmark by which to judge its performance. The second addresses the structure-agency relationship; more specifically it draws attention to the agents of change and the likely scope and limitations of their action given structural constraints and opportunities. The third has to do with time. What may seem revolutionary if pursued as an immediate objective, may turn out to be a series of incremental but cumulatively significant steps if measured over a prolonged time-span.

All three dimensions indicate the need for an historical-structural approach,[4] something that Knight himself acknowledges[5] but does not fully incorporate into his analysis. Historical structures refer to patterns of activity that entrench over relatively long periods of time a distinctive conjunction of materials interests, intersubjective meanings and institutional practices. Clearly, the scale and intensity of change are likely to be much greater between than within historical structures. The question immediately arises as to whether the confluence of events of the last ten to twenty years constitutes a 'threshold' in the evolution of the modern world system. A threshold here refers to that unique combination of influences which significantly alter the previously dominant pattern of interaction or historical structure. Placed in the context of multilateral reform, the question becomes: Is it possible to identify in this historical moment the conditions which point to a new way of visualizing and occupying political space,[6] a new normative framework, and presumably a new or substantially reconfigured set of institutions, rules and procedures? How one answers this question will greatly influence, if not wholly determine, one's approach to transformative change.

Structural impediments

The most obvious impediment to structural change stems from what Richard Falk has called 'geopolitical closure',[7] an institutional arrangement which cements the power configuration that notionally existed in the immediate aftermath of World War II, and gives any one of five states the power to block any initiative which it deems injurious to its interests. That having been said, it should not be thought that to bring the permanent membership of the Security Council more closely into line with the new geopolitical reality would of itself noticeably relieve the predicament of the UN.

The more fundamental obstacle has to do with the state-centric theory and practice which pervades the formal functioning of the UN system and other multilateral organizations. Based on the postulate that only 'sovereign' states occupy political space and can therefore qualify as members, the UN, as presently constituted, has at best limited capacity to incorporate non-state actors into its decision-making, to oversee – let alone regulate – the movements of transnational capital, or to respond effectively to the multidimensional character of contemporary conflicts. *De jure* global governance seems strangely out of step with an increasingly integrated yet simultaneously fragmenting international system.

By tying themselves so closely to the fortunes of the state, multilateral institutions are ill-equipped to retain their independence from what Cox has termed the 'nascent global historic bloc', in which he includes pivotal corporate economic players, states acting as agents of the globalized economy, and diverse intellectual and policy networks propagating the ideology of globalization.[8] As a consequence, the UN system is progressively marginalized, as are indeed most states, with the exception of a few powerful western states. Indeed, the transnational process of consensus formation among the guardians of the global economy increasingly resides in unofficial bodies such as the World Economic Forum, and official bodies such as the OSCE, the G7 and the IMF, over which the UN system – especially its most democratically structured organ, the General Assembly – has little or no influence.

The shift in the locus of economic decision-making from states to relatively unregulated markets has had one other far-reaching consequence. To the extent that transnational capital is able to impose its discipline on national economic policy, states – more specifically governments and political parties – are increasingly removed from the needs and preferences of their citizenry. To put it more accurately, the democratic process is visibly restricted by the state's diminishing freedom of action. There is little point in citizens taking advantage of consultative or participatory mechanisms, even voting in elections, if the capacity of governments to integrate social needs into fiscal and monetary policy is so narrowly circumscribed. If anything, the state has an interest in popular demobilization, since a mobilized public would simply exacerbate the state's already difficult predicament. Conversely, public disillusionment with conventional politics can only encourage depoliticization, apathy and even social rootlessness. The ensuing political void may be filled partly by covert politics (organized crime, drug-trafficking, security systems, undeclared private funding of political parties) or by 'exclusionary populism' based on varying mixtures of racial xenophobia, extreme-right political agendas, and religious cultism or fanaticism. These are not exactly ideal conditions for informed national or international citizenship to flourish.

One other impediment, closely linked to the threads of the preceding analysis, has had, and continues to have, a damaging effect on the prospects for UN reform. The state-centric conception of international society enshrined in the UN Charter has, as we have seen, privileged five states, of which by far the most influential has been the United States. Its dominant role owes much to its capacity to project military power on a global scale, but just as critical has been the size and dynamism of its economy, which is in turn intimately connected with the global reach of US capital. The United States, far from using its ascendancy to promote institutional reform, has instead used it to support institutions, regional or global (for example, IMF, NAFTA), which are consistent with narrowly defined interests, and to oppose or marginalize other institutions (notably the UN General Assembly, and the UN system more generally, including the prospective International Criminal Court) for fear that they might restrict its hegemonic role. Not surprisingly, the United States has remained an enthusiastic advocate of the power of veto in the Security Council and a determined opponent of any move which might enhance the UN's overseeing function in the area of economic policy.

To the extent that the United States has effectively portrayed itself, by virtue of its military and economic alliances, as leader of the western world, US dominance has become virtually synonymous with western dominance. Following so closely on the heels of European colonialism, the rhetoric and practice of US leadership, further encouraged by the demise of the Soviet bloc, has created a widely shared sense of an actual or impending civilizational fracture in international society. The forceful projection of western liberal values is proving highly damaging, for it acts in the name of a 'universalism' more likely to prompt unilateralism and resistance than a co-operative approach to global governance reform. As the increasingly tense relationship between Islam and the West suggests, the fact that religion and culture often disguise deeper economic, geopolitical and strategic cleavages does not lessen the negative impact of these civilizational cross-currents.

Countervailing tendencies

Daunting though they may be, the structural impediments to reform are in part offset by a number of contrary trends. Side by side with geopolitical and geoeconomic closure are the openings indicated by a new kind of universalism on the one hand, and the subtle but steady diffusion of power on the other.

The UN system has already acquired a degree of unprecedented universality as measured not only by the membership of states but the participation of an ever-widening range of other actors. UN activities and consultations have increasingly engaged villages and local communities, professional associations, labour and business organizations, humanitarian and human-rights agencies, scientists, educators and religious leaders, to name a few. This is not to say that the mechanisms of representation and accountability are effective or that they enjoy the necessary degree of legitimacy. There is no disputing the fact, however, that the last fifty or more years have seen a steady, and at times dramatic, expansion of the infrastructure of global governance in almost every area of human activity.[9] The innumerable negotiations, conferences, agreements and conventions sponsored by the UN and other international organizations have, especially over the last thirty years, brought together almost every relevant constituency in the world to deal with such issues as trade, development, social policy, human rights, women's issues, environment, population and much else. Mirroring the diversity of issues and constituencies has been the diversity of functions, from collection, interpretation and dissemination of data, to negotiation of norms and rules, the establishment of monitoring and inspection regimes, and limited attempts at enforcement.

The pronounced trend towards multilateralism reflects the state's declining capacity to manage the complex pressures generated by contemporary economic and technological change. What is in question is the competence of states, which are, by definition, boundary-maintaining systems, to act as self-contained entities when monitoring, interpreting and recasting the interaction between the social, economic and biophysical effects of human actions. It is precisely the limits to the efficacy of state action which has prompted states to transfer authority, functions and resources to a panoply of regional and international organizations. This does not mean that the global and regional tiers of governance have adequately offset the deficiencies of state intervention, or that they themselves can operate effectively except in collaboration with the local and national tiers. It simply means that the national state is increasingly obliged to operate within a complex mosaic of spaces characterized by multiple allegiances, new forms of identity, and overlapping tiers of jurisdiction.

The changing structures and processes of governance cannot, however, be reduced to the assessments and decisions of national policy-makers. They are as much the product of public sentiment, which is simultaneously expressed in the local, national and international domain. The globalization of the media is, in fact, contributing to the emergence of world public opinion just as it is facilitating the simultaneity of its expression.[10] Important, however, as the medium (for example, radio, television, Internet) may be to the dissemination of information, ideas and above all images, the message is also shaped by the growth of more complex societal forces which are as much transnational as they are national in scope and inspiration. In developed and developing societies the multiple crises of modernity and modernization respectively have resulted in the exponential growth of community action. Varying greatly in size, resource base, intellectual sophistication, longevity and mode of organization, citizen initiatives and popular movements have nevertheless had a cumulative impact on the context of both national and international decision-making.[11] The evidence, though not definitive, suggests the embryonic development of a global civil society. Such a society presupposes not a single set of values or beliefs, but a plurality of cultural interpretations which, in different ways and to different degrees, experience and respond to the same 'modern global circumstance'.[12] We may be seeing, in other words, the emergence of increasingly attentive publics occupying diverse but interactive political spaces and engaged in a politically influential process of global communication.

Paradoxically, this new universalism coincides with and stimulates the diffusion of power. Notwithstanding the military, economic and even cultural hegemony exercised by core interests, the evolution of the world system is not free of tension and contradiction. To begin with, the core is not monolithic. Despite several indicators pointing in the direction of a unipolar system (for instance, the collapse of the Soviet empire, the preservation of a number of US security arrangements, the relative success of the US-led coalition in the Gulf War, NATO's intervention in Kosovo, the resurgence of the US economy during the 1990s as the primary engine of world economic growth, the speed with which Washington forged a global coalition in its 'war against terrorism'), subtler but more enduring trends signal the development of a polycentric system, in which Europe, Japan, China, and in due course Russia, perhaps India and even an Islamic coalition, will play a more prominent role in defining the international security, economic or environmental agenda. Core states are adopting diverging policies with respect to such critical issues as trade, energy, global warming, debt-rescheduling, enforcement of international humanitarian law, sanctions policy in relation to Iraq, and handling of the Israeli–Palestinian conflict. Though this divergence is often obscured by secret diplomacy, it is intruding with increasing visibility in numerous international negotiations.

As for North–South relations, there remains, despite the South's continuing financial, technological and commercial dependence and the homogenizing influence of modernity, a marked disjuncture of interests and perceptions. The unrelenting competition between the major capitalist centres, coupled with the widening cleavage between core states and their respective civil societies, provides a new opening for elites in the periphery and semi-periphery to advance their interests. Clearly, their bargaining position is likely to be enhanced to the extent that they can co-ordinate their positions through multilateral forums and institutions. The North–South divide is likely to assume an even sharper profile as non-western civilizational perspectives are introduced with increasing vigour into world-order discourse.

A third distinguishing feature of this transitional period is the interplay of centripetal and centrifugal forces pushing towards regionalization. Though the trend is neither uniform nor universal, the last twenty years have seen the growth of several regional formations and the creation of new ones, with the focus on economic, security or functional co-operation. Though some of these arrangements tend to reinforce hegemonic power (for example, NATO, NAFTA) or to reconcile competing core interests (for example, APEC), others pose, potentially at least, a challenge to hegemonic power (for example, the EU), while others still provide the periphery and semi-periphery with an enhanced capacity for co-ordination (for example, ASEAN, OAU, the Arab League), or at least the opportunity to influence security or economic agendas (for example, ARF). Viewed from a global perspective, regionalism, which both markets and civil society are influencing to varying degrees, has become something of a melting pot, absorbing and integrating but also refining and differentiating the competing designs which will shape the future architecture of international security and the world economy.

Strategy for change

Global governance reform, if it is to make any headway, will have to take account of both structural impediments and countervailing tendencies. It will need to surmount or somehow bypass the former, while making full use of whatever openings are offered by the latter. Given the plurality of views and interests to be accommodated, the reform agenda and specific proposals we have outlined, however plausible and coherent, will have to be subjected to detailed and critical scrutiny, and inserted into a wider public discussion of options and strategies. This volume should be seen as simply adding a few more sentences to a rich and ongoing conversation. The first and decisive strategic aim of such a conversation must be to reach a normative consensus about the nature and purpose of the proposed transformative project. In the absence of such agreement it is difficult to see how the advocacy of change will gain the necessary legitimacy or generate the political will needed to translate ideas into action.

What exactly is meant by *normative consensus*? Just as the international community has over a long period of time developed something of a consensus around a number of key objectives – human rights and international humanitarian law readily come to mind – the time has come to strive for an equivalent meeting of minds on the norms that should govern the complex task of governance in the era of globalization. Here it is worth stressing both the scope and limitations of the normative consensus achieved in other areas. In the human-rights field, for example, the Universal Declaration has since been followed by a long list of resolutions, declarations, covenants, conventions and protocols which specify the international standards of conduct applicable in diverse circumstances. This is not to say that the normative consensus achieved thus far is definitive and all-embracing, or that it is universally supported and implemented. Far from it. Important differences of emphasis and interpretation persist. Nevertheless, a wide-ranging consensus may be said to have emerged, at least discursively, around a set of core principles – which is not to say that the consensus is frozen in time: on the contrary, it is subject to continuing review and renegotiation.

The aim here must be to forge a comparable consensus, but in this case one centred on the rediscovery, reinvigoration and renegotiation of the democratic idea, so as to make it relevant to the material and ideational conditions of a rapidly globalizing world. In striving for such a consensus, the analysis, scenarios and recommendations contained in this and other studies will need to be carefully considered. But the dialogue cannot be confined to the authors of such studies. It must engage key constituents of civil society, which Cox has rightly described as 'the base upon which a new or reconstructed political authority would have to rest'.[13] Here, civil society is understood in its broader sense to include the highly visible NGOs specializing in such issues as human rights, development, peace and the environment, but just as importantly a range of societal formations, including labour unions, farmers' and professional associations, student groups, and religious and cultural organizations, each with an obvious stake in the outcome of the dialogue. Experts, in particular lawyers, educators, communicators, political scientists, economists and scientists will no doubt have much to contribute to the process. The contribution of these 'epistemic communities', useful as it may be in developing, disseminating and legitimizing new knowledge and perspectives, must not, however, be overstated. The more critical function will be that served by 'organic intellectuals', a Gramscian category which refers to those who are closely ('organically') connected to societal constituencies, and engage with them in ways that clarify both current trends and future possibilities.

What of the role of the state? While it is hardly the engine driving the embryonic normative consensus, it may nevertheless play a part in the process. Different states, representing different political and cultural traditions, different economic and geopolitical interests, and different stages of economic development may, at least indirectly, promote different elements or dimensions of the normative framework. While core states may be reluctant to divest themselves of the status and privileges they currently enjoy, semi-peripheral and peripheral states (such as Sweden, Denmark, Finland, Ireland, Canada, New Zealand, South Africa, Malaysia, Iran, Venezuela) may be more open to notions of institutional reform. States are not in any case monolithic entities. Even where the state as a whole is unresponsive, key agencies and individuals located within the state apparatus and oppositional political formations (parties and popular movements) may be willing to lend weight to certain aspects of the reform agenda. States, it should be remembered, cannot but take account, however slowly or grudgingly, of the multifaceted pressures emanating from civil society (not just in its national, but increasingly regional and global dimensions). States, in any case, aware of the limitations on their capacity to handle global functions, find it increasingly necessary to extend the framework of international institutions. This has one important consequence. Though often restricted by political pressure and bureaucratic inertia, the international civil service is now a large and growing constituency with an intimate knowledge of the intricacies of regional and global governance and a substantial stake in its future development.

Civil society, in its diverse functional and geographic manifestations, the rapidly internationalizing intellectual communities which it spawns, the expanding international bureaucracy, and to a lesser degree the state, or at least particular states and fragments of states, are the major sites from which will be drawn the participants of the emerging global dialogue envisaged here. Such a dialogue will be mediated not only or even primarily by words, but also by actions and above all by symbols. While one might expect the dialogical project to resonate most sharply with those situated at the margins who have borne the main costs of globalization – in the North and in the South – we should not be surprised to find that it will also strike a responsive chord with a great many diplomats, generals and corporate managers who have come to see the value of more effective international regulation and more participatory decision-making institutions. Here, the challenge is to build bridges between these different agents and sites, effective channels of communication, and suitable fora where differences of perspective and emphasis can be productively negotiated. The strategic aim must be to maximize the number of participants, expand in ever-widening circles the arena of negotiation, and enhance the quality of the dialogue. The process itself will be at least as important as the outcome.

The September 11 attacks on the World Trade Centre and the Pentagon are in this respect extraordinarily rich in symbolism. They are but the latest and most dramatic in a series of events that point simultaneously to the vulnerability of the state (even the world's most powerful state), and the reflex reactions of states when confronted with their own insecurity, but also to the growing realization that no state, however powerful, can adequately cope with that insecurity. The global response thus far is an intriguing one. Much has been made of the need for a 'global coalition' against terrorism. But even within weeks of this disaster it had become painfully clear that the conduct of such a campaign would impinge upon a great many competing interests, priorities and strategies, all of which would need to be negotiated and somehow reconciled. Where, when and how remained unanswered questions.

While governments were frantically searching for answers, a multifaceted, world-wide dialogue had emerged with participants drawn from all the sites alluded to above. Key facets of that dialogue included: the changing face of terrorism, its social and political roots and the appropriateness of responses envisaged by the world's greatest power; the different approaches to the administration of criminal justice on a global scale; the relationship between Islam and the West; the Arab–Israeli conflict, its sources and possible resolution; the role of alliances and *ad hoc* coalitions on the one hand and of regional and global institutions on the other. Many of the answers offered were not in accord with the spirit or the letter of the reform agenda outlined in this volume, though a surprising number were. More importantly perhaps, a sharp and comprehensive debate on the future of governance in all its dimensions was now in full swing. Though still at an embryonic stage, a loose, heterogeneous, poorly organized, but symbolically potent coalition for institutional reform was beginning to take shape.

Three conclusions immediately suggest themselves. First, the dialogue will not end with this particular episode, with the multiple responses to it, or indeed with the next dramatic episode. It will be a prolonged, tortuous and contested process, with many watching the flow of events more closely, expressing their insecurities more openly, assessing the performance of existing institutions more critically than ever before. Secondly, the terrain for dialogue may be most fertile at moments of acute crisis – whether the crisis revolve around issues of physical, financial, economic, environmental or social security. Thirdly, for it to be at all viable, let alone legitimate, the dialogue will have to be universal, by which is meant not simply international but inter-civilizational. It will have to draw its insights as much from the non-western as from the western traditions. During this transitional period the political and cultural strands to which we have alluded may become sufficiently interwoven to enable the dialogue to be formalized. Over time a series of preparatory discussions, gatherings and projects convened within and across various sites may pave the way for a world summit by the end of the decade, at which the democratization of global governance would be the overriding theme. By itself such a process would take us only part of the way, but it could act as a catalyst for the strategically significant steps that must follow in this difficult but unavoidable journey.

Notes

1. This term, which neatly encapsulates the normative impulse of this study, was coined by Richard Falk in *Predatory Globalization: a Critique* (London: Polity Press, 1999), p.146.

2. The emphasis on the psycho-social dimensions of security and insecurity are discussed in J.A. Camilleri, 'The Security Dilemma Revisited: Implications for Asia Pacific', in W.T. Tow, R. Thakur, and I-T. Hyun (eds), *Asia's Emerging Regional Order* (Tokyo: UNU Press, 2000), pp.308–10.
3. W.A. Knight, *A Changing United Nations: Multilateral Evolution and the Quest for Global Governance* (Basingstoke: Palgrave [now Palgrave Macmillan], 2000), pp.26–36.
4. See R.W. Cox, 'Social Forces, States and World Orders: Beyond International Relations Theory', *Millenium: Journal of International Studies*, 10, 2 (Summer 1981), pp.126–55.
5. Knight, pp.4–6.
6. See J.A. Camilleri and J. Falk, *The End of Sovereignty?: the Politics of a Shrinking and Fragmenting World* (Aldershot, UK: Edward Elgar, 1992), pp.221–30, 251–6.
7. Falk, p.113.
8. R.W. Cox, 'Civil Society at the Turn of the Millenium: Prospects for an Alternative World Order', in R. Higgott and A. Payne (eds), *The New Political Economy of Globalisation*, Vol.II (Cheltenham, UK: Edward Elgar, 2000), p.460.
9. See K.W. Abbott and D. Snidal, 'Why States Act through Formal International Organizations', *Journal of Conflict Resolution*, 42, 1 (February 1998), pp.3–32.
10. See M. Shaw, 'Media and Public Opinion in International Relations', in B. Nacos and R. Shapiro (eds), *Decision-Making in a Glass House: Media, Public Opinion in American and European Foreign Policy* (Boulder, CO: Rowman & Littlefield, 2000).
11. See J. Boli and G.M. Thomas, 'INGOs and the Organization of World Culture', in P.F. Diehl (ed.), *Global Governance: International Organizations in an Interdependent World* (Boulder, CO: Lynne Rienner, 2001), pp.87–9.
12. This notion is at least implicit in the argument developed by R. Robertson and F. Lechner, 'Modernization, Globalization and the Problem of Culture in World Systems Theory', *Theory, Culture and Society*, 2, 3 (1985), pp.103–17.
13. Cox (2000), p.461.

Select Bibliography

Abbott, K.W. and D. Snidal, 'Why States Act through Formal International Organizations', *Journal of Conflict Resolution*, 42, 1 (February 1998), pp.3–32.

Abu-Lughod, J., *Before European Hegemony: the World System AD 1250–1350* (Oxford: OUP, 1989).

Aftergood, S., 'The Soft-Kill Fallacy', *Bulletin of the Atomic Scientists*, September/October 1994.

Agosin, M. and R. French-Davis, *Managing Capital Inflows in Latin America*, ODS Discussion Paper 8 (New York: UNDP/ODS, 1996).

Aitken, B., 'Have Institutional Investors Destabilized Emerging Markets?', *Contemporary Economic Policy*, 16 (1998), pp.173–84.

Akyuz, Y., 'The Debate on the International Financial Architecture: Reforming the Reformers', UNCTAD Discussion Paper No.148 (Geneva: UNCTAD, 2000).

Allison, G. and G.F. Treverton (eds), *Rethinking America's Security* (New York: Norton, 1992).

Annan, K.A., *Renewing the United Nations: a Programme for Reform* (New York: UN, 1997).

Annan, K.A., *We the Peoples: the Role of the United Nations in the 21st Century* (the *Millennium Report* of the UN Secretary-General) (New York: UNDPI, 2000).

Archibugi, D., 'The Reform of the UN and Cosmopolitan Democracy', *Journal of Peace Research*, 30, 2 (1993).

Attali, J., *Millennium: Winners and Losers in the Coming World Order* (New York: Times Books, 1991).

Azar, E. and J. Burton (eds), *International Conflict Resolution: Theory and Practice* (Sussex: Wheatsheaf, 1986).

Baker, D., G. Epstein and R. Pollin (eds), *Globalization and Progressive Economic Policy* (Cambridge: CUP, 1998).

Baker, J.A. with T.M. DeFrank, *The Politics of Diplomacy: Revolution, War, and Peace, 1989–1992* (New York: G.P. Putnam, 1995).

Barber, B., *McWorld versus Jihad* (New York: Random House, 1995).

Barnaby, F. (ed.), *Building a More Democratic United Nations* (London: Cass, 1991).

Barnett, M.N., 'The UN Security Council, Indifference and Genocide in Rwanda', *Cultural Anthropology*, 12, 4 (1997).

Bell, D., *The Coming of the Post-Industrial Society: a Venture in Social Forecasting* (New York: Basic Books, 1973 and 1999).

Bello, W., 'The End of a "Miracle": Speculation, Foreign Capital Dependence and the Collapse of the Southeast Asian Economies', *Multinational Monitor*, 19, 1–2 (1998), pp.10–17.

Bello, W., 'Asian Financial Crisis: the Movie', *Ecologist*, 29, 1 (1999), pp.28–32.

Bello, W., N. Bullard and K. Malhotra (eds), *Global Finance: New Thinking on Regulating Speculative Capital Markets* (London: Zed Books, 2000).

Bentley, J.H., 'Cross-Cultural Interactions and Periodization in World History', *American Historical Review*, 101, 2 (June 1996), pp.749–70.

Berdal, M. and D.M. Malone (eds), *Greed and Grievance: Economic Agendas in Civil Wars* (Boulder, CO: Lynne Rienner, 2000).

Bhagwati, J., *Anatomy and Consequences of Exchange Control Regimes* (Cambridge, MA: Ballinger, 1978).

Bidwai, P. and A. Vanaik, *New Nukes: India, Pakistan and Global Nuclear Disarmament* (New York: Olive Branch Press/Interlink Books, 2000).

Blomstrom, M. and B. Hettne, *Development Theory in Transition: the Dependency Debate and Beyond: Third World Responses* (London: Zed Books, 1984).

Bonanno, A., 'The Globalization and Theories of the State of the Agricultural and Food Sector', *International Journal of Sociology of Agriculture and Food*, I (1991), pp.15–25.

Bonanno, A., 'Diversity and Globalization: the Homogenization of Heterogeneity', Paper prepared for the seminar 'The Production of Diversity in a Global Context', Wageningen, The Netherlands, 26–28 October 1994.

Boulding, E., 'The Zone of Peace Concept in Current Practice: Review and Evaluation', Paper presented at the Inaugural Conference of the Centre for Peace Studies, Curtin University and University of Western Australia, 14–16 January 1991.

Boutros-Ghali, B., *An Agenda for Peace: Preventive Diplomacy, Peacemaking and Peace-keeping*, A/47/277-S/24111, 17 June (New York: UN, 1992).

Boutros-Ghali, B., *Supplement to An Agenda for Peace: Position Paper of the Secretary-General on the Occasion of the Fiftieth Anniversary of the United Nations*, A/50/60-S/1995/1, 3 January (New York: UN, 1995).

Boyle, J., *Shamans, Software, and Spleen: Law and the Construction of the Information Society* (Cambridge, MA: Harvard University Press, 1996).

Bring, O., 'Should NATO Take the Lead in Formulating a Doctrine on Humanitarian Intervention?', *NATO Review*, 47, 3 (Autumn 1999), pp.24–7.

Bullard, N., W. Bello and K. Malhotra, *Taming the Tigers: the IMF and the Asian Crisis*, Focus Paper (Bangkok: Focus on the Global South, 1998).

Burton, J., *Resolving Deep-Rooted Conflict: a Handbook* (Lanham, MD: University Press of America, 1987).

Cahill, K.M. (ed.), *Preventive Diplomacy: Stopping Wars Before They Start* (New York: Routledge/ Centre for International Health and Cooperation, 2000).

Camilleri, J.A., *States, Markets and Civil Society in Asia Pacific* (Cheltenham: Edward Elgar, 2000).

Camilleri, J.A. and J. Falk, *The End of Sovereignty?: the Politics of a Shrinking and Fragmenting World* (Aldershot: Edward Elgar, 1992).

Camilleri, J.A., K. Malhotra and M. Tehranian, *Reimagining the Future: Towards Democratic Governance* (Melbourne: Department of Politics, La Trobe University, 2000).

Carnegie Commission on Preventing Deadly Conflict, *Final Report* (Washington DC: Carnegie Corporation, 1997).

Cassese, A., '*Ex Iniuria Ius Oritur*: Are We Moving towards International Legitimation of Forcible Humanitarian Countermeasures in World Community?', *European Journal of International Law*, 10, 1 (1999), pp.23–30.

Castells, M., *The Information Society: Economy, Society, and Culture*, Vols 1–3 (Oxford: Blackwell, 1996–2000).

Cerny, P. (ed.), *Finance and World Politics: Markets, Regimes and States in the Post-Hegemonic Era* (Gloucester: Edward Elgar, 1993).

Chase-Dunn, C. and T.D. Hall, *Rise and Demise: Comparing World-Systems* (Boulder, CO: Westview Press, 1997).

Chavez, J.J., *The Asian Financial Crisis and Filipino Households: Impact on Women and Children* (Manila: Focus on the Global South and Save the Children UK, 2001).

Childers, E., 'Nations and Global Institutional Discourse and Reality', *Global Governance*, 3, 3 (September–December 1997).

Childers, E. and B. Urquhart, *Renewing the United Nations System* (Uppsala, Sweden: Dag Hammarskjold Foundation, 1994).

Commission on Global Governance, *Our Global Neighbourhood* (Oxford: OUP, 1995).

Cortright, D. and G.A. Lopez, *The Sanctions Decade: Assessing UN Strategies in the 1990s* (Boulder, CO: Lynne Rienner, 2000).

Cousens, E.M. and C. Kumar (eds), *Peacebuilding as Politics: Cultivating Peace in Fragile Societies* (Boulder, CO: Lynne Rienner, 2001).

Cox, R.W., 'Social Forces, States and World Orders: Beyond International Relations Theory', *Millenium: Journal of International Studies*, 10, 2 (Summer 1981), pp.126–55.

Cox, R.W. (ed.), *The New Realism: Perspectives on Multilateralism and World Order* (Tokyo: UNU Press, 1997).

Culpeper, R, *Systemic Instability or Global Growing Pains? Implications of the Asian Financial Crisis* (Briefing B-41, Ottawa: North–South Institute, 1998).

Curle, A., *Making Peace* (London: Tavistock, 1971).

Dhanapala, J. (ed.), *The United Nations, Disarmament and Security: Evolution and Prospects* (New York: UN, 1991).

Diehl, P.F. (ed.), *Global Governance: International Organizations in an Interdependent World* (Boulder, CO: Lynne Rienner, 2001).

Dillon, J., *Turning the Tide: Confronting the Money Traders* (Ottawa: Canadian Centre for Policy Alternatives, 1997).

D'Orville, H. and D. Najman, 'A New System to Finance the United Nations', *Security Dialogue*, 25, 2 (1994), pp.135–44.

Duchacek, I., *Conflict and Cooperation among Nations* (New York: Holt, Rinehart & Winston, 1960).

Dunning, J.H. (ed.), *Governments, Globalization and International Business* (Oxford: OUP, 1997).

Durch, W.J. (ed.), *The Evolution of UN Peacekeeping: Case Studies and Comparative Analysis* (London: Macmillan, 1994).

Eatwell, J. and L. Taylor, *International Capital Markets and the Future of Economic Policy*, Center for Economic Policy Analysis, Working Paper Series III, Working Paper No.9 (New York: New School for Social Research, 1998).

Ehrenberg, J., *Civil Society: the Critical History of an Idea* (New York: NYU Press, 1999).

Eichengreen, B., *Towards a New International Financial Architecture: a Practical Post-Asia Agenda* (Washington, DC: Institute for International Economics, 1999).

Eichengreen, B. and P. Kenen, *Managing the World Economy – 50 Years After Bretton Woods* (Washington DC: Institute for International Economics, 1994).

Eichengreen, B. and D. Mathieson, 'Hedge Funds and Financial Market Dynamics', IMF Occasional Paper (Washington DC: IMF, 1998).

Eichengreen, B. and M. Mussa, 'Capital Account Liberalization: Theoretical and Practical Aspects', IMF Occasional Paper 172 (Washington DC: IMF, 1998).

Etzioni, A., *The Spirit of Community: Rights, Responsibilities, and the Communitarian Agenda* (New York: Crown Publishers, 1993).

Evans, G., *Cooperating for Peace: the Global Agenda for the 1990s and Beyond* (NSW: Allen & Unwin, 1993).

Falk, R., 'Hard Choices and Tragic Dilemmas', *Nation*, 20 December 1993, pp. 755–64.

Falk, R., *On Humane Governance: Toward a New Global Politics* (University Park, PA: Pennsylvania University Press; Cambridge: Polity Press, 1995).

Falk, R., *Predatory Globalization: a Critique* (Cambridge: Polity Press, 1999).

Fawcett, L. and A. Hurrell (eds), *Regionalism in World Politics* (Oxford: OUP, 1995).

Feldstein, M., 'Refocusing the IMF', *Foreign Affairs*, 77, 2 (1998), pp.20–33.

Fowler, A., 'Capacity Building and NGOs: a Case of Strengthening Ladles for the Global Soup Kitchen?', *Institutional Development*, 1, 1 (1994), pp.18–24.

Frank, A.G., *ReOrient: Global Economy in the Asian Age* (Berkeley, CA: University of California Press, 1998).

Frank, A.G. and B.K. Gills (eds), *The World System: Five Hundred Years or Five Thousand?* (London: Routledge, 1993).

Friedman, J., *Cultural Identity and Global Processes* (Newbury Park: Sage, 1995).

Friedman, J. and S. Randeria (eds), *Worlds on the Move: Globalization, Migration, and Cultural Security* (London: I.B. Tauris, forthcoming).

Fry, G. and J. O'Hagan (eds), *Contending Images of World Politics* (London: Macmillan, 2000).

Fukuyama, F., *The End of History and the Last Man* (New York: Free Press, 1992).

Fukuyama, F., *Trust: Social Virtues and the Creation of Prosperity* (New York: Free Press, 1995).

Fuller, R.B., *Grunch of Giants* (New York: St. Martin's Press [now Palgrave Macmillan], 1983).

Galbraith, J.K., *American Capitalism: the Theory of Countervailing Power* (Boston, MA: Houghton Mifflin, 1956).

Galbraith, J.K., *The Culture of Contentment* (Boston, MA: Houghton Mifflin, 1992).

Garreau, J., *Edge City: Life on the New Frontier* (New York: Doubleday Press, 1991).

Giddens, A., *The Consequences of Modernity* (Cambridge: Polity Press, 1990).

Giddens, A., *The Third Way: the Renewal of Social Democracy* (Cambridge: Polity Press, 1998).

Gill, S., 'Global Hegemony and the Structural Power of Capital', Paper presented at the XIV Congress of IPSA, Washington DC, 1988.

Gill, S., 'Globalisation, Market Civilisation, and Disciplinary Neoliberalism', *Millennium*, 23, 3 (1995), pp.399–423.

Gill, S., 'New Constitutionalism, Democratisation and Global Political Economy', *Pacifica Review*, 10, 1 (1998), pp.23–38.

Gottweis, H., 'Genetic Engineering, Democracy, and the Politics of Identity', *Social Text*, 13 (1995), pp.127–52.

Habermas, J., *Legitimation Crisis* (Boston, MA: Beacon Press, 1973).

Hall, T.D., 'The World-Systems Perspective: a Small Sample from a Large Universe', *Sociological Inquiry*, 66, 4 (November 1996), pp.440–54.

Hamel-Green, M., 'The Uppsala Declaration on Nuclear Free Zones', *Pacific News Bulletin*, 15, 10 (October 2000).

Hampson, F.O. and J. Reppy (eds), *Earthly Goods: Environmental Change and Social Justice* (Ithaca NY: Cornell University Press, 1996).

Hanson, G., *Should Developing Countries Promote Foreign Direct Investment?*. Group of 24, Discussion Paper No.9 (February 2001).

Harmes, A., 'The Trouble With Hedge Funds', *Policy Studies Review*, 19, 1 (2001).

Harrod, J. and N. Schrijver (eds), *The UN under Attack* (Aldershot: Gower, 1988).

Harvey, D., *The Conditions of Postmodernity* (Oxford: Blackwell, 1990).

Held, D., *Democracy and the Global Order: From the Modern State to Cosmopolitan Governance* (Stanford, CA: Stanford University Press; Cambridge: Polity Press, 1995).

Held, D. and D. Archibugi (eds), *Cosmopolitan Democracy* (Cambridge: Polity Press, 1995).

Helleiner, G.K., *Markets, Politics and the Global Economy: Can the Global Economy Be Civilized?*, 10th Raul Prebisch Lecture, UNCTAD, December 2000.

Higgott, R. and A. Payne (eds), *The New Political Economy of Globalisation* (Cheltenham: Edward Elgar, 2000).

Hirsch, F., *The Social Limits to Growth* (Cambridge, MA: Harvard University Press, 1976).

Hobsbawm, E., *Age of Extremes – The Short Twentieth Century – 1914–1991* (London: Michael Joseph, 1994).

Hudson, H., *Global Connections: International Telecommunications Infrastructure and Policy* (New York: John Wiley & Sons, 1997).

Huntington, S.P., 'The Clash of Civilizations', *Foreign Affairs* (Summer 1993).

Huntley, J.R., *Pax Democratica: a Strategy for the 21st Century* (New York: Free Press, 1998).

Huxley, A., *The Perennial Philosophy* (New York: Harper & Row, 1944).

Ibn Khaldun, *The Muqaddimah, an Introduction to History*, 3 vols, tr. Franz Rosenthal (Princeton, NJ: Princeton University Press, 1967).

Independent Commission on Disarmament and Security Issues, *Common Security: a Programme for Disarmament* (London: Pan Books, 1982).

Independent Working Group on the Future of the United Nations, *The United Nations in its Second Half-Century* (New York: Ford Foundation, 1995).

Ismael, T.Y. and J.S. Ismael, 'Cowboy Warfare, Biological Diplomacy: Disarming Metaphors as Weapons of Mass Destruction', *Politics and the Life Sciences*, 18, 1 (March 1999).

James, E., 'Averting the Old-Age Crisis', *Finance and Development*, 32, 2 (1995).

Jishe, F., 'Nagging Uncertainty and Growing Concern: the Bush Administration's Arm Control Policy', *Disarmament Diplomacy*, 55 (March 2001), pp.3–7.

Jones, D.L., 'Mediation, Conflict Resolution and Critical Theory', *Review of International Studies*, 26, 4 (October 2000).

Kantrow, A.M. (ed.), *Sunrise ... Sunset: Challenging the Myth of Industrial Obsolescence* (New York: John Wiley & Sons, 1985).

Kaplan, R.D., 'The Coming Anarchy', *Atlantic Monthly* (February 1994).

Kimbrell, A., 'The Body Enclosed: the Commodification of Human "Parts"', *Ecologist*, 25, 4 (July–August 1995), pp.134–40.

Kindleberger, C.P., *Manias, Panics and Crashes: a History of Financial Crises*, 3rd edn (New York: John Wiley & Sons, 1996).

King, A. and B. Schneider, *The First Global Revolution: a Report of the Council of Rome* (New York: Pantheon Books, 1991).

Klare, M., *Rogue States and Nuclear Outlaws: America's Search for a New Foreign Policy* (New York: Hill and Wang, 1995).

Knight, W.A., *A Changing United Nations: Multilateral Evolution and the Quest for Global Governance* (Basingstoke: Palgrave, 2000).

Köchler, H., *Democracy and the International Rule of Law* (Wien: Springer-Verlag, 1995).

Kolodziej, E.A., 'The Great Powers and Genocide: Lessons from Rwanda', *Pacifica Review*, 12, 2 (June 2000), pp.121–45.

Korzenny, F. and S. Ting-Toomey (eds), *Communicating for Peace* (Newbury Park: Sage, 1990).

Kriesberg, L., A. Northrup and S. Thorson (eds), *Intractable Conflicts and Their Transformation* (Syracuse, NY: Syracuse University Press, 1989).

Krueger, A., *Liberalization Attempts and Consequences* (Cambridge, MA: Ballinger, 1978).

Krugman, P., 'What happened to Asia?', Mimeograph (January 1998).

Krugman, P., 'Balance Sheets, the Transfer Problem, and Financial Crises', Mimeograph (January 1999).

Kuperman, A.J., 'Rwanda in Retrospect', *Foreign Affairs*, 79, 1 (January–February 2000).

Lake, A., 'Confronting Backlash States', *Foreign Affairs*, 73, 2 (1974).

Lampen, J. (ed.), *No Alternative? Nonviolent Response to Repressive Regimes* (York, UK: William Sessions, 2000).

Langmore, J., 'Restructuring Economic and Financial Power', *Futures*, 27 (1995), pp.189–94.

Latter, R., 'Biological Weapons: the Growing Threat', Wilton Park Paper 124 (January 1997).

Leitenberg, M., 'Aum Shinrikio's Efforts to Produce Biological Weapons: a Case Study in the Serial Propagation of Misinformation', *Terrorism and Political Violence* (Winter 1999).

Leatherman, J., W. DeMars, P. Gaffney and R. Varyrynen, *Breaking Cycles of Violence: Conflict Prevention in Intrastate Crises* (West Hartford, CT: Kumarian Press, 1999).

Lederach, J.P., *Preparing for Peace: Conflict Transformation Across Cultures* (Syracuse, NY: Syracuse University Press, 1995).

Little, I., T. Scitovsky and M. Scott, *Industry and Trade in Some Developing Countries* (Oxford and New York: OUP for the OECD, 1970).

Mander, J. and E. Goldsmith, *The Case Against the Global Economy: and for a Turn Toward the Local* (San Francisco CA: Sierra Club Books, 1996).

Mansfield, E.D. and H.V. Milner, 'The New Wave of Regionalism', *International Organization*, 53, 3 (Summer 1999), pp.589–627.

Marsden, T.K. and A. Arce, 'Constructing Quality: Emerging Food Networks in the Rural Transition', *Environment and Planning A*, 27 (1995), pp.1261–79.

McQuaig, L., *The Cult of Impotence: Selling the Myth of Powerlessness in the Global Economy* (Toronto: Viking Press, 1998).

Mendelsohn, J., 'The Bush Presidency: Reconsidering the CTBT', *Disarmament Diplomacy*, 53 (December/January 2000/2001).

Mendez, R.P., 'Financing the United Nations and the International Public Sector: Problems and Reform', *Global Governance*, 3, 3 (September–December 1997).

Miall, H., O. Ramsbotham and T. Woodhouse, *Contemporary Conflict Resolution: the Prevention, Management and Transformation of Deadly Conflicts* (Cambridge: Polity Press, 1999).

Michalos, A.C., *Good Taxes: the Case for Taxing Foreign Currency Exchange and Other Financial Transactions* (Toronto: Dundurn Press, 1997).

Miller, J., S. Engelberg and W. Broad, *Germs: Biological Weapons and America's Secret War* (New York: Simon & Schuster, 2001).

Mitchell, C.R., *The Structure of International Conflict* (London: Macmillan, 1981).

Mittelman, J., *The Globalization Syndrome: Transformation and Resistance* (Princeton, NJ: Princeton University Press, 2000).

Montes, M.F., *The Currency Crisis in Southeast Asia* (Singapore: Institute of Southeast Asian Studies, 1998).

Moody, K., *Workers in a Lean World: Unions in the International Economy* (New York: Verso, 1997).

Mosco, V., *The Political Economy of Communication* (London: Sage, 1996).

Murphy, C.N., *International Organization and Industrial Change: Global Governance Since 1850* (New York: Oxford University Press, 1994).

Nacos, B. and R. Shapiro (eds), *Decision-Making in a Glass House: Media, Public Opinion in American and European Foreign Policy* (Boulder, CO: Rowman & Littlefield, 2000).

Nagy, T., 'The Secret Behind the Sanctions', *Progressive* (September 2001).

Nayyar, D. (ed.), *Governing Globalization: Issues and Institutions* (Oxford: Clarendon Press, 2001).

O'Brien, R., A-M. Goetz, J.A. Scholte and M. Williams, *Contesting Global Governance: Multilateral Economic Institutions and Global Social Movements* (Cambridge: CUP, 2000).

Otunnu, O.A. and M.V. Doyle (eds), *Peacemaking and Peacekeeping for the New Century* (Lanham, MD: Rowman & Littlefield, 1998).

Oxfam International, *Improving the UN's Response to Complex Emergencies*, Position Paper (November 1997).

Paolini, A.J., A.P. Jarvis and C. Reus-Smit (eds), *Between Sovereignty and Global Governance: the United Nations, the State, and Civil Society* (New York: St. Martin's Press [now Palgrave Macmillan], 1998).

Park, Y.C., 'East Asian Liberalization, Bubbles, and the Challenge from China', *Brookings Papers on Economic Activity*, 2 (1995), pp.357–71.

Peck, C., *Sustainable Peace: the Role of the UN and Regional Organizations in Preventing Conflict* (Lanham, MD: Rowman & Littlefield, 1998).

Polanyi, K., *The Great Transformation: Political and Economic Origins of Our Times* (New York: Octagon Books, 1975).

Pomerleano, M., 'Corporate Finance Lessons from the East Asian Crisis', *Public Policy for the Private Sector Note No.155* (Washington DC: World Bank, 1998).

Pomerleano, M., 'The East Asia Crisis and Corporate Finances: the Untold Micro Story', Mimeograph (Washington DC: The World Bank, 1999).

Potamaki, H., *Democratising Globalisation: the Leverage of the Tobin Tax* (London: Zed Books, 2001).

Prakash, A. and J.A. Hart (eds), *Globalization and Governance* (London: Routledge, 1999).

Prawitz, J. and J.F. Leonard, 'A Zone Free of Weapons of Mass Destruction in the Middle East: a Political Project', *Pacifica Review*, 11, 3 (October 1999), pp.258–9.

Putnam, R.D., 'What Makes Democracy Work?', *IPA Journal*, 47, 1 (1994), pp.31–4.

Radelet, S. and J. Sachs, 'The Onset of the East Asian Financial Crisis', Mimeograph (Harvard Institute for International Development, 30 March 1998).

Ratner, S.R., *The New Peacekeeping: Building Peace in Lands of Conflict After the Cold War* (New York: St. Martin's Press [now Palgrave Macmillan], 1995), pp.42–3.

Renner, M., *Fighting for Survival: Environmental Decline, Social Conflict and the New Age of Insecurity* (New York: W.W. Norton & Co, 1996).

Reychler, L. and T. Paffenholz (eds), *Peacebuilding: a Field Guide* (Boulder/London: Lynne Rienner, 2001).

Rieff, D., 'The False Dawn of Civil Society', *Nation* (22 February 1999).

Rifkin, J., *The End of Work: the Decline of the Global Labor Force and Dawn of the Post-Market Era* (New York: G.P. Putnam, 1995).

Rivlin, B., 'Regional Arrangements and the UN System for Collective Security and Conflict Resolution: a New Road Ahead?', *International Relations*, XI, 2 (August 1992), pp.95–110.

Roach, C. (ed.), *Communication and Culture in War and Peace* (Newbury Park: Sage, 1993).

Roberts, B. (ed.), *Weapons Proliferation in the 1990s* (Cambridge, MA: MIT Press, 1995).

Roberts, B., *Weapons Proliferation and World Order* (The Hague: Kluwer International, 1996).

Robertson, R. and F. Lechner, 'Modernization, Globalization and the Problem of Culture in World Systems Theory', *Theory, Culture and Society*, 2, 3 (1985), pp.103–17.

Rodrik, D., 'Five Simple Principles for World Trade', *American Prospect*, 17 (January 2000).

Rodrik, D., *The Global Governance of Trade as if Development Really Mattered* (New York: UNDP, September 2001).

Rosenau, J.N., 'Governance in the 21st Century', *Global Governance*, 1 (1995), pp.13–43.

Rosenberg, B., ' "Non-lethal" Weapons May Violate Treaties', *Bulletin of the Atomic Scientists* (September–October 1994).

Rummel, R.J., *Death by Government* (New Brunswick: Transactions Publishers, 1994).

Ryan, M.P., *Knowledge Diplomacy: Global Competition and the Politics of Intellectual Property* (Washington DC: Brookings Institute Press, 1998).

Scheffran, J., 'Moving Beyond Missile Defence: the Search for Alternatives to the Missile Race', *Disarmament Diplomacy*, 55 (March 2001), pp.21–6.

Schiller, D., *Digital Capitalism: Networking the Global Market System* (Cambridge, MA: MIT Press, 2000).

Schmidt, R., *A Feasible Foreign Exchange Transaction Tax* (Ottawa: North–South Institute, 1997).

Schmidt, R., 'Efficient Capital Controls', *Journal of Economic Studies*, 28, 3 (2001).

Shah, S., 'The Roots of Ethnic Conflict', *Nuclear Times* (Spring 1992), pp.9–15.

Shaw, M., *Theory of the Global State: Globality as an Unfinished Revolution* (Cambridge: CUP, 2000).

Singh, A. and A. Zammit, 'International Capital Flows: Identifying the Gender Dimension', *World Development* 28, 7 (2000).

Singh, K., *A Citizen's Guide to the Globalization of Finance* (Delhi: Madhyam Books, 1998).

SIPRI, *Yearbook* (New York: Oxford University Press, annual yearbooks 1994–2000).

Slaughter, A-M., 'The Real World Order', *Foreign Affairs*, 76, 5 (1997), pp.183–7.

Smith, H. (ed.), *International Peacekeeping: Building on the Cambodian Experience* (Canberra: Australian Defence Force Academy, 1994).

Smith, H., 'Intelligence and UN Peacekeeping', *Survival*, 36, 3 (Autumn 1994).

Smith, M., 'The MTCR and the Future of Ballistic Missile Non-Proliferation', *Disarmament Diplomacy*, 54 (February 2001), pp.19–25.

Smithson, A., 'Separating Fact from Fiction: the Australia Group and the Chemical Weapons Convention' (Henry L. Stimson Center, Occasional Paper No.34, March 1997).

Smithson, A., 'Toxic Archipelago: Preventing Proliferation from the Former Soviet Chemical and Biological Weapons Complexes' (Henry L. Stimson Center Report No.32, December 1999).

So, A., *Social Change and Development: Modernization, Dependency, and World Systems Theories* (Newbury Parks: Sage, 1990).

Soros, G., 'The Capitalist Threat', *Atlantic Monthly*, 279, 2 (1997), pp.45–58.

Soros, G., *The Crisis of Global Capitalism: Open Society Endangered* (London: Little, Brown & Company; New York: Public Affairs, 1998 and 1999).

[The] South Centre, *For a Strong and Democratic United Nations: a South Perspective on UN Reform* (Geneva: the South Centre, 1996).

[The] South Commission, *The Challenge to the South: the Report of the South Commission* (Oxford: OUP, 1990).

Stannard, D.E., *Before the Horror: the Population of Hawaii on the Eve of Western Contact* (Honolulu: Social Science Research Institute, University of Hawaii, 1989).

Stavrianos, L.S., *A Global History: From Prehistory to the Present* (Englewood Cliffs, NJ: Prentice Hall, 1991).

Strange, S., *Casino Capitalism* (Oxford: Basil Blackwell, 1986; reprinted by Manchester University Press, 1997).

Stremlau, J., 'Sharpening International Sanctions: Towards a Stronger Role for the United Nations', Report to the Carnegie Commission on Preventing Deadly Conflict (New York: Carnegie Corporation, November 1996).

Sutterlin, J.S., *The United Nations and the Maintenance of International Security: a Challenge To Be Met* (Westport, CT: Praeger, 1995).

Swyter, H., 'Political Considerations and Analysis of Military Requirements for Chemical and Biological Weapons', *Procedures of the National Academy of Sciences*, 65 (1970).

Tang, M. and J. Villafuerte, *Capital Flows to Asian and Pacific Developing Countries: Recent Trends and Finance Prospects* (Manila: Asian Development Bank, 1995).

Taylor, P., 'The United Nations System under Stress: Financial Pressures and Their Consequences', *Review of International Studies*, 17, 4 (October 1991), pp.365–82.

Tehranian, K.K., *Modernity, Space and Power: American City in Discourse and Practice* (Cresskill, NJ: Hampton Press, 1995).

Tehranian, K. and M. Tehranian (eds), *Restructuring for World Peace: On the Threshold of the 21st Century* (Cresskill, NJ: Hampton Press, 1992).

Tehranian, M., 'Global Communication and International Relations: Changing Paradigms and Policies', *International Journal of Peace Studies*, 2, 1 (January 1997), pp.39–64.

Tehranian, M., *Global Communication and World Politics: Domination, Development, and Discourse* (Boulder, CO: Lynne Rienner Publishers, 1999).

Tehranian, M. (ed.), *Worlds Apart: Human Security and Global Governance* (London: I.B. Tauris, 1999).

Tehranian, M. (ed.), *Asian Peace: Security and Governance in the Asia-Pacific Region* (London: I.B. Tauris, 1999).

Thranert, O. (ed.), *Preventing the Proliferation of Weapons of Mass Destruction: What Role for Arms Control?* (Bonn: Friedrich-Ebert-Stiftung, 1999).

Tingel, A.C., *Conflict Resolved? A Critical Assessment of Conflict Resolution* (London: Pinter, 1998).

Tow, W.T., R. Thakur and I-T. Hyun (eds), *Asia's Emerging Regional Order* (Tokyo: UNU Press, 2000).

Tucker, J.B. (ed.), *Toxic Terror: Assessing Terrorist Use of Biological and Chemical Weapons* (Cambridge, MA: Belfer Centre for Science and International Affairs, MIT Press, 2000).

Tunstall, J., *The Media Are America* (New York: Columbia University Press, 1977).

Ul Haq, M., I. Kaul and I. Grunberg (eds), *The Tobin Tax: Coping with Financial Volatility* (New York: Oxford University Press, 1996).

UNCTAD, *World Investment Report* (Geneva: UNCTAD, 1991–2000 annual reports).

UNCTAD, *Trade and Development Report* (Geneva: UNCTAD, 1996–2000 annual reports).

UNDP, *Human Development Report* (New York: Oxford University Press, 1990–2000 annual reports).

UNHCR, *The State of the World's Refugees* (Oxford: OUP, 1995).

United Nations, 'Report of the Independent Inquiry into the Actions of the United Nations during the 1994 Genocide in Rwanda' (the *Rwanda Report*), S/1999/1257, 15 December 1999.

United Nations, 'Report of the Panel on United Nations Peace Operations' (the *Brahimi Report*), A/55/305-S/2000/809, 21 August 2000.

United Nations Association of the United States of America (UNA-USA), 'The Preparedness Gap: Making Peace Operations Work in the 21st Century', January 2001.

UN Research Institute for Social Development (UNRISD), *States of Disarray: the Social Effects of Globalization* (Geneva: UNRISD, 1995).

U Thant, *View for the UN* (New York: Doubleday, 1978).

Waldheim, K., *The Challenge of Peace* (London: Weidenfeld & Nicolson, 1980).

Walker, J.P., 'Alternative Financing for the United Nations: an Idea whose Time Has Finally Come?', *Economic and Trade Policy*, Policy Staff Commentary No.10 (December 1995).

Wallensteen, P., 'Representing the World: a Security Council for the 21st Century', *Security Dialogue*, 25, 1 (1994), pp.63–75.

Wallerstein, I., *The Modern World-System*, Vol.1: *Capitalist Agriculture and the Origins of the European World-Economy in the Sixteenth Century* (New York: Academress, 1974).

Wallerstein, I., *The Capitalist World-Economy* (Cambridge: CUP, 1979).

Weiss, T.G., D. Cortright, G.A. Lopez and L. Minear (eds), *Political Gain and Civilian Pain: Humanitarian Impact of Economic Sanctions* (Lanham, MD: Rowman & Littlefield, 1997).

Weiss, T.G. and L. Gordenker (eds), *NGOs, The UN, & Global Governance* (Boulder, CO: Lynne Rienner, 1996).

Whitman, J. and I. Bartholomew, 'Collective Control of UN Peace Support Operations: a Policy Proposal', *Security Dialogue*, 25, 1 (1994), pp.77–92.

Whittaker, D., *United Nations in the Contemporary World* (London: Routledge, 1997).

World Bank, *Global Development Finance* (Washington DC: World Bank, 1990–2000 annual reviews).

World Bank, *Private Capital Flows to Developing Countries: the Road to Financial Integration* (New York: OUP, 1997).

Wright, S., 'Bioweapons: Cuba Case Tests Treaty', *Bulletin of the Atomic Scientists* (November–December 1997).

Wright, S., 'The Hijacking of UNSCOM', *Bulletin of the Atomic Scientists*, 55, 3 (May–June 1999).

Wright, S. (ed.), *The Biological Warfare Question: a Reappraisal for the 21st Century* (forthcoming).

Wright, S. and D. Wallace, 'Varieties of Secrets and Secret Varieties: the Case of Biotechnology', *Politics and the Life Sciences*, 19, 1 (March 2000), pp.33–45.

Zilinskas, R. (ed.), *Biological Warfare: Modern Offense and Defense* (Boulder, CO: Lynne Rienner, 1999).

Index